Praise for *Claude Lévi-Strauss* by Patrick Wilcken

"An illuminating study . . . The book offers clear, analytical descriptions of the basic tenets for which Lévi-Strauss is known. . . . This book, with an admiring but not slavish appreciation of its subject, thoughtfully analyzes the controversy that surrounded structuralism even during its glory days. . . . This book appreciates and communicates the grandeur of its subject's accomplishments." —Janet Maslin, *The New York Times*

"Patrick Wilcken's well-written biography, the first full-length treatment of Lévi-Strauss's life in English, provides an accessible and interesting overview of his career, personal life, intellectual development, contributions, and impact on thinking inside and outside of anthropology. Wilcken offers a clear explication and measured assessments of Lévi-Strauss's works as well as setting them within the broader context of twentieth-century French and European thought. . . . Wilcken is also a gifted storyteller and thoughtful analyst." —*Science*

"A surprisingly accessible account of life and work of Lévi-Strauss as he went from São Paulo to the Brazilian interior, from New York to Paris, in what can only be called a remarkable life. It provides a rare glimpse of one of the twentieth century's most influential minds." —*Tucson Citizen*

"Patrick Wilcken triumphs in tackling the daunting task of tracing the development of the ideas of French intellectual Claude Lévi-Strauss over more than sixty years." —*Shelf Awareness*

"An elegant, lucid account of an intellectual's life and work . . . this book delivers a bracing tour through an intellectual movement—structuralism." —*Somatosphere* blog

"Brilliantly assesses the great, original, creative ideas and their origins in the context of Lévi-Strauss's life." —*The Times* (Biographies of the Year)

"[Wilcken] lays out the life with clarity, efficiency, readability, and occasionally dissent. . . . A superbly thrilling life." —*The Guardian* (London)

"A beauty—pacey, eloquent, intelligent, always aware (unlike some modern biographies) who is the star of the show." —*Literary Review*

PENGUIN BOOKS

CLAUDE LÉVI-STRAUSS

Patrick Wilcken grew up in Sydney and studied at Goldsmiths College and the Institute of Latin American Studies in London. A contributor to the *Times Literary Supplement*, he works on the Brazil desk at Amnesty International. He is the author of *Empire Adrift: The Portuguese Court in Rio de Janeiro 1808–21*. He has spent periods in Paris and Rio de Janeiro and now lives in Stoke Newington, London, with his wife and child.

Claude Lévi-Strauss

The Father of Modern Anthropology

PATRICK WILCKEN

PENGUIN BOOKS

PENGUIN BOOKS
Published by the Penguin Group
Penguin Group (USA) Inc., 375 Hudson Street, New York, New York 10014, U.S.A. • Penguin Group (Canada), 90 Eglinton Avenue East, Suite 700, Toronto, Ontario, Canada M4P 2Y3 (a division of Pearson Penguin Canada Inc.) • Penguin Books Ltd, 80 Strand, London WC2R 0RL, England • Penguin Ireland, 25 St. Stephen's Green, Dublin 2, Ireland (a division of Penguin Books Ltd) • Penguin Books Australia Ltd, 250 Camberwell Road, Camberwell, Victoria 3124, Australia (a division of Pearson Australia Group Pty Ltd) • Penguin Books India Pvt Ltd, 11 Community Centre, Panchsheel Park, New Delhi—110 017, India • Penguin Group (NZ), 67 Apollo Drive, Rosedale, Auckland 0632, New Zealand (a division of Pearson New Zealand Ltd) • Penguin Books (South Africa) (Pty) Ltd, 24 Sturdee Avenue, Rosebank, Johannesburg 2196, South Africa

Penguin Books Ltd, Registered Offices:
80 Strand, London WC2R 0RL, England

First published in the United States of America by The Penguin Press,
a member of Penguin Group (USA) Inc. 2010
Published in Penguin Books 2012

1 3 5 7 9 10 8 6 4 2

THE LIBRARY OF CONGRESS HAS CATALOGED THE HARDCOVER EDITION AS FOLLOWS:
Wilcken, Patrick.
Claude Levi-Strauss : the poet in the laboratory / Patrick Wilcken.
p. cm.
Includes bibliographical references and index.
ISBN 978-1-59420-273-5 (hc.)
ISBN 978-0-14-312062-9 (pbk.)
1. Lévi-Strauss, Claude 2. Anthropologists—France—Biography.
3. Anthropologists—Brazil—Biogrpahy. 4. Structural anthropology. I. Title.
GN21.L4W55 2010
301.092—dc22
[B]
2010017301

Printed in the United States of America
DESIGNED BY MEIGHAN CAVANAUGH

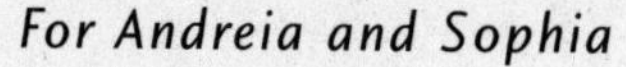

For Andreia and Sophia

CONTENTS

Introduction *1*

1. Early Years *15*

2. Arabesque *47*

3. Rondon's Line *79*

4. Exile *115*

5. Elementary Structures *149*

6. On the Shaman's Couch *180*

7. Memoir *202*

8. Modernism *225*

9. "Mind in the Wild" *249*

10. The Nebula of Myth 276

11. Convergence 308

Epilogue 341

Acknowledgments 347

Notes 349

Further Reading 385

Index 389

Claude Lévi-Strauss

Introduction

> Some people might ask whether I haven't been guided by a kind of quixotism throughout my career . . . an obsessive desire to find the past behind the present. If perchance someone some day were to care to understand my personality, I offer him that key.
>
> CLAUDE LÉVI-STRAUSS[1]

IN 1938, on the eve of his thirtieth birthday, Claude Lévi-Strauss was in Brazil, leading a mule train along the remains of a telegraph line. Its lopsided poles, rusted wires and porcelain adapters were strung out across the rugged scrublands of northwestern Mato Grosso state, on the fringes of the Amazon Basin. Bearded and sunburned, dressed in soiled dungarees, a colonial-style sun hat and high leather boots, Lévi-Strauss was heading an ethnographic expedition to study the Nambikwara—a loose designation for the nomadic groups who roamed the plateau, naked but for nose feathers, bracelets and waistbands. Farther up the line, as scrub turned to jungle and the team switched to canoes, Lévi-Strauss encountered other tribes encamped in rain-forest clearings—the survivors of the Arawak, Carib and Tupi cultures. He worked alongside a team of experts, including his first wife, Dina, the tropical-medicine specialist Dr. Jean Vellard, and a Brazilian anthropologist, Luiz de Castro Faria, on a mission that has become as celebrated as it is controversial.

Photographs from Lévi-Strauss's fieldwork look dated even for their era. Pack animals heaving crates of equipment through the wilderness, men in pith helmets mingling with virtually naked tribesmen, the exchanging of beads and lengths of cloth for bows, arrows and ritual objects, laden-down canoes and jungle campsites. The skinned carcass of a seven-meter boa constrictor stretches out across one plate, a dozen snake fetuses, its stillborn progeny, spilled out over the earth. "It took a lot of shooting," Lévi-Strauss recalled, "since these animals are impervious to body wounds and have to be hit in the head."[2] It all has the feel of some grand nineteenth-century scientific expedition.

The effect is doubly disjointed. Following the Polish anthropologist Bronislaw Malinowski's famous fieldwork in the Trobriand Islands off the coast of New Guinea, where he had studied ritual exchange across the archipelago, ethnography had already become strongly associated with solitary cultural immersion. By the 1930s, images from the field were more likely to show a single tent pitched within striking distance of a tribe, a trestle table strewn with notebooks, a rucksack with provisions, possibly some recording equipment stuffed into a satchel. The anthropologist's lonely vigil was expected to yield worthwhile results only after years of assimilation. In contrast, Lévi-Strauss's team clocked up more than a thousand kilometers, rarely pausing for more than a few weeks in any one place. His expedition would end up being one of the last ventures of its kind—an antiquated journey across a forgotten corner of Brazil.

Toward the end of 1938 the party broke up, Castro Faria traveling down the Amazon for Rio de Janeiro, Vellard and Lévi-Strauss taking a small steamship up the Madeira River, then boarding an amphibious plane for Cochabamba in Bolivia.[3] It had been at best a patchy experience. His field notes, now held at the Bibliothèque nationale in Paris, have a disorganized feel to them. Lévi-Strauss interspersed lists of basic vocabulary of different indigenous groups, confusing kin diagrams, illustrations of weaving techniques, and drawings of animals, faces and spears, along with inventories of the enormous quantities of provisions needed to sustain the expedition.[4]

Added to a brief, earlier spell of fieldwork among the Caduveo and the Bororo farther to the south, the trip had initiated Lévi-Strauss as an anthropologist, but in a peculiarly diffuse way. Instead of the in-depth analysis of a single group, Lévi-Strauss had briefly surveyed half a dozen different indigenous cultures, dotted across the Brazilian interior. That this should have been the starting point for his career was perhaps appropriate. From the fragments—an arabesque painted on a weathered Caduveo cheek, the Mundé's igloo-shaped forest huts, the ritual flute songs of the Nambikwara—Lévi-Strauss built a body of work that reflected not so much the intricacies of a single tribe, but features common to all culture.

The great irony was that his nineteenth-century-style expedition ended up being the handmaiden to one of the most avant-garde bodies of work in the humanities. In his memoir recounting the journey, *Tristes Tropiques* (1955), written a decade and a half after his experiences in Brazil, Lévi-Strauss put the then emerging discipline of anthropology on the map. From the scraps of his field notes, he pieced together a self-portrait of the anthropologist at midcentury: a cerebral pioneer on a quest to leave the confines of Western culture in order to know another world, another way of being; an outsider condemned to roam the cultural borderlands, forever restless, damaged ("*psychologiquement mutilé*"[5]) by chronic feelings of rootlessness; a forlorn traveler surveying the cultural ruins at the edge of European expansion. At the same time, he wrote of a new theoretical approach. The motley groups of Nambikwara, loitering around derelict telegraph stations, scrounging trinkets and leftovers from missionaries, the barely sustainable forest settlements, the heat, the dust—all this somehow crystallized into a highly stylized image of indigenous culture. The model was called structuralism—an approach that sought to uncover the hidden symmetries that underlay all culture. In *Tristes Tropiques* Lévi-Strauss captivated readers with early sketches of this method, in the process giving an unexpected coherence to the apparent confusion of indigenous ideas and practices.

"ON THE WHOLE, and all things considered, the interview is a detestable genre," Lévi-Strauss once said in an interview, "to which the intellectual poverty of the age obliges one to submit more often than one would like." Yet as his fame grew with the success of *Tristes Tropiques* and the subsequent march of structuralism, he spoke regularly to journalists and academic colleagues. In the 1960s and '70s he often appeared on French television, participated in a series of documentaries and, after his retirement, gave the writer and philosopher Didier Eribon extraordinary access, resulting in a book-length interview, published as *De près et de loin* in 1988.

The more one reads, though, the less one seems to be able to grasp the person behind the words and images. In print and on film Lévi-Strauss was at once forthcoming and elusive. Over the years he produced many details, but little substance. One is left with the impression of strong surface imagery—a vividness without depth. His anonymous Semitic features (he came from a Jewish family, originally from the Alsace) have been endlessly photographed in the same noncommittal pose. The images that have been staged—Lévi-Strauss standing in front of banks of metal card-reference drawers in a Paris archive, for instance, or in a jacket with a parrot perched on his shoulder—seem out of character, as if Lévi-Strauss was resistant to the crafts of publicity. In 1970, *Vogue* photographer Irving Penn posed Lévi-Strauss sunken into an overcoat, his head enveloped by artfully turned-up lapels, his glasses perched on his forehead, the left side of his face disappearing into the shadows. Compared to Penn's identically posed portrait of Picasso—whose one visible eye, unmoored from the rest of the face, fixes the viewer with a piercing stare—Lévi-Strauss's expression is difficult to read. Not even the manufactured intimacy of celebrity photography, with someone as talented as Penn behind the lens, could offer a glimpse of his inner being.

The effacement was in part deliberate: "I share the anti-biographical approach expressed by Proust in *Contre Sainte-Beuve*," Lévi-Strauss told the French anthropologist Marc Augé in 1990. "What matters is the work, not the author who happened to write it; I would say rather that it writes itself through him. The individual person is no more than the means of transmission and survives in the work only as a residue."[6] In Lévi-Strauss's case, though, this residue was a heavy one. His prose is instantly recognizable and impossible to imitate; his approach to his subject matter so idiosyncratic that for much of his career it defied systematic criticism.

On film, Lévi-Strauss had an easy, avuncular manner. He would appear on shows like *Apostrophes*, France's weekly cultural program that ran in the 1970s and '80s, explaining the ins and outs of his theories. The performances were fluid, at times monotone, at others more animated, when he produced an intellectual trump card or delivered the punch line of a well-worn tale. A dry humor and a certain Gallic charm shone through between patient explanations of anthropological conundrums. This is the image that was sedimented in France's popular consciousness—Lévi-Strauss as a much-loved national treasure, the father (perhaps now the grand- or even great-grandfather) of French anthropology, an icon from an age in which France's intellectuals were fêted internationally.

Wind the clock back, though, and a different Lévi-Strauss emerges. In a television interview given to Pierre Dumayet for the show *Lectures pour tous* in 1959, we see a far more serious, businesslike operator.[7] Dressed in a somber suit with a waistcoat, he shows an added edge, a hint of arrogance as he responds to Dumayet's straightforward, factual questions about North American ethnography; his features are stronger, better defined; his delivery fluent and humorless. Here was an intellectual in his prime, on the cusp of entering the prestigious Collège de France, an elite institution that had rejected him twice a decade before; a man who had already "unleashed"[8] his pen on several occasions with vitriolic responses to his critics.

Further back still, there are tantalizing glimpses of Lévi-Strauss in the field. Photographs from Brazil show a different kind of expression, one that seems less confident, more hostile. Against the backdrop of Brazil's dry savannahs, a young cosmopolitan man stares back at the camera, dusty and flea-bitten. In Brazil, Lévi-Strauss was an awkward *philosophe* standing out against the easy nakedness of the Indians; an embarrassed Frenchman bathing in a stream, fighting with giggling Nambikwara girls for the soap; an adventurer steeling himself against not so much physical discomfort as intellectual privation. In fleeting glimpses on film, he seems detached—an onlooker, an observer, but never a true participant. "My emotional states weren't that important to me," Lévi-Strauss later told Didier Eribon, when asked whether he kept a personal diary of his field trip.[9] Taciturn and courteous, Lévi-Strauss could also be aloof—"cold, stilted, in the French academic style," as his longtime friend and colleague the anthropologist Alfred Métraux noted in his diary on meeting him for the first time in the 1930s.[10] Though Lévi-Strauss mellowed with age, his reputation for traditional French reserve never left him. "Other than his family and school friends, were there people who addressed Lévi-Strauss in the familiar *tu* form? I doubt it," remarked his successor at the Collège de France, Françoise Héritier, after his death.[11]

I FIRST MET LÉVI-STRAUSS in 2005 at the Laboratoire d'anthropologie sociale, a research institute that he founded in 1960 located in Paris's fifth arrondissement. The fifth's streets are littered with references to centuries of learning, from the roads named after Descartes, Pascal, Cuvier and Buffon to the elite institutions that have cultivated France's most creative minds—the Lycée Henri-IV, the École normale supérieure and the Collège de France, all clustered around the Latin Quarter. At the east of the *quartier*, Paris's 1980s monument to inclusiveness, the Institut du monde arabe, with its mosaics of metal apertures dilating and contracting to filter the light, stands like a prematurely aging relic of another era; farther on, Mexican hothouses, Art Deco winter gardens and an old-fashioned zoo are arranged into the geometric plots of the seventeenth-century Jardin des plantes.

Lévi-Strauss's office was up a tight spiral staircase leading into a mezzanine, lodged in a section of the roof of a converted nineteenth-century amphitheater. On one side there was plate glass looking over iron light fittings hanging from a central beam; down below, researchers and librarians were at work on dark-stained desks, tapping on laptops or sifting through card catalogs. The back wall was stenciled with stylized flowers, strange coats of arms and medieval armor in burgundy, gold and light brown. The office contained almost no exotica—masks or feathers and the like—just books and loosely bound PhD theses. Lévi-Strauss appeared to be a faithful version of images stretching back decades, only shrunken and a little frailer. He wore a tweed jacket that was now slightly too big for him, and it hung loosely off his body. He was courteous and alert; only a pronounced tremor when he went to reach into his breast pocket to retrieve his address book betrayed his great age. Well into his nineties, Lévi-Strauss was still going into the office on Tuesdays and Thursdays, though no longer writing much. Our conversation, which focused on Brazil, was a strange combination of the stories I had read elsewhere, faithfully reproduced word for word, and a sentiment that I was not expecting: an acid, but ironic, nihilism.

We began by discussing *Tristes Tropiques*, the memoir of his fieldwork in Brazil that had brought him fame in the 1950s. It remains his only nonacademic book, written in a literary style that is only hinted at in his more formal work. I asked him why he suddenly lit out into this genre, never to return to it again. "I had a contract to write it, and I needed money" was his frank, though deflating, answer. (The response was atypical. Elsewhere he had given long and complex answers to the same question, going into detail about his motivations and literary aspirations at the time.) We talked about contemporary Brazil's indigenous populations. "What are their prospects?" I asked. "At my age, you don't think about the future," he deadpanned. But he went on to elaborate that, despite their rising population, land demarcations and, in some instances, greater self-determination within the Brazilian state, the indigenous peoples had been culturally impoverished, broken on the wheel of Western expansion.

I was intrigued by Lévi-Strauss's reaction to Brasília, the modernist capital that had not even existed during his fieldwork days, but which he briefly visited in the 1980s during a state visit with then president Mitterrand. I wondered whether the city might have chimed with his aesthetic sensibility, the formalism of his structuralist theoretical approach, his interest in patterns and designs. "There was not enough time and the visit was very programmed," he lamented, "but it would be a complete mistake to link my work with modernism"—an answer that has since come back to me again and again, in the light of the seemingly manifold interconnections between the modernist movement and Lévi-Straussian structuralism. Lévi-Strauss appeared not to want to talk about his theories. When I asked him about the legacy of his work, if there were other people pursuing his ideas, whether he thought his theories would live on, he was disarmingly blunt: "I don't know and I don't care." As I prepared to leave, the mood lightened and he talked effusively about the exhibition Brésil Indien, at Paris's Grand Palais, urging me to go and see it for myself.[12]

The following week, I wandered through the dazzling array of feather headdresses. There were plumes in electric reds and blues; fish, bird and jaguar heads fashioned in what looked like papier-mâché, molded around wicker frames; and four-foot-high porcelain funerary urns found on Marajó, a huge island at the mouth of the Amazon. Lévi-Strauss's collections closed out the exhibition. Under plate glass there were the Nambikwara nose feathers, the Caduveo's geometric-patterned urns, and ritual ornaments of the Bororo that I had read about in *Tristes Tropiques*. Beautifully composed black-and-white photos, taken on Lévi-Strauss's Leica, lined the room. The short films that he had shot in the field were projected onto the walls. Silent, overexposed, a little wobbly and interspersed with Portuguese intertitles, the footage was a cross between early newsreel and home movie. In one unforgettable sequence, an old Caduveo woman dressed in a tattered floral dress drew geometric motifs onto her face—designs that fascinated Lévi-Strauss throughout his career. There was little to connect the young bearded figure that flickered on the wall with the man I had just met. The great gulfs that time had opened up seemed unbridgeable, the mountain of work that Lévi-Strauss had produced in the interim only accentuating the sense of distance, the sense that these ghostly images related to another life, lived in another era entirely.

A second meeting at his home in the sixteenth arrondissement found Lévi-Strauss much more relaxed. In the intervening period we had corresponded regularly, with Lévi-Strauss diligently replying to questions about his experiences in Brazil. He lived in a large, haut-bourgeois apartment—solid, comfortable and in extremely good taste. The walls were adorned with an eclectic mix of beaux arts and indigenous artifacts—a wooden bowl from British Columbia, an antique rug, a romantic portrait of a girl in an ornate gold frame. We spoke in his study, a podlike room with solid parquet flooring and soundproofed door, a heavy writing table with thick, elaborately carved legs playing off against a modular black sofa. He took my coat and hung it in the hall—an operation carried out in the slow motion of extreme old age.

He spoke of his life in deliberate sentences, halting from time to time for breath. I asked questions about his experiences in Brazil, his flight from Nazi-occupied France and his formative years as a Jewish émigré in 1940s New York, where he mixed with exiled surrealist artists including André Breton and Max Ernst. I moved on to his return to academic life in Paris, and the stalling of his career in the 1950s when he contemplated quitting anthropology altogether and becoming a journalist. He was voluble at first, but when we got on to theoretical issues and the rise of structuralism, he began tiring and his answers became shorter and shorter.

We ended on a contemporary issue—the controversy surrounding the opening of Jacques Chirac's vanity project, the Musée du quai Branly. Housed in a vegetation-clad building across the Seine from the Musée de l'Homme, variously described as a giant intestine or a nave on stilts, the project pitted ethnographic purists against professional curators; academic fustiness against aesthetic theater. When the museum was first mooted, there was uproar at the Musée de l'Homme. Curators were said to have stashed prized objects in their living rooms rather than give them up to the fine-arts graduates charged with arranging the Quai Branly displays.

The collection, arranged in the grottolike penumbra of the museum's innards, contains some of Lévi-Strauss's Brazilian artifacts; in the museum's basement is the Lévi-Strauss Auditorium. When I put to him the criticism that the museum might exoticize the cultures whose artifacts it was displaying, he became animated once again. "Anthropology is an ethnocentric science par excellence," he parried. "If the Musée du quai Branly is displaying objects out of context, what about the Louvre and all the religious art there?" So you can approach indigenous art from a purely aesthetic perspective? "If you want," he replied. The thought seemed to have exhausted him, and the interview came to a halt. I took two pictures of Lévi-Strauss staring blankly back into the lens—identikits of scores of recent photographs.

I had found Lévi-Strauss open, even eager to help me, to fill in details, to recount (no doubt for the nth time) stories from his past. There were glimmers of a fully fleshed-out character, small breaches in the studied front, but still a kind of emptiness, an isolation. Old-world charm was matched by an inner reticence. In the end, the mask had barely moved. Later, when I strayed onto personal territory, asking in a letter about his second marriage and the final illness and death of his father, he politely, but firmly, closed the door.

LÉVI-STRAUSS CAME OUT of an age when universities housed tiny elites, when the branches of the humanities were only semiprofessionalized. Anthropology was in its infancy, fieldwork the preserve of a few score academics working on the edges of the still-extant European empires. The physical world had been mapped, but culturally whole regions were virtual blanks. Ethnographers were scouring the world not for unknown headwaters, sea passages or gorges, but for cosmologies, rituals and art. They were exploring the limits of human experience, documenting the rich alternatives that were emerging from the shadows of nineteenth-century prejudice.

An autodidact, Lévi-Strauss plowed through the classics, both Anglo-American and French—Edward Tyler, Robert Lowie, Sir James Frazer, Marcel Granet, Marcel Mauss—largely on his own. As one of the few French anthropologists of his generation not to attend Mauss's famous fieldwork seminars, he organized his own ethnographic expedition, deliberately choosing as remote a region as possible. His main thesis, later published in 1949 as *Les Structures élémentaires de la parenté* (*The Elementary Structures of Kinship*), was unsupervised, written in the New York Public Library while in exile from Nazi occupation. (Back in Paris, he had to go hunting for a supervisor after the fact so that he could be examined.) Initially blocked from ascending into the elite Collège de France, he spent much of the 1950s questioning his future as an anthropologist. What emerged were truly innovative ideas, spared the groupthink of a formal critical environment.

Drawing inspiration from surrealism, linguistics, aesthetics and music, Lévi-Strauss cut a fresh trail through the humanities. Through his career he subjected kinship, indigenous religious thought and myth to iconoclastic reinterpretations. He was an anthropologist in the broadest possible sense of the term, alternating between the minutiae of ethnographic detail and cultural universals, isolated tribes and the laws of the mind. An oeuvre that began with highly technical ethnographic analyses ended with meditations on the birth of the novel, the evolution of Western music and the irrevocable decline of the visual arts.

Through his encounters with Russian linguist Roman Jakobson while in exile in New York, Lévi-Strauss picked up on one of the most fundamental shifts in twentieth-century thought—the swing from meaning to form, the self to the system. His philosophical rationale, his mission "to understand being in relation to itself, and not in relation to oneself" (*de comprendre l'être par rapport à lui-même et non point par rapport à moi*),[13] which defined the structuralist project, heralded a belated modernist turn in the social sciences. It was through Jakobson that Lévi-Strauss discovered the ideas of the Swiss linguist Ferdinand de Saussure and began to apply them to his own research. Henceforth, language became *the* metaphor for cultural analysis; following Saussure, culture began to be viewed as a system of contrasting elements, like phonemes in language.

Lévi-Strauss also presaged the cognitive revolution in the social sciences, with his insistence that the way culture was organized was ultimately rooted in the workings of the brain. His dream was a convergence between areas of knowledge that had long been separated: the social and the hard sciences, culture and nature. Against the prevailing philosophical winds, he set out to study the mind rather than the individual, abstract thought in place of subjective experience—a radical rupture in an intellectual climate then dominated by the introspective philosophies, existentialism and phenomenology.

Lévi-Strauss is the only anthropologist to have achieved global fame. (Margaret Mead comes to mind, but, unlike Lévi-Strauss, her popular renown was largely confined to an Anglo-American audience.) From the mid-1960s on he became a fixture in the French press, giving interviews to publications such as *Le Monde*, *Le Figaro*, *Le Nouvel Observateur* and *L'Express*. Beyond France, American *Vogue* ran a Henri Cartier-Bresson photo-essay on him; he was on American television, and interviewed for *Playboy* magazine. Features came out in the pages of the *New York Times*, the *Washington Post*, *Newsweek* and *Time* describing his structural analyses of the workings of the "savage mind" as a revolution in the social sciences—a Copernican moment in which human culture was finally yielding to scientific method. In Britain, he was interviewed by the BBC, regularly appeared in the pages of the *Times Literary Supplement*, and was often referenced in the broadsheets. His death in November 2009 made front-page news around the world.

Although media celebrity is often unearned, in the case of Lévi-Strauss it was based on concrete achievements. Freud shook up the moribund discipline of psychiatry with his psychoanalytic revolution. Two generations later, Lévi-Strauss would have the same seismic effect on anthropology. Like Freud, his influence spilled over into neighboring disciplines, as he became the reference point for a new style of thinking. It was through his influence that the immediate postwar world of Albert Camus, Jean-Paul Sartre and Simone de Beauvoir ceded the high ground to the likes of Michel Foucault, Roland Barthes and Jacques Lacan in the 1960s, Lévi-Strauss's pointed attack on Sartre in the last chapter of *La Pensée sauvage* (*The Savage Mind*) hurrying the process along. Even though the next generation rejected Lévi-Strauss's grand theorizing style, it was still grappling with philosophical debates that he had initiated. Today's leading theoreticians, like the Slovenian Slavoj Žižek, France's Alain Badiou and Italy's Giorgio Agamben, can be understood only through the prism of Lévi-Strauss's decisive reorientation in the mid-twentieth century.

As a hinge figure of twentieth-century thought, Lévi-Strauss looked both forward and back. He rode the new wave with an early infatuation with the avant-garde. He was seduced by the promise of technology postwar, and by the possibilities this might have for future anthropological research. Early computing, cybernetics, atomic physics and mathematics seemed to offer new ways into the low-tech but highly complex social and cultural worlds of indigenous peoples. However much he might deny it, modernist techniques—narrative disruption, juxtaposition, collage—became staples of his work.

But he was equally fascinated by images from an earlier age: the hall of mirrors, the kaleidoscope, playing cards, hieroglyphics, the clocks and steam engines that continually crop up as metaphors in his work. In his middle age, the nineteenth century would exert a strong attraction through the music of Wagner, the romantic seaport pictures of Joseph Vernet and the novels of Balzac and Dickens. Lévi-Strauss repudiated nonfigurative art and rephrased his earlier interest in surrealism—the type of surrealism that had attracted him was not the bizarre, taboo-breaking dreamscapes of sex and death, but a more genteel, dandyish strain that looked back to the symbolists. By the time he retired, he said that he had largely lost interest in twentieth-century music, never went to the cinema and that the only novels he read were more than fifty years old.[14]

THIS BOOK is an assessment—an intellectual biography of Lévi-Strauss's long life of the mind. It follows him from Paris to São Paulo and into the Brazilian interior. It tracks his turbulent wartime years—his flight from Vichy France to New York and his eventual return to Paris—in search of the "residue" that made his thinking so beguiling and distinctive. It is not a blow-by-blow account of his career, which, postwar, would in any case amount to little more than the recounting of lecture series, book publications, conferences and awards. Nor does it attempt to excavate his private life. A traditional Frenchman, Lévi-Strauss was guarded about his three marriages—two relatively short-lived (Dina Dreyfus and Rose-Marie Ullmo) and one enduring (Monique Roman)—which produced two sons: Laurent, from his marriage to Rose-Marie Ullmo, and Matthieu, from his marriage to Monique Roman. What is interesting about Lévi-Strauss is not the minutiae of his life, but the way this ascetic figure, the very opposite of a Sartre-style charismatic intellectual, managed to capture the high ground of theory and ideas at a particular moment in the twentieth century. For someone whose work was often technical and demanding, Lévi-Strauss struck a powerful chord both within and outside the academy.

In the first half of the book I have looked in some detail at the formative, more eventful period of Lévi-Strauss's life, tracing the germination of his thought through his fieldwork days in Brazil and his life in exile in America to the publication of *Tristes Tropiques*. From the mid-1960s, his life settled, as he retreated into his own world of myths, masks and indigenous art. "I have no social life. I have no friends. I pass half my time in the laboratory, and the rest in my office," he could say to a journalist from *Le Monde* in the early 1970s, in a statement that, although exaggerated for effect, captures the progressive isolation of his later life.[15]

The second half of the book leaves behind the biographical detail to deal with his ideas. Reassessing his key articles and books, I have tried to steer a path between the dismissiveness of some of his critics and the reverence that he still inspires in France and, strangely enough, in Brazil. It is one thing to marvel at the output of an extraordinary mind, quite another to swallow whole what could at times be a quixotic project, and one that drifted in an increasingly idiosyncratic direction as he aged. His success in the 1960s speaks of a looser, perhaps more creative era—a time when big, experimental ideas could take flight, when the stream of consciousness of one mind could leave a deep cultural imprint. His great longevity means that his life has ended up tracing a vital intellectual thread back through the twentieth century. Whatever may have become of structural analysis, Lévi-Strauss's thought stands as an important promontory on the intellectual landscape of our time.

1

Early Years

> The "return to the primitive" was the return to the community, but also a return to the sacred, and even, perhaps, the return of the gods.
>
> MARCEL FOURNIER[1]

AT A BEND in the Seine, as the river turns southward before looping back around the Bois de Boulogne, two stone pavilions arc around a stone terrace. It was here that Adolf Hitler and Albert Speer posed for photographs in 1940, grinning in front of the Palais de Chaillot, the Eiffel Tower rising from the far bank of the Seine in the background. A year before the invasion, Lévi-Strauss, then a young anthropologist fresh from fieldwork in Brazil, had been at work in the Palais's recently installed Musée de l'Homme, cataloging the nose feathers, gourds and arrows that he had bartered for glass beads in the backlands of Mato Grosso, for an exhibition that would never go on display.

The site has resonance not just for the history of anthropology in France, but for the evolution of avant-garde art at the beginning of the twentieth century. Founded in 1938, the Musée de l'Homme marked the beginning of modern, professional ethnographic displays in France. Looking back at the museum's previous incarnation, the Musée de l'ethnographie, is like stepping back into another curatorial world. Occupying part of the Palais du Trocadéro, a Moorish, Byzantine folly on the same site as today's Palais de Chaillot, the Musée de l'ethnographie housed largely pre-Columbian artifacts, but later soaked up the spoils of the advancing French African empire—the spears, drums and masks that colonial traders hawked in ports up and down the west coast of Africa. Objects were classified by theme rather than by region or tribe. Curators piled up musical instruments in one corner and textiles in another; there were corridors of wood-carved statuettes, back rooms stacked up with fertility symbols, all displayed with little—if any—context.

"When I first went there, at Derain's urging, the smell of dampness and rot there stuck in my throat," remembered a young Pablo Picasso in 1907, of a visit to the museum's labyrinth of musty, dim-lit corridors. "It depressed me so much I wanted to get out fast, but I stayed and studied." Picasso had been drawn to the museum's clutter of artifacts by aesthetic instinct. A few years earlier he had acquired a West African mask, which he had studied not as an archaic fetish or a throwback to a bygone age, but as an artistic expression in its own right. But it was in the bowels of the Palais du Trocadéro that the penny had dropped. It was not just the plastic forms, distortions and poetic freedoms that struck Picasso, but the realization that art need not be an exercise in mirroring reality. Ethnographically speaking, it could have a "magical" role of capturing and controlling terrors and desires, pinning them down with color and form. "The day I understood that," Picasso said later, "I had found my path."[2]

A famous photograph dated a year after this revelatory experience—the year in fact of Lévi-Strauss's birth—has a twenty-seven-year-old Picasso seated in his studio in the Bateau-Lavoir in Montmartre with a pair of African wooden statues and what looks like a pig's skull on one side, and a bookcase filled with pre-Columbian figurines on the other. Gone were references to classical antiquity, Christian icons and the Renaissance. A new generation of artists was looking outside their immediate cultural surroundings for inspiration. Around the same time as Picasso's epiphany, artists like André Derain, Maurice de Vlaminck and Juan Gris were latching on to tribal art from Dahomey and the Côte d'Ivoire, and collector Paul

Guillaume was buying up African sculpture. By the time Brancusi's eerie totem pole–like *Endless Column* (1918) went on display, a strain of modern art had become virtually indistinguishable from indigenous artifact.

Somewhere between the ramshackle halls of the Musée de l'ethnographie and the professionalized galleries of the Musée de l'Homme, modern French anthropology was born. As Lévi-Strauss grew up, sociological investigations into ritual and religion were flowering into a peculiarly rich form of anthropological inquiry. Academics who had gathered around Émile Durkheim's influential *Année sociologique*—a journal promoting the sociological approach, founded at the end of the nineteenth century—were branching off into investigations of totemism, sacrifice and "primitive" religious thought. The new discipline both capitalized on and fed into the vogue for the exotic. It dabbled in the avant-garde—particularly the emerging surrealist movement, which had also become bound up in the idea of the primitive—even as it began moving off in a more scholarly direction.

Durkheim's nephew Marcel Mauss was a key early figure. At the turn of the twentieth century he had taken up a chair in the History of the Religions of Uncivilized Peoples (*Histoire des religions des peuples non civilisés*) at the Fifth Section of the École pratique des hautes études (which Lévi-Strauss would occupy half a century later) at a time of intense speculation about the origins of modern religion. Mauss had built up an encyclopedic knowledge of what was then known about tribal societies from compilations of reports of colonial administrators, missionaries and explorers, as well as the first professional ethnographic studies coming out of Britain and the United States. Throughout his career he mined these materials, producing a series of strange, but brilliant, synthetic studies: on personhood, prayer, bodily movements and the suggestibility of death. He wrote one short classic, *Essai sur le don* (published in English as *The Gift*), on which Lévi-Strauss would later draw heavily, but he also left behind a slew of unfinished works.[3]

Mauss was acutely aware that while *L'Année sociologique* was moving on to anthropological terrain, France lagged behind Britain and the

United States institutionally. He dreamed of creating a "bureau, institute, or department of ethnology, whatever you want to call it" to bring together a subject then strewn across different institutions—the École coloniale, the Musée national d'Histoire naturelle, and his own academy, the Fifth Section of the École pratique des hautes études. But it was not until well after the death of his uncle, along with several talented members of the *Année sociologique* school in the First World War, that Mauss finally won backing for the Institut d'ethnologie, which opened on the rue Saint-Jacques in 1926.[4]

With an athletic build, piercing eyes, a full beard and a "cavernous voice," Mauss gave dazzling, improvised lectures at the institute, teaching not just anthropology students, but missionaries and colonial administrators as well. He peppered his lectures with cultural minutiae from around the world, moving from anthropological sensationalism—cannibalism, priestess prostitutes and bizarre forms of circumcision—to a celebration of the prosaic: "A tin can characterises our societies better than the most sumptuous jewel or the rarest stamp."[5] At the same time he gave his students practical fieldwork advice—develop film quickly, write up an inventory of objects on index cards, keep a field journal, "don't be credulous, don't be surprised, don't lose your temper"—as well as possible areas of study: types of weapons, methods of preparing food (raw, smoked, dried, boiled, roasted, fried), varieties of fabrics. The irony was that Mauss disliked travel, even in Europe, and except for a brief period in Morocco, never did any meaningful fieldwork himself.

Mauss's ideas resonated not just with those wanting to study indigenous culture, but also with interested amateurs, philosophers and artists. Intellectuals in search of new ideas, like the writer Georges Bataille, turned toward the rich and varied veins that ran through the ethnographic record. What had once been relegated to an antiquarian pursuit was now considered quintessentially modern. Traffic flowed both ways. Out of hours, Mauss and his students would meet and talk late into the night on the terrace of the Café de Flore, a favorite haunt of avant-garde artists and poets; on Saturdays they would go to see African-American dancer Josephine Baker at the Bal nègre on the rue Bonnet.

In 1920s Paris, Africa—or some French metropolitan version of it—became a cultural touchstone. Paris's Belle Époque music halls, like the Folies-Bergères, the Casino de Paris and the Théâtre des Champs-Élysées, had once hosted a promiscuous mix of burlesque, animal acts, dance and theater. By the 1920s they were booked up with jazz bands, made up of African-American soldiers who had stayed on after the First World War. Writer, surrealist and ethnographer Michel Leiris, seven years Lévi-Strauss's senior, remembered being caught up in the experience: "Jazz was a rallying cry, an orgiastic banner in the colors of the moment," he recalled. "It was the first manifestation of the nègres, the myth of the coloured Edens which was to lead me as far as Africa, and, beyond Africa, to ethnography."[6]

ALTHOUGH FRENCH ANTHROPOLOGY was still only a suggestive collection of ideas and influences, the renewed interest in indigenous cultures inspired a rethink of the dusty collections in the Palais du Trocadéro. In 1928, sociologist Paul Rivet took charge of the museum and, assisted by amateur jazz player and curator Georges-Henri Rivière, began work. They cleared out exhibition spaces, sifted through the piles of artifacts, organizing them into metal cabinets, and glassed in a semicircular gallery on the second floor. Helped by high-society volunteers—well-heeled ladies of leisure—they modernized and expanded the library and began labeling exhibits. Rivet installed the collection he had brought back from Mexico, while trying to give some coherence to the vast backlog of nineteenth-century exotica.

Rivet and Rivière were resourceful, with a nose for publicity and fund-raising opportunities. They brokered agreements with the governor general of Algeria and North African colonial officials to mount the hugely successful Exposition du Sahara, showcasing ethnographic artifacts from across the region. At the opening of the Oceania hall, they invited Paris's top models to parade through the galleries. A fund-raising event pitted the "African" (in fact Panamanian) featherweight boxing star Al Brown against Marcel Mauss himself.[7]

Lévi-Strauss would become one of the most influential figures to emerge from this fertile amalgam of art and ideas—a tension between the aesthetic object and the ethnographic artifact that has run through the French tradition, recently resurfacing in the debates around the opening of the Musée du quai Branly.[8] Lévi-Strauss was one of the few early-wave French anthropologists not to attend Mauss's lectures, but his upbringing was suffused with the arts, and as a young man he got to know many in the surrealist movement, including André Breton. Although he would progressively disown his modernist roots, the texture of his early influences is present throughout his oeuvre. His path into the discipline would be circuitous. Like many who ended up in the field, Lévi-Strauss took a poorly signposted track leading off the arterial route of philosophy—still very much the main thruway of the French academic system—and kept on going.

LÉVI-STRAUSS WAS BROUGHT UP in a secular Jewish family, descendant on both sides from the Alsace, in an apartment on rue Poussin at the edge of Paris's sixteenth arrondissement. Wedged between the Bois de Boulogne and the Seine, the area was only semiurbanized; there were small farms down the end of the road, along with cheap-rent *brocantes* and artist studios in what was then a relatively poor corner of Paris. The apartment block itself was built only a few years before his birth. The only thing that now distinguishes it from the rows and rows of mid-nineteenth-century blocks that stretch across Paris are a few neo-Gothic touches: two black cast-iron vines that climb up the iron-and-glass doors at the front entrance; the ornamental foliage, molded from concrete, that supports the building's semicircular balconies.

Although the family was of modest means, Lévi-Strauss grew up hearing stories from a lost nineteenth-century idyll—an aristocratic world of orchestras and fine art. His great-grandfather Isaac Strauss had moved from Strasbourg to Paris in 1826 at the age of twenty and studied violin at the Paris Conservatoire. Starting out as a violinist at the Théâtre-Italien, he went on to make his name as a conductor, composer and orchestra director, running the spa orchestra in Vichy under Napoléon III, and ensembles at the Tuileries imperial balls and the Paris Opéra. He worked with Offenbach and even appears fleetingly in the memoirs of Berlioz. On his travels through Europe he bought up furniture and art, later focusing on Jewish ritual objects—Sabbath lamps, spice boxes and Esther scrolls—with which he filled the "Villa Strauss" in Vichy. The remnants of the collection are now displayed in the Salle Strauss at the Musée de Cluny in Paris.

Through the next generation, and the economic downturn of the 1880s, the family's fortunes waned. Lévi-Strauss's father, Raymond, was forced down a more prosaic route, studying at the École des hautes études commerciales and eventually finding menial work on the Paris Bourse. He married his second cousin Emma Lévy, the daughter of a rabbi, who had been sent to Paris to study typing and shorthand. A sensitive man with a passion for the arts, Raymond was not able to settle into the life of a minor functionary. Frustrated by his work at the Bourse, he made a bold decision: he enrolled at the École des beaux-arts and began portrait painting for a living. "His god was Maurice Quentin de la Tour," Lévi-Strauss later recalled, referring to the eighteenth-century rococo portraitist. "He did a lot of pastels and obviously was not in touch with his times."[9] It was while Raymond was working on a commission in Brussels, on November 28, 1908, that Emma bore him his only child, Gustave Claude Lévi-Strauss. Until his death Lévi-Strauss kept one of his father's paintings of the view from the window of the room in which he was born, as an *objet mémoire*. Raymond would go on to produce several evocative canvases of his son, including one as a young boy in a striped smock on a rocking horse and another soft pastel portrait of him as a young man.

While Lévi-Strauss's upbringing could not exactly be described as poor, his father's career choice meant that they would always be struggling bourgeoisie rather than solidly middle class. Raymond and Emma brought up their son in the classic bourgeois lifestyle, taking summer holidays on the beaches of Normandy and Brittany and even managing, in the 1920s, to buy a derelict property in the south of France, in the Cévennes, where they spent the summers. But there was periodic financial turbulence—the desperate months when the commissions dried up. The downturns were eased by the support of their extended family, with which they maintained strong ties. Given that Lévi-Strauss's parents were second cousins, the families were close—so close that "it would be more accurate to speak of one family, rather than two," Lévi-Strauss later recalled.[10] Each week they would gather at his paternal grandmother Léa Strauss's house. Once a year she would take the covers off the furniture in the dining room and the family came together for a meal. After lunch they would tour Paris's cemeteries, visiting the graves of their forebears.

When the First World War broke out, Lévi-Strauss's father was mobilized, securing the comparatively safe position of ambulance attendant due to his fragile health. Emma, fearing an invasion of Paris, left with her son, then five, traveling to Normandy and on to Brittany to join her sisters and their children. When the danger had abated, the entourage moved down to stay in Rabbi Lévy's huge house in Versailles, close to where Lévi-Strauss's father had been stationed.

In Versailles, Lévi-Strauss would have his first, contradictory, experiences of his Jewish roots. On one side was his grandfather, the rabbi—a timid but deeply religious man. His rambling house was both a home and a place of worship. In *Tristes Tropiques*, Lévi-Strauss recalled the sense of anguish he had felt as a child, walking down an inner passageway that led to the synagogue, from the warmth of the profane to the coolness of the sacred. He remembered the deadness of that room, only temporarily enlivened by his grandfather's services, as well as the few cryptic references to religion that punctuated his stay: his grandfather praying in silence before each meal; his grandmother fasting during Yom Kippur; a religious scroll on the dining room wall that read: "Chew your food well for the good of your digestion."[11]

Other memories were of his mother, who despite being the daughter of a rabbi had been educated along with her sisters in a Catholic convent school. She would surreptitiously hand out *sandwichs jambon* in the park, Lévi-Strauss and his cousins wolfing them down crouched behind statues so as not to upset their grandfather. On Lévi-Strauss's father's side, the Jewish legacy was more bizarre. One uncle, who became obsessed with biblical exegesis, committed suicide when Lévi-Strauss was three; another, in an act of rebellion, was ordained as a priest, but ended up working in a lowly position for the gas board.

As far as Lévi-Strauss's parents were concerned, religion was background noise to an otherwise secular family life. They did not observe holy days, "but they used to talk about them."[12] While in Versailles they gave Lévi-Strauss a bar mitzvah, largely for the benefit of his grandfather. At their core they were French patriots—in Versailles, encouraged by his parents, the young Lévi-Strauss donated his pocket money to the war effort. On Armistice, Lévi-Strauss remembered his father taking him to watch the victory parades from the vantage point of a building near the Opéra. Nevertheless, the family's vaguely conceived Jewish identity would play a decisive role in the rest of their lives. Lévi-Strauss learned early what it would mean to have a Jewish-sounding name in a still profoundly anti-Semitic culture. At school he was bullied by other children, who called him "a dirty Jew." "How did you react?" he was asked in an interview for *Le Magazine littéraire* in the 1980s. "With a punch"—*le coup de poing*—he replied. The bullying turned to persecution in the next world war, during which his family would lose everything and he would be forced to flee for his life.

LÉVI-STRAUSS WAS AN ONLY CHILD with a lively imagination at play in the clutter of the rue Poussin apartment-cum-atelier. The apartment was a storehouse of intellectual and artistic raw material—easels, canvases, tubes of paint, a makeshift darkroom where his father developed photos of his sitters, antiques and shelves of books. "My father and two of my uncles were painters [including the successful Belle Époque painter Henry Caro-Delvaille]. That is to say my mother and two of her sisters married painters and I was born and raised in artist ateliers . . . It was not at all an academic background . . . I had pencils and paintbrushes in my hands when I was learning to read and write," he later remembered.[13]

In the midst of his father's cultural bric-a-brac, the young boy constructed his own eclectic fantasies. He listened to records of American spirituals on the family gramophone and spent his pocket money on miniature Japanese furniture that he bought from a shop on the rue des Petits-Champs. Arranging the delicate pieces in a box lined with Japanese printed fabric that his father had given him, he conjured up a scaled-down version of a Far Eastern room. He became obsessed with a condensed version of Cervantes's *Don Quixote* with a pink-tinged cover, which he claims to have read and memorized by the time he was just ten years old. His parents would entertain guests by getting them to open the book at random and start reading, at which point Lévi-Strauss would continue without hesitation.[14] During lunches at his grandparents' place he would sit in a corner chuckling to himself as he read the nineteenth-century vaudeville plays of Eugène Labiche.[15]

Raymond Lévi-Strauss gave his son an enviable cultural grounding on slender means. He would book the cheapest obscured-view seats at the opera, introducing his son to Wagner's repertoire from an early age. They went every week to the Colonne and Pasdeloup classical concerts at Châtelet, spent long afternoons in the Louvre, and in adolescence Claude took violin lessons at the Opéra. His father's friends—a lively group of critics, writers and artists—would mill around the apartment in the evenings and on the weekends. Many took to the boy, indulging his curiosity, recommending books, paintings and music.

Encouraged by his father, the young Lévi-Strauss tried his hand at all the arts. "Working with bits of pastels that were lying around the studio, I began to draw what I imagined were cubist works . . . I can still see my naïve compositions—everything was flat, two-dimensional, with no attempt to convey volume."[16] As an adolescent he took and developed his own photographs, invented film scenarios and composed trios for two violins and piano. He drew costumes and painted sets for operas, and even began work on a libretto, which he abandoned after writing the prelude.

After the First World War, Lévi-Strauss enrolled in the Lycée Janson de Sailly, a few kilometers from his house, where he studied until sitting the baccalaureate. In contrast to the bohemian milieu of the rue Poussin, his education at Janson was strict, the atmosphere in the classroom imbued with an old-world formality. The beginning and end of lessons were announced by the beat of a drum; compositions were written "with anguish," with the results solemnly read out in front of the class by the headmaster accompanied by his deputy, "leaving us despondent or overjoyed." Indiscipline was severely punished.[17] In the afternoons Lévi-Strauss would range around Paris, exploring the neighboring arrondissements on foot, "like Jalles and Jerphanion in Jules Romains novels."[18] He would jump on buses and ride the open platforms at the back as the bus weaved through Paris. When he was older, he set off with friends on voyages of discovery into the outer suburbs, getting as far as the gypsum quarries of Cormeilles-en-Parisis, some sixteen kilometers from the sixteenth arrondissement.

As Lévi-Strauss edged toward adulthood, the avant-garde blossomed. At one of the first performances of Stravinsky's *Les Noces* at the Théâtre du Châtelet, he heard the spare abstractions, the choppy interchanges of chorus, percussion and piano that scandalized Parisian audiences when it debuted in 1923. Lévi-Strauss was fourteen years old, and was bowled over. The performance made such an impression on him that he went straight back the following night. Years later he wrote in his memoir that the experience "brought about the collapse of my previous musical assumptions."[19] In middle age, as he wrote in *Le Cru et le cuit* (*The Raw and the Cooked*), he still felt the "shattering" impact of hearing *Les Noces* along with Claude Debussy's symbolist opera *Pelléas et Mélisande*.[20]

He began making a pilgrimage up to Rosenberg's gallery on the rue La Boétie in the eighth arrondissement, where the latest Picasso would be propped up in the window. He later described seeing Picasso's still-life canvases of the mid-1920s as "the equivalent of metaphysical revelations."[21] When a friend of the family, the influential art critic Louis Vauxcelles, suggested that Lévi-Strauss write a piece for a review journal he was trying to launch, Claude proposed "the influence of Cubism on everyday life."[22] While researching the piece, Lévi-Strauss interviewed the artist Fernand Léger. "He received me with extreme kindness," remembered Lévi-Strauss. "Was the article ever published? I forget."[23]

What was fresh, irreverent and intellectually challenging for the young Lévi-Strauss spelled ruin for his father. Raymond Lévi-Strauss had been shocked by what he saw in the art salons on his return from Versailles after the war. In the interim, modern art had gone from the fringes of the avant-garde into the heartlands of the city's best-known galleries. Incomprehensible canvases of splintered shapes and clashing colors were being bought up by collectors like Daniel-Henry Kahnweiler, whom Lévi-Strauss's father had met during his years at the Bourse. By the 1920s changing tastes, along with the rise of mass photography, meant that the demand for realist portraiture was shrinking rapidly and Raymond Strauss's already precarious income was beginning to erode. He was left to improvise, often with the help of his son, turning his hand to a variety of more or less desperate business ventures, as Lévi-Strauss remembered years later:

> For a time the whole house became involved in printing fabrics. We carved linoleum blocks and smeared them with glue. We used to print designs on velvet on which we sprinkled metallic powders of various colours . . . There was another time when my father made small Chinese-style tables

of imitation lacquer. He also made lamps with cheap Japanese prints glued onto glass. Anything that would help pay the bills.[24]

Intellectually precocious, Lévi-Strauss started reading the master thinkers early. While still at Janson, he discovered Freud through Dr. Marcel Nathan, a pioneer of Freudian psychoanalysis in France and the father of one of his school friends, Jacques. It was through his recommendations that Lévi-Strauss read the early French translations of *A General Introduction to Psychoanalysis* and *The Interpretation of Dreams*. The influence would be profound and long-lasting. In the first half of his career Lévi-Strauss would revisit many of Freud's areas of theoretical interest—the incest taboo, the myth of Oedipus, and totemism; a late book, *La Potière jalouse* (*The Jealous Potter*), would be an extended dialogue with Freud, whom he admired and criticized in equal measure.

In the summer of 1925, when Lévi-Strauss was sixteen, another element was added: politics. It was then that he met the Belgian Workers' Party militant Arthur Wauters, through friends of the family. When Lévi-Strauss asked him to explain his ideas, Wauters took the young man under his wing "like an older brother," introducing him to the socialist cannon, from Karl Marx and Friedrich Engels to Jean Jaurès and Pierre-Joseph Proudhon.[25] He arranged for Lévi-Strauss to spend two weeks in Belgium as a guest of the Belgian Workers' Party, where he learned about how the party functioned institutionally and saw socialist ideals in action through party affiliations with workers' syndicates. Later he described the experience as "a complete revelation": a "new world was being unveiled to me, intellectually and socially."[26] Back in Paris, he read *Das Kapital* while studying philosophy at the lycée. "I didn't understand it all. In reality, what I discovered in Marx were other forms of thought also new to me: Kant, Hegel . . ."[27]

From political theory to the avant-garde to the classics, his reading was filling out, mixing French classics, such as Rousseau and Chateaubriand, with Dickens, Dostoyevsky and Conrad. He was not intimidated by sheer literary bulk, at one point becoming fixated on Balzac's *La Comédie humaine*—seventeen volumes of interlinked stories, which served as a kind of literary ethnography of France between the revolution and the reign of Louis-Philippe. He read it from beginning to end—ten times. Another major influence was Gide's *Paludes*—a literary satire of the symbolist movement, to which Lévi-Strauss would also become attracted.

By nature, Lévi-Strauss was proving to be an intellectual omnivore, a grazer eternally on the move, roaming the vast plains of Western culture—moving from French literature to philosophy to modernism across the arts. It was clear that he was gifted, capable of soaking up theories, new ideas and culture at a time of explosive change and creativity in Paris. But as he neared the end of his school days, it was not so clear what this inquiring mind would settle on and pursue. "I was too disorganized," he later confessed.

In the autumn of 1925, after passing the baccalaureate, Lévi-Strauss entered France's fast track into the intellectual elite. He moved from Janson to the Lycée Condorcet's *hypokhâgne*—the preparatory classes for the entrance exams of the prestigious École normale supérieure. The École normale supérieure on the rue d'Ulm in Paris's fifth arrondissement was founded after the French Revolution as the *grande école* for the humanities. Graduates—known as *normaliens*—have since filled the top positions in France's cultural elite. The high-flying academics, the heads of publishing houses, the directors of museums or government appointees to the top echelons of the education system—the vast majority have been members of an exclusive École normale supérieure club.

Lévi-Strauss was to have spent two years at Condorcet studying a broad range of subjects for some of the toughest exams in the French system, but faltered after the first. He later described being overawed by his fellow students, intimidated by the sense that he was surrounded by future *normaliens*. "I had the feeling that I could never be in their class," he remembered.[28] More practically, he felt unable to compete academically. He struggled with math, and Greek did not appeal—two subjects required for the entrance exams. In a fascinating glimpse into the eighteen-year-old mind of Claude Lévi-Strauss, his history and geography teacher Léon Cahen wrote notes on his progress, or lack thereof:

> Has worth, will develop. Knows a lot. Sharp, penetrating mind. But these qualities are often spoiled by a rigor that is, as a rule, almost sectarian, assertion of absolute, black-and-white theses, and sometimes the thinking makes do with a rather banal style, without precision or nuance.[29]

In the spring of 1926, on the advice of his philosophy teacher André Cresson, Lévi-Strauss gave up the idea of entering the École normale supérieure. Instead he enrolled in the law faculty, in the colonnaded neo-classical buildings on the place du Panthéon, while taking a parallel degree in philosophy at the Sorbonne.[30] It was there that he met his future wife, Dina Dreyfus, a French Jew of Russian extraction who had spent some of her early life in Italy. A strong-minded, introspective woman, she was, like Lévi-Strauss, an ardent socialist and philosophy student.

Lévi-Strauss later explained that he chose philosophy because it was easier and more open to his other interests: "I had a taste for painting, music, antiques—all that more or less married with the study of philosophy, more easily than another speciality which would have forced me to compartmentalize my existence and my curiosity."[31] There was also a more practical element—at that time philosophy offered "the only way for a young bourgeois intellectual to earn a living," a pressing concern given his family's shaky financial situation.[32] But after the excitement of growing up on the rue Poussin, his university years were uninspiring, spent learning thick law books by rote, ingesting philosophical formulae without truly understanding what they meant, and being trained in a style of exposition that sounded sophisticated but was ultimately empty and mechanical.

He filled the void left by Parisian academicism with a period of intense political engagement, just as the modern French Left was coalescing. In the wake of the Bolshevik Revolution of 1917 and the catastrophe of the First World War, blamed by many on capitalist infighting, the Left had become a force in French politics. The Parti communiste français (French Communist Party) was founded in 1920, but Lévi-Strauss leaned toward the more moderate Section française de l'Internationale ouvrière, or SFIO (French Section of the Workers' International). As Lévi-Strauss began working in the student movement, the SFIO was tasting real power as a part of the Cartel des gauches, a left-wing coalition that held a majority in the chamber of deputies in the mid-1920s.

Encouraged by Georges Lefranc, who headed a group of left-wing students at the Lycée Louis-le-Grand, another preparation school for the École normale supérieure, Lévi-Strauss began participating in the Groupe socialiste interkhâgnal—an assortment of socialists, communists and members of the Christian movement, La Jeune République. Each Thursday afternoon they would hold meetings at the Société de géographie on the Left Bank for talks and seminars about factory working conditions, workers' cooperatives, unions and colonialism. Prestigious guest speakers, including socialist luminaries Marcel Déat and Léon Blum, gave the forum a weight and credibility far beyond a mere student association. Lefranc later described it as a kind of "parallel university," run by "political and economic autodidacts."[33] Lévi-Strauss was active from the outset, contributing to debates, intervening from the floor and making speeches. His first published work dates from this period—a laudatory essay on the radical French revolutionary egalitarian, agitator and writer Gracchus Babeuf. Written originally as a dissertation for Léon Cahen at the Lycée Condorcet, it was published in the Belgian Workers' Party house journal, *L'Églantine*, as *Gracchus Babeuf et le communisme*—a piece that Lévi-Strauss later dismissed as "an accident," "which I would rather forget."[34]

During this period Lévi-Strauss alternated between the dry lectures at the Sorbonne and the excitement of the political meetings at the Société de géographie. He attended courses on psychology, morals and sociology, logic and the history of philosophy; at the place du Panthéon there were classes on civil, criminal and constitutional law. In his spare time he read socialist journals and grappled with Marx. Combining his interests, Lévi-Strauss chose to write his dissertation, "The Philosophical Postulates of Historical Materialism with Specific Reference to Karl Marx," under the direction of the sociologist and future head of the École normale supérieure Célestin Bouglé. Bouglé, himself a socialist and key collaborator in Durkheim's *Année sociologique* project, accepted what would have been a radical topic at a time when the ideas of Marx were not yet well established in France, with the proviso that Lévi-Strauss also write a dissertation on the safer, more classical thinker Saint-Simon. Lévi-Strauss was already thinking big. He saw himself as a potential philosopher of the Left, a synthesizer of classical and radical thought:

> The idea of building a bridge between the great philosophical tradition—by that I mean Descartes, Leibniz, and Kant—and political thought, as represented by Marx, was very seductive. Even today I understand how I could have dreamed of it.[35]

As he progressed through university, Lévi-Strauss's political engagement matured. In 1928 he became the secretary-general of the Fédération des étudiants socialistes (Federation of Socialist Students), a group that brought together *normaliens* from five Écoles normales supérieures. The same year he organized the Third Congress of Socialist Students of France and began contributing to the Federation's review, *L'Étudiant socialiste*. To earn money he read the bulletin of the Workers' International Bureau for Radio Tour Eiffel from a basement of the Grand Palais, on the Champs-Élysées. The following year he secured a job as secretary to the charismatic SFIO deputy Georges Monnet. His duties included running the office, typing up proposals for laws, attending debates at the Chambre des députés (France's legislative assembly) and writing articles. In 1930, as he neared the end of his studies, he became president of a kind of left-wing think tank, called the Groupe des onze (the Group of Eleven), whose aim was to discuss ways of mobilizing the Left on a global level, through unions, cooperatives and social insurance schemes. He was just twenty-one years old. It seemed at this point that Lévi-Strauss might have a promising political career ahead of him, in the vanguard of the new Left.

"Did you preach the revolution at the SFIO?" Lévi-Strauss was asked in an interview in the mid-1980s about this period. "It depends what you mean by the word," he answered diplomatically. "I wasn't a Leninist, so I rejected violent social change. In contrast, a small group of militants, of whom I was one, formed a movement—today you would call it a tendency [*tendence*]—which was called Constructive Revolution." The idea, as Lévi-Strauss later explained, was gradual, but nevertheless complete, transformation:

> If, day after day, we apply ourselves to create institutions in the socialist spirit, little by little they will grow, in virtue of their superiority, like a chrysalis in a capitalist cocoon, which will end up falling like a dead, dried-up envelope.[36]

Though he was spending more and more time on politics, Lévi-Strauss never lost sight of his broader cultural interests, inculcated into him by his father. He continued to read widely, visit galleries and think about art and aesthetics. By chance he did a brief spell of work as the assistant of the prolific novelist Victor Margueritte, whom he met through another novelist, André Chamson, then working in an office next door to Monnet's. Lévi-Strauss was drafted in to promote Margueritte's pacifist novel *La Patrie humaine* by hand-delivering specially inscribed editions of it to around a hundred influential Parisians and writing and sending out press releases to the media. Margueritte, then a crotchety seventy-year-old, was a cousin of the symbolist poet Stéphane Mallarmé and had mixed with Paris's literary elite all his life. In his grand apartment in the seventeenth arrondissement he regaled the young Lévi-Strauss with family anecdotes featuring Balzac, Zola, the Goncourts and Victor Hugo.

The new "Livres et revues" section of *L'Étudiant socialiste*, which Lévi-Strauss edited and regularly contributed to from 1930 onward, also gave him a more literary outlet. It was there that he wrote of the pleasure he derived from reading Trotsky's prose (in spite of the fact that he did not adhere to his views), eulogized Dostoyevsky and hailed Conrad as "the greatest novelist of the twentieth century." Among the many books he reviewed were the American pulp-fiction novel *Crime passionnel* by Ludwig Lewisohn, *Banjo*, a novel written by an African-American, and Louis-Ferdinand Céline's *Voyage au bout de la nuit*.[37] Céline's worldly pessimism would linger on in Lévi-Strauss's imagination, resurfacing in his descriptions of his own dystopian journey through Brazil in *Tristes Tropiques*.

One of his most interesting early pieces was "Picasso and Cubism," an article he ghosted for Georges Monnet for Bataille's short-lived avant-garde magazine, *Documents*. In an unconventional approach, Lévi-Strauss attacked cubism while heaping praise on Picasso. Cubism was not the radical rupture from impressionism that critics imagined, he argued—it was part of a long tradition of bourgeois art styles catering to a select group of insiders. Cubism had merely shifted the focus from visual to intellectual play. Like impressionism, it was a clever way of coding experience, "an aristocratic art, akin to earlier religious art." Picasso, however, was different. He was an aesthetic genius. He had an incredible eye and a gift for spontaneity. He cut to the heart of reality, bringing out its intensity. Picasso could evoke "the agonizing shame of the most complete nudity, like that of a man who, at the same time as taking off his shirt, is peeling away his skin." Women became "slabs of flesh" that Picasso somehow made eloquent. Even prosaic objects—bottles, glasses, pipes—were somehow edgy and full of suspense, "immersed in the still, apprehensive atmosphere that precedes accidents, riots and disasters."[38]

Through this article, Lévi-Strauss brushed against a milieu that would interest him more and more as he got older. *Documents* typified the strange fusions that were then coursing through French avant-garde culture. In its brief fifteen-issue life span, it mixed ethnographic artifact with modern art, popular culture with the bizarre. African masks, Aztec scripts, Picassos and covers of pulp-fiction novels shared pages with photos of slaughterhouses, a close-up of a big toe, and essays on dust and saliva. Michel Leiris described it as a "Janus publication," with one face turned "toward the lofty spheres of culture . . . the other toward a wilderness where one ventured with no map or passport of any kind."[39] Contributors to *Documents* included Mauss, Leiris and the ethnomusicologist André Schaeffner. Its editor, Georges Bataille, shared many interests with anthropology and developed a close friendship with the Swiss-French anthropologist Alfred Métraux, a future close friend and colleague of Lévi-Strauss.

Another coincidental contact with his future profession came about at around the same time, when Lévi-Strauss helped his father decorate the Madagascan pavilion for the Exposition coloniale. "I was taken on by him as it was done in the Renaissance ateliers," Lévi-Strauss recalled, "in which everybody got down to the work at hand—family, students and so on."[40] They worked in the halls of the Musée de l'ethnographie at Trocadéro, which Rivet had already begun remodeling and which would soon become the Musée de l'Homme. With thirty meters of wall space to cover, everyone pitched in. Lévi-Strauss posed for some of the figures in the mural and filled in portions of the vast backdrops, while his father did the more intricate work of painting groups of colonial officers and young Madagascan women.[41] It is not clear how Lévi-Strauss reacted to the idea of the exhibition itself. With its giant replica of the Angkor Wat temple in the Bois de Vincennes, mock-ups of African and Indochinese villages, and, in a bizarre twist, Missouri-born Josephine Baker featured as "the queen of the colonies," the Exposition coloniale was a popular success, but was not without its critics.

Some in the avant-garde and on the left were beginning to mobilize against colonialism. A group of surrealists, including André Breton and Yves Tanguy, both of whom Lévi-Strauss would later get to know personally, wrote and distributed a manifesto entitled "Ne visitez pas l'Exposition coloniale." The manifesto denounced France's atrocities abroad and called for "the immediate evacuation of the colonies and the putting on trial of the generals and administrators responsible for the massacres in Annam [North Vietnam], Libya, Morocco and Central Africa." One of the signatories, the poet and novelist Louis Aragon, organized a counterexhibition with displays of sculptures and artworks from Africa, Oceania and the Americas in a pavilion left over from the Art Deco fair of 1925.

At the time, Lévi-Strauss's own attitude to colonialism was far less radical. "By colonization we mean the subordination by force of less evolved groups, from the social and economic point of view, to more highly evolved, upstart groups," he wrote in a special edition of *L'Étudiant socialiste* dedicated to the issue. His line was paternalistic: he broadly accepted the need for colonialism, but argued that the profits should go toward helping the indigenous populations, which could be placed under the control of an international socialist protectorate.[42] It was precisely this Europe-centered vision of the world that Lévi-Strauss would later come to reject. Much of his work would be a rhetorical critique of colonialism, whose aftereffects he would soon be experiencing at first hand.

Although a voracious reader, he was still unaware of what was then called *ethnologie* in France. "I knew nothing about anthropology," he wrote in his memoir. "I had never attended any course and when Sir James Frazer [author of *The Golden Bough*] paid his last visit to the Sorbonne to give a memorable lecture—in 1928, I think—it never occurred to me to attend, although I knew about it."[43] Missing the chance to see Frazer—whose work Lévi-Strauss would critically reassess in the years to come—would end up being a source of profound regret.

AFTER REGURGITATING GREAT CHUNKS from law books and jumping through philosophical hoops for the examiners, Lévi-Strauss obtained his law and philosophy degrees. Ahead lay the ordeal of the *agrégation*—a set of competitive exams that qualify graduates to teach in the lycée system and eventually become university lecturers. The *agrégation* involved a battery of written and oral tests, which only a small fraction would pass. As a part of the process, Lévi-Strauss spent three weeks back at his old school, Janson, giving a series of probationary classes. His fellow trainees were two other future intellectual giants: the writer Simone de Beauvoir and the philosopher Maurice Merleau-Ponty, both (like Lévi-Strauss) in their early twenties. Lévi-Strauss remembered de Beauvoir as "very young, with a fresh, bright complexion, like a little peasant girl. She had a crisp but sweet side to her, like a rosy apple."[44] He sat the *agrégation* for philosophy in July 1931, along with Ferdinand Alquié (a future Sorbonne professor of philosophy and doctoral supervisor of philosopher Gilles Deleuze) and the tormented writer and philosopher Simone Weil. It might seem like a coincidence that so many future greats would find themselves together on the same course at the same time. But it is in fact more of an indication of how elitist, tight-knit and Paris-centric the French intellectual system was at that time, an arrangement that would begin to weaken only in the 1960s.

Lévi-Strauss's topics ranged from "The concept of causality in the work of Hume" to "Should philosophy be seen from an atemporal or historical perspective?"—a subject that he would frequently revisit throughout his career. For his *grande leçon*—a three-quarter-hour talk in front of a panel of examiners—he drew the topic "Is there such a thing as an applied psychology?" After being escorted to the library of the Sorbonne for the seven hours' preparation for the applied psychology question, Lévi-Strauss took a vial of medicine that the family doctor had given him to cope with the stress. He immediately began feeling nauseous and spent the entire preparation time lying stretched out between two chairs. "Seven hours of seasickness!" he remembered. "I appeared before the jury looking like death, without having been able to prepare a thing, and improvised a lecture that was considered to be brilliant and in which I believe I spoke of nothing but Spinoza."[45]

Lévi-Strauss had passed at his first attempt, coming third—a significant achievement at his age, especially for someone skeptical about the courses he took and who was pursuing a very active life outside the university. As a gesture of defiance, the day he got his results he went out and bought a book on astrology—"Not that I believed in it, but as a kind of retaliation and to prove to myself I hadn't lost my independence of mind."[46] But the celebrations were short-lived. Lévi-Strauss arrived home to a somber atmosphere. The Great Depression had finally taken its toll on the extended family's wealth, wiping out his uncle's stock investments, which had in the past eased his parents through their regular financial crises. Lévi-Strauss would soon be working as a teacher, but a large slice of his modest earnings would have to be plowed back into the family coffers.

On completing his military service—four months as a low-ranking soldier in Strasbourg, then a posting in Paris as a press monitor—he was offered a choice between teaching posts in Mont-de-Marsan and Aubusson. He opted for the Lycée Victor-Duruy in Mont-de-Marsan, a small town tucked away in the far southwest of France, on the edge of the great Landes Forest. In September 1932, on the eve of starting work, he married Dina Dreyfus. An intellectually oriented couple, they were both in their early twenties setting out on teaching careers in the lycée system, with the possibility of one day becoming university lecturers. Dina still had to sit the *agrégation*, but she would pass the following year. "It was both my first job and my honeymoon," remembered Lévi-Strauss of the trip down to Aquitaine.[47]

His brief spell in Mont-de-Marsan was a period of happiness. He was recently married, in a new job, exploring a corner of France that was completely unfamiliar to him. Teaching was still a novelty and he attacked the task of preparing his courses from scratch with enthusiasm. He also had space to pursue his interest in politics, building a lively social life around contacts with local socialist groups. He ran as a councillor (*conseil général*) in the local elections, but the campaign ended in farce when, driving without a license, he ran off the road in a Citroën 5CV given to him by his friend from childhood Pierre Dreyfus.[48] The following year he was posted to Laon, in Picardy, within striking distance of Paris. His wife was appointed to Amiens, so they moved back to the rue Poussin and traveled out to their respective lycées, scheduling their lessons for the same days.

As he began work in Picardy, Lévi-Strauss was immediately restless. The setup was less than ideal—on teaching days he was forced to take a room in a shabby hotel near the lycée. But his anxiety was more psychological. The realization that he would have to teach the same courses over and over again was sinking in. In October 1933 he made vague moves back toward a university career, enrolling for a doctoral thesis in philosophy, but this too seemed like more of the same. Outside teaching and academia, his interest in politics was drying up. In the spring of 1934, he left the Groupe des onze in protest against the group's radicalization and its hardening stance toward the SFIO. The decision effectively ended his political engagement—eight years of meetings, talks and publications, of youthful indignation and idealistic fervor.

ALTHOUGH GENERALLY SHORT of money, in the mid-1920s Lévi-Strauss's father had received a substantial payout for the Madagascar pavilion commission. From the proceeds he had bought an abandoned silk farm near Valleraugue in the Cévennes for five thousand francs. "It was in ruins, and all we ever did was camp there, but it was very important to me because I was a teenager. And that's when I realized what wilderness could be."[49] As a young man, Lévi-Strauss would unwind from the rigors of his life in Paris by hiking into the surrounding mountains. Heading off the paths, he followed the natural fault lines of these ruggedly beautiful landscapes, skirting limestone flanks, scrambling up escarpments and stumbling down the boulder-strewn hillocks, mapping the geological formations in his mind.

Away from Paris, his thinking synthesized. In different forms, the same idea kept coming back to him, an idea that he grasped hold of early, and never gave up on. For Lévi-Strauss there would always be two levels—reality and a kind of analytical subtext. Time and again their relationship would be found to be complex and counterintuitive: a random scattering of boulders, jagged cracks running through rock faces, a patch of dry brush turning to woodland—all this was an outward manifestation of tectonic movements, the ebb and flow of oceans, the heating and cooling of subterranean shafts. A landscape's surface was but a sea of fragments, transformations and analogues of a hidden geological "master-meaning"—what one writer has called "a kind of unconscious mind for the world."[50] The grotesque skewing of the economy's rewards, the resulting social and political unrest, this was one reality. Its analytical counterpart was Marx's ingeniously abstract schemes—his theories of value, surplus value, labor alienation and commodity fetishism. A patient presents with irrational feelings of hysteria and frigidity; she recounts strange dreams involving a house fire, the recovery of a jewelry box, a frustrating journey to a railway station, a dense wood. Again, the answer lay at another level of analysis, in Freudian relationships between the ego, the superego and the id.

Lévi-Strauss would later call geology, Marxism and Freud his *trois maîtresses*—three mistresses (rather coyly translated in the English version of *Tristes Tropiques* as his "three sources of inspiration"[51])—the muses that guided him through his intellectual life. Influenced by the philosopher Henri Bergson, his university lecturers had been wrapped up in their own perceptions, grappling with the very process of our access to reality—the mechanics of perception, meaning and reason. Lévi-Strauss systematically rebelled against this position. Aided by his "three mistresses," he found that he could look right through reality's confusing gloss. On the other side there was the tantalizing prospect of discovering the organizing principles that he would devote his life to deciphering.

As Lévi-Strauss searched for a career, he was dimly aware of the emergence of a new field of inquiry on the periphery of the humanities.

"At that time, it was known among the philosophy *agrégés* that ethnology offered a way out [*une porte de sortie*]," he said later.[52] In the 1930s, ethnographic research was finally opening up in France, decades after Anglo-American anthropologists had first ventured into the field. Much publicity had surrounded the Dakar–Djibouti expedition, a two-year sweep up the Niger River, through what was then a string of mainly French colonial possessions, and on to Ethiopia. Headed by a former pilot, Marcel Griaule, and joined by Michel Leiris as scribe, the team of nine scholars was instructed "to study certain black populations and their various activities" and "fill the gaps in the Musée d'ethnologie"—a duty they duly fulfilled, with a haul of thirty-five hundred artifacts. As the Dakar–Djibouti expedition wound up, the first generation of students to attend Mauss's influential courses on fieldwork technique were fanning out across the world. Jacques Soustelle, a philosophy *agrégé* like Lévi-Strauss, had left for Mexico to study Aztec civilization; Alfred Métraux had returned to Argentina, where he had grown up, to found an ethnology institute; and others traveled as far afield as Greenland, French Indochina and the Malay states.

The idea solidified after conversations with the writer Paul Nizan, who was married to one of Lévi-Strauss's cousins. Nizan had just published his first book, *Aden Arabie* (1931), a memoir of his Paris education and escape to Aden, shades of which would resurface decades later in Lévi-Strauss's own memoir, *Tristes Tropiques*. Like many left-leaning thinkers of the times, Nizan had been disillusioned with traditional French academia. In *Aden Arabie* he described the École normale supérieure, where he had studied, as a "ridiculous" and "odious" institution, and lamented the fraudulent emptiness of classical philosophy that he had been taught there. As a result of his elite education, he wrote, at the age of twenty he had been let loose on a "pitiless world" with nothing but "a few graceful accomplishments—Greek, logic and an extensive vocabulary."[53] A restless radical of his time, Nizan saw a certain authenticity in anthropology and suggested to Lévi-Strauss that this might suit his temperament. At the same time Lévi-Strauss was reading Robert Lowie's *Primitive Society* (a rather dry text to serve as an inspiration, it has to be said) and was struck by its freshness. Lowie's book described an intellectual endeavor that was not based on the juggling of worn ideas, but was charged with a reference outside itself—the anthropologist's experience in the field. The lure of fieldwork was potent. It combined travel and the intellect, theory and practice; in the French tradition, it could even include philosophy and art. Intellectually intriguing, anthropology could also free Lévi-Strauss from the treadmill of lycée teaching and enable him, for first time in his life, to leave Europe.

"BRAZIL WAS THE most important experience of my life," Lévi-Strauss said in an interview for *Le Monde* in 2005, "not only because of the remoteness, the contrast, but also because it determined my career. I owe that country a profound debt."[54] Yet as he admitted, the destination was arbitrary—if the offer had been the South Pacific or Africa, he would have taken the post without a second thought. When Célestin Bouglé phoned on an autumn morning in 1934 to say that the psychologist Georges Dumas was recruiting academics to teach at the newly formed University of São Paulo, Lévi-Strauss already had his bags mentally packed, but with no clear destination in mind. There was even, at this point, something arbitrary about his choice of anthropology. Before Bouglé's phone call he had written to Marcel Mauss for advice, saying that he wanted to travel, even if he could not do so as an anthropologist. Lévi-Strauss had suggested, interestingly, journalism as a possible alternative profession.[55]

Bouglé enticed Lévi-Strauss with a vision of São Paulo that was a century out of date, telling him that Indians still roamed the city's suburbs. Filled with his own fantasies of palm thatch, "bizarrely designed kiosks and pavilions," and the burning perfumes of the tropics (an association he later described, in an allusion to Proust,[56] as coming from the similarities between the words *Brésil* and *grésiller*, "to sizzle"), Lévi-Strauss contacted Dumas, who offered him the sociology chair.[57]

Lévi-Strauss traveled in the second of three batches of French scholars sent out to give European cultural credibility to the fledgling university. It included Fernand Braudel, then an up-and-coming historian, the philosopher Jean Maugüé, and the specialist in Portuguese and Brazilian literature Pierre Hourcade. With the exception of Braudel, all were provincial lycée teachers on the lower rungs of the academic ladder. Maugüé was amazed to receive a letter from Dumas out of the blue, tempting him with a post combining "the climate of Nice" with "substantial remuneration."[58] Even for Braudel, the trip was fortuitous: "They were looking for a professor at the Sorbonne and weren't finding one. I was an auxiliary professor at the Sorbonne, slightly above the level of the concierge—so they finally got down to me."[59]

In preparation for the trip, the young French academics attended a farewell dinner held in a disused mansion on avenue Victor-Emmanuel (now avenue Franklin Roosevelt), hosted by the Comité France-Amérique. In the musty atmosphere of the abandoned building, caterers cleared a space, setting up a small table in the middle of an enormous room. Dumas tried to put them at ease, explaining that, as French cultural ambassadors, they would be expected to hobnob with the Brazilian elite, frequenting casinos, racecourses and clubs—a surreal prospect for junior teachers who had been living a hand-to-mouth existence in the provinces. He finished by offering fatherly advice. Always be well dressed, he told them, recommending Á la Croix de Jeannette, a shop near Les Halles where he used to buy good-quality tailored suits in his youth.[60]

While still in Paris, Lévi-Strauss scavenged for information about a country about which he knew virtually nothing. He was introduced to the Brazilian ambassador, Luís de Sousa Dantas, who told him, contra Bouglé, that Brazil's native population had already been wiped out—strapped to cannons and blown apart—by barbarous sixteenth-century Portuguese colonists. (The irony was that the ambassador himself had indigenous ancestry.) He joined the Société des Américanistes and began reading up on the topic, mixing the work of North American anthropologists—Franz

Boas, Alfred Kroeber and Robert Lowie—with impressionistic accounts of explorers, shipwreck tales and early visitors to Brazil, such as the German soldier Hans Staden's experiences as a captive of the Tupinambá in the 1500s and the French historian André Thevet's descriptions of Villegagnon's ill-fated French colony in Rio de Janeiro, France Antarctique.[61]

But the book that really captured his imagination was Jean de Léry's *L'Histoire d'un voyage fait en la terre du Brésil.* Léry was a theological student who had spent eight months in France Antarctique, living in the colony and studying the native people around the bay. Published as a corrective to Thevet, Léry's book was a vivid proto-ethnography. It contained poetic descriptions of the Tupi Indians, a still-muscular and healthy people on the cusp of colonial catastrophe. As one of the strongest first-contact accounts of native Brazilians, Léry's book chimed with Lévi-Strauss's attraction to the romantic notion of the "noble savage" in the tradition of Rousseau—ideas to which he would cling, even after witnessing the cultural wreckage of the Brazilian frontier. "Reading Léry helped me escape my century," Lévi-Strauss later remarked, "and regain contact with what I will call the surreal—not the surreal that the surrealists talk about: it's a reality more real than the one I had witnessed."[62]

WHO WAS LÉVI-STRAUSS on the eve of his trip to Brazil? On the face of it, he was a newly married lycée teacher of modest means who had been given a lucky break to teach abroad. Like many before and since, his political idealism had dissipated, barely surviving to the end of his university years. He had been initiated into a range of French institutions, attending a famous Parisian lycée, studying at the Sorbonne, doing military service and beginning his teaching career in the provinces. Temperamentally, he had the severity of a young Parisian intellectual of the period, softened by a dry sense of humor. De Beauvoir remembered the young Lévi-Strauss's demeanor as a kind of mock seriousness: "[His] impassivity rather intimidated me, but he used to turn it to good advantage. I thought it was very funny when, in his detached voice and with a deadpan expression on his face, he expounded to our audience the folly of the passions."[63]

Below the surface there was already a deposit of ideas and influences building up. Culturally, he had been seduced by the avant-garde, but the modernist rupture would always be an ambivalent one for Lévi-Strauss. In the mid-nineteenth century, his forebears had been part of the cultural elite; by the 1920s his father was scraping by, building furniture in his living room and reliant on his newly qualified son for help, his chosen trade virtually extinguished by the vogue for modernism. Lévi-Strauss's early experiences straddled these two eras, a mix of his father's nostalgia for the ballrooms and opera houses of the Third Republic and his own fascination with the ramshackle artist studios of the new wave. As he grew older, his father's influence would reassert itself, but although Lévi-Strauss would subsequently repudiate modernism in the arts, certain elements of the avant-garde would be forever imprinted on his style of thought.

From the outset he was fascinated by the arts, especially music. "I have always dreamed since childhood about being a composer, or at least, a conductor," he said, but it was not to be. His early experimental compositions showed up a fundamental limitation—"something lacking in my brain."[64] In compensation, he would inject an artistic sensibility into his academic work both in form and content, from his use of textual collage and literary allusions to the parallels that he would repeatedly draw between indigenous cultural artifacts and classical music and art.

Lévi-Strauss often said that as a student he was in revolt against what he later called the "claustrophobic, Turkish bath atmosphere . . . of philosophical reflection" found in the French university system. Yet at the same time he had been grounded in this very style of thought. In spite of his oft-professed contempt for philosophical intellectual games, he was clearly at home with abstract arguments and metaphysical concepts, and all his subsequent work would end up having a philosophical ring to it. His study of the law, however halfhearted, had given him a systematic—at times dogmatic—approach to intellectual arguments. In skirmishes with intellectual opponents later in his career his approach could be bruising, like a barrister taking apart a witness.

Lévi-Strauss clearly had an exceptional intellect, but it was not without shortcomings. He absorbed ideas quickly and economically, but in the process stripped them of their content, converting them into a kind of intellectual shorthand. After consuming a huge amount of material, he would boil it down into a demi-glace of axioms and intellectual reflexes. His "three mistresses"—Freud, Marx and geology—had been reduced to simple principles: that surface reality deceives, that truth lies in an undergirding of abstraction. It is worth looking back for a moment at some of the words used in Léon Cahen's assessment: "knows a lot," "sharp, penetrating mind," a "rigour" that is "almost sectarian," a tendency to argue "absolute, black-and-white theses" and a lack of "nuance"—harsh, perhaps, but a recognizable assessment, especially in relation to Lévi-Strauss's early intellectual output.

It was Lévi-Strauss's great fortune that he had a chance early on to gain some perspective on his multiplicity of interests. As he prepared to leave for Brazil, after years cooped up in the French university system, the New World beckoned. But what he found there would at first baffle him. It would only be through the slow burn of intellectual discovery—more than a decade of reading and reflection—that he would finally grasp its significance.

Claude Lévi-Strauss in Brazil (1935–39)
Atlantic Ocean
Belém
Amazon River
Manaus
Xingu River
Madeira River
Tapajós River
BRAZIL
Carolina
Area of detail below
Porto Velho
TUPI-KAWAHIB
Araguaia River
Ilha do Bananal
Mato Grosso
Guaporé River
Juruena
MUNDÉ
NAMBIKWARA
Salvador
Mato Grosso
Cuiabá
KARAJA
Brasilia (est. 1960)
BOLIVIA
BORORO
Pantanal
Goiás Velho
Atlantic Ocean
Cochabamba
Santa Cruz
Corumbá
Porto Esperança
Pitoko
Miranda
CADUVEO
Serra da Bodoquena
Nalike
São Paulo
Bauru
Rio de Janeiro
Rio de Janeiro
PARAGUAY
São Paulo
Paraná
ARGENTINA
0 Miles 500
0 Kilometers 500
Porto Velho
Machado R.
Madeira R.
Juruena R.
TUPI-KAWAHIB
Xingu R.
Urupá R.
Presidente Pena
Pimenta Bueno
Barão de Melgaço
Três Buritis
BRAZIL
Guaporé R.
Vilhena
NAMBIKWARA
MUNDÉ
Juruena
Campos Novos
Utiariti
Serra do Norte expedition
(Rondon telegraph line)
Papagaio R.
BOLIVIA
Parecis
Mato Grosso
0 Miles 200
Rosário Oesta
0 Kilometers 200
Cuiaba
KARAJA
Pantanal
BORORO
Kejara aldeia
© 2010 Jeffrey L. Ward

2

Arabesque

> My memory calls them by their names, Caduveo, Bororo, Nambikwara, Mundé, Tupi-Kawahib, Mogh and Kuki; and each reminds me of a place on earth and a moment of my history and that of the world . . . These are my witnesses, the living link between my theoretical views and reality.
>
> CLAUDE LÉVI-STRAUSS[1]

IN EARLY FEBRUARY 1935, accompanied by his wife, Dina, Lévi-Strauss boarded the *Mendoza* at the port of Marseille, pulling out into the Mediterranean for the first leg of the journey. In his memoir, *Tristes Tropiques*, he recalled the moment as a haze of sensations, which was in reality a blend of memories of the many departures for the Americas that he would subsequently make. As the ship eased into the Mediterranean, the oily odors of the port vanished on the sea air. Drifting in and out of sleep, he breathed in a mix of salt, fresh paint and cooking smells rising from the galley while listening to "the throbbing of the engines and the rustling of the water against the hull."[2] He was twenty-six years old, leaving Europe for the first time, setting out for Brazil.

He traveled first-class as one of a handful of passengers on the eight-thousand-ton two-funneled steamer, which was freighting cargo across the Atlantic. Free to stroll the empty decks, he and his colleagues enjoyed long lunches in ballroom-sized refectories and smoking rooms, and spent hours reading in their substantial cabins. Mustachioed stewards dished out huge portions of *suprême de poularde* and *filets de turbot*; sailors dressed in blue overalls cleaned the empty corridors and dabbed paint onto ventilator shafts as the *Mendoza* slipped through the Mediterranean. From the passengers' perspective, it was a luxury ghost ship, whose limitless space and amenities Lévi-Strauss would fully appreciate only after he had suffered the squalor and overcrowding of the refugee boat that rescued him from Nazi Europe.

After calling at Algiers and ports along the Spanish and Moroccan coasts, loading cargo by day, sailing through the night, the *Mendoza* dropped down to Dakar. Once on the high seas, the schools of dolphins and seabirds vanished, leaving only the "adjoining surfaces" of ocean and overcast sky.[3] Lévi-Strauss spent much of the three-week crossing in a state of intense intellectual excitement, "strolling on the bridge, almost always alone, his eyes wide open, but his being shut off to the world, as if he was scared of forgetting what he had just seen."[4] In a strange inversion, he would later describe the ship as the fixed point around which the changing scenery was maneuvered—like rotating theater sets on a stage.

On one occasion he jotted down notes as he watched the sun sink behind the ocean in a welter of color. His long, lyrical description of the sunset survives, reprinted in *Tristes Tropiques*, a passage that is an intriguing intimation of what could have been. Like many early attempts at creative writing, it is a heaping of literary effects, a runaway production of images, metaphors and ideas. In the space of seven pages he likens clouds to pyramids, flagstones, dolmens, celestial reefs, vaporous grottoes and even, at one point, an octopus. There are invisible layers of crystal, ethereal ramparts, blurred blues, and "pink and yellow colours: shrimp, salmon, flax, straw." An extended theater metaphor involves floodlights, stage sets and a postperformance "overture" (as they apparently used to be performed in old operas).[5] Amid this overwrought experiment were stylistic elements that would later reappear. Even in his densest academic articles, Lévi-Strauss had an eye for descriptive detail and a fondness for metaphor, as well as a fascination for natural forms and processes.

Long before the Brazilian littoral was visible, he had picked up the scent of forest, fruit and tobacco, drifting off the landmass out into the ocean. In the early hours of the following day, a dim outline of the coast came into view—the jagged cordillera of the Serra do Mar escarpments. The *Mendoza* followed the ranges down the coast, gliding past stretches of beach, tropical forest and blackened rock. Dodging a scattering of globe-shaped islands, the ship approached the famous heads of Rio's Guanabara Bay, with its backdrop of polished mounds, fingerlike peaks and granite slabs.

Years later Lévi-Strauss wrote of the thoughts that ran through his mind as he viewed this spectacle, so alien from the European panoramas that he was familiar with. Here was landscape of a different order, on a grander scale than anything he had experienced before. Its appreciation, he wrote, required a mental adjustment, a rejigging of perspective and ratio, as the observer shrank before nature's immensity. But when the ship pulled into Rio's harbor, Lévi-Strauss was famously disappointed. Despite his mental efforts, the scenario offended his sense of classical proportions. The Sugarloaf and Corcovado mountains were too big in relation to their surroundings, like "stumps . . . in a toothless mouth," as if nature had left behind an unfinished, lopsided terrain. The towering rocks and supersized bay had left little room for the city itself, which was forced into the narrow corridors, "like fingers bent in a tight, ill-fitting glove."[6] Rio's palm-lined boulevards and turn-of-the-century architecture were like nineteenth-century Nice or Biarritz. "The tropics," he later wrote, "were less exotic than out of date."[7] (His dismissal of the beauties of Rio de Janeiro still smarts in Brazil, even featuring in a famous Caetano Veloso song: "*Claude Lévi-Strauss detestou a baía de Guanabara*"—meaning "Lévi-Strauss hated Guanabara Bay"). But Lévi-Strauss told me that this was merely a first impression, and that in subsequent visits he came to love the city.[8]

He spent a few days in Rio, exploring the city on foot. The walkways were inlaid with small off-white and slate-colored stones from Portugal hammered into the pavement, arranged into a repeating pattern of swirls and organic shapes, like a mosaic from antiquity. Wending his way through the backstreets, he was impressed by the apparent lack of distinction between inside and outside, with shops spilling onto the pavement and cafés piling up green coconuts on the street. "My first impression of Rio was of an open-air reconstruction of the Gallerias of Milan, the Galerij in Amsterdam, the Passage des Panoramas, or the concourse of the Gare Saint-Lazare," he wrote.[9]

Armed with a copy of Jean de Léry's *L'Histoire d'un voyage fait en la terre du Brésil*, Lévi-Strauss tried with difficulty to imagine the Tupinambá villages that had once dotted the bay. From the busy downtown commercial district, a smattering of favelas were visible on the hillsides—more like rustic wattle and mud villages than the breezeblock slums of today. The more affluent suburbs of Flamengo and Botafogo clustered around the bay, while on the ocean-facing side, through a connecting tunnel, lay Copacabana, then a bucolic town beginning its rapid ascent as a super-Cannes.

On his last evening in Rio, Lévi-Strauss took the funicular halfway up Corcovado Mountain, where he dined with some American colleagues on a platform with sumptuous views over the bay. Later that night he embarked on the *Mendoza* for the final leg to Santos. Rain sluiced down as the ship tracked down a barely settled coastline, passing run-down colonial ports built during the eighteenth-century gold rush. The flagstone roads that had once connected them to gold fields in the interior were now lost, hidden under the leaf litter of the rainforest. All that remained of the mule trains that had plied the route were rusty horseshoes strewn about the forest floor. The wealth that had built the towns was long gone, siphoned off across the Atlantic into the follies—the monasteries, palaces and villas—of the Portuguese court.

The *Mendoza* reached the port of Santos, docking beside cargo boats piled high with sacks of coffee beans. In pouring rain, the French entourage disembarked onto the quays where Júlio Mesquita, the owner of the newspaper *Estado de São Paulo* and one of the driving forces behind the establishment of the university, was waiting to receive them. Mesquita drove them on to São Paulo, a hundred-kilometer trip along the now disused Caminho do Mar. After crossing a humid plain of lush banana plantations, the road rose steeply through wisps of vapor into the cooler airs of the Serra do Mar tropical forests. Lévi-Strauss was captivated, marveling through the car window at the galleries of novel vegetation "arranged like tiers of specimens in a museum."[10] From the summit there were spectacular views back toward the sea; "water and land mingled like in the world's creation," wrote Lévi-Strauss, "veiled in a pink mist that barely cloaked the banana plantations."[11] From here the road rolled down the gently sloping plateau on the other side, past exhausted coffee plantations and the odd hut of a Japanese settler, down into the outskirts of São Paulo.

Mesquita delivered them to the suitably named Hotel Terminus, where the group would stay while they settled in. They had arrived with the carnival in full swing, and on their first night they ventured out into the soupy air to explore the surrounding streets. In a nearby neighborhood, music boomed out of the open window of a house. They approached and were told by a tall Afro-Brazilian man at the door that they could come if they wanted to dance, but not just to watch. Lévi-Strauss remembered dancing awkwardly, stumbling over Afro-Brazilian women who accepted his invitations "with complete indifference."[12]

WHEN LÉVI-STRAUSS ARRIVED in São Paulo, Brazil was modernizing, emerging from the shadows of its colonial past. But the process had been sporadic and uneven. Robbed of the lure of the Pacific, westward migration had ended inconclusively, petering out in the marshlands and forests of the South American hinterland. The bulk of the population still lived within striking distance of the sea—in cities and towns along the coast and around the coffee plantations, cane fields and cattle ranches that rolled back into the countryside.

There were just three million people in the vast interior through which

Lévi-Strauss would travel. Part-indigenous communities, the product of a now exhausted rubber boom, subsisted along the main waterways of the Amazon Basin. Clapboard mining towns had been left stranded in the scrublands of the central west. Farther south, colonization schemes were gradually opening up Paraná state, reducing great forests to pasturelands. Dwindling groups of indigenous Brazilians either had been drawn into settler society or were in flight from it. Herded into government reservations, they had become prey to missionaries, or exploited as cheap labor.

With an influx of European migrants and the beginnings of industrialization, Brazil's biggest cities were forging their identities: Rio as a pleasure city, São Paulo as its industrious cousin—a Milan to Rio's more sensual Rome. But the vestiges of traditional rural society were everywhere. On the outskirts of São Paulo there were campsites for mule trains arriving from the interior; saddle shops traded downtown. On Rio's hillsides, the poor tended their gardens, chicken coops and pigpens. There was little modern infrastructure. Trucks were only just beginning to replace the mule trains, spending days shuddering in low gear along rutted, overgrown dirt tracks. On a journey from Rio de Janeiro to Belo Horizonte in Minas Gerais state in 1940, the famous Brazilian modernist architect Oscar Niemeyer remembered having to yoke his sedan car to a team of oxen to drag it through the bog.[13]

The Great Depression had ravaged Brazil's commodity-based market, and by the time Lévi-Strauss arrived, the country was suffering the same political turbulence that was then spreading through Europe. Amid collapsing agricultural prices, *gaúcho* Getúlio Vargas had seized power by a coup in 1930. Flirting with fascism, he would survive the 1930s with difficulty, negotiating the demands of the Nazi-inspired Integralists and repressing the communists while placating the powerful farming block and the emerging urban elites. It was an environment in which left-wing intellectuals would become increasingly uncomfortable. Culturally, though, the French would be able to relax. In a hangover from the nineteenth-century empire years, France was still seen as the height of European refinement. Lévi-Strauss and his colleagues would not even have to worry about mastering Portuguese—they would lecture in French, a lingua franca among the educated urban elite.[14]

In contrast to Rio, Lévi-Strauss felt drawn to São Paulo. "It was an extraordinary city," he remembered much later, "still middle-sized, but in complete upheaval, where you crossed over within a few feet of each other from the Iberian world of the eighteenth century to the Chicago of the 1880s."[15] São Paulo was fast evolving into Brazil's industrial hub. The population had just topped one million, the first skyscrapers were appearing on the skyline and rapid expansion was in the air. With waves of mainly Italian immigration priming the pumps, houses were going up by the hour, turning the surrounding farmland into a patchwork of construction sites and garden plots, cow pastures and concrete. "The air is brisk; the streets clang; electric signs challenge the stars with hyperbole," wrote one traveler.[16] There were nouveau-riche extravaganzas, like a marina on an artificial lake and the luxury housing developments of the Jardim Europa that had begun springing up in what were then the suburbs. But there was old wealth too, dating back to the slave plantations of the nineteenth century. Weathered coffee-baron-built mansions lined the streets of the well-to-do suburbs, interspersed with gardens of eucalyptus and mango.

Lévi-Strauss captured the bustle of the immigrant town in a series of black-and-white images taken on a Leica that he had brought with him from Paris, occasionally adding a 75mm Hugo Meyer f1.5 lens, which he found "practically unusable because of its weight."[17] In the photos, a selection of which was later published in *Saudades de São Paulo*, crowds surge down the avenues: men in crumpled white suits; women wearing heavy frocks, brooches and pearl necklaces, clasping small leather handbags. Herders on horseback maneuver cattle past a downtown commuter tram. There are smokestacks, run-down buildings and slums. The pink Art Deco Martinelli Building, then nearing completion, stands alone as a symbol of things to come, topped by rickety neon advertisements.

Lévi-Strauss's father, who joined him in Brazil during his first year, appears enigmatically in two of the photos—one at the jasmine-laced iron gates of his son's house, looking down through the lens of his camera, and the other standing in front of a sign stenciled on a concrete wall saying "Plots of Land for Sale." According to Lévi-Strauss, they would go out together taking pictures, competing to see who could produce the sharpest images.[18]

GONE WERE THE POKY apartments of Paris and the provinces, the tight budgets, the freezing winters and the scrimping and saving of interwar rural France. Earning three times their salary in France, Lévi-Strauss and Dina lived in unaccustomed luxury. Soon after arriving, they moved into a substantial house with a walled garden just off Avenida Paulista. When they got there, Lévi-Strauss asked the owner to plant a banana tree "to give me the feeling of being in the tropics." Much later, after his expeditions into the interior, the garden would house his parrot, along with a capuchin monkey.[19] He furnished the house with late-nineteenth-century rustic pieces, fashioned from soft jacaranda woods. They even found they could afford a servant and an almost-new Ford. The historian Fernand Braudel went as far as employing a chauffeur to drive his Chevrolet into the university, while block-booking two hotel rooms—one for himself, the other for his books and papers.

The French mission saw themselves as cultural ambassadors, and initially formed an expatriate community at arm's length from their Brazilian counterparts. In the evenings they would go to French realist films staring Jean Gabin and Louis Jouvet.[20] On the weekends they explored the outskirts of São Paulo, from the coffee plantations in the north to the makeshift tracks through the ravines in the south. At the university there was an air of competition, and even of snobbishness. "All of us thought our careers were riding on our success or failure in Brazil, so we all attempted to surround ourselves with an exclusive court, more important than our neighbors," remembered Lévi-Strauss. "It was very French, very academic, but there in the tropics, it was a little ridiculous and not very healthy."[21]

From the outset, Lévi-Strauss trod a difficult intellectual path. Employed as a sociology lecturer, he was expected to teach the prevailing Durkheimian orthodoxy, an approach that he had rejected as politically conservative and too prescriptive. He had perhaps been influenced by the 1932 polemic *Les Chiens de garde* (*Watchdogs*), in which Paul Nizan had argued that, as a result of Durkheim's institutional success, "teachers taught children to respect the French nation, to justify class collaboration, to accept everything, to join in the cult of the Flag and the bourgeois Democracy."[22] In any case, through reading Lowie and Boas, Lévi-Strauss was already moving toward cultural anthropology and more Anglo-American, fieldwork-oriented methods of research. Sociologist Paul Arbousse Bastide, a nephew of Dumas, tried to force Lévi-Strauss to adhere to a traditional French approach, teaching not only Durkheim, but also nineteenth-century philosopher Auguste Comte's positivist sociology. When Lévi-Strauss bridled, Bastide attempted to fire him. But with the support of colleagues—the geographer Pierre Monbeig and especially Fernand Braudel—Lévi-Strauss survived with his independence intact.[23]

His early courses pointed toward the areas that he would go on to develop throughout his career. They included kinship (under the rubric of "domestic sociology"), totemism ("religious sociology") and cross-cultural research ("comparative sociology"), using a limited bibliography of Durkheim, Lowie, Van Gennep and Westermark. In a later conference he looked at the area with which he would eventually become synonymous: myth. The conference—The Tales of Charles Perrault—compared fairy tales with indigenous mythology and looked at how myths fit into the worldview of indigenous peoples. One area that he would subsequently abandon was physical anthropology—a discipline not yet tarnished by the racist strains developed in Nazi Germany. Like many foreigners, he became fascinated by the variations in skin color and physiognomy in

Brazil, the result of centuries of miscegenation. He envisaged Brazil as the perfect laboratory for the study of genetic inheritance and championed the idea of setting up a research department to produce an atlas of physical and cultural anthropology.[24]

Using materials at hand, Lévi-Strauss developed practical exercises. For the kinship course, the exam consisted of a series of family trees from which the students had to deduce the social rules of the group and work out who would be able to marry whom.[25] Another exercise involved a sociological analysis of the city of São Paulo circa 1820, working from the era's archives. "I put my students to work on their own city," remembered Lévi-Strauss. "We did monographs on districts, sometimes on single streets."[26]

Beyond teaching, for thinkers like Braudel and Lévi-Strauss, the Brazil years furnished space for contemplation, reading and research. It was "a paradise for work and reflection," Braudel remembered. In one of the first experiments in microfilm, he had paid a photographer to take pictures of thousands of documents, which he worked his way through in São Paulo. "I spent three marvellous years in this fashion: in winter, during the vacations, I was in the Mediterranean; the rest of the year, in Brazil, with leisure and fantastic possibilities for reading."[27]

In time, Lévi-Strauss and Dina broke out of their stifling expat environment. Forging links with a circle of Brazilian intellectuals and writers,[28] they began engaging with Brazil at a seminal moment in its modern evolution. In the 1930s, the country was rediscovering its roots. Artists, influenced by the symbolist/surrealist strain of the French avant-garde, were turning their attention to Brazilian subject matter: the rustic shantytown, samba groups, Afro-Brazilian coffee plantation workers, pineapples and toucans. Tarsila do Amaral's Léger-like tumescent women, cacti and palms crowned a homegrown modernist movement with the iconic image *Anthropophagy*, a tropical riposte to the avant-garde scene in Paris, where she had lived and worked. It was named after Oswald de Andrade's 1928 *Manifesto antropófago* (*Cannibalist Manifesto*), which rejected Western rationalism in favor of "liberating primitivism" and saw Brazilian culture's creativity as a process of devouring other cultures, absorbing their essences and reconfiguring them into something new and original—a kind of postmodernism *avant la lettre*. What had previously been denigrated as backward and provincial was now forming the basis of a cultural revival. Gilberto Freyre's revisionist classic—*Casa-Grande e Senzala* (*The Masters and the Slaves*) (1933)—which celebrated Brazil's racial mix, had just been published; Jorge Amado had begun producing his picaresque novels—such as *O País do Carnaval* (1931), *Suor* (1934) and *Jubiabá* (1935)—exploring the underside of life in Bahia; and the classical composer Heitor Villa-Lobos was turning to regional folk music for inspiration.

The Lévi-Strausses became close friends with poet and musician Mário de Andrade, the lynchpin of the group. Among his many cultural interests, Andrade had dabbled in what was then called folklore, sponsoring ethnomusicological expeditions to the northeast. In a similar way to John Lomax's salvaging of American folk music, he had built up a mammoth archive of recordings from the remotest Brazilian towns, from neo-slave-work chants to Afro-Brazilian dance and song and peasant folk music.

Dina Lévi-Strauss became an active member of the folklore society, which Andrade ran from his offices at the São Paulo municipal government's Department of Culture, attending meetings and contributing articles. She gave a course on the "science of ethnography," including physical anthropology, linguistics and archaeology. The focus was on the detailed study of the ethnographic artifact, based on the Maussian notion that "almost all phenomena of life can be decoded through material objects." To this end she taught how to make systematic documentary records, using tables of preset questionnaires, drawings, photography and film. The course, which attracted a devoted following, was held in a dingy attic in the Department of Culture from eight in the evening until midnight.[29]

According to Mário Wagner Vieira da Cunha, future economics professor at the University of São Paulo, who took both Lévi-Strauss's and

Dina's courses, tensions developed around the warm relationship that Dina had formed with Mário de Andrade:

> He [Andrade] had a soft spot for her, like we all had, because she was a beautiful girl, around our age. Lévi-Strauss was jealous of this situation—with reason . . . I used to go to their house on Cincinato Braga, because we had a lot of meetings about the Ethnographic and Folklore Society. With Dina, we would start talking and never stop. Lévi-Strauss used to check up on us. He wouldn't come into the room where we were. But he used to walk around in the adjoining rooms, stomping about as if to say I am here and I want the conversation to stop soon.

For da Cunha, Dina and Claude were chalk and cheese: "While he was cold, she was expansive and friendly. They were two people who you couldn't imagine being married."[30]

THE CITY OF SÃO PAULO was one reality for the Lévi-Strausses in Brazil, with their teaching duties, soirées with the Paulista elite and the more informal meetings with Brazilian intellectuals. The other reality was on the routes out of São Paulo, which Lévi-Strauss and Dina explored on weekends and in breaks from teaching. In the suburbs, where they found a miscellany of Syrian and Italian immigrant communities, along with Afro-Brazilians, they took footage of the Moçambique, Cavalhada and Congada dances, six minutes of which still exist in municipal archives in São Paulo.[31] Beyond the city, they reached the outlying German-, Italian- and Polish-dominated towns, along with the closed-off agricultural colonies of the Japanese.

The first long journeys were into the pioneer zones, which the British colonization company Paraná Plantations Limited was opening up by driving a railroad into the interior. Every fifteen kilometers or so, workmen cleared lots and small towns developed, with dirt roads and roughly constructed wooden houses, built by the Eastern European immigrants who were filtering into the area. The populations dwindled as the plots moved farther down the line, from a thriving town of fifteen thousand in the first settlement to five thousand in the second, followed by a thousand, ninety and forty, down to a solitary Frenchman living in the outermost clearing.[32]

The pioneer zone fascinated Lévi-Strauss. These dusty settlements taking shape in the ruddy soils of the interior were like proto-cities; "at the meeting point of nature and artifice," new entities were coming into being. As roads divided districts, and districts differentiated into the commercial and residential, the settlements self-organized along central and peripheral, parallel and perpendicular axes. Dreamed up by politicians and businessmen, the pioneer towns were as far as you could get from spontaneous, ad hoc development. But even so, Lévi-Strauss sensed a pattern, cut from a panhuman cloth—an involuntary reflex of the human condition. "Space has its own values," he wrote, "just as sounds and perfumes have colours and feelings weight."[33] And these values molded human behavior in profound ways. As innocuous as they might have looked to the casual observer, the pioneer towns hinted at a deeper truth that Lévi-Strauss would soon recognize in a more traditional ethnographic setting as he pondered the highly structured way in which tribes positioned their huts.

Farther to the west, the state of Paraná was still a wilderness, out of reach of the colonization projects. It was in this vast forest—today cane fields and cattle ranches—that Lévi-Strauss, accompanied by an agent from the Serviço de Proteção aos Índios, or SPI (Indian Protection Service), had his first contacts with native Brazilians. He had arrived in Brazil drunk with romantic expectation: "I was in a state of intense intellectual excitement," Lévi-Strauss described much later. "I felt I was reliving the adventures of the first sixteenth-century explorers. I was discovering the New World for myself. Everything seemed mythical: the scenery, the plants, the animals."[34] Eager to win his spurs as an anthropologist, he now stood on the brink of the exotic encounters that he had read about in Paris. But what he found when he entered a small Tibagy encampment in the forests of Paraná was sobering.

Scattered on the earthen floor of the huts were the flotsam of industrialization—enamel plates, poor-quality utensils and "the skeletal remains of a sewing machine." There were old-fashioned pistols alongside bows and arrows; matches were known, but rubbing sticks together was still the preferred method of making fire. In among the junk, Lévi-Strauss's collector's eye spotted a beautifully crafted stone mortar and pestle, possibly traded from another indigenous group. He left with the impression that they were "neither completely true Indians, nor, what was more important, 'savages.' " It was an experience that "took away the poetry from my naïve vision," Lévi-Strauss remembered.[35]

Continuing his tour, Lévi-Strauss spent days on horseback, stumbling up and down the narrow forest trails that wended their way under a thirty-meter forest canopy. From time to time their party would pass small groups of Indians, walking in single file through the forest in silence. At journey's end was the 450-strong São Jerônimo reservation—a series of broken-down sheds strewn across an open clearing, housing members of the Kaingang tribe. The Kaingang had experienced the full panoply of the native Brazilian experience: they had suffered flu pandemics and German colonists had hunted them down before the SPI subjected them to well-meaning but heavy-handed attempts at "pacification" and acculturation, only to abandon them to their run-down reservations.

The men wore tattered trousers, the women cotton dresses or "just a blanket tucked under their armpits."[36] They fished with half-learned versions of techniques picked up from the colonists, attaching hooks to the end of sticks and using scraps of cloth as nets, as well as harvesting bananas, sweet potatoes and maize from gardens in forest clearings. In the huts there was the same miscellany of cheap industrial products—pots, pans, cooking utensils and, in a surreal touch, an umbrella. Lévi-Strauss had been looking for exquisitely crafted material culture; what he had found was junk—an ironic allusion to nineteenth-century poet the self-styled Comte de Lautréamont's famous definition of beauty which inspired the surrealist movement: "the chance encounter, on a dissecting table, of a sewing machine and an umbrella." Lévi-Strauss tried to barter for the few traditional objects that remained—gourds fashioned from hollowed-out marrows—but "felt ashamed to deprive people who have so little."[37]

One traditional delicacy was still enjoyed—a type of pale grub known as *koro*, which thrived in the rotting hollows of tree trunks on the forest bed. After decades of prejudice and persecution, the Kaingang had become ashamed of their own culture, whisking away the delicacy when outsiders visited. Lévi-Strauss was determined to track some down and, coming across a fever-stricken Indian in a deserted village, resorted to questionable tactics: "We put an axe into his hands, shook him and pushed him." The Indian did not respond, so "we succeeded in dragging our victim to a tree trunk," where a single axe-blow revealed a heaving mass of *koro* inside the sodden wood. Hesitating at first, Lévi-Strauss popped one in his mouth and savored a taste that he described as a combination between "the delicacy of butter, and the flavour of coconut milk."[38]

He had had his first, bittersweet experiences of fieldwork—not the heroics of Léry's Tupinambá, but the tragicomedy of cultures on the fringes of the ever-expanding frontier. He had arrived too late. All that was left was the cultural gray water, a depressing mix of tradition and modernity, each corrupted by the other. The experience marked him, confirming his jaundiced view of the West, which he would come to see as a corrosive force that was dissolving mankind's cultural achievements. He realized that he would have to travel farther afield if he wanted to catch a glimpse of something less degraded, more authentic. He realized, too, that this would always be the anthropologist's fate. Like the indigenous peoples they were trying to study, they were compelled to embark on the ultimately futile exercise of outrunning the spread of their own culture.

IN NOVEMBER 1935, at the end of the university year when most of the French academics returned to spend the holidays in Europe, Lévi-Strauss and his wife stayed on to embark on their first real attempts at fieldwork in Brazil. Just a generation before, maps of São Paulo state were still being sold with blank spaces marked "unknown territories inhabited by Indians."[39] By the 1930s, Lévi-Strauss would have to cross the state lines into Mato Grosso—then a vast wilderness, loosely connected by train, river, dirt road and mule trail—to get firsthand experience of relatively isolated indigenous peoples. The trip was largely self-financed, with some help from Mário de Andrade at the São Paulo Department of Culture. Lévi-Strauss was instructed by the Museu Nacional in Rio to survey an archaeological site in the region, but his prime objective was to work among the Caduveo[40] on the Paraguayan border and to visit "by an as-yet-undetermined route"[41] the Bororo in central Mato Grosso, gathering data and material culture for the newly created Musée de l'Homme in Paris.

Accompanied by high school friend René Silz, who had come out from France for the expedition, the couple flew the first 350 kilometers to Bauru, a small town to the west of São Paulo. The light aircraft passed over rows of squat coffee bushes, furrowing the hillsides like vineyards. Pasturelands stretched out over the red soils of the interior, the vivid russet palette "so typical," noted Dina, that they "immediately take on a significance for the foreigner who arrives in Brazil."[42] From Bauru, they stowed their luggage—"a trunk, two bags, three navy bags, three tents, a medicine bag and a tent cloth"[43]—on a rickety wood-burning locomotive for the journey across the western portion of São Paulo state. A fine reddish dust blew off the desiccated landscape, coating the carriages, as the train rattled on toward Porto Esperança. After changing train companies on the Mato Grosso state lines,[44] the tracks straightened, and the landscape flattened out, leaving endless forests and fields against huge skies. The greens had deadened, the vegetation settled into dry bush, with scatterings of hardy trees and palms. The well-fed cattle that had sauntered across the Paulista pastures were now scrawnier, bony beasts picking through anthill-covered scrub. It was bleak, yet beautiful, "wild and melancholic, but how grandiose, how moving," as Dina wrote of these epic landscapes.[45]

After a few days carrying out an archaeological survey for the Museu Nacional, Dina was taken ill and returned to São Paulo. Lévi-Strauss and Silz continued on to Miranda, a few stops from Porto Esperança on the Paraguay River, where Lévi-Strauss had brief contact with a group of Terena Indians. From the terminus at Porto Esperança they took a secondary line—a precariously laid track skirting the Pantanal swamplands. The marshes sent the smell of rotting vegetation drifting up through the floorboards, along with swarms of mosquitoes. But this complex of rivers, muddy pools, embankments and shrub, covering an area the size of England, was also one of the world's great wildlife sanctuaries. To Lévi-Strauss's delight, *veados* (a type of deer), native emus and flocks of egrets scattered before the train.

As they pushed into the more remote regions, their demeanor and garb became more conspicuous. For their fellow passengers, most of whom worked on the railway, the idea that two foreign men were going to such lengths to track down indigenous peoples seemed outlandish. In their minds, the expedition was clearly a front for some kind of commercial survey—gringos prospecting for gold, precious stones or minerals.

They left the train at "kilometer twelve" and made their way to a ranch run by two Frenchmen—known locally as the Fazenda Francesa—their base for an expedition to Caduveo indigenous settlements. They spent six weeks on the ranch, time enough for Dina to rejoin the expedition.[46] They were now back in cattle country, on the Paraguayan borderlands. The Fazenda Francesa operated as a kind of colonial outpost, running an exorbitantly priced trade store and managing the *vaqueiros* (ranchers), many of them indigenous people, who tended the wandering herds of zebu cattle. Lévi-Strauss's party gathered supplies—rice, beans, *farinha*, *mate* and coffee, the staples of the Brazilian interior—along with "a heavy load of goods for barter." Among the diverse items were dolls and toy animals for the children, glass bead necklaces, little mirrors, bracelets, rings and perfumes for the women, and "more serious gifts" such as fabric, blankets and male clothing.[47] They set off with indigenous farmhand guides for the last leg of the trip, a three-day haul on horseback to Nakile, the largest Caduveo settlement.

Through grasslands and the muddy outskirts of the Pantanal, they scaled the Serra da Bodoquena, reaching a plateau of brush and cacti. From there they followed "the Indian road," down a track so steep they had to lead the horses on foot, to a clearing at the bottom of the slopes known as the *campo dos índios* (Indians' fields), where they made camp and ate. They were now in the Pantanal proper, an area so flat that much of the water accumulated on the plains, rather than draining off into the surrounding river systems.

A few of kilometers from the main village, the expedition party stopped off at a small Caduveo settlement on the Pitoko River—"a silent stream that arose mysteriously somewhere in the Pantanal, and disappeared just as mysteriously." There, they slung hammocks in a couple of derelict houses that had once served as SPI offices. Lévi-Strauss managed to barter a few examples of the ceramics that the Caduveo were still making, but the experience was disappointing. "The Indians of Pitoko are completely civilized, in the most disturbing sense of the word," wrote Dina, "that is to say very debased [*très déculturés*]."[48]

On the final stretch of the journey, they set off at midnight to take advantage of the cooler temperatures, only to be hit by a violent tropical storm—two hours of lightning and thunder, pounding and flaring "like shells from an artillery barrage."[49] The squall moved off, revealing the sodden outlines of a village up ahead: groups of wall-less dwellings—fibrous roofs mounted on wooden posts—standing on low hillocks. They were expected. News of their arrival had traveled on ahead through networks of indigenous herdsmen, spreading an age-old anxiety that the arrival of foreigners brought.

In many ways the Caduveo had reached a similar impasse to the Tibagy and the Kaingang—once an aristocratic tribe, dominating the region and enslaving the Terena, their less fortunate neighbors, they were now plagued by alcoholism, reduced to the impoverished life of Brazilian peasant ranchers. But there was a crucial difference. Elements of their material culture described by nineteenth-century travelers had survived the ravages of a predatory landgrab, the diseases that followed, as well as the Paraguayan War (1864–70), into which they had been coopted as cavalrymen.

The men were the sculptors, wrote Lévi-Strauss, the women the painters.[50] Among their artifacts were decorated ceramics, necklaces fashioned from beaten pieces of silver, and sculpted figurines, sometimes used for worship, sometimes given to children as playthings. Most striking, though, were the patterns—once tattooed, now painted on the faces of the women and girls. Lévi-Strauss had seen the late-nineteenth-century photographs by the Italian explorer and ethnographer Guido Boggiani, who had spent more than a decade on Brazil's far western borderlands before being killed in Paraguay by a tribe who believed he was a witch. But he had not expected to find Caduveo art still intact and actively practiced.

The women worked a fine bamboo spatula, tipped with *jenipapo* juice, producing clear lines that blackened on the face with oxidation. The patterns radiated from the mouth in scrolls and arabesques, then quartered the face with exquisite geometric motifs. As art, this was not the rough-cut primitivism that Lévi-Strauss would later document in the backlands of Brazil, but well-executed design, of a complexity and refinement that belied the squalid surroundings. At first he photographed them, but since they charged per image and demanded that he take a copious number of photos, he ended up feigning taking photographs and paying the fee, to preserve his film stock. He tried to draw the designs himself, and then handed out pieces of paper and got the women to reproduce them on the page, which they did without any difficulty whatsoever. He gathered several hundred, each alike, but none exactly the same—a register of

S-shapes, whorls, crosses and opposed spirals, convex and concave arabesques. For Lévi-Strauss it was not so much the motifs themselves that were unique (some were in fact reminiscent of the Spanish baroque style, elements of which the Caduveo may have borrowed), but the way they were combined in alternating curvilinear themes. The women's faces were a patchwork of slightly off-kilter symmetries and inversions that referenced each other with a hard-to-decipher logic.

So caught up in the Caduveo aesthetic world was Lévi-Strauss that the discomforts of travel off the beaten track began to fade: "Conditions are of course tough," he wrote in a letter, updating his friend and patron Mário de Andrade. "The heat is always overwhelming in the Pantanal. Some nights in Nalike we can't help shivering and the mosquitoes are as you would imagine. But there are so many interesting and admirable things here that other matters are not terribly important."[51]

During his two-week stay, Lévi-Strauss took a series of close-ups of the women's faces. On the older women, the designs play off wrinkles, the hollows of the cheeks, the creases on the forehead, like ornamental filigree on medieval parchment; while on the girls, pure lines swirl around the mouth with a seductive, flowerlike effect. There are also a couple of reels of film, a tantalizing glimpse backstage of his memoir, *Tristes Tropiques*. Only a few unsteady minutes of footage were shot, presented between silent-film-style explanatory text in Portuguese: *Entardecer* (Dusk), *Festa da puberdade de Nalike* (Nalike puberty celebration), *Confecção de rede* (Hammock making) and *Pinturas de face* (Face paintings). Black and white, shaky, slightly speeded up and at times overexposed, the footage has an antique vérité feel. A rapid opening pan across the village captures a glimpse of the backs of Lévi-Strauss and his French friend. They are dressed identically, looking like stereotypical nineteenth-century colonial expeditionists: white baggy overalls are fastened high up with a belt; hanging off the belt is a small leather sheath suitable for a hunting knife. The outfit is completed by sturdy hunting boots and sun helmets, of the type worn by Livingstone. Another shot has Dina Lévi-Strauss in animated conversation with one of the women. They seem to be talking about an object—perhaps a necklace—that Dina holds out between them.

The village looks more like a frontier campsite than anything resembling an indigenous settlement. A closer pan shows the eclectic cultural mix—inside the wall-less huts, a man sucks *mate* through a straw, a virtually naked woman weaves what looks like an ornamental belt, while in the background a figure dressed in cowboy gear sits by the campfire; as the camera turns toward him, he tilts his wide-rimmed cowboy hat to cover his face. More jerky footage has the women squatting together, drawing the disembodied designs on the sheets of paper that are scattered around them. An old woman in a tattered floral dress decorates her face using a pocket mirror; a younger, bare-breasted woman leans over a girl resting her head in her lap, applying *jenipapo* juice to the girl's cheeks from a small pot at her side. The film ends with a final close-up of the most spectacular design—an old woman bedecked in jewelry. Her wrinkled face is evenly covered with dotted lines and scrolls, as if she were "peering out from behind a complicated ornamental screen."[52] Her stare back into the camera is unwavering—an unreadable blank, to which hostility, defiance, world-weariness, indifference, boredom or a simple unfamiliarity with the act of being filmed could equally be ascribed.

The trip had been a success. To the surprise of the French *fazendeiros*, who had considered the Indians alcoholic layabouts, Lévi-Strauss's party arrived back from their expedition laden with superb indigenous artifacts, among them huge pottery jars, deerskins and wood carvings. From this point on, the French *fazendeiros* cultivated ties with the Caduveo, decorating their farmhouse with indigenous art. But the relationship ended in tragedy: ten years later one of the *fazendeiros* was killed by a local Indian. "It is unlikely that two bachelors were able to resist the charms of the young Indian girls," Lévi-Strauss speculated, "when they saw them half-naked on feast days, their bodies patiently decorated with delicate black and blue scrolls which seemed to fit their skin like a sheath of precious lace." Lévi-Strauss felt he bore some indirect responsibility for the death, for in the end the *fazendeiro* had been "not so much a victim of the Indians, as a victim of the mental confusion into which he had been plunged by the visit of a party of young anthropologists."[53]

More than the artifacts that he had collected, it was the Caduveo face designs that resonated with Lévi-Strauss. Over the following years he would come back to them often, writing articles and devoting a chapter of his memoir to his experiences. In a recent interview he described the women as "great artists."[54] In spite of the sorry state of their culture, the Caduveo had clung on to something that he found both aesthetically appealing and intellectually challenging. But it would be many years before he had the tools to analyze them. While he was in Brazil he toyed with conventional, if ambitious, explanations, trying to connect Caduveo design to the patterns on the pottery that had turned up thousands of kilometers away on the vast island of Marajó, which sits at the mouth of the Amazon, a line of inquiry that he later abandoned. By the time he had reached his conclusions, the phenomenon had slipped into history. The village was abandoned ten years after Lévi-Strauss passed through, the tradition of face painting disappearing in the cultural turbulence of the frontier.

FOR THE LAST YEAR, Lévi-Strauss had been on a slow, arduous journey away from the West—from Paris to São Paulo, from the frontier towns to the pitiful indigenous reservations of Paraná, and then on to the Caduveo, whose traditional culture was in its last stages of unraveling. The next phase would finally deliver him into the classic fieldwork scenario he had been hankering after since leaving Europe—a tribe remote enough to display the trappings of authenticity, the fetishized objects of the Western imagination: penis sheaths, multicolored headdresses, nose feathers, lip ornaments and body paint. Despite their long contact with Silesian missionaries and the beginnings of an influx of Western tools, clothes and diseases, the Bororo still looked the part—particularly the men, whose athletic bodies were smeared with vegetable dye and decorated with shells, palm fronds and feathers. The Bororo's highly ritualized lifestyle, their myths, their rich cosmology and material culture filled out the ethnographic possibilities for the young, ambitious anthropologist.

But Lévi-Strauss had to work hard for his prize. There were days in a steamer that took the Paraguay River's twists and turns upstream to the regional capital of Cuiabá. From there the Lévi-Strausses traveled by truck through rough gold-prospecting camps, then, taking a half-abandoned road, dropped down to the São Lourenço River. The last phase of the journey descended into chaos. The truck battled a boggy, overgrown track, often becoming marooned in the mud or blocked by foliage. Between digging the truck out of the mud and shifting fallen trees, the team spent uncomfortable nights sleeping on the bare earth, kept dry by rubber mackintoshes doubling as groundsheets.[55] Most of the bridges had been burned out by bushfires, forcing them to ford streams in the truck or to punt across rivers on rafts. When they reached the São Lourenço River, where the first Bororo camps were said to be, they found only five empty huts, obscured in the mists of the valley. Exasperated, they fanned out in all directions, but found nothing. Their only contact was a pale fisherman who told them that yellow fever had recently spread through the area, scattering the villagers. The nearest Bororo settlement—the Kejara *aldeia* (village)—was some way upstream.

The expedition spent a week canoeing against a swift current powered by tropical downpours as they ascended the Rio Vermelho, a tributary of the São Lourenço. Upstream they spotted naked figures—Bororo tribesmen—in the distance. "It's as if it were yesterday," Lévi-Strauss remembered in a television interview he gave some thirty years after the event. "Camped on the riverside, we saw two, three shapes, rather red, on the edge of the water—they were the first Bororo that we laid eyes upon."[56] The expedition members approached and tried to engage with them, but found that the only Portuguese word they seemed to know was *fumo* (tobacco). Communicating by gesture, they worked out that the Bororo village was but hours away. The tribesmen went on ahead to announce their imminent arrival, while Lévi-Strauss's party embarked on the final leg of their journey.

Later that day, climbing the steep banks of the river, Lévi-Strauss at last found himself among the "virtuous savages" he had philosophized about, a 140-strong indigenous village with few outward signs of acculturation. He was overwhelmed by fatigue and excitement, "hunger, thirst and mental confusion." He noticed the great huts, "not so much built as knotted together," woven into a kind of giant garment, of "grassy velvetiness," that protected their naked bodies.[57] Unlike the timid, broken indigenous peoples that Lévi-Strauss had already seen, the Bororo stood proud, glowing with a red pigment made from a mix of *urucu* seeds and animal fat, imprinted with black resin and dusted over with a mother-of-pearl powder. They laughed and joked as they stowed the expedition's luggage in a corner of the twelve-meter-by-five-meter hut, where Lévi-Strauss and his wife would sleep alongside the shaman's family and an elderly Bororo widow. (Dina, a slender, gamine figure who wore trousers and sported cropped hair, was apparently assumed to be a man by the Bororo, so special arrangements were not necessary.)[58] Lévi-Strauss was in a state of heightened sensitivity. "As I proceeded to settle into our corner of a large hut, I was soaking up these images, rather than grasping them intellectually," he later recalled.[59] He dozed off to the sounds of Bororo song—an elaborate ritual prelude to the eating of the *irara*, a type of badger that the expedition party had shot earlier and presented to the Bororo as a gift. Wind instruments, gravel-filled gourd rattles and the low chants of the men's voices played out their rhythms, which Lévi-Strauss later wrote were as sophisticated and subtle as those coaxed by Europe's finest conductors.[60]

The choice of the village had been somewhat arbitrary—the fisherman who acted as a guide had been keen to visit the *aldeia* because he had heard that the Bororo grew tobacco, a crop that was not cultivated downstream. He was right, and at the end of the expedition they returned with three hundred tobacco plants given to them by the Bororo.[61] On this somehow appropriate contingency rested Lévi-Strauss's first real experience of ethnographic fieldwork. The material he gathered would stay with him for the rest of his life, reemerging at intervals. Much later, Salesian missionary accounts of Bororo myth would provide the central thread of the *Mythologiques* quartet that crowned his academic career.

During his stay of just three weeks, he documented a spectrum of Bororo ritual and cosmology—weddings, funerary rites and myths—and added to his collection of indigenous artifacts. "We were immersed in the wealth and fantasy of an exceptional culture . . . It was a society that had abolished time, and after all what greater nostalgia could we have than to abolish time and then to live in a sort of present tense which is a constantly revitalized past and preserved as it was dreamt in myth and belief," Lévi-Strauss remembered in the 1960s, when he was interviewed in his office at the Collège de France.[62]

Yet what caught his eye was something altogether more prosaic. As in the frontier zone, he became fascinated with the layout of the village—a circle of family huts around a central longhouse reserved for the men. Quizzing the Bororo through an interpreter, Lévi-Strauss surveyed each hut and plotted their relationships to one another. He drew diagrams in the earthen yard of the various imaginary dividing lines, the sectors they formed and the complex network of rights, duties, hierarchy and reciprocity through which they were defined.

The emergent scheme was involved, yet elegant. An invisible north–south axis divided the village into moieties (that is, two intermarrying descent groups); within the moieties were clans, and within the clans, a tripartite system of castelike grades. Marriage was permitted only between moieties and within grades, with a procession of men, once married, crossing the yard to live on the other side—in their in-laws' huts. The village circle was then quartered by an east–west axis running parallel to the river, the upstreamers organizing the downstreamers' funerals, and vice versa. What resulted was "a ballet in which two village moieties strive to live and breathe each through and for the other; exchanging women, possessions and services in fervent reciprocity; intermarrying their children, burying each other's dead . . ."[63] So integral was this system to the Bororo that Salesian missionaries had learned early on that changing the village layout led to a rapid cultural meltdown.

Just as with the Caduveo face designs, Lévi-Strauss was struck by the geometry of human culture. In this small tribal settlement on a scrubby clearing in a remote corner of Mato Grosso, a set of rules—computerlike in their dispassionate symmetry—had evolved over time. Guided by a "smokescreen of institutions," the Bororo lived out orderly lives.[64] What looked like a motley rural hamlet was in fact a precision machine. The circular-hut plans spread out across the vast central Brazilian plateau as a common feature of the Ge linguistic group. Lévi-Strauss could only hint at what this might mean in broader anthropological terms, but he would later look back on the Bororo with affection and an exaggerated sense of their influence on the development of his theories. In the early 1990s, he explained to a French documentary crew:

> I have the feeling now when I try to reconstitute my intellectual history—it's very difficult because I have a terrible memory—I have the feeling that I was always what later became known as "structuralist" even when I was a child. But meeting the Bororo who were the great theoreticians of structuralism—that was a godsend for me![65]

An old-fashioned ethnographic inventory survives on film, similar to the footage of the Caduveo, with the natives acting out life scenes for the camera: a Bororo pulling back the string on his bow (but not actually firing it); two men laboriously making fire by rotating a stick on a wooden base; a shuffling dance; Bororo men testing their physical strength by balancing 1.5-meter-high discs made of grasses and dried palm stalks on their heads; a canoeing scene. The flickering, speeded-up images carry the strange power of the amateur-shot silent film—a mystery, an emotional charge, a melancholy—reinforced by a fleeting glimpse of Lévi-Strauss himself. The camera tracks the Bororo as they paddle long, slender canoes down the river. For a few stray frames a figure in colonial garb appears leaning back on a branch, smoking a cigarette as he watches the canoes glide by.

In November 1936, Lévi-Strauss and Dina sailed for Europe to winter in France. Stowed in the hold were crates of indigenous artifacts, sourced mainly from the Caduveo and the Bororo, with a handful of objects from the Terena (neighbors of the Caduveo) and the Kaingang. In one case was a set of Bororo bull-roarers, slender wooden boards tapered at each end and painted with arcs and dots. The bull-roarers made a low humming sound when spun from a length of twine—the drone of spirits greatly feared by the women. The Bororo had reluctantly traded them on the condition that Lévi-Strauss lock them in a chest and not open it until he had reached Cuiabá.

Along with the bull-roarers, the Lévi-Strausses had amassed a spectacular ethnographic collection of hides, headdresses and musical instruments from a poorly documented part of Brazil. Indiens du Matto Grosso[66] would be the first exhibition organized under the auspices of the Musée de l'Homme, although as the museum was not yet opened to visitors, the collection was put on display at the Wildenstein Gallery, at the corner of the rue du Faubourg Saint-Honoré and the rue La Boétie. But perhaps there was something appropriate in the alternative arrangements—a year later the same gallery would host a major exhibition featuring leading surrealist artists.

According to Lévi-Strauss, the exhibition received "a polite appraisal,"[67] but a review in the Brazilian *Jornal do Comércio* was effusive:

> Many intellectuals, travelers, artists and curious people visited the art gallery in the evening, admiring around a thousand objects—ceramics, skins, masks, hammocks, flutes, hunting bows and arrows and other examples of indigenous art gathered by the Strausses from their visit to the Bororo

> and other tribes. Professor Lévi-Strauss gave explanations of these objects fascinating to the visitors, who were astonished and seduced by the originality and the beauty of this exhibition.[68]

Some of these objects—a shuttlecock, a funerary clarinet, a spectacular armadillo-claw pendant adorned with feathers, mother-of-pearl discs and porcupine quills—can still be seen today, in a glass case in the Musée du quai Branly. What remains striking are the colors of the decorative feathers: shocking reds and yellows that, after decades in storage, are still vivid enough to pierce the museum's penumbra.

More than the exhibition, Lévi-Strauss's first significant academic publication, "Contribution à l'étude de l'organisation sociale des Indiens Bororo"—a detailed analysis of the Bororo clan/moiety structure and its relationship to the village layout for the *Journal de la Société des Américanistes*[69]—signaled his entry into the small world of 1930s French anthropology. Marcel Mauss, no less, hailed the Lévi-Strausses as "the great hopes for French study of the Americas."[70] The article, which appeared late in 1936, was greeted with excitement by specialists and would travel widely, being remarked on in Brazil, the United States and France. Even hardened field-workers, like the great German anthropologist Curt Unckel, who had adopted the native name Nimuendajú and spent years on solo expeditions into central Brazil, were intrigued. Nimuendajú wrote him an encouraging letter saying that he hoped Lévi-Strauss would have the opportunity to carry out a proper long-term study in the future. He also wrote to Robert Lowie in the United States about Lévi-Strauss and his work, opening up a link to American academia that would soon prove vital.

Lévi-Strauss later said that the enthusiasm around his early work was not so much due to its "slim merit"[71] as its good timing—South America was the new frontier of western-hemisphere anthropology, and U.S. scholars were looking with interest at the work that was beginning to come out of Brazil. In truth he was disappointed by the brevity of his contact with the Caduveo and the Bororo, and modest about the significance of his findings. Replying to Nimuendajú, he explained: "My stay among the Bororo was unfortunately very short; I could only get an idea of certain problems, but I need to return and stay for a long period this time, to try and solve them. I hope you will excuse the poverty of my responses"—a self-deprecating tone that, although absent from *Tristes Tropiques*, he would later cultivate when questioned about the quality of his fieldwork.[72]

On more sensitive issues, where the building up of trust was crucial, his fleeting visits were not enough. Bartering for artifacts sometimes degenerated into farce. When Lévi-Strauss began negotiating for a hairpiece—the only object passed from mother to daughter among the Bororo—the women flew into a rage.[73] He tried, and failed, to collect a full set of physical anthropological data from the Caduveo and the Bororo (a part of his research that was written out of subsequent accounts), as he explained in an interview with a journalist from the Brazilian newspaper *O Jornal* on his return from the field:

> We collected only a few anthropometric measurements, and only from male Indians, because the women were shy and reserved. It was impossible to obtain measurements of skeletons and bones from both the Caduveo and the Bororo of Rio Vermelho . . . Blood type was also not obtained, because the Indians refused to cooperate, and they also made it difficult to obtain photographic negatives as they feared death and curses.[74]

These early, impressionistic spells of fieldwork set the tone of Lévi-Strauss's whole method as it later developed. He combined rapid assimilation of situations and ethnographic materials with boldly intuitive model-building. Time and again these hit-and-run tactics would pay off, bringing out fresh perspectives. Anthropologists could get bogged down in detail, trapped inside their own stale arguments; after years of patient cultural excavation, there was a tendency to lose sight of the overall design. In contrast, Lévi-Strauss captured a culture through fragments, filling the gaps in his mind, conjuring models as if from thin air.

IN MARCH 1937, Lévi-Strauss returned with his wife to São Paulo for his third and final academic year, determined to make the most of what he knew would be his last spell in Brazil. While making plans for a major, long-term ethnographic expedition, he went on a number of smaller trips, on one occasion even fitting in some impromptu fieldwork. In July, he went on the road with Jean Maugüé and René Courtin, a law graduate from the University of Montpellier who had just joined the French mission. Traveling in Courtin's new Ford, their goal was to go "as far as his car would take us" in a roughly northerly direction out of São Paulo.[75] They dressed for the part: Maugüé in boots, a cotton cloth shirt, a wide-brimmed straw hat, armed with a knife and a revolver; Courtin in flannel trousers and a woolen jacket, with a shotgun and cartridges "as if he were about to set off on a hunting trip in the Cévennes"; while Lévi-Strauss was in his familiar colonial explorer's uniform with his camera about his neck and a "Sherlock Holmes–style" sun helmet.[76]

They drove up through the coffee plantations of Campinas, on to Uberlândia and across the rapids of the Paranaíba River. From there Courtin's Ford broke free, motoring across semiarid plains studded with giant anthills. Stranded in empty fields, they passed by the building blocks of Goiânia, the future state capital. A hundred or so half-built houses stood alongside a hotel—a massive cement box dumped on the red flats. It was a brutalist architectural statement that took Lévi-Strauss aback: "Only the fear of disaster could justify the existence of the block-house," he later wrote, a disaster that "had, in fact, occurred, and the silence and immobility all around was its ominous aftermath."[77] They pushed on to the diamond-trading center of Goiás Velho, a baroque town of cobbled streets and pastel-fronted Italianate eighteenth-century houses set in rolling palm-topped hills. Farther north still, the road petered out at the Araguaia River, a major waterway that disgorged into the mouth of the Amazon a farther thirteen hundred kilometers downstream.

It was there, on the riverbank, that they came across a small outpost of semiacculturated Karaja Indians. Karaja villages spread up the immense Araguaia Valley, across the world's largest interfluvial island, the two-million-hectare Ilha do Bananal. For centuries the Karaja had moved through this region, fishing, hunting turtles and cultivating maize, manioc and watermelons in forest gardens. Now some groups had dropped down into the outskirts of Brazilian frontier towns, hawking artisanal wares to passing travelers. Lévi-Strauss sat down with them and tried to communicate, apparently with some success. "I marveled at how he could decipher gestures that for Courtin and me were merely picturesque," remembered Maugüé.[78] While Lévi-Strauss asked questions and took notes, a timid little girl fashioned two clay dolls with giant phalluses for Courtin and Maugüé. Lévi-Strauss collected several other examples of the unbaked dolls, with their black wax hair, bark loincloths and ballooning thighs. He was impressed by the formal similarities between these dolls and statuettes dug up in prehistoric Aurignacian culture, also drawing parallels to short, distended thighs found in Mexican Gualupita terra-cotta figures.[79] He took pictures—one of a Karaja woman in a loose patterned dress inspecting a doll; another of a native woman at work, sitting on fibrous mat with a knife, a pot of dye and a ball of string lying about her.

After a few days among the Karaja, they turned the car around. On the return trip, Courtin's Ford, which had battled from town to town down fifteen hundred kilometers of rutted tracks more normally used by mule trains and oxcarts, began to deteriorate. The front suspension snapped, leaving the engine balancing on the axle. They managed to make it a hundred kilometers farther before carrying out makeshift repairs in a small town where a mechanic fitted a strip of metal to hold up the engine. Then it was an anxious six-hundred-kilometer slog home. As the car bumped its way through São Paulo state, Maugüé caught a glimpse of his companions. "From the back of the car, I watched Lévi-Strauss, sitting beside Courtin," he remembered. "His sober expression nonetheless betrayed the jubilation we shared on being back in the city with all its comforts and above all a bathroom."[80]

As LÉVI-STRAUSS set his sights on more intensive fieldwork, the political turbulence of the 1930s was already threatening to intervene. In the streets of Rio de Janeiro, the Nazi-styled Integralists were goose-stepping in uniforms emblazoned with a swastika-like emblem, the sigma (Σ), the mathematical sign of the integral. They churned out crude anti-Semitic propaganda, with books like *Brazil: Colony of Bankers* and *The São Paulo Synagogue*, and branded refugees from Hitler as "human garbage." In a bizarre ethnographic reference, they hailed one another with a strong-arm salute, accompanied by the word *anauê*, a native Tupi greeting. To the far left, communist agitators threatened insurrection, staging wildcat strikes and violent protests. President Getúlio Vargas was adopting an increasingly authoritarian path through the morass. After being courted in Europe and brought over to teach in Brazil, the French were now viewed with suspicion. Lévi-Strauss's links to French socialism, as well as his connection to the well-known leftist and antifascist campaigner Paul Rivet at the Musée de l'Homme, put him in a particularly sensitive position. "We had interminable difficulties renewing our contracts," remembered Maugüé.[81]

In France, the pendulum was moving in the other direction. Listening to the news on shortwave radio, Lévi-Strauss was elated to learn of the victory of the socialist Front populaire and the ministerial post of Georges Monnet, for whom he had worked as a secretary in the 1920s. He was expecting to receive the call to work for Monnet and, had it come, Lévi-Strauss later recalled, "I would have boarded the first outward-bound ship."[82] In retrospect, it was a fork in the road: "My former comrades had forgotten me. Events, the new course my life was taking, did the rest . . ."[83] In the historical cauldron of the mid-1930s, Lévi-Strauss's political aspirations died at the very moment that his career as an anthropologist was lifting off.

3

Rondon's Line

> Imagine an area as big as France, three-quarters of it unexplored, frequented only by small groups of native nomads who are amongst the most primitive to be found anywhere in the world, and traversed, from one end to the other, by a telegraph line.
>
> CLAUDE LÉVI-STRAUSS[1]

LÉVI-STRAUSS BEGAN SCOUTING for field sites for a major ethnographic expedition. He had two points of reference: his own brief stay among the Bororo, and Nimuendajú's more detailed studies of the indigenous groups in central Brazil. Through correspondence with Nimuendajú, it seemed that even though they were describing tribes more than a thousand kilometers apart, their findings tallied; the assumption was that the scattered tribes of central Brazil made up one vast cultural/linguistic area—the Ge. It was thought that the Ge had once occupied the coastal zone, but had been pushed back into more inhospitable terrain by the Tupi-Guarani before European colonization. When the Portuguese arrived, they found Tupi cultures spread out along a great arc running along the Amazon corridor, down the Brazilian littoral and back up the Paraguay River into the interior. The Ge had been left with the rugged savannah of the central plateau, now at the anthropological frontier.

Ambitiously, Lévi-Strauss conceived of a "cross-section through Brazilian anthropology" traversing this region, from Cuiabá to the Rio Madeira. Accompanied by a team of experts, he planned to spend a year crossing an immense stretch of wilderness in an attempt, as he immodestly put it, "to understand America" rather than "study human nature by basing my research on one particular instance." Lévi-Strauss's goal was not just to survey the western outer reaches of the Ge, but—once over the rim of the Amazon Basin and into the forest—to contact little-known outposts of the Arawak, Carib and Tupi cultures as well. Later he would consider even this enterprise inadequate. "Today," he wrote in the 1950s, "I realise that the western hemisphere must be studied as a whole."[2]

The route that Lévi-Strauss eventually chose was forbidding. Beginning in Cuiabá, it traced a diagonal running in a northwesterly direction, roughly parallel to the border with Bolivia. Dirt tracks first crossed an arid scrub, broken by the orchardlike *cerrado*, where evenly spaced trees with gnarled trunks and contorted branches squatted along the plains. Farther north, thickets concealed a series of Amazon tributaries, which gushed down the otherwise parched plateau. At the halfway mark, Vilhena, the terrain changed again; dust turned to vapor, the biscuit-colored scrub to the deep greens of the great Amazon rain forest. In the 1930s this was still a virtual blank on the map. The frontier had stalled somewhere between the exhausted goldfields of the south and the impoverished riverine communities of rubber-tappers to the northwest. So little was known about this region that it was named after a mountain range—the Serra do Norte—that is, in fact, no more than a rocky outcrop. It might have seemed like inauspicious terrain in which to travel, let alone mount a large-scale ethnographic mission, but there was one potential route through—a single telegraph line whose filaments looped their way across the plateau, threading along a narrow *picada* (trail) hacked through the forest a quarter of a century before.

Its origins lay in the life of Cândido Rondon (1865–1958), a military officer and the founder of the SPI, the predecessor of today's federal agency the Fundação Nacional do Índio, or FUNAI (National Foundation for the Indian). A short, upright man with a bushy mustache, Rondon was a rare breed for the times—a frontiersman who was sensitive to the plight of the indigenous peoples, who he believed could become assimilated

Brazilians, working as clerks or seamstresses. He placed his faith in positivism, a secular religion based on the theories of Auguste Comte, which stressed progress through the dispassionate application of science and technology. Through his long career, he single-handedly explored much of the state that now bears his name, Rondônia, making peaceable contact with many indigenous groups whose only previous exchanges with Europeans had been running skirmishes with frontiersmen.

In 1907, Rondon was put in charge of the extension of Brazil's telegraph system from Cuiabá into the Amazon, with a view to connecting the then federal capital, Rio de Janeiro, all the way up to the Bolivian frontier. Crews began by cutting a trail. They dug a series of holes for the crooked tree trunks that served as telegraph polls, attached the porcelain elements to the tops of the posts, and slung them with reels of wire. At intervals they established telegraph stations, equipped with leather chairs, telephone exchanges and Morse code machines. Over the first stretch the going was relatively easy, but when the line entered the forest, cutting involved felling hardwoods and clearing solid vegetation, all in a sodden ninety-five-degree heat. Malarial fevers swept through the work crews, livestock began dying off, morale slumped, but Rondon drove his men on with strict military discipline. In the middle of the jungle he would insist on lecturing his workers for hours on end, showing slides of the Brazilian president and playing the national anthem on gramophone records.

Indigenous peoples, many of whom would only ever have seen lone rubber-tappers passing through, periodically approached the construction site as it shifted slowly through the forest. It is difficult to know what they would have made of several hundred men with pack animals and mountains of equipment hewing a corridor through the forest. From later reports it seems they ended up attaching a naturalistic significance to the telegraph line itself—equating the rounded shape of the transformers and their humming sound with beehives.

Some indigenous groups, however, did make contact. Photos from the line-building expedition show an enthusiastic Rondon handing out pairs of white cotton trousers and draping indigenous children in Brazilian flags. Various "improving" habits were taught—one photo has a group of Paresi children in rows balancing awkwardly on one leg with arms outstretched, performing calisthenics, a type of Swedish gymnastics. In others, a teacher instructs a small brass band made up of indigenous children trying to master trombones, trumpets and clarinets. Children were taught to read and write, along with basic mathematics. The boys also learned potential trades, such as shoe repair and Morse code, while the girls practiced sewing, embroidery and typing.

The Rondon line never really worked properly. Loose connections, power failures and substation breakdowns made the service intermittent and unreliable. In any case, as the last posts were being driven into the ground, the seven hundred kilometers of wood and wire were already obsolete. After a decade of work and the deaths of hundreds of men, the telegraph line was quietly superseded by shortwave radio. As Lévi-Strauss prepared to journey up the line, all that was left of Rondon's *grand projet* was a handful of employees stranded in lonely telegraph stations, unable to leave because of the debts they had racked up to backland traders. At other posts, in a rebuke to Rondon's positivist ideology, missionaries had filled the vacuum, proselytizing the local indigenous population. The line itself—with its lopsided posts and sagging wire—had begun its long decline.[3]

RETURNING TO PARIS in November 1937 at the end of the Brazilian academic year, Lévi-Strauss read what little had been published on the so-called Serra do Norte and the Ge-speaking groups that he hoped to study: a classic ethnography by the Brazilian anthropologist Edgar Roquette-Pinto, who had accompanied Rondon; work done by Curt Nimuendajú on central Brazil; the first volumes of the Rondon Commission, a documentary project set up in conjunction with the building of the telegraph line; and the memoirs of Theodore Roosevelt, whom Rondon had hosted on a game-hunting expedition in the 1910s. With financial backing through Paul Rivet at the Musée de l'Homme in place and letters of introduction to the Brazilian authorities, Lévi-Strauss stocked up on trinkets for bartering in wholesale outlets at the Carrefour Réaumur-Sébastopol. After his experiences among the Bororo, he had some idea of what was likely to be prized—small beads in a spectrum of colors that the Indians were already familiar with: blacks from palm nuts, whites from mother-of-pearl river shells, yellows and reds from the *urucu* dyes.

Back in Brazil, Lévi-Strauss faced an uphill bureaucratic battle to mount the expedition. The major hurdle was the Conselho de Fiscalização das Expedições Artísticas e Científicias (Council for the Monitoring of Artistic and Scientific Expeditions), formed in 1933 to oversee and control research in Brazil in an increasingly xenophobic era. Lévi-Strauss tried to apply first through the Museu Nacional in Rio and then under the auspices of the University of São Paulo, as a "Franco-Brazilian" expedition that would share results and ethnographic collections. Part of the process involved the agreement of the SPI, which was at first reluctant. None of their agents were in the region, and there was a feeling that the expedition might disturb the already fragile relations between frontiersmen and the Indians. The nomadic Nambikwara, whom Lévi-Strauss was planning to study, had killed seven telegraph workers in 1925 and another six members of a Protestant mission in 1933. A few years before Lévi-Strauss's trip there had been rumors that a line worker had been found buried waist-deep, with scores of arrows sticking out of his chest and his Morse keypad on his head.[4] Eventually, after interventions from Mário de Andrade and writer Sérgio Milliet, agreements were made between the SPI, the Museu Nacional, the Department of Culture and the University of São Paulo. The SPI warned that the service could not guarantee Lévi-Strauss's safety and that he should not retaliate in the event of an attack.[5]

Lévi-Strauss initially proposed a team of five experts from various disciplines—an anthropologist (Dina Lévi-Strauss), an ethnographer (himself), a naturalist/biologist (Dr. Jean Vellard), a linguist (Dr. Curt Nimuendajú) and his high school friend who had traveled on the previous expedition,

René Silz, whom he put down as "cartographer." But recruitment did not go according to plan. Silz was unavailable and Nimuendajú turned him down, saying that he needed time to write up results from fieldwork among the Canela and Xerente, and that he had already arranged with Robert Lowie to travel to the south of Bahia to continue studying another branch of the Ge. The real reason, though, was the presence of Vellard. Nimuendajú had read one of Vellard's reports in the *Journal de la Société des Américanistes* that described some distinctly nineteenth-century methods he had used while on an expedition in Paraguay. In the report, Vellard related how his party had counterattacked with guns when they had come under arrow-fire from an encampment of Guayaki Indians. The Guayaki fled, leaving a small boy behind. Vellard described ransacking the village for artifacts and taking the boy, whom he measured, weighed and photographed. Vellard wondered whether he could find a family in the Paraguayan capital, Asunción, to take care of the boy and speculated that it might be interesting to study his development. Nimuendajú was shocked by this account, and flatly refused to have anything to do with Vellard.

In his stead, the Museu Nacional insisted that a Brazilian anthropologist, the twenty-five-year-old intern Luiz de Castro Faria, join the expedition. From his field notes published in 2001, *Um outro olhar: diário da expedição à Serra do Norte* (*Another Look: The Diary of the Serra do Norte Expedition*), a belated and rather dry account of the expedition, Castro Faria comes across as a young man overawed by his selection. In contrast to Lévi-Strauss, he cultivated a more down-to-earth interest in regional Brazilian music and folk culture. He ended up in a difficult role as an unwanted team member—seen, as he put it years later, as "a nuisance," and a potentially dangerous one. Part of his job was to monitor the progress of the party and report back to the Museu Nacional. "I had the power to stop the expedition," he said in an interview in 1997, shortly before his death.[6] Lévi-Strauss was uncomfortable with the inclusion of a rival anthropologist, writing to the director of the Museu Nacional, Heloísa Alberto Torres, that "an ethnographer will have little work to do, because the scientific data, in this area, will be used in my doctoral thesis."[7] He was also unhappy about Castro Faria's secondary role as the eyes of the Brazilian state, or "tax inspector" as Lévi-Strauss disparagingly put it.[8]

By April 1938 final preparations were under way in São Paulo. Castro Faria met Lévi-Strauss and gathered together the vast amount of equipment needed for the expedition—some 1,470 kilos of it, including a bulky radio transmitter, a typewriter, a large-format Contaflex camera, an arsenal of hunting rifles and three thousand rounds of ammunition. By now there was considerable press interest. Lévi-Strauss and Castro Faria gave interviews, with the evening papers trumpeting an expedition that would, according to the *Diário da Noite*, "collect all possible knowledge about Amerindian peoples who are on the brink of destruction." "In among the many trunks of goods that will be used on the expedition," added the *Folha da Noite* with a lighter touch, "there are numerous toys which will be handed out to the indigenous children."[9]

Unable to find a seat on the plane up to Cuiabá, Castro Faria was forced to take the arduous train trip through the interior to Corumbá, the route Lévi-Strauss had traveled to the Caduveo, and from there up the Paraguay River to Cuiabá. At dusk on May 2, 1938, he boarded the *Eolo*—a two-story paddleboat slung with hammocks. He inspected his cramped cabin and was disappointed to find that, although he had expressly asked to be alone, someone else's things were already in the room. Two books were lying on the lower bunk bed—one by the nineteenth-century German ethnographer Karl von den Steinen, the other by the Brazilian anthropologist Estevão Pinto. Incredibly, among the diamond traders, Syrian peddlers and assorted Mato Grossenes, there was another anthropologist on board—Buell Quain, an ethnographer from Columbia University in New York.

A young man with an almost Latin complexion and strong, even features, Quain was the son of a well-off medical family from the Midwest, and had done his first spell of fieldwork in Fiji, where he studied the island's literature and epic poetry. Castro Faria had already come across him while he was researching at the Museu Nacional in Rio de Janeiro.

He'd even fetched a book for Quain—Vincenzo Petrullo's *Primitive Peoples of Mato Grosso, Brazil.* As the paddleboat began its weeklong meander upstream they fell into conversation, Quain talking of his plans to do a year's fieldwork in the Upper Xingu. "An extraordinary coincidence had resulted in us meeting here," Castro Faria noted down in his diary, "both on the way to distant regions, driven by the same desires."[10]

Buell Quain was one of several Columbia students who were turning their attention to Brazil. While he was in the Xingu, Ruth Landes was studying the Afro-Brazilian religion Candomblé in Salvador and the Texan Charles Wagley was beginning ethnographic work among the Tupi-speaking Tapirapé of central Brazil. To the west of the Tapirapé, William Lipkind was on the Araguaia River working with the Karaja Indians—the same group that Lévi-Strauss had chanced upon on his road trip through Brazil the previous year.

In Cuiabá, Castro Faria, Quain and Lévi-Strauss stayed at the same hotel, the Lebanese-run Esplanada. Quain and Lévi-Strauss, as two foreign anthropologists out in the sticks, struck up a brief but warm friendship. As they got to know each other, Quain unburdened himself to Lévi-Strauss, explaining that after he had left Rio he had begun to develop disturbing symptoms and was convinced he had contracted syphilis. Lévi-Strauss advised him to return to Rio and seek specialist help, but after a long stay in Cuiabá, Quain set off for his fieldwork site in the Upper Xingu.

While waiting for the arrival of Vellard from Asunción, Lévi-Strauss and Castro Faria filled their days trying to gather up-to-date information on the indigenous groups along the telegraph line. Around a hundred line workers still manned the substations, operating sections of the line that still functioned—a motley crew of semi-Westernized Paresi Indians, impoverished Brazilians, along with a handful of eccentric Europeans. They had intermittent contact with the Nambikwara, communicating with them using a forty-word half-Portuguese, half-Nambikwara pidgin.

Lévi-Strauss sent telegrams to the functioning substations with a series of simple questions: "Are there Indians in the vicinity? Are they friendly or do they mount attacks? Do they bring goods to sell? Do they ask for gifts? Do they show up regularly? Do they speak Portuguese? Do they dress like civilized people? Do they invite civilized people to their villages?"[11] After a lengthy delay, replies began trickling in. A shadowy group, the Beiços de Pau (literally "wooden mouths," after the plugs they wore in their lower lips), had recently attacked one of the stations. They were thought to live some distance from the line, spoke no Portuguese, and it was unclear what their native language was. Another station reported that the local Nambikwara regularly cut through the wires on the line "to show that they are enemies" and at times threatened violence. Indigenous groups near Vilhena seemed friendlier, but were prone to infighting. A line worker who happened to be in Cuiabá at the time confirmed the reports, but other lines of inquiry were less successful. Castro Faria went to the SPI offices, but was told that the government posts had closed down and that they had lost contact with operatives in the region.[12]

Buell Quain had lit out into the Amazon alone. Lévi-Strauss would set off with his wife, Castro Faria, Jean Vellard and a team of twenty men, fifteen mules, thirty oxen, a few horses, tons of equipment and a truck. Throughout the month they spent in Cuiabá preparing for the expedition, they had scoured the region for suitable recruits, with Lévi-Strauss's ending up buying every mule for sale within a fifteen-kilometer radius of the city. The men, poor locals of conservative Portuguese stock, were promised a rifle and a small daily allowance.[13] Out on the plateau, they would subsist on salt beef, dried fruit and any game that might come their way. Guides would be employed en route, as and when needed. When the crew and equipment were finally assembled on fields on the outskirts of Cuiabá, the herds of pack animals, the boxes, bags and saddles, the bearded men in loose cotton shirts and leather boots looked more like a traveling country fair than a scientific expedition.

In the pages of *Tristes Tropiques*, this large supporting cast often vanishes into the background, leaving Lévi-Strauss center stage. In reality, the Serra do Norte expedition was as far from the Malinowskian ethnographic gold standard—the early-twentieth-century loner, painstakingly learning the native language, submerging himself in their culture—as was possible. In contrast to the Conradesque journey to the extremes of humanity, much of the time Lévi-Strauss's entourage would outnumber the natives he was trying to study. So large and complex were the logistics that Castro Faria ended up doing a kind of ethnography on the mechanics of the expedition itself—documenting "the precise science of the porters," how they rearranged the saddle to load the crates, balancing packing cases across the oxen's back using specially designed wooden frames.[14]

Lévi-Strauss had barely set off before he was asking Rivet for extra money to cover spiraling costs. Prices had risen since his last visit to Cuiabá, he explained. The region was so dangerous that he had been forced to expand his team, and therefore the provisions and the number of oxen. As it stood, the thirty oxen were not enough to haul the tons of equipment required to subsist for six months in a region with no resources. (The team would in fact end up spending only short periods in the wilderness, with regular stop-offs at telegraph stations.) He calculated that he had just enough to get to the end of the expedition, but not enough to send the team back or freight his ethnographic collections. "I am therefore obliged to ask you for a supplementary credit of 40,000 francs,"[15] he concluded, to be deposited into his bank account at the Royal Bank of Canada, 3 rue Scribe, Paris, before December 1. Lévi-Strauss hoped that he would be able to cash checks somewhere on the upper Madeira River.

The scale of the expedition gave Lévi-Strauss's enterprise the feel of a nineteenth- or even eighteenth-century South American scientific venture, harking back to the journeys of Alexander von Humboldt and Charles Marie de la Condamine with their pack animals, porters and canoes. Like them, he sought enlightenment through mobility, an explorer's overview rather than an obsessive's single case study. There are also obvious parallels with the Mission Dakar–Djibouti, launched a few years before Lévi-Strauss had set off. In contrast to the intense engagement of the Anglo-American method, expedition leader Marcel Griaule had approached that trip as a documentary exercise. The mystique of "going native" was entirely absent, with translators used throughout. That team's goal had been not so much to render a lived reality as to map a mind-set, a cosmology, a civilization: *l'homme noir*.

THE MAIN BODY of the expedition set off to the shouts of the herders, the pack animals kicking up dust as they moved slowly off into the distance. The idea was to give the drovers a week's head start. Lévi-Strauss and the others would truck up to the Utiariti telegraph station, joining the mule train five hundred kilometers north of Cuiabá, where the first group of Nambikwara could be found. The truck would be abandoned on the banks of the Papagaio River, its contents loaded onto the oxen, and the expedition would then set off into the backlands.

After loading up the truck with crates of medical supplies, ammunition, tools and provisions, the anthropologists set off on June 6, in the predawn hours of a Monday morning. To Lévi-Strauss's dismay, only a couple of hours into their journey they overtook the mule train; the herders had advanced just fifty kilometers in the week since they had left. "I lost my temper for the first, but not the last time," recalled Lévi-Strauss.[16] The pace, it seemed, was being dictated by the whims of the oxen. Lévi-Strauss never adapted to the languid rhythms of backland travel—the constant loading and unloading, grazing and herding, the rest days that could hold up the expedition for an age in the middle of nowhere.

Leaving the mule train, they continued by truck through a string of dismal satellite towns. In Rosário Oeste they met a well-built *caboclo*, an ex-line worker who had just arrived from Utiariti. "He was the first person to talk about the Indians, even the Nambikwara, without that sense of apprehension, an almost involuntary fear," wrote Castro Faria in his diary.[17] Even better, the *caboclo* told them there were currently some fifty Nambikwara around the Utiariti station. This was a relief, given that they might have to wait anything up to three weeks there for the mule train to catch up.

A little farther on from Rosário Oeste, grinding up a rocky path at the Serra do Tombador, the chainwheel of the driving shaft snapped. The party found themselves stranded in the bush, while they sent word to Cuiabá to have a new part flown up from Rio. They slung their hammocks and waited, with nothing to do "but sleep, dream and hunt."[18] The hunting was good: the drivers managed to kill a small deer ("a wonderful dish," according to Castro Faria[19]) and an armadillo (an "explorers' club menu," Lévi-Strauss joked in a letter to Mário de Andrade[20]), which they dined on. Drinking *mate* around a campfire, they listened to the drivers tell fantastic stories of the backlands—popular legends involving anteaters, jaguars and Indians.

An image from this brief interlude taken by Castro Faria sets the scene. The boyish Dina Lévi-Strauss, wearing a loose jacket, jodhpurs and high leather boots, sits on her haunches jotting down something ("field notes," according to Castro Faria, although at this stage they had not yet begun ethnographic research). Around her, on the rocky scrub, lies a pile of charred branches, metal plates, a tin can and pots. A hammock is slung loosely from the back of the truck. Behind it, an expressionless Lévi-Strauss stands looking out from under his sun helmet.

When the new chainwheel finally arrived and was fitted, they made for the line. At Pareci they came across the abandoned weapons of the much-feared Beiços de Pau Indians and were told by telegraph workers that they had recently been spotted in the distance. Lévi-Strauss's group camped in nearby marshlands, but slept fitfully; a few kilometers off, wisps of smoke rose into the night sky, almost certainly from native campfires.

They had reached the line. From here onward, twisted telegraph poles stretched into the distance over a wasteland of sand, gravel and scrub. The combination reminded Lévi-Strauss of Yves Tanguy's landscapes, with their mysterious, soft-focus contraptions set against a woozy backwash, an effect created by thinning paint with turpentine. Lévi-Strauss's *tristes tropiques* were not the lush rain forests up ahead, but this dusty plain, doused during the four-month rainy season and then baked dry for the rest of the year.

The line was scored by a series of rivers flowing down the plateau into the Amazon Basin, each requiring a cumbersome crossing. Unloading the truck at the Cuiabá River, they eased it onto a rickety raft, made up of a wooden platform mounted on four shallow-bottomed canoes. During the crossing the ferryman confirmed that there was a group of Nambikwara in Utiariti, just three leagues up ahead. When the dirt track ended at the next river, Lévi-Strauss caught his first glimpse of members of the group that would end up being the focal point of the expedition. There were three of them, "completely naked, medium height, well built," according to Castro Faria's diary entry, waiting on the far bank of the river, accompanied by a Jesuit priest from the mission farther up the line in Juruena. (Lévi-Strauss remembered just two.)[21] The Nambikwara laughed as they helped carry their luggage to a straw hut that had been used to store equipment while the line was being constructed, which the mission had prepared for their stay.

In marked contrast to the highly charged descriptions of entering the Bororo village for the first time, Lévi-Strauss skips over his first impressions of the Nambikwara in his memoirs, moving straight on to ethnographic descriptions. But a candid account of the first day among the Nambikwara survives in a letter sent from the field to Mário de Andrade in São Paulo:

> Of the journey, I will say nothing. This region of Brazil is a god-forsaken, deserted bush land, through which we drove for 700 km. We were warmly welcomed by the telegraph team in Utiariti, who had prepared a beautiful hut on the banks of the river, situated, in a very thoughtful gesture, right next to the Nambikwara encampment. I am writing to you in the midst of fifteen men, women and children who are stark naked (but that's a shame since their bodies are not beautiful), with an extremely welcoming nature given that they are the same group (and probably the same individuals) who had slaughtered a Protestant mission in Juruena five years ago. Unfortunately, work promises to be extremely difficult: there is no interpreter at hand, a total ignorance of Portuguese and a phonetic language that seems impossible to understand. But we have only been here for 24 hours.[22]

As with the Bororo, the Nambikwara celebrated the anthropologists' arrival with a night of music. Seated about a fire, they listened to the songs' mesmerizing rhythms while the Nambikwara stamped their feet in the earth to the beat.[23]

AMONG THE CADUVEO, Lévi-Strauss had found aesthetic excitement in the women's exquisitely tattooed faces. When he entered the Bororo village, with its hangar-sized longhouse and highly evolved metaphysics, he was humbled. Virtually bereft of any cultural overlay, the Nambikwara offered no easy entry point.

The Nambikwara spoke a hushed, whispered tongue. They slept naked on the bare earth, rolling toward their smoldering night fires as the temperature dropped in the early hours of the morning. Powdered by ash, their skin took on a ghostly pallor as they crisscrossed the savannah, their worldly possessions scarcely filling the cylindrical baskets that they hitched, Sherpa-style, to their foreheads. Their "houses" during the dry season (the nomadic phase of the Nambikwara year) consisted of bunches of angled palm fronds jammed into the ground, periodically repositioned throughout the day to protect them from the sun, wind or rain. They made no pottery and few manufactured items. Instead there were hatchets dating back to Rondon, empty gasoline cans, tins and assorted cooking utensils scrounged during intermittent contacts with telegraph line workers. Canoes were unheard-of; when necessary, the Nambikwara floated across rivers on bundles of driftwood. They used no spices or salt, and cooled cooked food before eating it. Their main technological achievement was the use of poison-tipped arrows, but on the exposed grounds of the savannah the hunting was often difficult. When there was no game, they survived on berries, palm nuts, grasshoppers, microscopic lizard eggs and mouse-sized bats.

Even the penis sheath—common among South American hunter-gatherer groups—was not generally used. Nambikwara men and women were completely naked save for a set of accessories: nose feathers, bamboo-fiber labrets, arm- and waistbands made out of dried palm leaf, simple shell necklaces, armadillo-tail bracelets, and the occasional jaguar-skin hood for men. As if sampling from an extensive wardrobe, the Nambikwara regularly changed their ornaments, mixing and matching to suit their moods.

On the move, the Nambikwara filed across the savannah "like a column of ants."[24] They were accompanied by an eclectic menagerie: cocks and hens perched on the lips of their baskets (descendants of Rondon's efforts to encourage poultry farming), parrots, small monkeys balancing on the women's heads and babies strapped loosely to their mothers' thighs. The small-statured Nambikwara women were dwarfed by their baskets, which contained only the bare essentials: kindling, balls of wax, bones, teeth and porcupine quills, along with pebbles and shells. It was a nomad's survival kit, the raw materials for on-the-go invention—slim pickings for Lévi-Strauss's ethnographic collection.

In place of the rigid rules of a Bororo-like tribe, Lévi-Strauss found a casualness, a lightness of touch, an atmosphere of easy intimacy and banter. In broad daylight the Nambikwara rolled around on the ground in amorous play, fondling each other in twos and threes. Lévi-Strauss observed these joyous embraces carefully: "I never once noticed even an incipient erection," he noted, though it seems that he found it hard to share the native insouciance. "It was difficult . . . to remain indifferent to the sight of one or more pretty girls sprawling stark naked in the sand laughing mockingly as they wriggled at my feet."[25] In the mornings he was embarrassed when the Nambikwara women groped him while he bathed in the river, trying to steal his soap. (A comical picture survives of Lévi-Strauss, naked, pale and bearded, surrounded by a group of Nambikwara at the river's edge.)[26] Throughout the day he would find women taking a siesta in his hammock, leaving the fibers stained with *urucu* dye. "People who live in a state of complete nudity are not unaware of modesty," concluded Lévi-Strauss. "They define it differently"—just as, in the other direction, the burka merely leads to "a shifting of the threshold of anxiety."[27]

The team got down to work, making observations throughout the morning. After lunch, as the heat peaked at over a hundred degrees, they would take a siesta before checking their findings during the afternoon. They took photos, Lévi-Strauss with his Leica, Castro Faria using a more unwieldy Contaflex, and drew pictures—"really bad ones, but good for documentary record," according to Castro Faria.[28] He later lamented that although they had brought with them a bulky, hard-to-transport radio transmitter and a record player, they had no recording equipment for interviews or indigenous music.

Lévi-Strauss was a copious note-taker, but he never followed the strict formulas that his wife had taught her students in São Paulo, with their tables of set questions and standardized responses. Instead, he filled French-style graph paper exercise books with a mélange of information. He mixed diary-style entries with kinship diagrams, staves of music recording indigenous songs and lists of basic vocabulary—*feu*, *eau*, *terre*, *soleil*, *lune*, *vent*, *nuit*; *petit*, *grand*, *près*, *loin*, *beaucoup*, *joli*, *laid*, for instance, and their indigenous equivalents.[29] Expedition lists were thrown in promiscuously. "Luiz: ice, socks, throat medicine, Agfa film . . . ; Me: sunglasses, alcohol, razor," he scribbled at one point, next to which he had written, "Done, done, done." Every so often he noted down bulk provisions, "60 kg rice, 10 kg salt, one *arroba* [just over fourteen kilograms] of sugar" and so forth, along with miscellaneous articles—tents, Winchester rifles, axes and radio sets. On other pages there were short excerpts from books in French, English, German and Portuguese, references to articles and books about Brazil, and names of contacts, including Buell Quain. Drawings were scattered through the pages—of plants, penis sheaths, a monkey's head, a pregnant woman, along with rough maps and settlement plans.[30]

In contrast to the rich evocations in *Tristes Tropiques*, written fifteen years after the event, in more discursive moments the style of his notes was businesslike: "See indigenous people and distribute small gifts. Dinner at night. In the evening we visit the Indians. Songs and dance," he wrote of their first contact with the Nambikwara. In these short, staccato entries Lévi-Strauss complained often about the rigors of travel: "Very cold night—moonlight quickly covered by clouds—and a very hard bed . . . return to camp at the end of the day where it is teeming with insects . . . a day of anxiety and inaction." He referred back wistfully to his native country—certain escarpments in the Brazilian interior were like those found in the Haut-Languedoc; a wooded area reminded him of forests in central France.

"My notebooks are rough," Lévi-Strauss later admitted. "I am horrified how poorly put together they are."[31] There is indeed a kind of a haphazardness to his field notes. Apart from the general disorganization, the entries are uneven. Some of the sketches, for instance, are well executed—a detail of hand and twine to demonstrate weaving techniques, close-ups of spear tips, a spherical nose flute, palm fronds, a face densely tattooed around the chin and lower lip. But others are more like doodles, childlike drawings of jaguars, armadillos, birds and fish.[32] The overall impression is of an artist trawling for ideas rather than an academic at work.

Focusing on material culture, Lévi-Strauss bartered for the simple artifacts—nose feathers, bows and arrows—that were available, while Vellard conducted experiments using native curare, a poison used to asphyxiate prey. Vellard watched as the Nambikwara made their preparation, first shaving off the rust-colored outer casing of roots, then boiling them in a billycan over the campfire. The liquid immediately turned an intense red, frothing up before reducing to a thick, murky substance. The Nambikwara dipped their arrowheads into the concentrate before setting off on hunting expeditions. Vellard tried it out on a dog, plunging the arrowhead into muscle tissue in its leg and holding it in for five minutes. The dog immediately became groggy, its leg stiff and anesthetized. After a second jab, it died of asphyxiation. "A positive result," Castro Faria noted in his field diary, alongside a forlorn picture of a dead dog.[33]

As night fell, the Nambikwara gathered about their fires in animated conversation, which Lévi-Strauss tried with great difficulty to understand, while children milled around, goading the newcomers to join them in their games. When the Nambikwara lay on the ground to sleep, the team retired, Lévi-Strauss slinging his hammock, around which he hung a curious, box-shaped mosquito net, specially designed by a seamstress in Cuiabá.

It seems there was little collaboration. "I work alone . . . ," Castro Faria wrote. "Individualism, as a method of work, is absolute." Lévi-Strauss was "silent, introspective," he remembered later. "He had no true relationship with Vellard or me. It was absolute individualism: each kept his own notes. Vellard had no idea what Lévi-Strauss was writing down and vice versa. For a Brazilian it was a very unusual experience."[34] Lévi-Strauss was solitary by nature, more suited to the Malinowskian-style fieldwork to which he aspired, begging the question of why he had ended up organizing such a large and logistically complex mission. He was also guarded about his own findings in front of the Brazilian anthropologist, for both professional and political reasons. But in the rough campsites on the plateau, with the team struggling to understand the worldview of the Nambikwara, the scenario has a strange, almost neurotic feel to it.

AFTER ONLY TWO WEEKS' WORK, a gonorrheal eye infection spread by the *lambe-olho* fly began to afflict the Nambikwara. The group was soon in agony, sitting on their haunches or lying in the sands clutching their foreheads while family members administered some kind of herbal remedy through a leaf rolled up into a cone. By July 10, Dina Lévi-Strauss had caught the infection and her eyes were full of pus. Lévi-Strauss ordered medical supplies from Cuiabá, and then, in consultation with Vellard, decided that Dina's condition was too severe for her to continue in the field. They accompanied her back to Cuiabá, from where she returned to São Paulo for treatment. There, Mário de Andrade received a letter from a friend, Oneyda Alvarenga, describing her condition in alarmist terms:

> Did you know that Mme. Lévi-Strauss is almost blind and will perhaps lose her sight? She caught a purulent conjunctivitis in Mato Grosso which her husband avoided, they told me, by wearing glasses (which I thought was ridiculous). I don't know any more. She's here and might be leaving for France. Lévi-Strauss is going ahead with his work among the Indians.[35]

Although, after returning to Paris, Dina did in fact make a full recovery, the infection could have caused blindness if it had been left untreated. It was also very contagious, and over the following weeks it spread through the rest of the team, with the exception of Lévi-Strauss. Castro Faria's diary entries plot the ailment's progress. August 7: "Everyone is terribly affected by a purulent ophthalmia." August 8: "I have contracted the ophthalmia that afflicts the rest of them. It really is excruciating." August 10: "A night of terrible suffering. I didn't sleep a wink, tormented by an almost unbearable pain."[36] After months of preparation, fieldwork had ground to a halt almost as soon as it had begun.

Lévi-Strauss went on ahead up the line to Campos Novos—"Journey very long and without interest . . . long and difficult crossing of dry forest," he scribbled in his field notes—where he spent a despondent fortnight waiting for the others to recover.[37] Alone on a poverty-racked substation, living off wild pigeons, guava and *caju*, Lévi-Strauss became dejected. The few inhabitants there were riddled with hookworm and malaria. Unlike the indigenous families at the Utiariti station, the local Nambikwara groups that he had come to study were at one another's throats, and took a particular dislike to Lévi-Strauss. Retreating to the sidelines, he watched the spectacle of a Nambikwara feud. The two groups confronted each other, yelling insults, holding their penises and pointing them in aggression, and trying to steal bows and arrows, before eventually exchanging bracelets, *urucu* paste and gourds in reconciliation.

Disillusioned, unable to work, Lévi-Strauss marked time by rereading his notes, checking his diagrams and jotting down ideas, but he soon tired of recycling his own material. He fell into a depression, taunted by regret and self-doubt:

> It was now nearly five years since I had left France and interrupted my university career. Meanwhile, the more prudent of my colleagues were beginning to climb the academic ladder: those with political leanings, such as I had once had, were already members of parliament and would

soon be ministers. And here was I, trekking across desert wastes in pursuit of a few pathetic human remnants.[38]

Exasperated, he began work on a play, written on the reverse sides of his field notes. It was called *L'Apothéose d'Auguste* (*The Apotheosis of Augustus*), an involved companion piece to the seventeenth-century French playwright Pierre Corneille's classical tragedy *Cinna*.[39] Beginning as the senate discusses Augustus's possible deification, it centers around Cinna, the object of affection of Augustus's sister Camille. Although in love with Camille, Cinna has rejected society, spending ten years on the road in self-imposed exile, subsisting off lizards and snakes. His hard-won outcast status will enable him to return and claim Camille authentically and not merely as a result of social convention.

As the story progresses, Cinna seems more and more like a cipher for Lévi-Strauss himself and his predicament—a drifter who is beginning to doubt the validity of his adventures. Enlightenment through travel, Cinna concludes, is a lie, "a snare and a delusion." Stories of adventure exist only in the mind of the listener; in reality "the experience was nothing; the earth resembled this earth and the blades of grass were the same in this meadow." Cinna ends up filling his days reciting Aeschylus and Sophocles until they become meaningless, stripped of their beauty, now only reminding him of "dusty roads, burnt grass and eyes reddened by the sand"—just as Lévi-Strauss found that he could not shake the melody of Chopin's Étude no. 3, op. 10 from his head as he tramped through some of the remotest regions of western Brazil.[40] Moving into the third act, the plot pushes forward in a typically classical direction. Augustus, told by Jupiter's ragged eagle that becoming a god would involve a Cinna-like journey into oblivion, talks to Cinna about his dilemma. They come up with a solution to their respective problems: Cinna must assassinate Augustus. Augustus will achieve lasting public veneration, while Cinna will realize his goal of social rebellion.[41]

At the end of act three, inspiration deserted him. Like Cinna,

Lévi-Strauss had reached an impasse. Travel had promised a new world of ideas and experiences, yet here he was, holed up in a banal two-horse town in the Brazilian backlands, trapped inside his head. Had he hacked hundreds of kilometers down the telegraph line seeking the truths of indigenous nomads, only to return to the myths of antiquity?

Loneliness, depression, the weight of expectation, the sense of futility, the shadow of madness—Lévi-Strauss was finally experiencing the truth about modern fieldwork. Unlike any other discipline, that era's anthropological research was based on a situation of maximal alienation. The feeling of being cut off, stranded both geographically and culturally, was thought to be the route to true knowledge. Lévi-Strauss was fortunate that he could return to the rest of the expedition. However formal his relationships with the rest of the team were, there was at least the prospect of familiar references and conversation.

AMERICAN ANTHROPOLOGIST BUELL QUAIN had no such option as he began fieldwork in the Xingu. He had chosen difficult hosts. The Trumaí lived in fear, besieged by their neighbors, the Suyá and the Kamayurá. "All death is murder," he wrote in a letter to his supervisor at Columbia, Ruth Benedict. "Nobody expects to live longer than the next rainy season." The small group was also riven with sexual tensions—a paucity of available women had turned a girl whom no one would claim as a relative because of her ringworm into the tribe's prostitute. Struggling with the language, Quain compiled notes with little assistance from the Trumaí themselves. "There is nobody among them who volunteers information of ethnological value," he wrote to Benedict. "For three months I dug for structure and got very little."[42]

Quain's fieldwork ended prematurely when he was recalled by the SPI; he did not have the requisite paperwork to be in the region and was forced to return to Rio de Janeiro. In Rio he took a run-down rooming house, the Pensão Gustavo, on the Rua do Riachuelo in Lapa, a bohemian district full of bars and flea-bitten brothels, just as the carnival celebrations were getting under way. In his diaries the anthropologist Alfred Métraux, who had just arrived in Rio on his way to Buenos Aires, remembered dining with "Cowan," along with his Columbia colleague Charles Wagley, at his hotel, the Belvedere, in Copacabana:

> Cowan told us about his journey to the Xingu, and then spoke extravagantly on the subject of his syphilis. I detected a hint of desperate bravado in his brutal frankness and in the jokes he made about his condition . . . Cowan is quite drunk and fills the dining room with his booming voice. Wagley calms him with a delicate, courteous hush, hush.[43]

After sorting out his paperwork, Quain set off for the Upper Xingu again, this time to study the Krahô. He began fieldwork, but fell into a deep depression after receiving a series of letters from home. Having burned the letters, he left the village abruptly, accompanied by two Indian boys. The journey ended two days later, near the town of Carolina, now situated on the Maranhão/Tocantins state lines. It was from here that he wrote his last letter back to Heloísa Alberto Torres of the Museu Nacional in Rio de Janeiro: "I am dying of a contagious disease. This letter will arrive after my death. It should be disinfected. I would like my notes and tape recorder (unfortunately with no recordings) to be sent to the Museu. Please forward my notes to Columbia."[44] After his indigenous companions had retired for the night, Quain tried to commit suicide by slashing his arms and legs with a razor. When this failed, he hanged himself with the rope of his hammock from a nearby tree.

Intrigue still surrounds Buell Quain's death. Lévi-Strauss, among others, attributed his suicide to his belief that he had contracted syphilis. But according to a local barber who had befriended Quain during his last spell of fieldwork, this was a fantasy—he was in good health and showed no physical signs of illness.[45] There was also speculation about his drinking habits, family problems and guilt over casual sexual encounters in Rio, possibly homosexual.[46] Whatever the truth, Quain remains a tragic figure in the annals of anthropology, a testament to the pressures of fieldwork, as it was then conceived, as a long-term solitary exercise in an unpredictable and sometimes hostile environment. "A feeling of aloneness permeates the Quain notes," summarized the anthropologist Robert Murphy, who edited his Trumaí findings for publication after his death.[47] Where many others had soldiered on, Quain had buckled under the strain.

LÉVI-STRAUSS ABANDONED *The Apotheosis of Augustus* a short way in. It was time to bury his doubts and return to work. Traveling back to the rat-infested Jesuit mission station of Juruena, he rejoined the rest of the expedition, minus Dina.

They were studying a moving target, a nomadic group ranging across their enormous territories. Lévi-Strauss wanted to see the Nambikwara in situ, on the plains, rather than as hangers-on around the substations. As it happened, the chief of the group at Utiariti, who had traveled up to Juruena, was just about to set out on a trip across the plateau to a traditional meeting with disparate Nambikwara groups. The meeting place was a few days out of Juruena, in the very same region where the Nambikwara had massacred the seven telegraph workers in the 1920s. The chief was reluctant to let the expedition accompany them, nervous about how the other Nambikwara groups would react to the sudden arrival of Lévi-Strauss's party. But after much negotiation, he agreed on the condition that Lévi-Strauss scale back his entourage, taking just four oxen as pack animals.

Soon after setting off, traveling down a different route from their normal one to accommodate Lévi-Strauss's oxen, Castro Faria noticed that there were no women in the Nambikwara group—just taciturn men with hunting weapons. Lévi-Strauss's party nervously fiddled with their Smith & Wessons as they were led with few provisions out into a vast and featureless landscape. At midday they were relieved to catch up with the women, who, laden with animals, children and baskets, had in fact been sent off earlier.

When they finally pitched camp, the chief faced an open revolt after an unsuccessful hunting expedition left the Nambikwara hungry and irritable. Lévi-Strauss hoarded his provisions, while the Nambikwara were forced to dine on crushed grasshoppers, a dish even they considered frugal.

After a difficult two-day journey, they arrived at an opening by a stream, a gravelly campsite peppered with Nambikwara gardens. The atmosphere was tense. Families filtered in intermittently off the plateau. By nightfall Lévi-Strauss had counted around seventy Nambikwara in all, many of whom had apparently not seen a Westerner since their encounter with the telegraph workers more than a decade before. As the temperature dipped, Lévi-Strauss's party bedded down on the sands in the Nambikwara mode for a long, restless night, racked by mutual suspicion.

The uneasy cohabitation lasted a few days. In this unpromising environment, Lévi-Strauss carried out a surreal ethnographic experiment. He handed out blank sheets of paper and pencils, as he had done among the Caduveo, a strange move since the Nambikwara neither wrote nor drew, aside from rudimentary decorations—the dots and jagged lines with which they adorned their gourds. After initially ignoring the paper, the Nambikwara began scribbling a series of wavy lines, from left to right across the page. Unprompted, they had begun "writing." The chief went one step further, requesting a notepad from Lévi-Strauss. Quizzed on ethnographic points, he "wrote" answers in the pad, handing his doodles to Lévi-Strauss. When the bartering began, the chief made a great show of "reading" the list of exchanges and beneficiaries from a sheet of scribbles.

Somewhere in those scrawled lines lay meaning, not of the literal kind, but in a metaphorical sense. The Nambikwara had intuitively grasped the power of paper, notebooks, pens and markings in Western culture, and the mysterious rituals of ethnography. The chief's approach had been a pragmatic one, slotting into an alien culture with a certain ritual fluency, trading symbols alongside beads, arrowheads and lengths of cloth. Writing, Lévi-Strauss concluded, was first about power, and only afterward used for the purpose of aesthetic or intellectual enlightenment. Far from being mankind's crowning cultural achievement, it had initially been used to create hierarchies between the scribes and the illiterate masses. "The primary function of written communication," Lévi-Strauss concluded, "is to facilitate slavery."[48]

The return journey almost ended in catastrophe. Battling with an uncooperative mule, Lévi-Strauss fell behind the group and quickly became lost in the scrub, an episode recounted as farce in *Tristes Tropiques*.[49] As the sun set, he was contemplating a long, worrying night alone in the bush, without provisions and with uncertain prospects of rejoining the party the following day, when two Nambikwara tracked him down and led him back to the encampment. From Juruena, they made their way back up the line through Campos Novos to Vilhena, where they studied two Nambikwara groups—the Sabané and the Tarundé. "Excellent work," Lévi-Strauss later wrote in a memo referring to this period—so good, in fact, that when the Nambikwara wanted to leave, Lévi-Strauss gave them sacks of flour to stay put so that he could complete his research.[50]

Fifteen years later, Lévi-Strauss sifted these fragments of Nambikwara life, looking back on the weeks spent in and around the telegraph stations, the days out on the plains, remembering his relationships—fraught by communication problems—with a handful of Indians. In *Tristes Tropiques*, he searched for a philosophical synthesis. Whether he had seen the dying embers of traditional Nambikwara culture or been witness to the fallout of postcontact demographic collapse was irrelevant. For Lévi-Strauss, these ragged families alone on the plateau represented the end point of Rousseau's quest for man in the state of nature, uncorrupted by society. They were human society in embryo, stripped of its trappings, pared down to its core. What Rousseau had suggested as an ideal "which perhaps never existed," Lévi-Strauss claimed, rather extravagantly, to have found in flesh and blood. But uncovering a kind of ur-culture only led on to deeper problems. "I had been looking for a society reduced to its simplest expression," he wrote; "that of the Nambikwara was so truly simple that all I could find in it was individual human beings."[51]

THEY WORKED their way up the line through late September. From the substations of Três Buritis to Barão de Melgaço, the sun-blasted colors of the plateau slowly began saturating; dry savannah gave way to lush grasslands with palms, wild pineapple and clusters of native chestnut trees. Sands turned to mulch, the air humidified and a strong, organic odor rose off what was now the forest floor. At Barão de Melgaço they could look down into the Machado Valley, sinking into the fringes of the Amazon rain forest. The changing environment offered new gastronomic possibilities. They gorged on an exotic range of game, given a Gallic culinary treatment—roast parrot *flambé au whiskey*, *jacu* (a pheasantlike native bird) *rôti au caramel*, along with grilled caiman's tail—and freshened up, changing their encrusted dungarees for the first time in days.[52]

Thus began the second phase of the Serra do Norte mission. With the forests thickening and the trails narrowing into overgrown tunnels, they dispensed with the surviving pack animals. (Half would continue on to be sold in rubber-tapping villages in the forest; the other half would make the long trip back to Utiariti.) Much to Lévi-Strauss's relief, from here on the pace would quicken. A slimmed-down ethnographic team would travel by canoe.

The commander of the Barão de Melgaço substation lent them two light dugout canoes for the onward journey, half floating, half punting down the Machado River. The boats carried around five men, along with wooden crates and a couple of Nambikwara baskets for provisions and equipment. Clamped to Lévi-Strauss's boot was Lucinda, a tiny capuchin monkey, immortalized in a fine pencil sketch in his field notes, that he had been given by the Nambikwara when she was only a few weeks old. Hardwired to cling to her mother's back, Lucinda had at first tried to live in Lévi-Strauss's hair, the way the Nambikwara traveled with small monkeys. But he had managed to train her to accept his boot, an arrangement that would prove painful once they began hiking through dense rain forest. After trying in vain to get her to move to his arm, Lévi-Strauss was forced to stride through the forest to the constant squeals of Lucinda, as she was lashed by the thorny undergrowth.[53]

Two days downstream they reached the telegraph station at Pimenta Bueno in pouring rain, furiously bailing out their canoes. There, over their first sit-down lunch since setting off from Cuiabá, Indians working at the station told them about two tribes in the vicinity still living in the forest. After five more days gliding up a tributary of the Machado, they reached the first—a breakaway group that had fallen into obscurity and was now camped in the forest a kilometer back from the river.

A set of igloo-shaped thatch huts spread out across a rough-cut oval clearing where twenty-five men, women and children who called themselves Mundé subsisted. Lévi-Strauss was the first academic to contact them, a professional milestone that would quicken the pulse of any aspiring anthropologist. Yet the honor was largely symbolic—he spent just four days among the Mundé, with no interpreter. Stretching credibility, he claims to have gained an insight into "aspects of the Mundé way of thinking and social organisation . . . the kinship system and vocabulary, the names of parts of body and the colour vocabulary, according to a chart I always carried with me."[54]

In contrast to the disheveled, ash-powdered Nambikwara, the Mundé were fastidious depilaters. Their stocky bodies were neatly adorned with translucent resin labrets, mother-of-pearl necklaces and beaded nasal septa. Unlike the muted sounds of the Nambikwara tongue, the Mundé language was sharp and zesty, "like the clashing of cymbals."[55] The Mundé's exoticism was compelling, yet enigmatic. "They were as close to me as reflections in a mirror," wrote Lévi-Strauss, musing on the paradox of fieldwork. "I could touch them; but I could not understand them."[56] And the very act of understanding—the questionnaires, the descriptions of ritual, myth and religion, the charting of kin systems—would have broken the spell.

The expedition was nearing its end. After Vellard came down with malaria and withdrew to Urupá to recuperate, the scientific team was reduced to just Lévi-Strauss and Castro Faria. But there was one last indigenous group that Lévi-Strauss wanted to see. Working from reports from rubber-tappers, Tupi line workers back at Pimenta Bueno, a scattering of references from the Rondon Commission papers and Curt Nimuendajú's ethnographic works, Lévi-Strauss set his sights on contacting the Tupi-Kawahib, whom he believed to be the last descendants of the great Tupi civilization of the middle and lower Amazon. In the first decades of the sixteenth century, ancestors of the Tupi-Kawahib had met the Portuguese and French as they stumbled off their ships onto the beaches of the Brazilian littoral, becoming the subjects of some of the earliest experiments in ethnography. In a romantic gesture, Lévi-Strauss hoped his descriptions would close a four-hundred-year-old ethnographic circle.

First contact was discouraging. Deep in the forest, the party bumped into two natives traveling down the trail in the opposite direction—one wearing a tattered pair of pajamas, the other naked but for a penis sheath. They learned through their interpreter that the Tupi-Kawahib were about to abandon their village for the substation of Pimenta Bueno. "This did not suit our purpose at all," wrote Lévi-Strauss, so after promising gifts, he convinced the extremely reluctant chief to stay put, so as to afford them a more "authentic" ethnographic experience.[57]

At around twenty members strong, two of whom were severely disabled, the Tupi-Kawahib were barely a viable group. Their soon-to-be-abandoned houses stood in the undergrowth, adorned with symbols in red and black *urucu* dye—striking images of toads, dogs and jaguars, depicted as if they were climbing the walls. In the background a large wooden cage on stilts housed a harpy eagle whose feathers were periodically plucked for use on ornaments. In hints of earlier conflicts, the women wore necklaces studded with spent cartridges.

Just as the team settled down to work, disaster struck. Emídio, one of the young herders they had recruited from Cuiabá, leaned on his rifle while shooting pigeons in the forest. The report was heard in the village, followed by screams of pain. Emídio had blown his hand apart. "It was incredible," wrote Castro Faria. "Shattered bones, exposed nerves, severed fingers."[58] They debated what to do, considering amputation, but since he was a herder by trade and reliant on both hands, they could not bring themselves to do it. They decided instead to clean out the wound, dousing it with disinfectant and wrapping it in cotton and gauze, then retrace their steps back to the river. Delirious, Emídio stumbled down the trail ahead of them as they struggled to keep up. By the time they reached the riverbank, Emídio was in extreme discomfort. Peeling off the dressing, they tried to clean out the maggots that had already infested the wound. Castro Faria ferried Emídio back downriver, from where he was taken to Porto Velho for treatment and later flown back to Cuiabá. Meanwhile, Lévi-Strauss stayed on to complete his fieldwork. The whole incident clearly disturbed him. In the midst of his field notes there is a surreal drawing in the style of Dalí inspired by the accident—a writhing ball of fingers, thumbs, limbs and teardrop eyeballs.[59]

Lévi-Strauss camped by the side of the river with the Tupi-Kawahib, who were still planning to leave the forest shortly. In an expressive image, the now thickly bearded Lévi-Strauss, wearing round black-rimmed glasses, stands awkwardly, his left hand scrunched into a nervous fist. Lucinda, the small monkey given to him by the Nambikwara, clings to his right boot, attached by a lead to his belt strap. On his right is a roughly constructed wooden table, with camping equipment neatly lined up—blackened billycans, a tin plate with a large fruit of some kind and what looks like half a manioc root. In the background, the broad river feeds off into the distance. On the left-hand margin, a naked Tupi boy looks back at Lévi-Strauss—a figure absent from an almost identical image reprinted in the photo album *Saudades do Brasil.*[60]

In another lightning spell of ethnography, Lévi-Strauss spent two weeks documenting a culture that was unraveling before his eyes. An elaborate ritual involving virgins spitting into a 1.5-meter-tall barrel to ferment maize wine had been reduced to three little girls hawking into a cup. Their polygamous kin system had reached the limits of its sustainability, with the chief monopolizing four of the six available women—the other two being his sister and an old woman. Lévi-Strauss was intrigued by the fact that the Tupi-Kawahib neither cultivated nor used tobacco, a rare omission in central Brazil. The Nambikwara had been keen smokers; the Mundé had blown powdered tobacco through a meter-long pipe into each other's nostrils. The Tupi-Kawahib, in contrast, were horrified by the substance: "On seeing us unroll our supply of tobacco, the village chief sarcastically exclaimed, '*Ianeapit!*' ('This is excrement!')."[61] This strong aversion was apparently long-standing. When Rondon had first encountered the Tupi-Kawahib years before, the Indians had angrily yanked cigarettes out of the mouths of anyone smoking.

The visit climaxed with the performance of what Lévi-Strauss described as a kind of operetta, "an exotic version of *Les Noces*." The chief, becoming possessed, began impersonating a series of different characters in what Lévi-Strauss likened to alternating arias, leitmotifs and brooding melodies reminiscent of Gregorian chants. Through an interpreter, Lévi-Strauss apparently followed the convoluted plot—which involved the *japim* bird, various forest animals, and "a stick, a pestle and a bow"—sufficiently difficult to test the most proficient native linguist, working through Portuguese, a language in which Lévi-Strauss was never comfortable. Nevertheless, he managed to fill twenty pages of his notebook with the plot, and also jotted down more than forty airs, corresponding to different characters.[62] The performance was Wagnerian in scale, lasting eight hours over two nights. At the end, the chief, exhausted and in a deep possession, rushed at his wife with a knife and had to be restrained as she fled into the forest.[63]

The chief's near-homicidal finale marked the end of the ethnographic part of Lévi-Strauss's journey. The return trip took them through a string of rubber-tapping villages. At Urupá, as they waited for a motorboat to take them to the Madeira River, Vellard threatened to leave early and make his own way overland. "This will completely disrupt our plans—it amounts to absurd and condemnable obstinacy," wrote Castro Faria in his diary.[64] In the event, they talked Vellard around and made their way by boat to Jacaré. Once on the Madeira, they were back on a steamship, which transported them up to Porto Velho. It was the end of the line for Castro Faria, who took a steamer down the Amazon to Belém, from where he traveled back to Rio. Lévi-Strauss and Vellard boarded an amphibious plane for Cochabamba in Bolivia. In a light aircraft filled with peasants tending chickens, hens and ducks, they braved Bolivia's domestic services before recrossing the border at Corumbá and heading back up to Cuiabá. By January 1939, Lévi-Strauss was back in Utiariti, where the Nambikwara were building huts for the rainy season. It was time to wind up the expedition. Laden with his ethnographic collections, his truck heaved its way back to Cuiabá, from where he freighted crates of indigenous artifacts down to São Paulo. Lévi-Strauss would never again return to the field.[65]

"THE TRIP WAS LONG AND DIFFICULT," wrote Lévi-Strauss to Mário de Andrade back in São Paulo, "but I will never forget these eight months; they were full of fascinating experiences. In scientific terms I think we brought back good material, a lot of it new—material that will profoundly change current thinking. I sincerely believe that the expedition will make its mark."[66] From a professional perspective, though, Lévi-Strauss's fieldwork fell well short of the standards of the time. It had been considerably shorter than he had originally planned. One year had shrunk to eight months—two of which were spent in Cuiabá preparing the mule train and equipment. Illness, accidents and logistical problems had pared contact time down even further. He spent a large amount of the remaining time describing and collecting indigenous artifacts, something he later regretted. When he had been preparing his expedition at the Musée de l'Homme, Marcel Mauss had instilled in him "a truly mystic reverence for the cultural object"; in the field he had felt duty-bound to focus on material culture, hampering his work on beliefs and institutions.[67] Even among the Nambikwara, on whom he would subsequently base one of his theses, practical problems prejudiced the research. A few snatched months of observation, captured through an interpreter via Portuguese, could hardly measure up to the kind of in-depth ethnography that was already being produced by British and American anthropologists.

As the discipline of anthropology matured through the twentieth century, Lévi-Strauss's enterprise aged rapidly. By the 1950s no serious anthropologist could have gotten away with such a whimsical journey, dotted with brief periods of contact with a series of indigenous groups. In the intimate settings of the ethnographic encounter, the expedition's sheer scale militated against the collection of data. Much later, in an interview he gave to the BBC in the mid-1960s, Lévi-Strauss was at pains to claim that he had worked in a very different way. Asked if the very presence of ethnographers changed the culture they studied, Lévi-Strauss responded:

> Of course if you send an enormous anthropological team into a small tribe with photographers, cameraman, tape recorders and the like, you would alter the culture. I've never worked that way and I don't believe in working that way. I think that the anthropologist, and I am still Malinowskian in that respect, should work alone with as little apparatus as possible, just a notebook and a pencil and make himself as unobtrusive as possible.[68]

But after retirement, he responded to his critics with disarming frankness. "I don't want to overemphasize the importance of my fieldwork," he said in an interview at the end of the 1990s. "I did more than certain critics allege, but I am the first to admit that in total my work is still modest." He described the paucity of material that he came away with on the Nambikwara as "fieldwork taken to its negative limit" and likened his experiences in the field to self-analysis undertaken as a part of psychoanalytic training.[69] The months spent traveling through the Brazilian interior took him into the discipline's subconscious; it gave him insights into the process of writing ethnography and expertise in evaluating the work of others. It would aid his subsequent modus operandi—a kind of meta-ethnography, based not so much on his own fieldwork as on large-scale comparisons, pooling data on indigenous peoples from around the world and synthesizing the findings. "Finally, why not admit it?" he concluded to Didier Eribon in the late 1980s. "I realised early on that I was a library man, not a fieldworker."[70] Interview-based research was indeed never ideal for his more traditional, academic sensibility. He found the whole process of ethnography intrusive, involving "an embarrassing degree of indiscretion."[71]

Of those involved in the expedition, Castro Faria left the fullest impressions of Lévi-Strauss in the field. In a late interview he characterized Lévi-Strauss as a philosopher, a man of ideas who had stoically endured the fieldwork experience as a kind of unpleasant induction into the profession. "It was the price Lévi-Strauss paid to be recognized as a real anthropologist," Castro Faria explained to a journalist with the French newspaper *Libération*.

> As the saying goes, he wasn't cut out for the job. He had difficulties communicating, and that made it boring for him to be so far from civilization, from his own comforts . . . The expedition was actually more like traveling than doing fieldwork: there were months of preparation for very brief periods with indigenous groups . . . For Lévi-Strauss, it was difficult to accept such uncomfortable conditions. Camps were set up and dismantled all the time, it was too much for him. He was truly a "philosopher among the Indians."[72]

Castro Faria eulogized the Brazilian doctor and anthropologist Roquette-Pinto, who had traveled with Rondon through Mato Grosso and had written what is still considered a classic ethnography of the region. He was also impressed with Lévi-Strauss's wife—"Our findings would have been very different had Dina Lévi-Strauss stayed with us"—and said that the expedition suffered greatly when she was forced to return to São Paulo. I put this to Lévi-Strauss, seated on a modern black leather sofa in the study of his sixteenth-arrondissement apartment. His response was unequivocal: "Dina had no interest in ethnology. In her heart of hearts she was a philosopher, not an ethnologist." Her active role at the University of São Paulo and then in the field was more a question of strategy than passion. "São Paulo and Brazil were virgin territory," Lévi-Strauss explained. "To be cynical, we were occupying the terrain. She took on folklore and physical anthropology; I took on sociology."[73]

By far his most trenchant critic, though, was Vellard. He had disliked the general disorganization of the voyage, had never gotten along with Castro Faria and had fallen ill with malaria in the latter stages of the expedition. His assessment was blunt: "The expedition was a complete failure," he told Alfred Métraux.

LÉVI-STRAUSS'S FIELDWORK was indeed limited—but it added up to far more than the mere stamping of his anthropological papers. He had explored Brazil, traveling thousands of kilometers by rail, car and mule train, traversing jungles on horseback, in canoes and on foot, in an era when backland travel was difficult and dangerous. He was a gifted writer and photographer who, with scant materials, produced iconic portraits of a range of Brazilian tribes. Unlike the fixation on the minutiae of a single group that often makes ethnography virtually unreadable outside specialist circles, Lévi-Strauss's vivid descriptions of the Caduveo, Bororo, Nambikwara, Mundé and Tupi-Kawahib revealed the richness and variation of Brazilian indigenous culture, which he likened to "a kind of Middle Ages which lacked a Rome: a confused mass that emerged from a long-established, doubtless very loosely textured syncretism."[74]

Much has been made of the brevity of his contact time, but as the French anthropologist Alban Bensa wryly remarked, "Anthropologists can spend ten years in the field and end up with nothing interesting to say." In contrast, Lévi-Strauss was "a good observer, and more importantly an intelligent analyzer of his own observations."[75]

ON THE EVE of his return to Europe, Lévi-Strauss went down to Santos to meet fellow Americanist Alfred Métraux, who was stopping off in Brazil for a few hours on the way to Argentina. They had exchanged letters, but this was the first time they would meet in person—the beginning of what was to become a long, close friendship. They left behind a ramshackle port teeming with prostitutes and strolled along the sweeping sands of Santos's beachfront. Métraux's first impressions were lukewarm:

> Lévi-Strauss arrived. He looked like a Jew who had stepped out of an Egyptian painting: the same nose and a beard trimmed *à la sémite*. I found him cold, stilted, in the French academic style . . . Lévi-Strauss hated Brazil. He thought Vargas was an unprincipled dictator who just wanted to cling on to power. His dictatorship was essentially a police state. Lévi-Strauss saw no hope in South America. He was almost inclined to see in this failure a kind of cosmic curse. He had decided to leave Brazil, where all work seemed impossible.[76]

Lévi-Strauss had had his fill. President Vargas's Estado Novo (1937–45), modeled on Salazar's dictatorship in Portugal, had seen Brazil turn into a country of secret police, informants and phone tapping. The regime had banned political parties and begun jailing left-wing dissidents. There was suspicion about foreigners, who had to register with the police, justifying their presence in the country. Censors went though their letters, some of which were mysteriously "lost" in the post. Although it lacked the aggression and energy of Mussolini's Italy or Nazi Germany, Brazilian fascism was nevertheless stultifying and toxic to a young left-leaning intellectual like Lévi-Strauss.

All that remained for him to do was to pack up and leave for France. This was easier said than done. In a farcical coda to the bureaucratic wrangles with the Museu Nacional, when he tried to board the ship for Europe, Lévi-Strauss was arrested and confined to his cabin by a Brazilian naval officer, accompanied by two officers carrying rifles with fixed bayonets. The dispute was over export licenses for the ethnographic materials Lévi-Strauss was taking out of the country. In the hold lay the fruits of his research—irreplaceable artifacts, books and field notes—now in danger of being seized and left behind on the docks. The matter was eventually settled when he explained that, as agreed, he had left half the expedition's artifacts with a scientific institute in São Paulo.[77] Part of Vellard's collection, however, including indigenous bones, native hummingbirds and a selection of invertebrates, was impounded.

The ship set sail, stopping off in Rio de Janeiro, Vitória and Salvador, where Lévi-Strauss disembarked and strolled the famous streets of the city's historic center, the Pelourinho. Outside one of the hundreds of baroque churches that spread out through the upper quarter of the port of Salvador, he stopped to take pictures, followed by a group of "half-naked negro boys" begging him to have their photo taken. He took a few snaps, only to be arrested and briefly detained again for defaming Brazil. "The photograph, if used in Europe, might possibly give credence to the legend that there were black-skinned Brazilians, and that urchins of Bahia went about barefoot," Lévi-Strauss later wrote in his memoir.[78]

The ship pulled out into the bay. The Brazilian littoral shrank back to a green outline, flickered and then disappeared over the horizon. Ahead lay Europe of the late 1930s—Europe on the brink. In the mid-Atlantic, passenger ships powered past them, bound for the Americas. Crammed into their second-class cabins were Jews, their life's possessions stuffed into battered suitcases.

4

Exile

> No one had told me . . . that New York was an Alpine city. I sensed it on the first evening of October, when the setting sun ignited the heights of the skyscrapers with that ethereal orange-like colour that one sees on the crests of the rocky walls while the valleys fill up with cool shadow. And there I was at the bottom of a gorge, in that street of blackened brick through which there passed a bitter yet cleansing wind.
>
> DENIS DE ROUGEMONT[1]

LÉVI-STRAUSS ARRIVED BACK in Paris toward the end of March 1939, with a post as a teacher at the Lycée Henri-IV held for him for the autumn term. For the last five years he had been on the move—crisscrossing the Atlantic, wandering the wastes of central Brazil. He had returned with a second collection of indigenous artifacts, thousands of photographs, as well as a stack of field notes, still smelling of the creosote he doused his canteens in to protect them from termites. Now, at thirty years old, it was time to take stock, exhibit his collections, put his notes in order and begin writing up his thesis.

In his absence, the Musée de l'Homme had opened as a part of the 1937 Exposition internationale des arts et techniques dans la vie moderne. In retrospect, the exhibition had been a foretaste of what was to come. The colossal swastika-draped German pavilion designed by Albert Speer had faced the equally monolithic Soviet pavilion, with its giant statue of peasant workers holding aloft a hammer and sickle. Ironically, Speer had taken the Grand Prix for his model of the Nuremberg rally grounds.

Installed at the Musée de l'Homme, Lévi-Strauss unpacked the half dozen crates he had shipped from Brazil and laid out some seven hundred objects that he had exchanged for colored beads and lengths of fabric. Coming mainly from the Nambikwara, they lacked the theater of his earlier haul. In place of the Bororo bull-roarers, ornamental rattles and clarinets were nose feathers, chipped gourds and rough-weaved baskets. After surveying his collection, he began the painstaking process of sorting and labeling each object, however prosaic, preparing it for display in the new, professional environment of Rivet's museum.

Perhaps as a counterweight to the rather dry and bureaucratic cataloging exercise, Lévi-Strauss used his spare time to make a start on a novel, a "vaguely Conradian" tale with an ethnographic angle. Based on a newspaper report he had read, the plot was to involve a cargo cult–like situation: a group of refugees would use a phonograph to dupe a tribe on a Pacific island into believing their gods were about to return to Earth. All that remains is the title, *Tristes Tropiques*, the lyrical description of a sunset, written on board the *Mendoza* en route to Brazil, which would later be recycled for his memoirs, and a handful of pages in Lévi-Strauss's archive held at the Bibliothèque nationale de France. The pages follow the character Paul Thalamas as he sets off on a voyage to the tropics, just as Lévi-Strauss had done a few years before. The extract is intriguing, combining melodrama—"He breathed deeply" was Lévi-Strauss's opening sentence—with awkwardly introduced philosophizing: "In a vague way, Paul Thalamas turned his thoughts to Berkeley and the famous theory in which the English bishop tries to prove the relativity of our visual perceptions, by the apparent differences in the size of the moon at the zenith and on the horizon."[2] Clearly Lévi-Strauss had not yet mastered the flow of fiction, but who knows what he might have been able to achieve had he plowed his formidable intellectual energies into a literary career instead of an academic one. What the extract does show is that Lévi-Strauss's modus operandi was the same whatever he turned his hand to—a very Gallic blend of drama and philosophy.

Like the many other artistic projects he had started, the novel was abandoned fifty pages in, "because it was so bad," in Lévi-Strauss own words.[3] "I very quickly realized that I wasn't able to do it, because I lacked imagination and didn't have the patience to write the descriptive details needed to flesh out a character and create atmosphere."[4]

Engrossed in his work at the museum and struggling with his novel, Lévi-Strauss seemed strangely disconnected from the events brewing across Europe. "Did you feel that the war was coming?" he was asked in the 1980s. "No," he replied. "No more than I sensed the dangers of Hitler or the Fascist threat. I was like most people, totally blind."[5] Nor did the mounting threats to Europe's Jewish population strike a personal chord. As German Jews continued to flee across the border into France, Lévi-Strauss explained away Nazi anti-Semitism as petit bourgeois jealousy against Jewish bankers who had profited from the era's high inflation rates. The ongoing persecution he likened to a kind of natural disaster to be weathered—like a volcanic eruption—rather than some fundamental, catastrophic social change.[6]

Lévi-Strauss's second exhibition never took place. As he finished documenting his collections, war broke out. The forlorn wail of sirens sounded across Paris skies as civilians went through the paces of air raid drills; barricades and checkpoints sprang up along the boulevards; soldiers piled sandbags high around the city's famous monuments and carried artwork into storage. For Lévi-Strauss, the drift toward war was accompanied by personal upheaval. In the spring of 1939, he separated from Dina. An eleven-year marriage, a good proportion of it spent in Brazil, was over. The couple had worked closely together, enduring the hazards and pleasures of backland travel, the thrill and tedium of ethnographic fieldwork. Seventy years after they had split, I asked Lévi-Strauss what had happened. At the age of ninety-eight, he spoke in short sentences, with long pauses in between. "She lived in her head," he told me. "I never knew what she was thinking." He went on to hint at other problems. Sometime after they had divorced he had been told of the existence of "romantic letters" between Dina and Mário de Andrade.[7]

By September, British Expeditionary Forces began arriving in northern France, marching over fields still pitted with the divots left from the First World War. French conscripts dug trenches and constructed shelters from the Channel down to the Ardennes, trying to paper over defenses to the north of the Maginot Line. Lévi-Strauss was drafted. He has described his war experience as a kind of continuation of fieldwork. Just as he was settling back into Paris, to the museum, his writing desk and the prospect of the teaching job in the autumn, he was on the move again. Over the next months there would be more travel to uncertain destinations, more bivouacking and tinned food, boredom and discomfort.

He spent the first months of the *drôle de guerre* censoring telegrams for the postal ministry ("utter buffoonery"[8]) before he asked to be trained as a liaison officer for the incoming British Expeditionary Forces. His English was rudimentary, but he managed to pass the exams and was posted behind the tail of the Maginot Line on the Luxembourg border. In the months leading up to the German invasion, there was little to do. During the spring he whiled away his time on long hikes through the surrounding wooded fields. It was on one of these excursions, at the beginning of May, that he claims to have had his first, sketchy intimations of the philosophical basis of structuralism. Gazing at a bunch of dandelions, he fell into intense intellectual contemplation. He examined the gray halo of a seed head with its hundreds of thousands of filaments sculpted into a perfect sphere. How was it that this plant, along with all others, had come to such a regularized, geometric conclusion? "It was there that I found the organizing principle of my thought," he later remembered.[9] The dandelion was the result of the play of its own structural properties, calibrated into a unique and instantly recognizable form. Subtle variations, changes at a deep genetic level, could give rise to other forms, the different species that multiplied through nature. The idea that culture,

Claude Lévi-Strauss as a boy in a painting by his father, Raymond. It was one of many portraits Raymond would produce at different stages of Claude's life.

Lévi-Strauss's father, Raymond, c. 1936. An old-style portrait painter, Raymond's aesthetic sensibilities would leave a deep impression on his son.
[Claude Lévi-Strauss Archive]

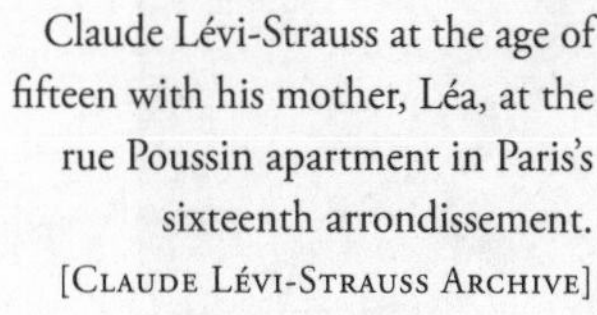

Claude Lévi-Strauss at the age of fifteen with his mother, Léa, at the rue Poussin apartment in Paris's sixteenth arrondissement.
[Claude Lévi-Strauss Archive]

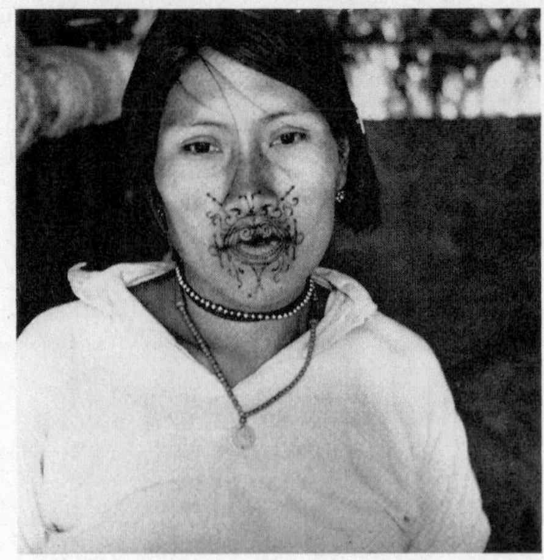

Among the Caduveo, Lévi-Strauss became fascinated by the volutes and scrolls painted on the women's faces, which made them look as if they were "peering out from behind a complicated ornamental screen." [Claude Lévi-Strauss Archive]

Lévi-Strauss's chief informant and interpreter among the Bororo. Raised by missionaries, he claimed he had been to Rome and visited the pope. [Claude Lévi-Strauss Archive]

Lévi-Strauss and his first wife, Dina, in the field in December 1935, studying the Caduveo in what is today Mato Grosso do Sul state, Brazil. [Musée du Quai Branly, photo Claude Lévi-Strauss/Scala, Florence]

A corridor is hewn through the forest during the construction of the Rondon telegraph line in the early twentieth century. In the 1930s the line would become the setting for Lévi-Strauss's Serra do Norte expedition. [Museu do Índio Archive/FUNAI—Brasil]

A group of Paresi Indians being taught callisthenics, a type of Swedish gymnastics, in ill-fated early efforts to "civilize" and assimilate them into Brazilian society. [Museu do Índio Archive/FUNAI—Brasil]

Lévi-Strauss photographs a Nambikwara Indian firing an arrow against the backdrop of a rustic telegraph station in Utiariti. [Luiz de Castro Faria Archive/MAST–RJ]

Above: Twenty-five-year-old Luiz de Castro Faria, a Brazilian anthropologist whom the Museu Nacional sent to accompany the Serra do Norte expedition. [Luiz de Castro Faria Archive/MAST–RJ]

Left: Tropical-medicine specialist Dr. Jean Vellard, who also took part in the Serra do Norte expedition. [Luiz de Castro Faria Archive/MAST–RJ]

Lévi-Strauss stands at the river's edge during fieldwork among the Tupi-Kawahib. Clinging to his boot is a capuchin monkey, Lucinda, connected to his belt strap by a leather lead. [Getty Images]

Lévi-Strauss washes in a river with a group of Nambikwara Indians: "I was often embarrassed by a concerted attack on the part of half-a-dozen or so females—young or old—whose one idea was to appropriate my soap, of which they were extremely fond." [Claude Lévi-Strauss Archive]

Portrait of a Nambikwara boy, which subsequently became the cover of a reprint of *Tristes Tropiques*. [Claude Lévi-Strauss Archive]

Nambikwara men mill around their makeshift camp in the aftermath of a successful hunting expedition that bagged four toucans. [Claude Lévi-Strauss Archive]

Simone de Beauvoir and Jean-Paul Sartre have tea in a café in Paris, May 1946. Initially enthusiastic supporters of Lévi-Strauss's ideas, they would come under attack in the early 1960s as Lévi-Strauss turned on existentialism. [Time & Life Pictures/Getty Images]

Above: A young Michel Foucault in Uppsala, Sweden, in the mid-1950s. At first Foucault acknowledged his debt to the work of Lévi-Strauss, but he would later distance himself from the label of structuralism. [Jean-François Miquel]

Left: Psychoanalyst Jacques Lacan, pictured here in the late 1970s, was profoundly influenced by Lévi-Strauss. The two were friends, though Lévi-Strauss confessed that he never really understood Lacan's theories. [© François Leclaire/Sygma/CORBIS]

Maurice Henry's illustration published in the literary journal *La Quinzaine littéraire* in 1967 defined an era. It features (*from left to right*) Michel Foucault, Jacques Lacan, Claude Lévi-Strauss and Roland Barthes.

Lévi-Strauss in Paris in 1949 after his return from New York, where he was influenced in turn by fellow exiles André Breton and Roman Jakobson. [AFP/Getty Images]

Lévi-Strauss sits in the front row of a lecture theater at the Collège de France with Georges Dumézil, listening with rapt attention to the Russian linguist Roman Jakobson. [All rights reserved. Photograph taken from Cahier de l'Herne *Lévi-Strauss*, 2004]

Lévi-Strauss hosts one of his famous seminars at the old Laboratoire d'anthropologie on the place Marcelin-Berthelot. Among the participants are Jean Pouillon, Maurice Godelier and Isac Chiva. [All rights reserved. Photograph taken from Cahier de l'Herne *Lévi-Strauss*, 2004]

Shot from a Henri Cartier-Bresson photo essay published in American *Vogue* in 1968, a time when Lévi-Strauss was achieving global fame. [HENRI CARTIER-BRESSON/MAGNUM PHOTOS]

Lévi-Strauss gives his opening address at the Académie française. In May 1973 he became the first anthropologist to enter France's elite intellectual institution. [AFP/GETTY IMAGES]

Lévi-Strauss, aged ninety-six, with his third wife, Monique. As Lévi-Strauss reached the end of his life he grew more pessimistic about modernity, a sentiment first aired in his postwar classic *Tristes Tropiques*. [AFP/GETTY IMAGES]

like nature, could have its own structuring principles—hidden, yet ultimately determining, like the genetic codes that produced the geometry of nature—would inform much of Lévi-Strauss's subsequent work, as he began his analysis of sociological/cultural phenomena such as kinship, totemism and myth.

Lévi-Strauss was awoken from his intellectual reveries by the dramatic opening of Germany's westward offensive. With news of strikes into Belgium and Holland on the airwaves, a little to the north of where Lévi-Strauss was stationed, columns of tanks sped down the narrow lanes of the Ardennes Forest. Crossing the Meuse at Sedan, German panzer divisions punched effortlessly through the French defenses, leaving a trail of dust and diesel fumes as they broke into open countryside.

The surprising ease of the German conquest traumatized the French. "It was horrible . . . ," remembered Jean Rouch, who would go on to become a renowned ethnographic filmmaker. "We discovered that what we had learned at school—the invincibility of the French army—was false. The old officers were afraid and were escaping. There was not a real battle. In just one month the whole of France was occupied. We were ashamed to have lost the war." Then a student of civil engineering, Rouch spent the first months of the occupation traveling around France by bicycle from the Marne River to the Massif Central, blowing up bridges to slow the German advance.[10]

With the German blitzkrieg penetrating deep into French territory, Lévi-Strauss was relieved by a Scots regiment, which arrived with its own set of liaison officers. Lévi-Strauss's group set off in search of their corps, tracking them down to a village in the Sarthe. "It probably saved our lives," he remembered, "for the [Scots] regiment was decimated a few days later."[11] In the confused weeks that followed, Lévi-Strauss found himself caught up in huge movements of people across France. Cars weaved cross-country through the trees to avoid the lengthening traffic jams. Streams of refugees choked all routes south, trying to outpace the Germans' spectacular advances. Overnight, eight million were on the move. The historian Gaston Roupnel watched the catastrophe unfold:

> I started *Histoire et destin* [*History and Destiny*, his last book] at the very beginning of July 1940. In my little village of Gevrey Chambertin, I had just seen waves of refugees go past along the main road, the whole sorry exodus of unfortunates, in cars, in carts, on foot, a miserable muddle of people, all the wretchedness of the roads, and mixed up with all this were the troops, soldiers without their weapons . . . and this great panic, this was France![12]

Lévi-Strauss's corps traveled by rail and cattle truck, from the Sarthe through Corrèze and Aveyron as their officers bickered over whether to head for Bordeaux and surrender to the Germans or escape to the Mediterranean. Fortunately, they opted for the south and the trip ended in the relative safety of Béziers. They were quartered on the Larzac plateau. After a disorderly retreat, Lévi-Strauss had miraculously landed on his own doorstep, near the family home in the Cévennes, where his parents had already taken refuge.

He was moved with his corps on to Montpellier. There he left his barracks in search of work at the university, offering his services as an examiner in philosophy for the upcoming baccalaureate examinations. He was hired and, after being demobilized, divided his time between the university and his family home. In Montpellier he met up with René Courtin again, his traveling companion in Brazil. Courtin was in the process of setting up a Resistance network, and after the war would be one of the founders of *Le Monde*.

Lévi-Strauss had escaped unscathed, his only experience of the fighting being the splintering of tiles overhead when his position was strafed by German Stukas during the retreat. He was secure in Vichy France, with family nearby and a university job. Yet by the beginning of September he was courting danger once more. He traveled up to Vichy to ask to be reassigned to his old job at the Lycée Henri-IV in Paris. Just as French Jews were escaping south, Lévi-Strauss requested to be sent back north, into Nazi-occupied territory. It was an extraordinary move, given the times. In France forty thousand foreign Jews were already interned in camps—makeshift wooden huts in muddy fields, which froze during the winter.[13] Although official persecution of French-born Jews had not yet begun, the screws were tightening under the Nazi occupation.

In the 1980s Lévi-Strauss claimed that it was his "lack of imagination" that led him on this potentially disastrous attempt to return to Paris. "That helped me during my fieldwork," he told Didier Eribon. "I was unaware of the danger."[14] Scarcely believing such an offhand reply, I went back over this with him. "I did know that the Jews were threatened," he told me, "but I thought you had to hide in the most direct, thorough way possible, by carrying on as normal."[15] Fortunately for Lévi-Strauss, the official dealing with the request, the director of secondary education, refused to send anyone with such an obviously Jewish name back into occupied France, suggesting a college in Perpignan instead. When Lévi-Strauss arrived in Perpignan, a new mood was in the air. Colleagues were wary, studiously avoiding the subject of the Jewish situation and the Nazi race laws. A gym teacher, who privately sympathized with Lévi-Strauss's position, became his only confidant.

After only a few weeks in Perpignan, Lévi-Strauss returned to Montpellier, where he taught what would turn out to be the last philosophy classes of his career for a preparatory course at the École polytechnique. It turned into a purely ritualistic exchange between a set of students with no interest in philosophy and Lévi-Strauss, who had already mentally fled the discipline for anthropology. He read out his lecture notes against the hubbub of students chatting among themselves.

Outside classes he caught up on his reading. One book in particular, *Catégories matrimoniales et relations de proximité dans la Chine ancienne* (*Matrimonial Categories and Kin Relations in Ancient China*), written by the doyen of francophone Far Eastern studies, Marcel Granet, struck a chord, setting in motion a train of thought that would follow him into exile. Granet was the leading sinologist of his day, studying Chinese classical texts, traditional numerology and feudalism. *Catégories matrimoniales* was one of the first attempts to rigorously map out classical Chinese kinship relations. Lévi-Strauss had already grappled with kinship in Brazil, observing the Bororo's fine-tuned moiety system and the small, densely interrelated nomadic families of the Nambikwara. Unlike Lévi-Strauss's fumbling efforts to pin down their significance, Granet had tried to move beyond description. His goal was to unveil the very mechanics of kin systems, to find a set of objective rules that underpinned what at first glance appeared to be merely the arbitrary outcome of tradition. His book drew together concepts that Lévi-Strauss would later revisit: the symmetry of kinship systems as a kind of mathematical inevitability; the incest taboo as a positive prohibition—a magnetic field of repulsion propelling a system of exchange. Granet also hinted at universality (albeit through an evolutionist paradigm), drawing parallels between ancient Chinese systems and present-day Australian Aboriginal arrangements. The arguments were dense. There were complex diagrams—spirals inside cones, stars embedded in circles, crisscrossing arrows. "I was spellbound," Lévi-Strauss later recalled.[16] Yet he was also frustrated. He found Granet's solutions obscure and overly elaborate; complexity had generated yet more complexity; untidy data could be described only by invoking baroque rules. The goal, which would remain a lifelong quest for Lévi-Strauss, was to descend to the next level of abstraction, into a clarifying world beyond description, a purer universe of simple imperatives.

Three weeks later, Lévi-Strauss was fired under the first Jewish Statute introduced by the Vichy government on October 3, 1940. He returned to his parents' house, this time with some sense of the very real danger that he and his family were in. "I already felt myself to be potential fodder for the concentration camp," he later confessed.[17] He entertained romantic notions of being able to survive on the run, scavenging in the countryside, sleeping rough, Nambikwara-style, roaming the Cévennes. But inevitably thoughts turned toward exile. After Georges Dumas intervened to secure him a new posting at the University of São Paulo, another spell in Brazil was an option.[18] He might even have been able to resume fieldwork among the Nambikwara. The nomadic period had shown him only one aspect of Nambikwara life; intensive study of the sedentary camps during the wet season would fill out the picture.

Lévi-Strauss traveled back up to Vichy, where the Brazilian embassy had set up offices in a cramped ground-floor room. There, in an episode later recounted in *Tristes Tropiques*, he tried, but failed, to renew his visa. In an excruciating scene the ambassador held the stamp in midair, ready to hammer it onto Lévi-Strauss's open passport, but—reminded by a zealous official of the new rules in place—could not follow through. Lévi-Strauss left empty-handed.

With his options dwindling, he received a letter that turned out to be as life-defining as Bouglé's phone call had been six years earlier. It was an invitation from the Rockefeller Foundation to teach at the New School for Social Research in New York. Founded after the First World War, the New School had been taking in European intellectuals under threat from the rise of fascism and anti-Semitism. With the outbreak of the Second World War, it began receiving waves of intellectuals from across Europe fleeing war and persecution. Lévi-Strauss was fortunate to have the backing of both Alfred Métraux and Robert Lowie, who had been impressed by his work on the Bororo, as well as family connections in the States—his aunt Aline, widow of the painter Henry Caro-Delvaille, raised money through a wealthy friend to support the application. After the offer Lévi-Strauss wrote to Dina, who was also Jewish, saying that if she wanted to get out of France she could travel with him as his wife.[19] She elected to stay on and ended up playing a role in the Resistance. Lévi-Strauss's parents would remain in Vichy France, stranded in their holiday house in the Cévennes and unable to return to the rue Poussin apartment until after the war.

Lévi-Strauss could now enter the States; the problem lay on the French side. As the war progressed, leaving the country was becoming more and more difficult. After the occupation of the north, some Jews and perceived undesirables hiked over the Pyrenees, traveling across Spain and into Portugal to the neutral port of Lisbon, from where they packed onto Cunard liners or, money permitting, took the newly established twelve-hour Pan American Clipper air service. The other route, out through Marseille, was more direct, but still involved mountains of paperwork: affidavits of support, proof of job in the host country, visas, proof of passage and Vichy exit papers, with each document depending on the others in a dispiriting bureaucratic chain.

Artists Max Ernst and André Masson, writer Arthur Koestler and Nobel physicist Otto Meyerhof, among thousands of others, gathered in Marseille to get their papers in order and find a berth out of Europe. They were aided by the inspired work of the American Quaker Varian Fry and his Emergency Rescue Committee, another privately funded organization aimed at rescuing European intellectuals from the deteriorating situation in Europe. Vichy military police scoured the port with orders to arrest any "subversive" who could not produce proof of passage. People had begun disappearing. Russian revolutionary Victor Serge, who sailed with Lévi-Strauss, described lives "hanging by slender threads" in Marseille, where the "talent and expertise of Paris . . . in the days of her prime" were reduced to "hunted, terribly tired men at the limit of their nervous resources."[20] Despite the difficulties, the artistic communities that would soon set up in exile—in New York, Buenos Aires and Mexico City—were already forming before they set sail. André Breton and assorted surrealists along with Victor Serge and Varian Fry rented the eighteen-room Villa Air-Bel, where they hosted exhibitions, "auctions," theater and comedy nights.

The unusually mild autumn of 1940 gave way to one of the coldest winters on record. A biting mistral blew off the Massif Central, streaming down the Rhône Valley. Snow dusted the Mediterranean. Shortages of food and heating oil signaled the beginning of the long, hard slog through the war years. His papers now in order, Lévi-Strauss came down from the Cévennes and did the rounds of Marseille's drafty shipping offices. He heard rumors that a ship was about to leave for Martinique and tracked it down to the Compagnie des transports maritimes—the very same shipping company that he and his academic colleagues had used on half a dozen trips to and from Brazil. A company official who remembered Lévi-Strauss from the Brazil days confirmed that a ship was setting sail for the Caribbean the next month, but tried to dissuade him from taking it, being "unable to tolerate the idea that one of his former first-class passengers should be transported like livestock."[21]

Lévi-Strauss packed up the remains of his ethnographic materials—notes, card indexes, a travel diary, maps, diagrams, photographs and negatives—for the trip to America. With the help of a smuggler, the crate was spirited into the hold. On March 25, 1941, he boarded the *Capitaine Paul-Lemerle*, ushered down the quai de la Joliette and out of the country by a fascist guard of dishonor:

> We went on board between two rows of helmeted *gardes mobiles* with sten guns in their hands, who cordoned off the quayside, preventing all contact between the passengers and their relatives or friends who had come to say goodbye, and interrupting leave-takings with jostling and insults. Far from being a solitary adventure, it was more like the deportation of convicts.[22]

A creaking steamer ("a can of sardines with a cigarette butt stuck in it," according to Serge[23]), the *Capitaine Paul-Lemerle* was loaded up with 350 "undesirables"—"a kind of floating concentration camp"[24] of German, Austrian, Czech, Spanish and French Jews and political agitators whose paperwork had finally come through. Among the hundreds jammed into the hold on makeshift pallets and straw mattresses were Breton, Cuban artist Wifredo Lam, German novelist Anna Seghers and Victor Serge, one-time colleague of Lenin. Serge, with his "clean-shaven, delicate-featured face" and a "strangely asexual" voice, confounded Lévi-Strauss's image of the virile revolutionary.[25]

Arrangements were primitive. Two sets of unventilated cubicles had been rigged up—one on the port side for men, the other on the starboard side for women. A zinc trough leading off into the sea served as the toilet, a miserable dribble of water as the shower. Nevertheless, Lévi-Strauss told me that the mood was not bleak, but excited—"more like setting out on an adventure."[26] A surviving photo from the *Capitaine Paul-Lemerle*'s deck bears this out. Behind a heavy coil of ship's rope young women smile gaily, chatting and smoking. Men look confidently back into the lens, and a couple of toddlers have been hoisted up at the back of the group, appearing against a backdrop of the open sea.

Through his connections with the Compagnie des transports maritimes, Lévi-Strauss managed to secure one of the bunk beds in the only two cabins on the vessel. He shared with an Austrian metal magnate and a wealthy Martinican returning home ("the only person on board who could reasonably be presumed to be neither a Jew nor a foreigner nor an anarchist"[27]). The last bunk was occupied by a mysterious North African with a Degas stashed away in his suitcase. While most of the other passengers were treated with disdain, he seemed to have an inside track with all the officials throughout the trip. The man claimed that, after a voyage of several months, he would be spending only a few days in New York. Lévi-Strauss later learned through photos published with his obituary in 1974 that he was Henri Smadja, a French-Tunisian Jew who ended up editing *Combat*, the Resistance paper founded during the war by Albert Camus. It remains unclear exactly what he was doing aboard the refugee ship.

The *Capitaine Paul-Lemerle* docked briefly at Oran in Algeria and at Casablanca before skirting the African coast for Dakar. While waiting to go ashore in Casablanca, Lévi-Strauss was surprised to hear André Breton give his name to passport control ahead of him in the queue. Breton was by then famous in France, Lévi-Strauss virtually unknown. Nevertheless, Lévi-Strauss immediately introduced himself and the two became friends.

They were both serious intellectual aesthetes, both cool and somewhat formal in their approach to the world, yet intrigued by a midcentury modernist infatuation with the primitive and the subconscious. Deprived of books, they passed the rest of the voyage chatting on deck, handing each other long, densely theoretical notes, exchanging ideas on art, surrealism and aesthetic appreciation. Lévi-Strauss wrote a detailed commentary on Breton's doctrine of spontaneous creativity, trying to resolve the contradictions between surrealist "automatic" art (in which the artist simply writes, draws or paints with no preplanned ideas, guided by chance and random events) on the one hand, and the idea of artistic technique or expertise on the other. How could artistic creativity express itself through what was merely a reflex of the subconscious? He concluded with the notion of "irrational awareness" (*prise de conscience irrationelle*)—a kind of creative inspiration that the true artist smuggles into a spontaneous work of art. In reply, Breton wrote of the "para-erotic" aesthetic pleasure derived from art, which distinguished it from impulsive doodles, and concluded that Lévi-Strauss's idea of irrational awareness might itself be produced at a subconscious or "pre-conscious" level.[28] Even in the difficult circumstances of the crossing, Breton was always on the lookout for random aesthetic events. At one point he was struck by the combination of a hanging carcass of an ox that had been slaughtered on board, flags fluttering over the ship's aft and the rising sun. "Their somewhat hermetic assembly, in April 1941," observed Breton, "seemed rich with meaning."[29]

Conditions became primitive as the ship descended into the tropics. Rising temperatures forced everyone up onto deck, now a clutter of clotheslines, children's nurseries, bedding and open-air dining arrangements. Passengers began using the toilets in the small hours of the morning so as to avoid "collective squatting"; the dribble of water in the shower boxes turned to steam in the tropical air.[30] Breton's aristocratic sensibilities were tested to the limits. "André Breton, who was very much out of place *dans cette galère* [in this hell]," wrote Lévi-Strauss in *Tristes Tropiques*, "strode up and down the few empty places left on deck; wrapped in his thick nap overcoat, he looked like a blue bear."[31] Lévi-Strauss, now a veteran of primitive living conditions and in any case traveling in the relative luxury of a cabin, was philosophical. "I learned some anthropology there,"[32] he quipped to a *Washington Post* reporter decades later.

On the run in to Martinique, relief spread through the decks at the prospect of landfall and the first bath in weeks. Hopes were short-lived. A crude French nationalism reigned in the colony, loyal to Vichy France, rather than any notion of embryonic resistance. Paranoid officials, brooding in their colonial outpost, finally had a group of "traitors" on whom to vent their anger and frustration. As soon as the *Capitaine Paul-Lemerle* docked, heavily armed troops in tropical kit flooded onto the decks. There were show interrogations, consisting mainly of eyeballing and shouting abuse, followed by internment in prison camps.

Breton was singled out for special treatment. He was forced to pay a nine-thousand-franc "deposit" to enter Martinique, which was subsequently revoked, although he ended up paying fifteen hundred francs in "internment fees" for the pleasure of being imprisoned in the former leper colony Pointe-Rouge. When he presented his invitations to speak in America, one official scoffed, "A fat lot of good *that'll* do the Americans." Breton was eventually freed with the parting shot: "We don't need any Surrealist or hyperrealist poets in Martinique."[33]

Lévi-Strauss was accused of being "a Jewish Freemason in the pay of the Americans" and was apparently told that "so-called French Jews are worse than foreign Jews."[34] But his luck held. At the request of the ship's captain, who had served as chief officer on the Brazil trips, he was spared the rigors of the camps and was, along with the Martinican and Smadja, allowed ashore. They toured the island in an old Ford, grinding up mountain roads in low gear past fern fronds and fruit trees set against pale mists and volcanic earth. Lévi-Strauss found the landscapes pleasing, more in tune with his idealized vision of the tropics than Brazil's mix of the baking *cerrado* and the claustrophobia of the forests.

From Martinique, he took a Swedish banana boat to San Juan, Puerto

Rico. For the first time he sensed America on the air, albeit from the edge of the Caribbean:

> I breathed in the warm smell of car paint and wintergreen . . . those two olfactory poles between which stretches a whole range of American comfort, from cars to lavatories, by way of radio sets, sweets and toothpaste. I tried to guess what the girls in the drug-stores with their lilac dresses and mahogany hair were thinking about, behind their mask-like make-up.[35]

Lévi-Strauss's official welcome, though, was hostile. His immigration paperwork was already out of date, and while he cabled New York for fresh assurances, he was placed under a loose form of house arrest, accompanied by two bored police officers wherever he went. Three weeks passed before the Americans could arrange for an FBI expert to inspect his crate of fieldwork notes. The agent, though highly suspicious of a card-index reference to Karl von den Steinen's classic work on Mato Grosso, *Unter den Naturvölkern Zentral-Brasiliens*, eventually passed the collection. Months after being bundled on the refugee ship in Marseille, Lévi-Strauss was cleared to proceed to New York.

As he embarked on the last leg of his voyage, another Jewish intellectual, Russian linguist Roman Jakobson, was fleeing Europe by boat. After passing the wreckage of the recently sunk *Bismarck*, Jakobson's liner plowed across the North Atlantic, bound for New York. The two men's subsequent meeting would mark the beginning of a new intellectual matrix; two disciplines—anthropology and linguistics—would come together, as the study of kinship and phonemics, of systems of sound and marriage, became unlikely bedfellows.

AT THE END OF MAY 1941, Lévi-Strauss disembarked in New York with his crate of ethnographic materials, a few personal effects and a small amount of currency. The long journey into exile that had begun a year before in the deceptively tranquil woods behind the Maginot Line was finally over. He checked in at the New School for Social Research, which had by then adopted the role of a welcoming center, helping disoriented exiles find their feet. By the time Lévi-Strauss arrived, some thirty thousand French men and women had fled to New York. Some were *émigrés de luxe*—the rich avoiding the inconvenience of war—others penniless artists or academics. French newspapers, journals and a small book publishing industry were taking root; there were concerts, exhibitions and plays featuring French artists.

In a reprise of May 1939, Lévi-Strauss found that he had a salaried summer ahead of him before classes began in the autumn. Through an unseasonably humid spring, he set out to explore the city. He strolled up and down the avenues, ducked into cross streets, hopping from Chinatown to the Puerto Rican neighborhood around West Twenty-third Street; from Little Italy to the garment district off Union Square and the rows of sweatshops, still "charged with the stale odours from Central Europe." He visited the fading Upper West Side and its grand turn-of-the-century apartments, now subdivided for poorer tenants, and walked through streets of East Side mansions. "One changed country every few blocks," Lévi-Strauss later wrote, marveling at the novelty of an urban multiculturalism that European cities would only begin to experience on the postwar collapse of empire.[36]

As he walked, he turned his ethnographer's eye on New York. Aside from the cluster of skyscrapers around Wall Street, he found the urban landscape "astonishingly slack."[37] Manhattan was not yet the corridor of high-rises that it would become, and in the shadow of that era's tallest buildings lay a mishmash of villagelike residential areas, cottages, redbrick apartment blocks, greenery and vacant lots. Rio had been quaint, out of date—a tropical version of nineteenth-century Paris. In New York, the temporal was warped and bent, its social fabric rent by immigration, money and mobility. It was not so much modern as multilayered, a riveting mix of retro and provincial American styles, promiscuous European and Asian influences, and the hint of what was to come: "obscene" advertising for deodorant, dramatized department store window displays and eclectic couture.[38]

Nosing around secondhand bookshops on Lower Broadway, Lévi-Strauss was moved to find issues of the *Annual Report of the Bureau of American Ethnology* on sale for a few dollars. "I could scarcely describe my emotion at this find," he later remembered. "That these sacrosanct volumes, in their original green and gold bindings, representing most of what will remain known about the American Indian, could actually be bought and privately owned was something I had never dreamt of."[39] He scrimped and saved, and gradually built up his collection—ranging from Mesoamerican pictographs to Pacific Northwest Coast Tsimshian mythology—ending up with every volume except one.

Lévi-Strauss toured the museums. What they lacked in range and depth, they made up for in solidity and attention to detail. He became fascinated by the hyperrealist dioramas in the American Museum of Natural History, with their too-perfect arrangements of stuffed animals and plants from around the world, re-created, like a freeze-frame of a zoo exhibit, down to their last leaf and whisker. The ground floor of the museum, curated at the turn of the century by the father of American anthropology, Franz Boas, was given over to the Indians of the Pacific Northwest Coast—a string of indigenous settlements stretching from Alaska through British Columbia down as far as Oregon, which had produced some of the finest pre-Columbian art in the Americas. The museum's broad corridors housed rows of heavy totem poles, obsidian masks and wooden chests carved with a mix of formal and figurative designs. Lévi-Strauss spent hours wandering through these galleries, looking at each artifact in detail.

One object, a *sxwaixwe* mask from the Salish people around Vancouver, particularly disturbed him. With its plug-shaped eyes—two cylinders projecting out from the face as if the eyeballs were mounted on stalks—and its gaping mouth, the mask was an exceptional piece. "It looked so different from the rest," Lévi-Strauss remembered thirty years later. "Not the same shape, not the same style, and especially these protruding eyes—and my problem was, why these protruding eyes? What is their meaning? What are they there for?"[40] These were questions that he would be able to answer only toward the end of his career, with the help of the theoretical tools he would develop in the interim, when he returned to the subject in the 1970s in *La Voie des masques* (*The Way of the Masks*). In the intervening period he developed what he described as a "carnal bond" with Pacific Northwest art, which intrigued him as much aesthetically as intellectually.[41]

WHILE VISITING SURREALIST PAINTER Yves Tanguy, Lévi-Strauss found a small studio in Greenwich Village near the corner of Eleventh Street and Sixth Avenue, which he immediately rented. Down a dingy basement corridor and up a staircase, the studio gave onto an overgrown garden. The accommodation was basic—a single room with a bed, a table and two chairs, with a sitting room annex. For decorations, Lévi-Strauss painted his own artwork, "a large surrealist-inspired canvas in somber tones, with giant interlocking hands dissolving into other features." It was a reworking of the manic sketch he had produced in the Amazon after the herder Emídio had blown his hand apart.[42] On the coffee table there was a glass ashtray along with a small wooden statue of a golden-eyed warrior and a miniature British-Columbian totem.[43] The desk on which he wrote much of his five-hundred-page thesis was barely a meter wide.[44] Unbeknownst to Lévi-Strauss, Claude Shannon, the father of cybernetics, was renting an apartment on the same block, "inventing an artificial brain," according to one of Lévi-Strauss's neighbors.[45] Over the next years, the two men—one working on computer circuit boards and the other on tribal kin relations—would labor away on the same fundamental problems completely unaware of each other's existence.

As the artistic hub of New York—a network of cold-water flats, poky studios and crumbling tenement apartments—Greenwich Village was quickly colonized by the surrealist émigrés. Yves Tanguy joined Breton on Eleventh Street and Roberto Matta on Ninth. After a spell uptown in Peggy Guggenheim's Hale House, Marcel Duchamp had eventually settled nearby in his famously minimalist one-room studio, decked out with a table, a chair, a packing case and two nails hammered into the wall with a piece of string hanging off one of them. American artists were also moving into the neighborhood. A few blocks away was the young and then relatively unknown Jackson Pollock, along with Gordon Onslow Ford, Arshile Gorky and Robert Motherwell.[46] Life in the village was convivial. Italian delicatessens sold homemade spaghetti, traders laid out fruit and vegetables on carts, and the clubs along MacDougal Street played gravelly, slow-tempo jazz into the night. Nevertheless, the French complained bitterly about the lack of cafés, which had formed the backbone of their bohemian lifestyle in Paris. Lévi-Strauss's own nostalgia was different. Although French to his core, his long spell in South America had left him rootless. "I dreamt a lot about the map of France," he later recalled, "a France I hardly knew."[47]

Through Breton, Lévi-Strauss soon became an honorary member of a celebrated artistic set. He was invited to soirées where the surrealists played their infamous parlor games: *vérité*, a psychoanalytic version of "truth or dare"; charades using only analogies; tarot card readings; and *cadavres exquis* (exquisite corpses), a game in which textual and visual fragments produced by members of the group were agglomerated into bizarre images and narratives. The artists visited one another's houses, dined out, went to cocktail parties hosted by Peggy Guggenheim and late-night dancing sessions at the Savoy Ballroom in Harlem.

Lévi-Strauss warmed to Max Ernst from the outset, and became friends with André Masson. He admired Tanguy the painter, but found him difficult to get along with. Duchamp "had great kindness," and Lévi-Strauss's friendship with the poet and art critic Patrick Waldberg—who would later become one of surrealism's chroniclers—outlasted the brief bohemian sojourn in wartime New York.[48] Waldberg remembers touring the exotic restaurants of Manhattan Island with Lévi-Strauss, sampling Panamanian tortoise eggs, moose stew, oyster soup, Mexican oil-palm grubs and "silky textured octopus."[49] It is through Waldberg's eyes that we see Lévi-Strauss at this crucial stage of his life—an exile, a thinker still on the periphery, but on the brink of greatness:

> He appeared to me imbued with what I would call an air of dignity: tall and slender with a long chiseled face, a look at once profound and searching, sometimes dreaming and melancholic, sometimes fixed and alert . . . For those who didn't know him well, his manner could be difficult and at times even cold . . . I also remember the weight of his silence, as soon as an unwelcome presence tried to get him to say something he didn't want to say. But if he was with trusted friends, he knew how to turn on the charm with warm, sometimes passionate, words.[50]

Lévi-Strauss's association with the surrealists was a fertile coming together of ideas. He was interested in midcentury artistic preoccupations: the subversive power of the subconscious, the importance of myth, irrationality and juxtaposition. The surrealists saw anthropology and psychology as the key modernist disciplines. They fed off half-digested ethnography and idolized tribal art. Just before the outbreak of the war, the artist Kurt Seligmann had spent almost four months at a trading station in British Columbia observing the ritual life and artwork of the Northwest Coast Indians, shipping an eighteen-meter-high totem pole back to the Musée de l'Homme in Paris. Breton was a keen collector of indigenous artifacts, which had lined his studio in Paris. And while driving back across America from Santa Monica in Peggy Guggenheim's Buick convertible, Max Ernst stopped off to witness Hopi dances and collect Zuni *kachinas* (figurines) carved from cottonwood root.

In New York, Ernst chanced upon even richer pickings. He was walking past a shop on Third Avenue, run by a German antiques dealer named Julius Carlebach, when a spoon caught the corner of his eye. It was of Northwest Coast indigenous provenance and was being displayed as a part of a collection of spoons from around the world. Ernst spoke to the dealer, who told him he would put together a collection of Northwest Coast tribal artifacts, which Ernst subsequently snapped up. At first he kept the shop's location hidden from his fellow artists, turning down Seligmann's offer to reveal the source in exchange for his collection of witchcraft illustrations, but eventually Breton tracked the shop down.

Soon Lévi-Strauss, along with all the surrealists, were descending on Carlebach's store, pooling their money to buy up the Teotihuacán stone masks, Northwest Coast wood carvings, and Inuit and Melanesian art. Carlebach was a man of simple tastes, only interested in "old German chinaware and quaint curios of the *Gemütlich* type," but, guided by the surrealists, he bought up wooden carved masks, bowls and clubs with built-in visual puns. His source was the Museum of the American Indian's warehouse in the Bronx, which was filled with so-called duplicates that the director was selling off for fifty dollars apiece. One afternoon two taxis full of surrealist artists—among them Ernst, Breton, Matta, Tanguy and Seligmann, along with Lévi-Strauss and Georges Duthuit, the art critic and son-in-law of Matisse—set out for the Bronx warehouse. With the help of a guard, they toured the museum's stores, selecting choice artifacts, which would then mysteriously end up for sale in Carlebach's shop.[51]

For the collector, New York at midcentury was a treasure trove. A spectacular range of global flotsam had washed up in what had already become one of the world's most cosmopolitan cities. With the right connections, there were trunks of Peruvian antiques, shelves piled high with Nazca vases, boxes of jewelry salvaged from the Russian Revolution or packing cases of rare Utamaro Japanese prints on offer, sold informally from apartments, garages and sheds in the backstreets of midtown Manhattan. The secondhand shops were piled high with sixteenth-century Spanish and

Italian furniture. Though relatively poor at the time, Lévi-Strauss found he could afford an antique Tuscan sideboard, on sale for just a couple of dollars. After the war he had it shipped back to Europe, where it furnished his apartment in Paris.[52]

In 1942 American surrealist artist David Hare, working with Breton and Ernst, launched the journal *VVV*, a *Documents*-like combination of poetry, art, anthropology, sociology and psychology. Their stated aim was "to distinguish what is dead from what is living in all fields relevant to art and action," an enterprise requiring "the very different skills of coroner and midwife."[53] The first issue is like a time capsule representing the artistic tics and obsessions of an era, containing pieces on mythology, childhood, dream imagery and discussions about the possibilities of purity through spontaneity. Incongruously wedged between poetry by Aimé Césaire and a collection of surreal images—a clock in fragments, an umbrella on a staircase, bathtubs in a field, a New England church with pews outside—was a piece by Lévi-Strauss.

It was titled "Indian Cosmetics" and returned to the mysterious volutes and coils—the "expert bruisings" and "graphic surgery," as he put it—that he had photographed on the faces of the Caduveo women in backland Mato Grosso years before. By now, his analysis was beginning to focus on formal, aesthetic aspects:

> These highly developed compositions, at once unsymmetrical and balanced, are begun in one corner or other, and carried out without hesitation, going over, or erasure, to their conclusion. They evidently spring from an unvarying fundamental theme, in which crosses, tendrils, fretwork and spirals play an important part. Nevertheless, each one constitutes an original work: the basic motifs are combined with an ingenuity, a richness of imagination, even an audacity, which continually spring afresh.[54]

The extract is an intriguing window on his thinking on the eve of his theoretical breakthrough. It was as if he was groping toward a way of reconciling unity and difference, genre and originality.

Also in the issue was Lévi-Strauss's appreciation of Bronislaw Malinowski, the recently deceased father of modern fieldwork. He heaped praise on Malinowski's contribution to anthropology, both in terms of his pathbreaking ethnographic work and his twinning of "the two most revolutionary disciplines of our time: ethnology and psychoanalysis." From now on, wrote Lévi-Strauss, all ethnography would be viewed as "pre- or post-Malinowski." But the review had a sting in the tail, and a highly ironic one, given Lévi-Strauss's future orientation. He criticized Malinowski's "inexplicable disdain for history" and "absolute contempt for material culture."[55] Lévi-Strauss would always be interested in material culture, but would go on to reject outright historical approaches to ethnography.

THROUGH THE SUMMER MONTHS Lévi-Strauss tried to pick up the thread of his academic career. He finally began writing up his fieldwork notes, working them into a publishable thesis. He decided to write in English, to master a language in which he still felt clumsy. In the meantime he made contact with the leading lights of anthropology in the United States. He got in contact with Alfred Métraux, who was teaching at the Smithsonian Institute in Washington. The two became close friends. Métraux would stay in the Greenwich Village studio when he was visiting New York, with Lévi-Strauss sleeping on a camp bed in the sitting room. At the time Métraux was organizing the *Handbook of South American Indians*, an encyclopedic overview of the region's ethnography, and he invited Lévi-Strauss to contribute sections on the indigenous groups of central Brazil. Robert Lowie, who had supported his application to the New School, and Alfred Kroeber were teaching in California but made contact on visits to New York. Lévi-Strauss met anthropologists Ralph Linton and Ruth

Benedict and got a taste of the departmental politics at Columbia University. Linton and Benedict's mutual loathing was legendary, and they would invite Lévi-Strauss to dinner to bitch about each other.

But, most important, he had the opportunity to meet Franz Boas, then in the last years of his life. Boas had begun fieldwork among the Inuit on Baffin Island in the 1880s, before working with Pacific Northwest groups, including the Kwakiutl (now known as the Kwakwaka'wakw). He became the first professor of anthropology at Columbia—a post he held for thirty-seven years. A small-framed, intense figure with his bushy mustache, goatee beard and swept-back gray hair, Boas was the first to back up a professional interest in Native American culture with detailed fieldwork research into language, physical anthropology and material culture. His students, among them Margaret Mead, Ruth Benedict, Robert Lowie and Edward Sapir, defined the first wave of institutionalized anthropology in America. "All of American anthropology issued from him," Lévi-Strauss later said, without exaggeration.[56]

Lévi-Strauss wrote to Boas as soon as he arrived in New York. Boas received him cordially, as the young, unknown, virtually unpublished French anthropologist he then was. Lévi-Strauss subsequently went to Boas's house in Grantwood across the Hudson, where he admired Boas's collections of Kwakiutl wood carvings. Boas liked to tell the story of when he brought a Kwakiutl informant to New York for the first time. The Native American seemed unimpressed by the heaving avenues, rows of skyscrapers, subways and the steam rising through pavement vents. What caught his attention were the freak shows that still ran on Times Square, with their dwarves and bearded ladies. He also developed specific aesthetic interests—becoming fixated on the brass balls on staircase banisters and on tumble clothes dryers in Laundromats—just as the anthropologist was wont to fetishize certain aspects of the indigenous cultures he visited.[57]

Much later, at the end of 1942, Lévi-Strauss and Boas met on one final occasion at a lunch that has gone down in the annals of anthropology. The lunch was organized in honor of another French exile, Dr. Rivet of the

Musée de l'Homme, with guests including Boas's protégés Mead, Benedict and Linton. Rivet had been working in South America in Colombia and was passing through New York en route to Mexico. On a bitter winter's day they settled around a large dining table at the university faculty club. "Boas was very jovial," remembered Lévi-Strauss. "In the middle of a conversation, he shoved himself violently away from the table and fell backwards. I was seated next to him and bent down to lift him up. Rivet, who had started his career as a military doctor, tried in vain to revive him. Boas was dead."[58]

LÉVI-STRAUSS BEGAN WORK in the autumn at the New School for Social Research, his name chopped down to Claude L. Strauss, to distinguish himself from the jeans. "The students would find it funny," he was told by way of explanation. The confusion would plague him throughout his life. "Hardly a year goes by without my receiving, usually from Africa, an order for a pair of jeans," he told Didier Eribon in the 1980s—though, with fame, Lévi-Strauss found he could almost hold his own. When he gave his name while queuing for a restaurant in San Francisco in the 1980s, the waiter shot back, "The pants or the books?"[59]

The New School brought together émigrés from around Europe, great minds working in a looser, cross-disciplinary milieu. It was a vibrant environment, in which new music, theater and film mixed freely with academia. Lévi-Strauss gave lectures on the contemporary sociology of South America, a subject in which he had little grounding, beyond his experiences in Brazil. He had boned up on the topic over the summer and managed to pull together a series of evening classes, skipping from Argentina to Peru to Bolivia. He still struggled with the language, but since most of the students were also foreign refugees, broken English became the lingua franca.

In early 1942 the École libre des hautes études de New York—a kind of French university-in-exile—was inaugurated next door to the New School.

Backed by De Gaulle's Free French, as well as the Belgian government-in-exile, the university opened to great fanfare at the Assembly Hall of Hunter College with three thousand in attendance and Metropolitan Opera singers on hand to sing the American, Belgian and French national anthems. The *New York Times* compared the École's role to Constantinople's sheltering of scholars after the fall of Rome. The historical subtext was clear: in response to the boorish Nazi empire, French-speaking Jews—barred by racist laws from working in France, Belgium and Eastern Europe—were being welcomed in the New World. It became a major francophone institution in New York, with ninety professors teaching almost a thousand students in subjects ranging from cinematography to law.[60]

Lévi-Strauss lectured in French on anthropology—a relief after cobbling together sociological talks in English. The topics were broad: General Ethnography, The First Totalitarian State: The Incas, The Study of Material Culture in the Museum and in the Field. Yet Lévi-Strauss often found himself lecturing in near-empty rooms. Not that it seemed to bother him—he spoke "as if he were in a vast auditorium," according to Patrick Waldberg's wife, Isabelle, who attended his course. She remembered Lévi-Strauss's lecturing style as competent, but by no means electrifying: "One feels that Lévi-Strauss takes great trouble to work through the issue, and even if he doesn't reach startlingly original conclusions, he at least offers plenty of detail, expresses himself with clarity and often makes very interesting comparisons."[61]

Toward the end of the war Lévi-Strauss also taught at Barnard College, a women's campus affiliated to Columbia University in Morningside Heights, his first, nerve-racking foray into the mainstream U.S. university system. Thirty years later, during a talk to the college's alumnae, he could afford to joke about his disastrous debut:

> When I settled myself behind the table and started lecturing on the Nambikwara Indians, my fright changed to panic: no student was taking notes; instead of writing, they were knitting. They went on knitting

> until the hour was over as if they were paying no attention to what I was saying—or rather trying to say in my clumsy English. They did listen, though, for after the class was over a girl (I can still see her: slender, graceful, with short and curly ash-blonde hair, and wearing a blue dress) came up to me and said that it was all very interesting but she thought I should know that *desert* and *dessert* are different words.

This confusion, he playfully concluded, showed that even back then he was mixing the ecological and the culinary, "which later served to illustrate some of the structural properties of the human mind."[62]

Whether or not, on some subconscious level, Lévi-Strauss was already drawing his ideas together, the raw materials of future analyses were gradually building up. In a faint echo of Karl Marx's time in the Reading Room of the British Museum a century before, each morning from nine till midday he would sit in the now defunct American room of the New York Public Library.[63] In contrast with the cavernous main reading hall, the American room was a smaller, more intimate setting for Lévi-Strauss's research. A high portal with an austere marble architrave led into the room of a dozen reading desks, a counter behind which the librarian would sit and banks of card catalogs. Natural light streamed through the skylights, illuminating floor-to-ceiling book casing, with a mezzanine for access to the upper shelves.

It was there, in the classic beaux arts building on Fifth Avenue, with its murals, decorated ceilings, carved oak and tiled floors, that Lévi-Strauss hoovered up the vast store of ethnography that had accumulated in the library's subterranean stacks. "What I know of anthropology I learnt in those years," he later recalled.[64] On breaks he browsed scientific journals, trying to keep abreast of the latest developments in other fields. As he digested ethnography after ethnography, memorizing obscure native beliefs and practices, a Native American in full feather headdress and buckskin jacket sat a few tables along, jotting down notes with a Parker pen.[65]

It was during this period that he came across another book that fit like a key into his evolving thought: D'Arcy Wentworth Thompson's *On Growth and Form*, an eccentric classic that looked at the mathematics of morphology. A Scottish polymath, D'Arcy Thompson showed how both natural and human engineering had arrived at similarly elegant geometric solutions to design challenges thrown up by physical conditions in the world. In a series of beautifully written illustrations of his ideas, D'Arcy Thompson compared the shape of a falling drop of water to a jellyfish, plant fiber to wire, the metacarpal bone from a vulture's wing to a certain type of truss. Nature's diversity was generated out of different applications of classical proportions and ratios, which had subsequently been rediscovered in the geometry and mathematics of Pythagoras and Newton. Although some have considered the book scientific heresy because it played down the role of Darwinian evolution, it continues to fascinate to this day.[66] For Lévi-Strauss, D'Arcy Thompson's blend of aesthetics and theory was hugely appealing.

PRIMED WITH RAW MATERIAL, Lévi-Strauss was ripe for theory. He was in search of a framework, some organizing principle, the inner structure that he had sensed during his fieldwork in Brazil. He was looking for what had triggered the powerful sensations that he had felt while gazing into the bunch of dandelions on the Luxembourg border and while reading Granet's kinship book. "At the time I was a kind of naïve structuralist," he later explained, "a structuralist without knowing it."[67]

The catalyst was the Russian poet and linguist Roman Jakobson. He was fluent in a dozen languages and had been a key member of both the Moscow and Prague linguistic schools. The world Lévi-Strauss had recently been introduced to in New York had long been Jakobson's natural milieu—a mix of academia and modern art, lecture halls and bohemia, avant-garde poetry and the then emerging field of structural linguistic analysis. In revolutionary Moscow, Jakobson had mixed with the futurists; in Prague, with Czech surrealists and modernist cabaret artists. He had even dabbled in anthropology, studying folklore in and around Moscow, alongside the Russian ethnologist Petr Bogatyrev.

A bon vivant, "a veritable globe-trotter of structuralism,"[68] Jakobson had arrived in New York after a tortuous flight across Central Europe and Scandinavia, never more than a few paces ahead of the galloping Nazi frontier. On the German invasion of Czechoslovakia, Jakobson had been teaching at Masaryk University in Brno. Well known as a Jewish antifascist intellectual, he burned his papers and went into hiding. He wound up in Prague, spending a month living in a wardrobe at his father-in-law's apartment. Accompanied by his wife, Svatava, Jakobson traveled on to Denmark, where he had been invited to teach at the University of Copenhagen. The journey took the couple through the Nazi heartlands, forcing them at one point to change trains in Berlin. There, Jakobson took perverse delight in drinking a beer on the platform while posting off letters to friends who were astonished to see a Berlin postmark days after Hitler's fiftieth birthday celebrations.

Jakobson worked at the University of Copenhagen for six months before being forced to flee with his wife to Norway. On the German invasion, they were on the run again, reaching the Swedish border without a passport or any identity papers. After a week imprisoned in a customs post, they were allowed into neutral Sweden to settle in Uppsala, where Jakobson researched aphasia and child speech patterns. A year later he was on a steamer bound for America, but his ordeal was not quite over. German soldiers boarded the ship en route to check the identity of the passengers. As Jakobson and his wife were stateless, they were in a potentially dangerous position, but they managed to convince the officers that they were Russian émigrés and were allowed to proceed to New York.[69]

When Jakobson arrived in New York, Lévi-Strauss was still struggling with his thesis on the Nambikwara, trying to fit together scraps of kinship and linguistic data collected on his journey across Mato Grosso. In his field notes, he had experimented with a series of different models for describing kinship systems—the conventional family tree, columns of relationships headed "*mon père appelle*," "*ma mère appelle*," "*mon frère appelle*," "*j'appelle*," "*mon mari appelle*" and so on, as well as a checkerboard design that cross-referenced rows and columns of kin terms. He sometimes used stick figures (a stick penis added to distinguish between the sexes) with lines, circles and arrows connecting up relatives across generations.

There was an air of desperation in the successive tables of basic native vocabulary, listing kinship terminology in yet another language with which Lévi-Strauss would have had only fleeting contact. At one point he jotted down "*langue semble différente*" (language appears to be different), suggesting that he was having problems even identifying which linguistic group he was dealing with.[70] When he talked about his difficulties to Alexandre Koyré, a French-Russian academic specializing in the history and philosophy of science, Koyré suggested that he should see Jakobson, who had just begun lecturing at the École libre des hautes études. Koyré had sensed a possible affinity between the two, but he could not have imagined the impact his introduction would have. Lévi-Strauss was expecting technical advice; what he got was a whole new way of thinking.

Jakobson was twelve years older than Lévi-Strauss, and with his vast and varied academic experience in universities across Europe, he became a kind of mentor to the young anthropologist. At first Jakobson thought he had found an ideal drinking partner with whom he could talk into the night, but he soon discovered that Lévi-Strauss, despite cavorting with the surrealists, was a moderate at heart, who didn't drink and preferred to get to bed early. Yet Jakobson's hedonism somehow meshed with Lévi-Strauss's more subdued asceticism and their friendship blossomed, developing into a lifelong attachment. They dined out frequently together, exploring New York's Chinese, Greek and Armenian restaurants.[71] Jakobson also introduced Lévi-Strauss to a new circle of intellectuals. Through Raymond de Saussure, the son of the great linguist, he made contact with New York's leading psychoanalysts, including Rudolph Loewenstein, Ernst Kris and Herman Nunberg.

From the autumn of 1942, they attended each other's courses—Jakobson's on phonetics and Lévi-Strauss's on kinship. Speaking virtually without notes in fluent French, Jakobson skipped from the poems of Edgar Allan Poe to Knut Hamsun's *Hunger*, tossing in philosophers Edmund Husserl and Jeremy Bentham along with the Scholastics. He gave examples of liquids, labiodentals, nasals, hissing and hushing sibilants from the Slavic languages, illustrating his arguments with words drawn from French, Finnish and Korean. And amid this display of European cosmopolitanism and erudition, Jakobson told the story of the emergence of structural linguistics, an approach first outlined by Ferdinand de Saussure and then developed by the Russian linguist Nikolai Trubetskoy and Jakobson himself. "The discipline practised by Jakobson enthralled me like a detective story," remembered Lévi-Strauss. "I had the feeling I was taking part in a great adventure of the mind."[72]

At its core, structural linguistics worked with a simple yet revolutionary idea: the notion that language consisted of a formal system of interrelated elements, and that meaning resided not in the elements themselves, but in their relationships to one another. The solidity of language—of the word, its sound and referent—was dissolved. At root was a system of differences. The classic examples came from phonetics, a field that had forged ahead under the new approach. In the nineteenth century, linguists had focused on the production of sound and describing the sounds themselves. They studied the position of the tongue, the lips and teeth during a given utterance; they filmed, photographed and eventually were able to X-ray speakers' larynxes; they monitored each subtle modulation, building up finer and finer-grained data, more and more complex notations of subtly different sounds. The end point was a virtual continuum of sound and motion—a jelly of data that offered no theoretical purchase. Under the strictly empiricist approach, "the phonic substance of language becomes as dust," as Jakobson put it.[73]

Jakobson likened the previous generation to a character in a story written by the romantic Russian writer Vladimir Odoevsky (and later reprised by Borges in the short story "Funes the Memorious"). A man is given the gift of being able to see and hear everything and promptly descends into a supersaturated, empiricist hell: "Everything in nature became fragmented before him, and nothing formed whole in his mind," and for this unfortunate man "the sounds of speech became transformed into a torrent of innumerable articulatory motions of mechanical vibrations, aimless and without meaning."[74]

Structural phonology, Jakobson went on to explain, offered a way out of this exponential explosion of data. The key problem was to identify the "quanta of language": the smallest units able to change meanings. Sounds with a "differentiating value" were called phonemes. Pairs of opposing phonemes—like *b* and *v* in "bat" and "vat"—operated like gates on a circuit board, switching between alternate meanings. Crucially, it was the relationship between the phonemes that generated meaning, not the phonemes themselves; thus the paradox: "Language . . . is composed of elements which are signifiers, yet at the same time signify nothing."[75] Jakobson went on to demonstrate the progress over the past decade, and the systematization of the phonemes into bundles of features, which could be paired off into basic oppositions—compact and diffuse, open and closed, acute and grave—which underlay all languages. He would later elaborate these relations in an ingeniously simple schema: two triangles, one for vowels and the other for consonants, which distilled fundamental phonetic differences. As newborns gradually tuned in to these distinctions, they began standardizing their multiple combinations into meaningful sounds, the words of their native language, be it French, Japanese or Turkish.

For Lévi-Strauss, the idea that thousands of languages were rooted in an essence—small sets of opposed phonemes—was seductively reductionist. Like the nineteenth-century linguists, Lévi-Strauss had also felt overwhelmed by the sheer quantity of empirical data, condemned "to the endless task of searching for things behind things."[76] The change in focus from objects to the relationships between objects seemed potentially liberating. Structural linguistics had shown that a deliberate foray into abstraction and experimentation with higher-order modeling could yield dramatic results.

As Lévi-Strauss continued his course on kinship, the fit seemed uncanny. Kinship was, after all, a relational system par excellence. Kin diagrams naturally lent themselves to simple oppositions: male/female; in marriage/out marriage; opposing moieties, clans and grades. Running underneath the drama of human relations were unspoken rules, unconsciously observed, which allowed groups of people to communicate with almost mathematical efficiency down the generations. Although the array of bizarre marriage rules seemed baffling in isolation, taken as a set—as contrasting strategies within an overall system—Lévi-Strauss could begin to see the outlines of a grand scheme. Jakobson encouraged him to write down his ideas, and while Lévi-Strauss finished off his thesis on the Nambikwara, he also began work on *Les Structures élémentaires de la parenté* (*The Elementary Structures of Kinship*).

The different strands of Lévi-Strauss's thought were coming together. The new linguistics drew a common thread through his early intellectual history—his fascination for Marx and Freud, as well as his interest in geology. He realized that ethnographic reports that he had been reading, as vivid as they appeared, were mere surface phenomena—as landscape is to geology, historical events are to the Marxist, or desire, revulsion and neurosis to the psychoanalyst.

To these three "mistresses," he could now add another: the Swiss linguist Ferdinand de Saussure. Through Jakobson's influence, Saussure's famous *Cours de linguistique générale*, which had been compiled by students and posthumously published in 1915, became a cornerstone of his thinking. Key ideas from the *Cours* became permanent features of Lévi-Strauss's intellectual arsenal: the distinction between *la langue* (language as an abstract system) and *la parole* (language as it is spoken) and the differences between the synchronic (snapshot) and diachronic (historical) approaches were transposed into the ethnographic setting. Henceforth,

Lévi-Strauss would focus his attention on comparisons between abstract cultural systems drawn from the ethnographic record rather than individual ethnographies, just as linguists privileged grammars over the background noise of idiosyncratic usage and gradual linguistic drift. Saussure's concept of "binary pairs"—the contrasts that generate meaning—that had been so useful in phonetics became another Lévi-Straussian staple.

Saussure's insights, filtered through Jakobsonian structural linguistics, gave Lévi-Strauss the tools with which to float free from the morass of descriptive data and observe the patterns that cut across continents and cultures. The exercise required a massive leap of faith. As Lévi-Strauss began importing wholesale concepts from linguistics into the social sciences, he was setting off on a path into the intellectual unknown.

5

Elementary Structures

Social life imposes on . . . mankind an incessant traveling back and forth, and family life is little else than the expression of a need to slacken the pace at the crossroads and to take a chance to rest. But the orders are to keep on marching.

CLAUDE LÉVI-STRAUSS[1]

THE WAR LEFT deep scars across France, its progress a source of constant anxiety for those living in exile. In New York, Lévi-Strauss obsessively read news reports and listened to the radio, raking over the situation in Europe. The Jewish question, which he had only recently treated so casually, was now a matter of survival for the friends and family he had left behind. In the early years, Lévi-Strauss received intermittent news from his parents in the Cévennes. He wrote them long letters in his spidery handwriting, replete with photos pasted onto the page and little drawings—street maps and a floor plan of his apartment in Greenwich Village. But all correspondence had come to an abrupt halt upon the invasion of the free zone in 1943.

In retrospect, Lévi-Strauss had been fortunate to leave when he did—a few days after he had embarked from Marseille, the Vichy government had created a General Commissariat for Jewish Affairs, followed later by a census and special police force to deal with the Jews. Had Lévi-Strauss somehow managed to secure his teaching job in Paris, as he had wanted to, he might not have survived the war. His involvement with the Musée de l'Homme, where he had worked through the summer of 1939 preparing the Nambikwara artifacts for exhibit, would have placed him at extreme risk. It was there, at the beginning of the occupation, that one of the first Resistance cells had formed. Researcher Anatole Lewitzky, a student of Mauss, led the group with his librarian fiancée, Yvonne Oddon. In December 1940 they had begun printing and distributing the bulletin *Résistance* on a duplicating machine installed by Rivet in the 1930s for the production of antifascist propaganda. The group was eventually broken up, and despite Mauss's protestations, Lewitzky was tried and later shot on the Mont Valérien near Nanterre, along with seven accomplices from the Musée network; three women, including Yvonne Oddon, had their death sentences commuted and ended up in Germany's labor camps.

Even the great Marcel Mauss had difficulties, surviving the war in increasingly straitened circumstances. At the age of seventy, in August 1942, he and his bedridden wife were evicted from their spacious apartment on the boulevard Jourdan, which was requisitioned for the greater comfort of a German general. Students helped Mauss salvage his library, which he stashed at the Musée, before moving into a "cold, dark and dirty" ground-floor flat on the rue Georges de Porto-Riche in the fourteenth arrondissement. That autumn, along with all Parisian Jews, he was forced to sew a yellow star onto his overcoat.[2]

In New York, the complexities of the wartime politics were projected back onto those who had fled; the exile community became a microcosm of the schisms that would define French political culture for the next generation. There were strong opinions on every aspect of France's capitulation, as well as on America's initial policy of recognizing the Vichy government and refusing to negotiate with de Gaulle. For some the terms of Armistice were a betrayal, for others an understandably pragmatic move. Few openly supported Pétain, but some were privately sympathetic. The writer and pilot Antoine de Saint-Exupéry was hounded for his tacit acceptance of Pétain and his refusal to back de Gaulle, whom he saw as an illegitimate leader. Many supported de Gaulle as a military man, but worried that his dictatorial tendencies made him a dangerous politician. Gaullists mounted witch hunts against waverers, but also engaged in bitter infighting of their own.

Lévi-Strauss joined the Free French and attended the odd Gaullist meeting in New York. But when Jacques Soustelle tried to recruit him to join the Resistance in London, he politely declined. His mind was buzzing with new ideas. He wanted to write. Besides, the political rigidity of his youth had drained away. A pacifist before the war, Lévi-Strauss had lost faith in his political judgment. "I lived through *la drôle de guerre* and the French collapse and I realised that it was a mistake to pigeonhole political realities in the framework of formal ideas," he recalled.[3]

After the United States entered the war, Lévi-Strauss found work through Waldberg, reading out propaganda broadcasts on the French desk of the Office of War Information on Fifty-seventh Street for the francophone version of the Voice of America. There, an extraordinary collection of French exiles—headed by the future editor of *France Soir* Pierre Lazareff and including André Breton, philosopher Jacques Maritain, writer Denis de Rougemont and Dolorès Vanetti (who would become Sartre's lover after the war)—came together a few times a week to write and broadcast. At around $250 a month, work at the Office of War Information was a valuable boost to exiles' income.

Rougemont remembers working in a room with thirty typewriters, the stutter of teletext machines and harsh lighting. Men with green visors and rolled-up sleeves edited copy before passing the scripts on to the announcers in Studio 16. Each broadcast began, "*Voici New York, les États-Unis d'Amérique. Nous nous adressons aux gens d'Europe!*," followed by war news, commentary and speeches by key politicians. Breton, a pacifist, was a reluctant participant. True to his surrealist principles, he refused to read out any references to the pope. "He lent us his noble voice," remembered Rougemont, "but retained a sense of irony." Lévi-Strauss read out French translations of Roosevelt's speeches because it was felt that the clarity and precision of his diction carried best over the jamming.

Recorded broadcasts were sent to the BBC in London, from where they were retransmitted in France. It is unclear how many listeners in France actually managed to tune in, but, according to Lévi-Strauss, the broadcast was picked up by a friend of his, who contacted his parents to reassure them that their son was alive and well.[4]

AT THE ÉCOLE, Lévi-Strauss continued toying with the new ideas to which he was being exposed. He quickly realized that the tools of structural linguistic analysis could be used for any set of systematic relationships. While continuing to analyze kinship data, he turned his hand to another area—the aesthetic properties of indigenous artwork—where morphological relationships opened up the possibilities of a more formal style of analysis.

"Split Representation in the Art of Asia and America," first published in *Renaissance*, the École's house journal, saw him groping toward a different method of cross-cultural comparison. Examining Northwest Coast Indian masks, motifs on ancient Chinese art, Caduveo face painting and Maori tattoos, Lévi-Strauss drew out formal similarities. Boas had described Northwest Coast Indian portrayals of bears, sharks and frogs, depicted as if sliced lengthwise, flattened out and inverted into two profiles, facing each other as mirror images. Similar patterns featured in ancient Chinese masks, and bronze urns of the Shang dynasty. "Splitting techniques" were also at play in Caduveo face painting, with its complex axes of inverted patterning, and in the more rigorous symmetry of Maori face tattoos. The parallels were striking: the quartered face, the spirals and frets mirroring across the forehead and blossoming around the lips.

Were these patterns, following Boas, due to the gradual diffusion of cultural traits over space and time? Or could the various "splitting techniques" be related to underlying structures, emerging spontaneously through the ages and across continents? Interestingly, at this stage Lévi-Strauss's explanation was still more classically sociological than cognitive.

Maori tattoos "stamp onto the mind all the traditions and philosophy of the group," just as the more dislocated symmetries found on the Caduveo faces represent the "dying echo" of the group's decaying feudal order—a transformation running parallel to similar developments in Chinese art and society.[5] But there was also a cognitive edge. The "common denominator" was dualism. Lévi-Strauss's analysis boiled down to sets of Jakobson-like binary pairs, stacked up in analogous relationships: representational and abstract art; carving and drawing; face and decoration; person and impersonation.[6]

On June 6, 1944, Lévi-Strauss switched on the radio in his studio flat in Greenwich Village. Over the hiss and crackle of the airwaves, the announcer read the morning news, leading with the latest events from Europe. At first Lévi-Strauss struggled to understand what seemed like an incoherent jumble, "a kind of soup of words, place names and figures,"[7] but as the truth dawned he was overwhelmed by emotion. Under heavy fire, Allied troops were scrambling up the beaches along the Normandy coast. In a rare display of sentiment, Lévi-Strauss broke down sobbing.

When the Allies had wrested their way off the Normandy beaches, they advanced into northern France, which was once more embroiled in heavy fighting. Soon afterward American and French troops landed in Provence in the south, from where they began an advance up the Rhône Valley and into the Alps. By the end of August, Paris had been liberated and two million Allied soldiers were on French soil. As the fighting continued into the autumn of 1944, France slowly emerged from years of occupation.

The run of events in Europe placed the future of the École libre des hautes études in doubt. As it had been founded as a university-in-exile, it was unclear what its postwar role would be. Negotiations over its future were complicated by a rift between the Gaullists, who saw the university as an adjunct to the French government-in-exile, and those wanting to maintain academic neutrality. After all, there were many francophone academics who were not French—such as Jakobson and Koyré—and who had no particular interest in politicizing the university. Nevertheless, Henri Seyrig, the cultural attaché for the French Committee of National Liberation (de Gaulle's government-in-exile), following orders from Algiers, tried to bring the École under Gaullist control. Lévi-Strauss supported Seyrig, and when the U.S. Department of Justice asked for the École's political affiliation to be officially registered under the Foreign Agents Registration Act, he argued that the university should comply. The measure was deeply resented by an opposing faction led by the Catholic philosopher Jacques Maritain, who claimed that this was a threat to the principles of academic freedom and impartiality. In an angry board meeting just after the Normandy invasion, the Gaullists won through, and Lévi-Strauss was appointed as secretary-general.[8] A few months later he was sent to the Directory of Cultural Relations in the newly liberated Paris for talks on the institution's future.

In the dying months of the war, Lévi-Strauss boarded an American naval convoy, which churned its way through the gray seas of the North Atlantic, docking at the port of Cardiff. On clearing customs, he set off through the narrow lanes for the railway station, passing the rows of low, dilapidated houses, taking in the scenes of wartime dereliction. After his years in exile, he was finally back on European soil, his homecoming somehow intensified by a lonely landing in a foreign port.

Lévi-Strauss took the train from Cardiff across Wales and into England, past barren fields, blacked-out villages and war ruins. In London, the last of the V-1 rockets were still buzzing across the skyline; piles of bricks, gutted buildings and shabby, makeshift defenses belied the closeness of victory. He took another train down to the Channel and crossed over to Dieppe, from where he rode into Paris in an American military truck. It was January 1945. Pockets of fierce fighting continued in Dunkirk, Lorient, Saint-Nazaire, La Rochelle and Royan; severe rationing was still in place, and the *épuration sauvage* was under way: the hastily arranged firing squads, the shearing of women's hair. After the blazing neon lights of New York City, Paris was a ghost town of rolling blackouts and daily shortages. Horse-drawn carts clip-clopped down the boulevards; street urchins rummaged in garbage cans. Liberation celebrations papered over the poverty and collective neurosis of a people recovering from the rigors of the years of Nazi occupation.

Lévi-Strauss met his parents, from whom he had received no word for more than a year, finding his father aged by the privations of the occupation and in poor health. He caught up on the dismal news. Upon the German occupation of the south, they had been forced to leave their house in the Cévennes and hide in a property owned by René Courtin in the Drôme. In the meantime, the family home in the sixteenth arrondissement had been ransacked, and they had been left with nothing, "not even a bed."[9] The studio flat at 26 rue des Plantes, where he had briefly lived on his return from Brazil, had also been pillaged—among the losses, the field notes he had taken among the Caduveo.[10]

Lévi-Strauss met up with Henri Laugier, who then headed the Directory of Cultural Relations, and began negotiations on the future of the École libre. They agreed that the École had outlived its useful existence and concluded that, one way or another, it should be wound down or perhaps amalgamated with the Alliance française. Lévi-Strauss was making himself redundant, but with Laugier's help he managed to maneuver himself into the position of France's cultural attaché in New York. He was originally offered the post in Mexico, but through his own connections with Seyrig he secured the ideal job: a not-too-demanding diplomatic post a few blocks down from the New York Public Library.

While negotiations continued, Lévi-Strauss set up an office at the Directory of Cultural Relations in a town house on the rue Lord Byron, off the Champs-Elysées. There, working under Laugier, he acted as a liaison officer for French people wanting to visit America. He later recalled processing the then famous soprano Jeanine Micheau, who strolled into his office "heavily perfumed, leading two enormous dogs on leashes."[11]

He also remembered meeting Maurice Merleau-Ponty, whom he had not seen since they had taught classes together during the three-week probationary period in the run-up to the *agrégation* more than a decade earlier. In the intervening years, Merleau-Ponty had become one of the most influential philosophers working in France. Their meeting was pure coincidence, he having wandered into Lévi-Strauss's office in search of advice about visiting America.

They talked philosophy, Lévi-Strauss asking Merleau-Ponty to explain what existentialism was. Merleau-Ponty apparently satisfied him with the vague answer: "It is an attempt to re-establish philosophy as it was in the times of Descartes, Leibniz and Kant." Asked later by Didier Eribon what he thought of the response, Lévi-Strauss replied: "Nothing. Philosophy didn't interest me anymore, even existentialism"[12]—a typically dry but hardly credible answer. Lévi-Strauss had been away for more than a decade, with only intermittent contacts with the French academic system, to which he hoped one day to return. Philosophy was the intellectual ballast of the humanities, and despite his later protestations to the contrary, Lévi-Strauss was still a typically French, philosophically oriented thinker. He would surely have been curious to hear about developments in his absence.

Several milestones had passed him by. The publication of Sartre's *L'Être et le néant* (*Being and Nothingness*) (1943) and Merleau-Ponty's own increasingly influential work, culminating in *La Phénoménologie de la perception* (*The Phenomenology of Perception*) (1944), were at the head of a revival and reassessment of the work of the German philosophers Edmund Husserl and his onetime assistant Martin Heidegger. While at one end of the spectrum Lévi-Strauss had begun grappling with overarching, abstract systems, at the other Merleau-Ponty was talking about the centrality of the body in intimate acts of perception. For Merleau-Ponty, a person's most private or even banal thoughts were the raw material of philosophy. Pages of reflections on his experiences of his own body—from the impossibility of treating his eyes as objects (even using a mirror, "they are the eyes of someone observing") to the mysterious sensations of simultaneously touching and being touched when his left hand grasped his right[13]—were indeed remote from Lévi-Strauss's intellectual instincts.

Back in New York, Lévi-Strauss worked out the last months of his contract at the École against a backdrop of hostility. There was widespread criticism of his role in negotiations over the future of the École. The physicist Léon Brillouin complained that Lévi-Strauss had been "unfaithful to his mission, since far from defending the interests of the École . . . he appeared to bring back with him the death sentence for our institution."[14] The faculty eventually voted to block Lévi-Strauss's last month's salary.

Lévi-Strauss was beginning to reveal a deft, pragmatic side—a kind of coolness toward events, which he was about to apply to ethnographic data. A fascinating window into his state of mind at the close of the war comes from a classified report on the politics of the École, filed by an agent from the American Office of Strategic Services (the forerunner of the CIA). The OSS agent had originally intended to interview the film producer Jean Benoît-Lévy, but as he was away, Lévi-Strauss stepped in. The agent was charmed by Lévi-Strauss, finding him "a most attractive and agreeable personality," loyal toward General de Gaulle, but with some harsh views on recent events in Europe. France had "lost the war" and "the sooner that people realised this the better for all concerned," Lévi-Strauss told the agent, adding that "it might have been better to kill 50,000 collaborationists immediately" rather than get bogged down in the niceties of gathering evidence and mounting trials[15]—an astonishing statement for someone who had just returned from France and seen for himself the postoccupation tensions and ambiguities. Lévi-Strauss had traveled a long way from the idealism of his youth. His political commitment had "faded away."[16] What remained was a conservative instinct that would never really leave him for the rest of his life.

IT WAS IN THIS TRANSITIONAL PHASE of Lévi-Strauss's life, as the war wound down and his exile status evaporated, that he produced a short paper, "L'Analyse structurale en linguistique et en anthropologie" (Structural Analysis in Linguistics and Anthropology).[17] Published in *Word: Journal of the Linguistic Circle of New York*, which had been founded by Roman Jakobson and his colleagues, the article consecrated Lévi-Strauss's intellectual partnership with Jakobson, drawing parallels between structural linguistics and anthropology and fusing them in the area of kinship. Although on the face of it a dry, technical and strictly anthropological essay, the piece introduced the kind of theoretical radicalism that Lévi-Strauss would become known for.

He likened the state of the study of kinship to the extreme empiricism of nineteenth-century linguistics, when the analysis of sound had collapsed under the weight of its own endlessly subdividing data. "Each detail of terminology and each special marriage rule is associated with a specific custom as either its consequence or survival," he wrote; "we thus meet with a chaos of discontinuity." Where both anthropology and traditional linguistics had erred "was to consider the terms, and not the relations between the terms."[18] He then addressed the classic anthropological conundrum of the differing attitudes between a man and his sister's children, a relationship known as "the avunculate." The argument is involved and difficult for the nonspecialist to grasp, but it is worth following through step by step, since this reinterpretation set the methodological tone for much of Lévi-Strauss's later work.

British anthropologist Alfred Radcliffe-Brown had observed two sets of inversely correlated relationships. A boy's relationship with his maternal uncle—be it strict obedience or jesting familiarity—was the reverse of the same boy's relationship with his father. If the boy had an easy, joking relationship with his maternal uncle, he would be submissive toward the father, and vice versa. Radcliffe-Brown had argued that the distinction had to do with descent: in matrilineal[19] societies the maternal uncle, as a member of the descent group, becomes an authority figure, the father a source of familial tenderness; in patrilineal societies the situation is the opposite—the father embodies traditional authority of the descent group, and the maternal uncle becomes a kind of "male mother." This seemed like a tidy solution, but it was spoiled by numerous exceptions to the rule.

Lévi-Strauss reframed the question by adopting the linguist's approach. He looked at all possible permutations of relationships within the system as a whole—not just within the family unit, as Radcliffe-Brown had, but across interlocking family groups. The "atom of kinship," as Lévi-Strauss coined it, became a complex of consanguinity (blood relations), affiliation (marriage) and descent (generational relations)—in its most stripped-down form, a man, his wife, their child and the child's maternal uncle.[20] He then drew up a table of possible attitudes, marking them "+" for free and familiar and "–" for strict and reserved. Like crystalline structures of compound molecules, the pluses and minuses seemed to follow a pattern, balancing off against each other in a complex yet ultimately symmetrical manner.

This approach revealed certain structural echoes—sets of relationships that ran in parallel to each other. Lévi-Strauss summarized his findings in the following "law": "In both groups, the relation between the maternal uncle and nephew is to the relation between brother and sister as the relation between father and son is to that between husband and wife," he wrote.[21] Or, in more condensed form, *maternal uncle/nephew* is to *brother/sister* as *father/son* is to *husband/wife*. And the model seemed to work, at least in the examples that Lévi-Strauss put forward. From Tonga to the Trobriand Islands, the Lake Kutubu groups of Papua New Guinea to the Siuai of Bougainville, the African Kipsigi to the Melanesian Dobuans, relationships of respect and familiarity were distributed through the kinship system with an eerie symmetry.

Radcliffe-Brown had focused on a specific problem to tease out the meaning of its content. But Lévi-Strauss simply dissolved the problem and its content within a network of relationships.[22] It was a maneuver that he would use again and again in his analyses—not just of kinship systems, but when he moved into the more conceptual realm of religious thought and mythology. The method hinted at the more profound truths that Lévi-Strauss had long sensed but had struggled to articulate. His use of linguistic models for social systems was more than metaphorical; it was based on what he believed to be a concrete affinity. The bridge between linguistics and kinship was cognition. At root a kinship system existed "only in human consciousness" as "an arbitrary system of representations," like a language or a system of sounds.[23] Beyond the hard-to-follow kinship analysis, the *Word* article was theoretically suggestive; it pointed toward a revolutionary way of understanding human culture. The full demonstration, though, would have to wait until 1949 with the appearance of the first copies of *Les Structures élémentaires de la parenté.*

AT THE END OF 1945, Lévi-Strauss took up his new post as cultural attaché. His first task was to refit a mansion on Fifth Avenue near Seventy-fourth Street, acquired by the French government before the war but empty since the mayor of New York had barred Vichy officials from using the building. Working with the architect Jacques Carlu, who had designed the monumental Palais de Chaillot in Paris—now housing the Musée de l'Homme—he drew up plans, consulted with builders, even carried out some of the manual work himself, a job he apparently relished. The hands-on practicality appealed to him, a vestige of growing up on the rue Poussin surrounded by his father's various artisanal projects.

While the work went on, he was forced to improvise, running his office out of what had been a ballroom—an eccentric salon done out as a replica of a Roman palazzo, with painted ceilings and elaborate woodwork. Later, when hosting the great modernist architect Le Corbusier, Lévi-Strauss asked what he should do with the room. "Don't touch it," Le Corbusier told Lévi-Strauss. "It's a fine piece of craftsmanship, let's respect that." The advice left an impression on Lévi-Strauss. From then on, wherever he lived, he would leave previous owners' architectural follies intact.[24]

Once they were installed, Lévi-Strauss settled into his diplomatic duties. Much of his job involved hosting French cultural figures passing through New York, entertaining them and dealing with the logistics of their stay. In the course of his work, he met French writers and intellectuals, including Jean-Paul Sartre, Simone de Beauvoir and Albert Camus. Already intellectual stars, Sartre and de Beauvoir needed little assistance, but he showed Camus around New York, dining in a restaurant in Chinatown and ending up in a club—probably Sammy's Bowery Follies on the Bowery at Third Street, a cabaret featuring aging divas belting out old standards. Among the many other people Lévi-Strauss received in New York were the celebrated neurologist and future director of the Collège de France, Yves Laporte; the head of the Bibliothèque nationale, Julien Cain; the psychiatrist and writer Jean Delay; as well as Gaston Berger, a philosopher and the writer of an acclaimed study on Husserl, who would go on to run the university system at the ministry for education. After the years of exile, Lévi-Strauss was rapidly reconnecting with France's cultural elite.

In other areas, he tried to bend his newfound powers to his own interests, proposing that the government buy up a collection of Northwest Coast Indian art, to be had from a collector in exchange for "a few Matisse and Picasso canvases instead of taxable dollars."[25] (He was unsuccessful, and the collection ended up going to a West Coast museum.) He was also involved in negotiations between the Rockefeller Foundation and the French government for the resumption of their funding of French academic institutions driven to their knees by war and occupation. He sat in on meetings discussing the creation in Paris of something akin to the London School of Economics. The result was the establishing in 1948 of the Sixth Section of the École pratique des hautes études (where Lévi-Strauss would soon be teaching), seeded by ten thousand dollars of Rockefeller largesse a year for the first three years.

His life settling once more, with a respectable job and a steady income, Lévi-Strauss married for the second time soon after his return to New

York. His new wife, Rose-Marie Ullmo, gave birth to a son, Laurent, in early 1947. The birth coincided with Simone de Beauvoir's visit to New York. Lévi-Strauss invited her for lunch. "I remember it very well—my son had just been born—she looked at the crib with such revulsion! A baby was not the thing to show her!"[26] Rose-Marie Ullmo remains an enigmatic figure. The relationship was evidently troubled from the outset (they were separated by 1948 and divorced six years later), but Lévi-Strauss and his immediate family have always refused to comment on the marriage and its dissolution.

Cut some slack by Paris, Lévi-Strauss came to an arrangement whereby he worked in the office in the mornings, leaving the afternoons free for his research and writing. As he was lodged in an upstairs suite, he was on hand to meet and greet visiting dignitaries if necessary. "I cruised through it all," he later recalled. "I was a very bad cultural attaché; I did the minimum."[27] Some afternoons he kept clear for work at the New York Public Library, where he continued compiling the staggering number of sources that would eventually find their way into *Les Structures élémentaires de la parenté*. On other afternoons he put the finishing touches on his entries for the *Handbook of South American Indians*, whose six volumes appeared between 1946 and 1950. He wrote short descriptive pieces on the Nambikwara, the Tupi-Kawahib, as well as the tribes of the Upper Xingu tributaries that irrigate the central Brazilian savannahs. A later piece described the ingenious uses that indigenous Brazilians had made of their natural environment—the razors fashioned from blades of tough savannah grasses; the gums, glues and oils harvested from the forest; the methods of grinding certain roots and fibers and mixing pulp from seeds and bark to form pigments, shampoos and poisons.[28]

There is something rather aristocratic about this period of Lévi-Strauss's life. "I was working on a grand scale in a magnificent setting and in what amounted to a virtual Embassy of my own," he recalled.[29] Duties at the embassy barely interrupted his academic research, and he found time to attend conferences at Harvard, and in Chicago and Paris. In Chicago he stayed with leading American sociologist Robert Redfield in his dilapidated farmhouse, with its peeling paint and filthy bathrooms, perched on the edge of the outer suburbs.[30] Redfield offered him a job at the University of Chicago. It was one of many academic posts in the United States that Lévi-Strauss would turn down.

His time in America—an intense and formative period in his intellectual life—was coming to an end. In his final months he completed the first draft of his thesis, ordering his surge of creativity in New York into one satisfyingly bulky manuscript. Soon afterward Alfred Métraux, visiting from Washington, noted in his journal:

> We [Métraux and the German anthropologist Paul Kirchoff] visited Lévi-Strauss and discussed the state of ethnography. He wants a return to philosophy, to one unified idea. Anthropology in the U.S. is a social illness, which afflicts people incapable of tolerating their own civilization. I was overwhelmed by a deep depression. A very bad night.[31]

It is unclear whether Lévi-Strauss's ideas triggered Métraux's bout of melancholy; a manic-depressive, he often ended his journal entries with a comment on his mental state. What is remarkable is Lévi-Strauss's insistence on "a return to philosophy," a discipline he had fled in his youth and from which he spent much of his subsequent career distancing himself. What, perhaps, he meant was a return to a philosophical approach to anthropology—to grand systems rather than piecemeal work, to a different style of writing reflecting the philosophical aspirations of his forebears, such as Montaigne and Rousseau.

New York and his association with Roman Jakobson had had a liberating effect on Lévi-Strauss. In a sense he had come of age as an anthropologist not in the rugged scrub of the Brazilian *cerrado*, but in the reading rooms of the New York Public Library in midtown Manhattan. America was his true culture shock, involving a new language and another way of thinking, and it was in this intellectual climate—part Anglo-American, part continental émigré culture—that structural anthropology had begun to take on a recognizable shape. On one side he had absorbed vast quantities of ethnographic minutiae; on the other, Jakobson had exposed him to new ways of systematizing his accumulating data. Dry model-making had been leavened by the flare and unpredictability of the surrealists. As he hunched over piles of books in the New York Public Library, leafing through ethnographic reportage from around the world, Lévi-Strauss's ideas had coalesced. The United States was the second country to which he would feel indebted. "The help I received there probably saved my life," he remembered, "and for several years I found there an intellectual climate and the opportunity for work that to a large extent have made me who I am."[32]

LÉVI-STRAUSS RETURNED to Paris in the autumn of 1948—"a sullen, grumbling, drizzling city," as the American writer Saul Bellow described it during his postwar sojourn. "The city lay under perpetual fog and smoke could not rise and flowed in the streets in brown and gray currents. An unnatural smell emanated from the Seine."[33] The war had ended, but its aftereffects lingered in the run-down façades, the rationing of fuel and food, and the air of a recently defeated nation—a stark contrast to New York's glass and steel shop fronts and bustling avenues.

Lévi-Strauss was turning forty. Since his late twenties he had been on the move—from São Paulo into the Brazilian interior; from Paris to Montpellier, Marseille to New York. This extended "walkabout" for a man who spent the rest of his life in Paris, the bulk of it in the sixteenth arrondissement, a stone's throw from his childhood home, is crucial for understanding Lévi-Strauss's intellectual trajectory in the postwar years. While in the Americas, Lévi-Strauss had missed out on a fundamental intellectual shift in French philosophy. Before he left, Durkheim, Bergson and the philosopher Léon Brunschvicg had reigned; when he returned, phenomenology was dominant. Jean Hyppolite's translations of Hegel's *Phänomenologie des Geistes*, which came out on the eve of the Nazi invasion, had signaled an (as it turned out) ironic turn toward the German philosophical outlook. In 1947, Alexandre Kojève published his celebrated 1930s lectures, *Introduction à la lecture de Hegel: leçons sur la phénoménologie de l'esprit*. Kantian idealism had been displaced by the "three Hs": Hegel, Husserl and Heidegger; philosophical systems for interpreting the world had given way to a philosophizing of the very act of interpretation, of being and knowing. Sartrean existentialism was becoming deeply rooted in the broader culture, although among academics it was Merleau-Ponty who was idolized. "It was fashionable to affect scorn for Sartre, who was fashionable," remembered Michel Foucault of the postwar era. "When we were young it was Merleau-Ponty who counted, not Sartre. We were fascinated by him."[34]

Lévi-Strauss's experiences had been very different. Through Jakobson, he had been exposed to Saussure and the Prague and Vienna linguistic schools—a genealogy that had largely bypassed France, where linguistics was still relatively backward. In Brazil he had worked an anthropological terrain that was only beginning to be studied seriously, while in New York he had absorbed the best of Anglo-American ethnography, with all its layers of dry description and attention to detail. After his travels, Lévi-Strauss would reenter the Parisian scene at an oblique angle, with a unique synthesis that would startle his contemporaries.

While he found his feet, he organized stopgap work at the Centre national de la recherche scientifique (CNRS) as *maître de recherche* before returning to the Musée de l'Homme as assistant director of ethnology. As Rivet was retiring and the other assistant director, the archaeologist André Leroi-Gourhan, was teaching in Lyon, Lévi-Strauss pretty much ran the museum, while lecturing to students at the Institut d'ethnologie. The Musée de l'Homme had been virtually abandoned during the war. After years in wealthy U.S. institutions, Lévi-Strauss was made acutely aware of how backward the social sciences were in France at the time. "At the Musée de l'Homme I found French ethnology in its infancy," he recalled, "struggling to survive in a musty atmosphere that was a little provincial."[35]

He began mixing with a new circle of friends, some of whom would subsequently prove influential. On the recommendation of Jakobson, he met the great philologist and scholar of myth Georges Dumézil, with whom he would form a lifelong intellectual bond. At the Musée de l'Homme there was the poet and ethnographer Michel Leiris, an ever-present figure in the early developments of prewar French anthropology, whom Lévi-Strauss finally got to know both as a colleague and as a writer. And through Koyré, Lévi-Strauss met the psychoanalyst Jacques Lacan. Lévi-Strauss would profoundly influence Lacan; after they met, Lacan began reading Saussure and exploring structural linguistics, and when Jakobson visited Paris, the three would form a close set. Lacan would soon be setting off on a parallel track to Lévi-Strauss's developing work on kinship, injecting linguistic theory into psychoanalysis and extending the metaphor of language to the subconscious.

While at the Musée, Lévi-Strauss scouted for professors who could supervise his already written theses: the draft of *Les Structures élémentaires de la parenté* and his shorter, complementary thesis, or "*petite thèse*," *La Vie familiale et sociale des Indiens Nambikwara* (*The Family and Social Life of the Nambikwara*), which he had completed over his first summer in New York. Back in 1944 he had written to Marcel Mauss asking him to be his supervisor, but by the time he had returned to Paris, Mauss's mind had deteriorated. "He did not recognise me," remembered Lévi-Strauss. "He thought I was Soustelle."[36] He eventually prevailed upon the dean of the Sorbonne, Durkheimian sociologist Georges Davy. The composition of the rest of the jury was complex—such was the breadth and originality of the work that it was difficult to find scholars equally at home with linguistics, global ethnography, the Asian subcontinent and Australasia, or who were familiar with even a small portion of the vast number of sources Lévi-Strauss had used, many of which were published only in English, some unavailable in French libraries. The jury ended up comprising a suitably eclectic group: the linguist Émile Benveniste, the sinologist Jean Escarra and the sociologist of religion and morals Albert Bayet. Marcel Griaule, who had headed the famous Dakar–Djibouti ethnographic expedition in the 1930s and was continuing his work among the Dogon, examined the complementary thesis on the Nambikwara. In June 1948, Lévi-Strauss was passed, an event that he considered a rite of passage. "Successfully defending my thesis not only opened doors for me in the university system," he remembered, "but it also gave me the feeling that I had become an adult"[37]—this, on the eve of his fortieth birthday. *La Vie familiale et sociale des Indiens Nambikwara* was published by the Société des Américanistes at the end of 1948. The following year *Les Structures élémentaires de la parenté* appeared in print.

LES STRUCTURES ÉLÉMENTAIRES was hugely ambitious. From its title—a reference to Durkheim's classic *The Elementary Forms of Religious Life*—and its dedication to one of the founders of American anthropology, the nineteenth-century anthropologist Lewis Henry Morgan, it was a pitch for glory. It took on big questions: the relationship between nature and culture, the meaning of the incest taboo, the cognitive basis of dualistic thinking and reciprocity, parallels between language and kinship, words and women. Wide-ranging discussions of Jean Piaget's work on child development and Freud's *Totem and Taboo* filled out a book that was much more than an academic thesis.

Referencing more than seven thousand articles and books, *Les Structures élémentaires* was a work of prodigious scholarship. Lévi-Strauss boasted that for a brief period in his early career he managed to keep up with the entire output of anthropological literature, before the growing volume of publications outpaced him. Much of this early erudition was on display in *Les Structures élémentaires*, a book that roams the globe, citing ethnographic examples from Arnhem Land to Assam, Fiji to Peru, but, interestingly, touching only briefly on his own fieldwork in Brazil.

Kinship was a natural target for Lévi-Strauss. At midcentury it was the discipline's one area of technical expertise, its single claim to professionalism. On one level, kinship had an earthy intimacy. It was the staple of the ethnographic experience, covering the myriad ways in which small-scale societies married, reproduced and defined who their relatives were and how to behave toward them. On another, as Jakobson had immediately realized, it had the potential for mathematical exactness, for modeling, for the systematizing that Lévi-Strauss had craved since his introduction to structural linguistics. The labyrinth of obscure notation and conceptual conundrums was an invitation to abstraction, as his earlier Jakobsonian sketch in *Word* had shown. So complex were some of the Australian Aboriginal systems that even indigenous specialists had tried to model their own kin systems, practicing a form of ethnography in neighboring tribes. Native anthropologists traveled widely, spending days in conversation with distant kin, arranging broken twigs and scraping lines in the ruddy sands of the outback to represent their involved familial arrangements.[38]

Against this often byzantine backdrop, Lévi-Strauss proposed a series of simple, all-binding principles. The "elementary structures" in question had a linguistics-like rigor to them. Defined in the very first sentence of the book's preface, they were either systems that "prescribe marriage with a certain type of relative or . . . which divide them into two categories, viz., possible spouses or prohibited spouses."[39] The key was incest avoidance. For Lévi-Strauss, the incest taboo was *the* social rule, from which all kin systems flowed. It distinguished humanity's rule-bound existence from nature's promiscuity; it marked the passage from nature to culture. In a mysterious way, the incest taboo was "at once on the threshold of culture, in culture, and in one sense . . . culture itself."[40]

Lévi-Strauss took his second principle from Marcel Mauss's influential *Essai sur le don* (*The Gift*), which argued that reciprocity was a central feature of all "primitive" societies. According to Mauss, there were no truly free or pointless gifts. Drawing from the ethnographic record, he showed that all gifts were really social symbols, imbued with a power that bound groups together in mutual obligation and solidarity. "Things create bonds between souls," wrote Mauss, "for the thing itself has a soul, is part of the soul." Sometimes gifts were simply swapped between clans; in more complex societies, they traveled along elaborate chains of givers and receivers. The drive toward reciprocity was not merely custom, it was deep-rooted and intuitive. Observing gift-giving was "to catch the fleeting moment when the society and its members take emotional stock of themselves and their situation as regards others."[41]

Reworking this idea, Lévi-Strauss argued that, in kin systems, women operated as gifts. The incest taboo stimulated their constant circulation between groups; reciprocity structured their movements. In mathematical terms, incest was the limit of reciprocity, "the point at which it cancels itself out."[42] Observance of the prohibition set up a displacement effect, which rippled through the system: "As soon as I am forbidden a woman, she thereby becomes available to another man, and somewhere else a man renounces a woman who thereby becomes available to me."[43] It was, therefore, a positive rule, driving out-marriage, forcing groups into complex alliances. What resulted was a finely equilibrated machine that seesawed between groups, rotating women down the generations.

Focusing on a subset of ideal types, taken from Granet's divisions between *chassé-croisé* (restricted exchange, or a more-or-less straight swap) and *échanges différés* (generalized exchange, or a longer chain), Lévi-Strauss took on a wholesale reinterpretation of the anthropological data he had patiently sifted through in the New York Public Library. What had been traditionally conceived of vertically, in terms of descent through the nuclear family, was upended. Placing exchange at the heart of the system gave Lévi-Strauss a panoramic view across interlocking kinship structures.

In the more restricted system, the dualism that Lévi-Strauss had already noticed in Northwest Coast masks, Maori tattooing and Caduveo face painting seemed to be infused through whole social setups. As he had observed firsthand among the Bororo, the two halves of the village choreographed their reciprocal duties in an intricate interplay of give and take. In other societies the circuit was longer, more complicated and risky, involving four, eight or even sixteen groups in circuits of exchange. But it was also potentially more profitable, widening circles of alliances. The resulting structures were naturalized in indigenous sayings, appropriate unions likened in one instance to "a leech rolling toward a wound," inappropriate ones to "water flowing up to its source." Whole systems of symbolic relationships echoed kin structures, from the way a buffalo was carved up and distributed among relatives in Burma to the prevalence of twins in the native mythologies of tribes organized around moieties.

Just as the structural linguistic models had switched emphasis from terms to relations, so Lévi-Strauss performed the same shift for the social sciences. "The relationship of reciprocity which is the basis of marriage," he wrote after a discussion of an apparent anomaly from the Trobriand Islands, "is not between men and women, but between men by means of women, who are merely the occasion of this relationship."[44] Men, as both "the takers of wives and the givers of sisters," "the authors and the victims of their exchanges," were nodal points in a web of exchange; women an aspect of its workings. (Much later, when under attack from feminists for the apparent male-centric character of his kinship models, Lévi-Strauss casually inverted his terms: "One could just as well say that women exchange men; all you have to do is replace the plus sign with the minus sign and vice-versa—the structure of the system would not change.")[45]

As the book progressed, the analyses thickened. There are pages of kin diagrams—obscure repeat patterns, as if lifted from a native design, undulating in diagonals across the page. Rotating obligations and exchanges of women run clockwise and counterclockwise around circular diagrams, sometimes shifting into three dimensions, spinning on the equator of a sphere. Systems are subdivided into "harmonic" and "disharmonic," according to the convergence or otherwise of residence and descent. In among colorful ethnographic examples, Lévi-Strauss illustrates native kin systems by drawing analogies to the Duponts of Paris and the Durands of Bordeaux—the only two families in a fictitious France. The principle of reciprocity is evoked both by the exchange of coconuts and dried fish in Polynesia and by an old Marseille café tradition whereby peasants swap their tumblers of wine before drinking.

The buildup of evidence is numbing, as is the language, twisting and turning through kinship conundrums of increasing complexity. At times examples read like a riddle: "In the great majority of cases there is marriage with the father's sister's daughter who is *at the same time* the mother's brother's daughter (where the father's sister has married the mother's brother)."[46] In other parts, kinship is pared down to a biblical simplicity: "All told, two men and two women; one man creditor, one man debtor; one woman received and one given."[47]

In the end, Lévi-Strauss had mapped out a vast area, covering the Asian subcontinent, Siberia and Oceania, where elementary systems predominated. The geographical extent was supposedly arrived at "without prior design or foreknowledge," although it was in effect a reinterpretation of previous research done by Frazer, William Rivers, Radcliffe-Brown and Granet, who had looked at distributions of the phenomenon of cross-cousin marriage. In the final pages he likened his analysis to that of the phonologist, drawing parallels between exchange and communication, women and words. For Lévi-Strauss, the properties of these structural systems were ingrained in a whole way of thinking. Kinship, as a rule-bound system operating below the threshold of consciousness, held up a mirror to the inner workings of the human mind.

Lévi-Strauss had sketched a world of rules and obligations, of imposed collaboration, of compulsory to-ing and fro-ing. Depending on which way you looked at it, this was either an expression of a long-lost instinct for community or a necessary but claustrophobic web of responsibilities. Lévi-Strauss left it to a final, mischievous paragraph of a five-hundred-page book to hint at the latter: "To this very day, mankind has always dreamed of seizing and fixing that fleeting moment when it was permissible to believe that the law of exchange could be evaded, that one could gain without losing, enjoy without sharing." It was a perennial dream "eternally denied to man, of a world in which one might *keep to oneself*."[48]

For the appendix, Lévi-Strauss asked the mathematician André Weil, brother of the philosopher and writer Simone, to analyze a particularly convoluted Australian kinship system. The resulting rows of mathematical notation seemed a long way from actual human relations—the easy intimacy of the ashen-faced Nambikwara, rolling in the dust of their campsites—but, as the logical end point of Lévi-Strauss's quest for abstraction, it was a fitting way to close out his first full-length book.

Les Structures élémentaires created an impact well beyond academic circles. No doubt this was due to the book's own structure—the broad, more accessible opening chapters on incest and reciprocity, adapted from lectures he had given in New York, gave the book a lofty intellectual flavor, before the descent into technical kinship analyses blotted out the narrative for all but a handful of specialists. But it was also due to Simone de Beauvoir's early interest in the project. She had heard about *Les Structures élémentaires* even before it was published, through Leiris, who was working with Lévi-Strauss at the Musée de L'Homme. At the time de Beauvoir was finishing off writing *Le Deuxième sexe* (*The Second Sex*) and she wanted an overview of the latest anthropological research, so she arranged to spend a few days at Lévi-Strauss's apartment going through the manuscript. It is unclear how useful *Les Structures élémentaires* was for de Beauvoir's own book, since sections on anthropology in *Le Deuxième sexe* rely on an outdated nineteenth-century evolutionary scheme. But much later her thank-you note, in the form of a long, glowing review in *Les Temps modernes*—the highly influential journal of politics and philosophy founded by Jean-Paul Sartre in late 1945—would launch Lévi-Strauss's ideas on the Parisian intellectual stage.

The oft-quoted opening line set the tone: "For a long time French sociology has been slumbering; Lévi-Strauss's book, which marks its dazzling awakening, must be hailed as a major event."[49] This is not just a book for specialists, wrote de Beauvoir. Beyond the baffling diagrams lies the "mystery of society as a whole, the mystery of mankind itself." No adulation was too great—the book was reminiscent of a young Marx; it reconciled Engels and Hegel. Strangely, de Beauvoir located Lévi-Strauss's thought "in that great humanist mainstream, that considers human existence bearing within itself its own justification," even claiming that it echoed certain existential arguments. Lévi-Strauss's long battle against both humanism and existentialism had not yet begun, but was surely implicit in a text in which human lives dissolved into models, their most intimate decisions an epiphenomenon of the system. Philosophical contradictions notwithstanding, de Beauvoir was impressed. The final sentence of the review was a simple, unambiguous endorsement: "*Il faut la lire*" (It has to be read).[50]

Soon afterward, Georges Bataille wrote another long piece on *Les Structures élémentaires*, the incest taboo and eroticism, titled "The Enigma of Incest," in the literary-philosophical review-journal *Critique*, which he had founded. In a largely positive review, Bataille included some uncharacteristic honesty when dealing with dense but supposedly great intellectual work:

> A dogged patience is called for, able to take in its stride the tangled data . . . It goes on and on and alas, it is desperately tedious: roughly two-thirds of Lévi-Strauss's big volume are devoted to the detailed examination of the multiple permutations and combinations thought up by primitive humanity to resolve one problem, the problem of the distribution of women . . . Regrettably, I myself am obliged to enter this maze; for a clear conception of eroticism we must struggle out of the darkness that has made its significance so hard to assess.[51]

A kind of aura developed around *Les Structures élémentaires*, aided by the fact that very few copies of the first edition were printed.[52] Looking back, French scholars remember it as a landmark publication, a parting of the waters for the humanities as a whole. Decades later, the French anthropologist Marc Augé recalled being impressed by the book's "will to scientificity" and its "quest for the most encompassing model to account for phenomena that do not appear, initially, to be a part of the same categories of analysis." "This was an important, decisive moment," remembered the philosopher Olivier Revault d'Allonnes. "At the time I saw a confirmation of Marx in *Les Structures élémentaires de la parenté*." Much later, after copies of the first edition had dried up, the anthropologist Emmanuel Terray remembered borrowing a friend's first edition and transcribing the first hundred pages of the book by hand. For Terray, *Les Structures élémentaires* was as important as Freud's *Interpretation of Dreams* and Marx's *Das Kapital*.[53]

Although much of *Les Structures élémentaires* was written in the United States and was based on American sources compiled in the New York Public Library, it took almost twenty years for the book to appear in English.[54] In the meantime, two French-speaking British anthropologists, Rodney Needham at Oxford and Edmund Leach at Cambridge, were reading the book in the original.

Needham had come across a copy of *Les Structures élémentaires* in Blackwell's bookshop in Oxford and took it with him on his fieldwork among the Penan forest nomads of Sarawak in Borneo. "At that time the scene was arid in the humanities, staid, unexciting, dry," he told me, sipping on a pint of ale at the Turf, the famous, low-beamed seventeenth-century tavern hidden down a series of meter-wide passageways in the heart of the Oxford colleges. "Suddenly there was this new wave—Lévi-Strauss, Dumézil, McLuhan, Borges—who breathed life into a flat postwar intellectual world." To this meticulously tidy man, who kept cross-indexed scrapbooks of all his notes and publications, Lévi-Strauss's formal modeling must have been immediately attractive. Needham recalled being "seduced" by Lévi-Strauss—a word that crops up repeatedly in intellectuals' reminiscences of first coming across his work—and began developing his own brand of structuralist analysis in Britain.

For Leach at Cambridge, reading *Les Structures élémentaires* was a paradoxical revelation. He had spent the war in Indochina, arriving in 1939 and traveling up to the northern Burmese hill tribes. He conducted an initial eight months' fieldwork among the Hpalang, a small Kachin community on the northeastern Burmese border, who practiced shifting monsoon cultivation, overlooking the paddy fields of the Chinese Shan states. Later, working as a British intelligence agent, he returned to the Kachin hills, where he spent long periods studying remote communities that had had little contact with Westerners. Through the chaotic years of the Japanese invasion, he lost all his field notes, photos and a draft of his manuscript, but later managed to reconstruct his findings, publishing them in the postwar classic *Political Systems of Highland Burma*. As it happened, the central section of *Les Structures élémentaires*, the chapter that contained the very nub of Lévi-Strauss's arguments, related to the Kachin, a group about which Leach had recent firsthand ethnographic knowledge.

Leach quickly recognized that Lévi-Strauss had based his analysis on earlier, poorly researched ethnographic accounts that were factually inaccurate. He also became concerned at the way Lévi-Strauss had marshaled his evidence, drawing questionable parallels between a hodgepodge of different hill tribes. In a review essay, Leach concluded that the book's huge ambition of establishing "the general laws of development governing all Asiatic societies, ancient and modern, primitive and sophisticated" was achieved only "by adopting a decidedly cavalier attitude towards the facts of history and ethnography." He criticized Lévi-Strauss's "inexcusable carelessness" of assuming customs among the Haka Chin were applicable to the Kachins—two entirely different groups separated by hundreds of kilometers. He also questioned Lévi-Strauss's use of sources: Head's *Handbook on Haka Chin Customs*, which Lévi-Strauss had described as "an unrecognised treasury of contemporary ethnography," was in actual fact a "pamphlet of forty-seven pages, originally priced at eight *annas*" written by "a Frontier Service administrative officer with no professional competence as an ethnographer."[55]

And yet there was something about Lévi-Strauss's account that intrigued Leach. In spite of the inaccuracies, he found certain insights—specifically, the way marriage circuits had a tendency to break down and morph into caste systems—that even he had not realized in the field, but which with hindsight fit the evidence. Curiously, in a kind of inadvertent structuralist effect, Lévi-Strauss's model had somehow been inverted in the process—"He'd got it back to front and upside down," laughed Leach in an interview given to the literary critic Frank Kermode in the early 1980s. "This fascinated me," he continued, "as how someone could be wrong about the facts, but right somehow about the theory."[56]

Writing in a review essay for the *New Left Review* in the mid-1960s, Leach described *Les Structures élémentaires* as "a splendid failure," with one very good idea drawn from Lévi-Strauss's reading of Marx, Freud and Jakobson—that social behavior is conducted with reference to a logically ordered conceptual scheme, "a model in the actor's mind of how things are or how things ought to be." For Leach, Lévi-Strauss's structural method was like psychoanalytic dream interpretation. "The basic assumption is that the actual dream . . . is an ephemeral, trivial matter, but is at the same time a precipitate of something much more important and enduring, a logical puzzle in the dreamer's conceptual system."[57] Taking the analogy a step further, Leach grafted Freud's triad, the id, the ego and the superego, onto Lévi-Strauss's nature, culture and human mind. There is indeed a similar flavor to the works of Freud and Lévi-Strauss: both chose their arena of intellectual invention at a remove from surface reality; both invented a set of logical interrelations that were said to exist beyond the threshold of consciousness.

Leach and Needham would later emerge as the key interpreters of Lévi-Strauss in the English-speaking world, a role that would become fraught with mutual suspicion and, in Needham's case, personal animosity, when Lévi-Strauss began questioning their interpretations of his work in the 1960s.

In France, criticism was couched in more conceptual terms. In a piece for *Les Temps modernes*, the philosopher Claude Lefort, a student of Merleau-Ponty, launched what would become a standard line of attack. *Les Structures élémentaires* was overly abstract—it reduced behavior to rules, meaning to mathematics. For Lévi-Strauss, this was exactly the point. "Is there any need to emphasise that this book is concerned exclusively with models and not with empirical realities?"[58] he hit back in the introduction to a later edition of *Les Structures élémentaires*—an extraordinary statement that was a measure of how far he had traveled from conventional anthropological analysis. By the end of the 1940s, Lévi-Strauss's experiences among the Caduveo, the Bororo and the Nambikwara were dissolving. Their day-to-day lives, their relationships, their struggle for survival on the margins of twentieth-century Brazil, so evocatively captured on film and in his field notes, had shrunk to a pinpoint on a graph.

Les Structures élémentaires remained Lévi-Strauss's favorite book throughout his life, although interestingly he did not include it in Gallimard's Bibliothèque de la Pléiade selection of his works, published in 2008. In many ways, though, it was the least convincing application of the structural method. The central claims, made with such gusto in the opening chapters, have not stood up well over the years. Anthropologists have since questioned the universality of the incest taboo, citing examples from ancient Egypt and Achaemenid Persia where brother–sister, father–daughter and mother–son relations were actually encouraged. Though the incest taboo is deep-rooted in human societies, evidence now points toward its biological, adaptive foundations, an argument ridiculed by Lévi-Strauss. Once seen as "a cultural taboo, putting a break on innate desires," incest prohibition is now viewed "as an innate tendency, which is being eroded by culture."[59] Advances in primatology have destroyed Lévi-Strauss's strict distinction between promiscuous animals and rule-bound humans, the cornerstone of the nature/culture divide.[60] Indeed Lévi-Strauss would later completely recast the book's central claim—the elemental division that he believed existed between nature and culture. This, he came to realize, was an opposition in the mind, rather than an empirical reality.[61]

More fundamentally, the idea that these structures were truly "elementary"—that is, forming the building blocks of all kin systems—has never progressed. At the time Lévi-Strauss envisaged a second volume (*Les Structures complexes de la parenté*), but he eventually realized that the combinatory possibilities of less restricted systems were so vast that the task was beyond him. He also wanted to extend the work introduced in his essay for *Word*, systematically mapping attitudes between members of kin systems, but this too would remain on the drawing board.

When Lévi-Strauss had sent his manuscript to Robert Lowie, the great American anthropologist told him that it was a work "in the grand style." Lévi-Strauss at first took this as a compliment, but with the passing of time he would become less sure about what Lowie really meant.[62] Much later, when he had begun to understand Lowie's backhanded compliment, he could admit that the project had been overambitious.

But the grand edifice of *Les Structures élémentaires* took decades to crumble. Its originality, the confidence of its assertions, the sense of a long-overdue theoretical reorientation, made it the landmark publication of its times. Only a handful of specialists (like Leach) were equipped to evaluate Lévi-Strauss's sometimes fast-and-loose use of ethnography; the rest were left to marvel at the book's theoretical implications, which seemed to offer a way out of a double bind—the logjam of empiricism and the subjectivity of contemporary philosophical thought—while promising the birth of leaner, more scientific humanities. Lévi-Strauss's own summaries of his work, many of which imply, to the untutored eye, that *Les Structures élémentaires* had demonstrated that *all* kinship systems (not just the very restricted and in some ways atypical set that Lévi-Strauss had examined) were but variations on limited sets of structural laws, periodically primed the pump.[63] But as a pioneering, if flawed, attempt at using the tools of linguistics in a completely different domain, *Les Structures élémentaires* levered open new theoretical space.

In the book, Lévi-Strauss had criticized Freud's famous account of the origins of the incest taboo as a myth. Yet he had produced his own kind of myth: a peculiarly mid-twentieth-century appeal to abstraction, displacement and mathematics. Like Freud, Lévi-Strauss's claims were ambitious, though not always fully backed up by the evidence. But they were endlessly suggestive. Against the intellectual current, Lévi-Strauss had introduced a series of ideas that were destined to change the intellectual ecology for decades to come.

6

On the Shaman's Couch

> Most of us regard psychoanalysis as a revolutionary discovery of twentieth-century civilisation and place it on the same footing as genetics or the theory of relativity. Others, probably more conscious of the abuses of psychoanalysis than the real lesson it has to teach us, still look upon it as one of the absurdities of modern man.
>
> CLAUDE LÉVI-STRAUSS[1]

LÉVI-STRAUSS WAS AS FASCINATED by the work of Sigmund Freud as he was skeptical of the practice of psychoanalysis—then becoming an established, if left-field, treatment for psychosexual problems and neuroses. In New York, he had met the famous Freudian psychoanalyst Raymond de Saussure through Jakobson, and back in Paris his friendship with Jacques Lacan was blossoming. In the 1960s he would make the distinction between the psychoanalyst's "theory of the mind" and "theory of the cure," saying that it was only the former that interested him.[2] But in the late 1940s he began exploring the borderlands between psychoanalysis and anthropology, the therapist and the shaman, analysis and ritual cure. It offered him a way back to the matrix of the unconscious, the irrational and the primitive—the aesthetic hunting ground of the surrealists. It also opened up another area that was occupying his thoughts more and more: myth.

He set down his ideas while teaching at the newly established Sixth Section of the École pratique des hautes études—an autonomous social science research center, the institutional home of the famous Annales school of historical research. He had been recruited by founder of the Sixth Section Lucien Febvre in the winter of 1948–49, the first fully functioning year of the institution, to give a seminar on the Religious Life of Primitives. In two essays—"The Sorcerer and His Magic" and "The Effectiveness of Symbols"—he placed ethnographic examples from Brazil, Panama, Mexico and the Pacific Northwest against Freudian psychoanalysis.

"The Sorcerer and His Magic" followed the story of Quesalid, one of Franz Boas's informants from the Kwakiutl group near Vancouver. Quesalid is a native skeptic who becomes a shaman in order to unmask "the false supernatural," the fakery of the shaman's art—the hidden nails, the tufts of down concealed in the corner of the mouth, the use of "dreamers" (spies) to find out information about the patient who is being treated. But through the course of his debunking quest, as Quesalid himself becomes a great shaman renowned for his cures, he begins to doubt his own skepticism. He finds that some deceptions work better than others, that certain rituals do in fact make patients better. Through his cures Quesalid discovers that the power of performance is in some sense real. The interactions between the patient, the shaman and the group, the structuring of a psychic universe, however achieved, bring about concrete results.[3]

This point was vividly demonstrated in Lévi-Strauss's companion piece, "The Effectiveness of Symbols," written at around the same time. Dedicated to Raymond de Saussure, the essay worked through a ritual incantation used to assist difficult childbirths in Panama, which had been recorded by Swedish ethnologists. The incantation describes the shaman's and his spirit assistants' journey into the woman's vagina and up to the uterus on a quest to release the unborn child. The child must be liberated from the Muu—the spirit who forms the fetus, but who in this case has abused her powers. The shaman sings the woman's predicament as she lies in a hammock, knees parted, pointing eastward, "groaning, losing blood, the vulva dilating and moving." He calls on diverse spirits, "of the winds, waters and woods," as well as, in a Conradesque touch, "the spirit of the silver steamer of the white man."

As the torturous labor continues, the shaman embarks on his journey. Through blood and tissue, into a uterine "hell *à la* Hieronymous Bosch," he marshals his spirits in single file along "Muu's way." The group struggles up the woman's birth canal, the shaman calling on "Lords of the wood-boring insects" to cut through the sinews, clearing a path through a jungle of human fiber. After defeating Muu and her daughters with the use of magic hats, and thus releasing the child, the shaman's troop begins the descent, another perilous journey, analogous to the act of childbirth itself. The shaman urges his troop on toward the orifice, employing more "clearers of the way," such as the armadillo. After the delivery of the child, the shaman throws up a cloud of dust, obscuring the path to prevent Muu's escape.[4]

The myth, rich in literary effect, worked by focusing the woman's mind and body, by organizing—structuring—the otherwise chaotic experience of an interminable labor. Lévi-Strauss likened the process to the psychoanalyst's "abreaction," whereby the patient, guided by the analyst, relives painful past experience in order to unblock subconscious impasses. Based on the same elements, the shamanistic cure was actually a tidy inversion of psychoanalysis: while the analyst listens, the shaman speaks. Guided by the analyst, the patient elaborates his own personal myth, normally a stylized version of vague childhood memories. The shaman, on the other hand, declaims an equally formulaic social myth. With transference, the patient articulates through the analyst, while the shaman speaks on behalf of the patient. But both approaches were ultimately premised on the assumption that the unconscious—that apparently mysterious, subterranean place of inchoate feelings, the bizarre and the unexpected—was in fact a logically structured universe. Both shamanism and psychoanalysis worked by eliciting this symbolic structure, evoking the hidden order of experience.

Lévi-Strauss's point was that modern techniques were merely reworkings of ideas that have been with us from the dawn of time. When Europe was still chaining up the mad, shamans in "primitive" societies were already treating patients on the metaphorical psychoanalyst's couch.[5] (Much later, he would argue in *La Potière jalouse* that many of Freud's psychoanalytic theories, such as the oral or anal character, effectively recycled indigenous Jivaro myths.) In fact, it was only in the then most experimental branch of psychoanalysis, namely group therapy, that modern practitioners were beginning to approach the most sophisticated techniques that had been known to shamans for millennia.

Lévi-Strauss's concluding remarks moved from psychoanalysis to the unconscious to myth, making perhaps his strongest appeal yet to the kind of structuralism of symbolic and mythic thought that would end up dominating the rest of his career. Memories, strange incidents, and personal histories related to the unconscious like words to a language, where "the vocabulary matters less than the structure." Myths, whether embodied in individual neurotic complexes or social narratives, were stocks of unconscious representations, structured by a limited set of laws. He ended by drawing a direct parallel between language and myth, already hinting at a project that would culminate in the *Mythologiques* quartet:

> There are many languages, but very few structural laws which are valid for all languages. A compilation of known tales and myths would fill an imposing number of volumes. But they can be reduced to a small number of simple types if we abstract from, among the diversity of characters, a few elementary functions. As for the complexes—those individual myths—they also correspond to a few simple types, which mold the fluid multiplicity of cases.[6]

Lévi-Strauss's brief foray into the world of psychoanalysis left an indelible mark on the future of the profession. The essays deeply influenced Jacques Lacan, who cited them in his early theoretical breakthrough lecture delivered in Zurich, "The Mirror Stage as Formative of the Function 'I' as Revealed in Psychoanalytic Experience," as well as in his 1953 Rome discourse, a polemic calling for a return to the analysis of the patient's language. Lacan's intervention signaled a break from the psychoanalytic establishment and the opening up of a new form of practice—as abstruse as it was influential—that spread through the humanities in the 1960s and '70s.

MANY HAVE NOTED the extraordinary unity of Lévi-Strauss's intellectual output. These early essays, packed with hints of the future direction of his work, are a testament to his steady progression and the internal consistency of his ideas. By the end of the 1940s, he had eased into position the foundation stones on which he would construct his life's work; many of the theoretical set pieces that would crop up again and again in books, interviews and articles were already in place. For Lévi-Strauss, language, as a formal system of differences, had become more than just an analogy. It was a template that could draw out new truths from diverse domains: kinship, the unconscious, symbolic thought, myth and aesthetic composition.

Lévi-Strauss's remarkably coherent theoretical outlook was twinned with the conviction that the whole of the humanities, following the lead of linguistics, was on the brink of a scientific revolution, destined to move in his direction. He even read back into previous key works the beginnings of a struggle toward structuralist thought. When, in 1950, Lévi-Strauss was asked by the sociologist Georges Gurvitch to write an introduction to the work of Marcel Mauss as part of a series of books on recently deceased intellectual greats (Mauss had died three years earlier, at the age of seventy-seven, after a bout of bronchitis), Lévi-Strauss tried to portray him as a proto-structuralist. In this rewriting of French intellectual history, the *Essai sur le don* (*The Gift*) was the breakthrough—a work in which anthropology finally moved beyond mere observation and crude comparisons to look at its subject matter as a system, alive with correlations, formal equivalences and interdependent parts, and reducible to a limited set of operations. "The *Essai sur le don* therefore inaugurates a new era for the social sciences, just as phonology did for linguistics," wrote Lévi-Strauss, and "can be compared to the discovery of combinatorial analysis for modern mathematical thinking." Mauss had provided the inspiration, but had not been able to follow through. "Like Moses conducting his people to the promised land whose splendour he would never behold," Lévi-Strauss concluded, Mauss had halted "at the edge of . . . immense possibilities."[7]

Gurvitch was unhappy with this interpretation, which did indeed seem to willfully manipulate the legacy of France's most celebrated anthropologist. Claude Lefort cut to the heart of Lévi-Strauss's sleight of hand in *Les Temps modernes*, in the same review in which he had taken on *Les Structures élémentaires*. For Lefort, Lévi-Strauss's reading "seems foreign to his inspiration: Mauss aim[ed] at meaning, not at symbols," wanted to understand "behavior without leaving the realm of experience" and was never trying to construct a Lévi-Strauss-type superstructure of logic.[8]

ON THE STRENGTH of *Les Structures élémentaires* and a now respectable body of published articles, Lévi-Strauss's reputation was growing, and moves were already afoot to have him admitted to the prestigious Collège de France. Founded in the sixteenth century by Francis I for the king's lecturers, the Collège de France remains an elite institution, the pinnacle of French intellectual life. Part of its attraction is that it functions at a remove from the university system. It does not award degrees or administer exams, nor is there a syllabus or student body. The day-to-day bureaucracy of university life is eliminated in favor of pure, original research, presented in a series of twelve two-hour lectures, open to the public. Membership is for life, voted by existing members. In the secure but open-ended environment of the Collège, with its mission "to teach science in the making,"[9] academics either flatlined or innovated. Lévi-Strauss, who was already furrowing his own idiosyncratic intellectual path, would surely thrive.

At the time, admission to this elite intellectual sect still seemed a surreal prospect for Lévi-Strauss. "I hardly knew what the Collège de France was," he recalled, remembering it from his youth as "a fearsome place, off limits," which he had avoided even setting foot in as a student.[10] But unbeknownst to him, even before he arrived back in Paris, his supporters had begun mobilizing on his behalf. As he was leaving New York, Gaston Berger had made the throwaway remark that Lévi-Strauss was returning to France to enter the Collège. At the time, Lévi-Strauss had dismissed it as banter, but when he arrived back in Paris, the psychologist Henri Piéron called him for a meeting and told him that he had supporters in the Collège who wanted to see him elected. Lévi-Strauss was seen as a modernizing force, both in terms of his theories and his progressive politics—progressive, that is, in comparison with the sclerotically conservative hierarchy that still dominated the institution. The old guard was epitomized by Edmond Faral, who had held the chair in Latin Literature of the Middle Ages since 1924 and was then the Collège's administrator.

When a chair became vacant, Piéron put Lévi-Strauss forward for election, in November 1949, but he was defeated. One year later another chair at the Collège came up. The linguist Émile Benveniste nominated Lévi-Strauss once more, but again he was turned down. By coincidence, Lévi-Strauss was giving the Fondation Loubat lecture series at the Collège as his application was being considered for the second time, delivering six talks on the Mythic Expression of Social Structure. In the audience were Max Ernst, André Breton, Maurice Merleau-Ponty and Georges Dumézil. It was during these talks that Lévi-Strauss cemented his friendship with Dumézil—a key influence and ally in the years to come.

"Not naming any names," Lévi-Strauss told me, "there was an element of anti-Semitism in my failure." Faral, who during the occupation had barred Jews from the Collège even before the October 1940 law had required him to do so,[11] apparently told Lévi-Strauss to his face that he would never enter the Collège. More generally, Lévi-Strauss had been caught up in a struggle between conservatives and progressives. "I had been an innocent," he told Didier Eribon, "brought in to a quarrel between ancients and moderns: the traditionalists still included men who, by their spirit or arrogance, belonged to another century."

The double blow at the Collège was compounded by the separation from his second wife, Rose-Marie, a marriage that had lasted only a few years. "I broke with my past, rebuilt my private life" is as forthcoming as Lévi-Strauss ever was on the subject.[12] Short of money, he moved into the then working-class eleventh arrondissement—one of his rare spells outside the sixteenth. He was also forced to sell part of his treasured collection of indigenous artifacts—the masks and bowls for which he had scrimped and saved in New York. Half went to his friend Jacques Lacan, with other objects being sold to André Malraux, the Musée de l'Homme and a museum in the Dutch university town of Leiden.

BETWEEN THE TWO REJECTIONS from the Collège, Lévi-Strauss traveled to the subcontinent. He had secured funding through Métraux, who was then working for UNESCO's Bureau for Racial Relations, for a two-month mission to Pakistan and India studying the possibilities for future research in the region, for UNESCO's social sciences division. Lévi-Strauss traveled in the aftermath of one of the most cataclysmic partitions in history—Britain's rapidly concocted division between India and Pakistan, which had erupted in bloodletting and left millions destitute in refugee camps, scattered on both sides of the borders. He visited Karachi, Dacca, the Chittagong Hills, Calcutta, New Delhi, Lahore and Peshawar, later condensing the six hundred pages of notes he took into two sections in *Tristes Tropiques*.

He flew to Karachi via Egypt, over the pale pinks—"peach bloom, mother of pearl, the iridescence of raw fish"—of the desert sands before rolling mists dissolved into the night.[13] A dawn flight took him across the newly created partition, floating over a patchwork of pink and green agricultural fields, akin to "the geographical musings of Paul Klee." Down to the mouths of the Ganges globular fields clustered together, surrounded by the viscous waters of the floodplains and the mangrove forests of the Sundarbans.[14]

In Calcutta he found himself mobbed by stump-waving beggars, rickshaw touts, shoeblacks, pimps and porters, while in the Chittagong Hills, where he stayed in a luxurious room in a Swiss-style chalet called the Circuit House, he was smothered by the attentions of teams of manservants. They preempted his every whim, serving five meals a day, continually offering to bathe him, even waiting outside the privy "to snatch the master's substance from him." He was repelled by their unctuousness—"There is something sexual in this anguished submission," he observed—imprisoned in a colonial bubble that had survived independence intact.[15]

Traveling into the tribal areas north of Chittagong, Lévi-Strauss engaged in another short spell of on-the-hoof ethnography among the Kuki. He stayed in a bamboo house perched on a hillside, with ample verandas where women pounded paddy in a giant mortar with two-meter-high pestles. Deer, monkey, boar and panther skulls were used as decorations. On the evening of his arrival, the festivities began. They were served rice beer in oxen horns and treated to "extremely monotonous" dance songs, which Lévi-Strauss later transcribed. The boys wore loincloths, sashes and glass bead necklaces; the girls, knee-length skirts loaded with copper tubes, beetle-wing-fringed breastplates and ivory earplugs.

Lévi-Strauss's experiences generated two almost apologetic papers, which remain elegies to his earlier forays into ethnography in Brazil. The first outlined a set of kinship terms for the Cakma, Kuki and Mog tribes, a list that remained incomplete "on account of the briefness of our stay in the native villages"; the second consisted of "highly fragmentary" descriptions of the Kuki village.[16] Interestingly, the Kuki had already featured in *Les Structures élémentaires* as one of the key examples of a simple form of "generalized exchange."[17]

Lévi-Strauss's impressions of the subcontinent were bleak. In some of his most misanthropic writing, he recalled teeming cities, festering slums and dull, functional apartment blocks, like the half-built concrete cube he had driven past in the abandoned city in Brazil's interior. All that he saw around him was "filth, chaos, promiscuity, congestion; ruins, huts, mud, dirt; dung, urine, pus, humours, secretions and running sores."[18] In a disturbing image, he likened the city slums to goose pens for producing foie gras, which he had seen in Mont-de-Marsan during his first year teaching at the Lycée Victor-Duruy. Each goose was wedged in a box, "reduced to the status of a mere feeding tube." But there was an important difference—while the geese were being fattened up, the poor were being slimmed down. Like some sinister structuralist model, their tiny cubicles were "mere points of connection with the communal sewer," reducing human life "to the pure exercise of excretory functions."[19]

Was it temperament, culture shock or the difficult phase of his life—the disappointment at the Collège and his unraveling marriage—that produced such a toxic response to his experiences on the subcontinent? Whatever his reasons, the trip confirmed his growing disillusionment with modernity. Overpopulation would become thematic in Lévi-Strauss's evolving critique. Man had once been in proportion to the natural landscapes he inhabited, roaming through vast forests, settling along thousand-kilometer littorals and roaring rivers. He was now reduced to "life on a pocket handkerchief scale," in the drab uniformity of the world's rapidly expanding cities.[20]

BLOCKED FROM ASCENT in France's hierarchical academic system, Lévi-Strauss felt himself adrift. He said that at this point he was convinced he would not have a "real career," that he even entertained doubts about continuing to pursue anthropology, thinking again about journalism or writing.[21] This seems difficult to square with his growing reputation in France and abroad. Even though he had failed entrance to the Collège, his career was progressing. At the end of 1950, on the heels of his second rejection at the Collège, he was appointed director of studies of the more conservative Fifth Section of the École pratique des hautes études, devoted to *sciences religieuses* (religious studies). He filled the chair left vacant by the retiring Maurice Leenhardt, the same chair that had been held by the great Marcel Mauss from the turn of the twentieth century up until the Second World War. It was another hard-fought appointment process. Leenhardt, a missionary-turned-anthropologist who had studied the Kanak people in New Caledonia, opposed Lévi-Strauss's selection, favoring one of his student protégés to succeed him. But with the help of Georges Dumézil, Lévi-Strauss finally secured tenure. There he would become part of an illustrious intellectual heritage, which included several figures who influenced the formation of his own thought—Mauss, Dumézil as well as Marcel Granet and Alexandre Kojève.

The chair signaled a major change of direction for Lévi-Strauss, which in retrospect would split his career into two distinct phases. Perhaps fortunately, the post steered him away from the shoals of kinship and into the open waters of religious thought, an area that was looser, more to do with ideas, not so bound to the specifics of field data. Although Lévi-Strauss would continue to come back to kinship periodically, and still harbored a desire to write the *Structures complexes* companion piece to his thesis, future work would increasingly develop a more interpretive flavor. When I asked him why, after years dedicated to decoding kinship systems, he had lit out into new intellectual territory, he replied in a typically fatalistic fashion. There had been no real choice involved, as the shift in direction was imposed upon him. He had to fulfill his duties in a chair that was devoted to religious studies, he explained, as if he were merely a drone in the academic hive. But in retrospect the pull on the tiller seems rooted in Lévi-Strauss's own evolving sense of where he wanted to end up. A trail of earlier articles on shamanism, myth and symbolism, written in the late 1940s while he was giving his Religious Life of Primitives seminars at the Sixth Section, had already signaled intent. By the 1950s, Lévi-Strauss was angling toward more interpretive areas of investigation, better suited to his aesthetic, literary frame of mind.

His decade of Wednesday afternoon lectures and seminars at the Fifth Section was a crucial road test for this new line of thinking. Following the method he had adopted in New York, he used his lecture cycle as an opportunity to think aloud, toy with new ideas, giving verbal expositions of what would later turn into essays and books. He worked from a rough outline but would go off on tangents when the mood took him, following chains of associations across the globe, bringing his now considerable ethnographic knowledge to bear on conceptual hypotheses. He was searching, he told Didier Eribon, for "small islands of organisation," in among "a vast empirical stew."[22] I was curious to know how he had identified these islands. The process, he told me, was essentially one of trial and error.

For this reason he banned the use of tape recorders, so as "to feel at liberty to engage in mental struggle, explore odd byways, submit tentative ideas to the test of oral formulation"—a test he said he often failed.[23] He didn't want what he considered risky, malformed ideas preserved on tape, to contradict him after he had ironed out the inconsistencies. Perhaps he need not have worried—time and again former students have commented on how incredibly clear his expositions were the first time around. "He spoke as he wrote," said Philippe Descola, Lévi-Strauss's student and in many ways his natural successor as the current director of the Laboratoire d'anthropologie and professor of anthropology at the Collège. Descola spoke to me in what had been Lévi-Strauss's office, still containing the low-slung leather chair on which a much younger Descola had sat, terrified, when he had asked Lévi-Strauss to be his supervisor.[24] "It was like seeing Kant, Hegel," Descola told me. "He was one of the great geniuses of the twentieth century." The office was now book lined and adorned with South American indigenous artifacts, including a mask with clumps of straw for hair and, in a cheeky, postmodern reference, the Arumbaya fetish from *Tintin and the Broken Ear*. "He built up complex sentences, piling up subclauses, but always landed on his feet," Descola explained.[25]

As a method, it was rather like Breton's automatism—a kind of intellectual free association, which uncovered the hidden links between apparently unrelated data. Through this free jazz of the mind, Lévi-Strauss began exploring the connections that reproduced themselves in a metaphysical world of myth and mysticism. The first course he taught at the Fifth Section, the Visitation of the Souls, returned to his fieldwork in Brazil, looking at relations between the living and the dead among the Bororo. Lévi-Strauss had arrived too late to witness the early stages of Bororo funeral rites—the rotting of the body in an open grave, covered over with loose branches; the washing of the deceased's bones in the stream, and their painting and adorning with feathers. But he had been present at the long and complex rites that followed.

Fifteen years later, Lévi-Strauss dissected what he had seen. Combining his own fieldwork with his library research in New York, he drew comparisons between the Bororo rituals and those of the North American Algonquian and the Sioux-speaking Winnebago and Omaha, looking at the spatial directions (east–west, up–down, left–right, etc.) as well as certain colors, animals and vegetables that proliferated through the rites. Recurrent symbols, such as the use of a shell for water, a rounded stone for the earth or a star for the sky, were for Lévi-Strauss a kind of "algebra" that could give mathematical shape to these apparently inchoate rituals. Using structural analysis, rich belief systems could be boiled down, reduced to simpler, more formal systems of fundamental oppositions. The resulting dual and tripartite configurations echoed the social organization of the groups. It was a kind of inversion of Durkheimian method, linking ideas, rituals and myth back to the social, rather than the other way round. "The relationship between the living and the dead," Lévi-Strauss concluded with a kind of proto-structuralist simplification, "is no more than the projection, on the screen of religious thought, of real relations between the living."[26]

The following year Lévi-Strauss moved on to mythology, comparing the origin myths among the Hopi, Zuni and Acoma of the western/central Pueblo Indians. It was the beginning of his life's work—a two-decade-long obsession that would take him further and further into the more obscure recesses of the indigenous imagination. The *Mythologiques* quartet would begin to appear only in the 1960s, but fragments were already coming together as early as 1952.

In the middle of 1952 Lévi-Strauss traveled to Bloomington, Indiana, to speak at a conference that brought together linguists and anthropologists. There, he began putting a cognitive, even neurological gloss on what he saw as the growing rapprochement between linguistics and anthropology. He made theatrical references to "the uninvited guest, the human mind," arguing that language and culture had to be related in some way; otherwise the mind would either be "a complete jumble" or would consist of "compartments separated by rigid bulkheads."[27] The quest lay in a systematic cultural analysis that would ultimately shed light on how the brain worked. "For centuries the humanities and social sciences have resigned themselves to contemplating the world of the natural and exact sciences as a kind of paradise which they will never enter," he concluded, with an allusion to his introduction to the work of Marcel Mauss. "All of a sudden there is a small door which is being opened between the two fields and it is linguistics which has done it."[28] It was through this "small door" that Lévi-Strauss entered, searching for a communicating passage between anthropology and the hard sciences. His enormous influence as a postwar thinker would rest on this initial gamble, and his boldness in bringing together two very different types of inquiry. Over the next decade, scores of scholars from neighboring disciplines—literary criticism, psychoanalysis, philosophy—would follow in behind him, looking for the rigor that linguistics had achieved.

In the same year, Lévi-Strauss's contributions to a major anthropology symposium in New York drove his arguments further. The event, sponsored by the Wenner-Gren Foundation, brought together eighty scholars to discuss the state of the art in anthropology. It featured many of the discipline's leading lights, academics such as Margaret Mead, Alfred Kroeber, Robert Lowie and Julian Steward, whom Lévi-Strauss had met in New York during the war. They were joined by scholars from neighboring fields, such as the sociologist Robert Redfield and Lévi-Strauss's friend and collaborator Roman Jakobson, for a wide-ranging discussion of the discipline's achievements and its future.

Transcripts of Lévi-Strauss's contributions show a mind sparking with new ideas, pushing the insights from structural linguistics in novel and eccentric directions. When asked to discuss how structural analysis could be used in domains outside linguistics, he returned to his half-formed thoughts on the differences between plant species that had occurred to him while he idled on the Maginot Line on the eve of the fall of France. Postwar research had confirmed his intuitions. Differences between species could indeed be systematically described in terms of permutations of core features. Just as in linguistics, scientists had nailed down small sets of contrasts—petals and carpels were either separated or united, stamens numerous or few, the corolla regular or irregular, and so forth—which, in different combinations, generated abundant diversity.[29] For Lévi-Strauss, the same genetic principle could be equally applied to a range of cultural domains, from fine art to tools, clothing to kinship and mythology.[30]

Wherever Lévi-Strauss looked he saw formal connections. It was the early days of television, and the snowy images that the sets produced were still a novelty. He was intrigued to notice that low-frequency bands yielded only an outline, a mere sketch of a figure or an object, whereas high frequencies filled in the image, giving it the appearance of solidity. In a far-fetched analogy, he likened the contrast to art's fundamental properties: the division between drawing and painting. Culture and technology, science and art were blending in the structural echo chamber of Lévi-Strauss's mind, each revealing the other's hidden properties.

Lévi-Strauss was already supplementing his prodigious ethnographic reading with Norbert Wiener on cybernetics and Claude Shannon and

Warren Weaver's *The Mathematical Theory of Communication*. Through the prism of early digital theorizing, crossovers into the social sciences seemed plausible. "Communication is not only a field for linguistics," Lévi-Strauss explained in the symposium, "but it can be said that society is, by itself and as a whole, a very large machine for establishing communication on many different levels between human beings."[31] The image revealed one wing of Lévi-Strauss's early thought: a mechanistic outlook that refused to grant cultural phenomena any special metaphysical status. As chief engineer to this "very large machine," Lévi-Strauss was tinkering with its components, drawing up blueprints of its various interlocking devices, measuring each rotation and monitoring the engine's rhythms. Yet at the same time—and this disjuncture runs through the whole body of his work—Lévi-Strauss was not ultimately interested in the machine's functions or outputs. Like Niki de Saint Phalle's Stravinsky Fountain mobiles beside the Centre Pompidou, with their spouting hoses and whirring wheels, Lévi-Strauss's cultural engine was an aesthetic contraption that worked, but to no discernible end.

In his concluding remarks at the symposium, Lévi-Strauss was asked to sketch anthropology's progress so far and its prospects for the future, a task that he warmed to with an interesting take on the discipline's formation. In the past, anthropology had fed off the scraps, the garbage left over by the established disciplines. In the Middle Ages virtually anything outside Europe was considered, in a philosophical sense, anthropological. With the rise of classical studies, mainstream scholars commandeered Indian and Chinese thought, restricting anthropology to Africa, Oceania and South America. In the modern setting, professional anthropology has been pushed further to the fringes, scavenging in the dustbins of academia. Paradoxically, the "ragpickers" had found gold. Driven to the extremes of human culture, anthropology was now on the point of making profound intellectual discoveries. (Margaret Mead took immediate exception to what she saw as Lévi-Strauss's equation between indigenous culture and garbage, but his analogy was innocent. It was meant only in the sense that anthropologists were rummaging through the offcuts of other disciplines, as he subsequently explained, "picking up odds and ends.")

Kant had envisaged the world as a division between the "starry skies" (Newtonian physics) and "moral law" (Kant's own philosophy); anthropology, via linguistics, Lévi-Strauss concluded, was poised to unite these realms into a federated union of diverse, but related, disciplines:

> Linguists have already told us that inside our mind there are phonemes and morphemes revolving, one around the other, in more or less the same way as planets go around the solar system; and it is in the expectation that this unification may take place that I feel anthropology may really have a meaningful and important function not only in the development of modern society but also in the development of science at large.[32]

By the early 1950s, Lévi-Strauss's vision was filling out. He believed that he was living in an era of massive theoretical convergence. In Paris he was meeting regularly with Jacques Lacan, the mathematician Georges Guilbaud and the linguist Émile Benveniste in cross-disciplinary discussions around the concept of structures and how principles in mathematics could be carried over into the human sciences.[33] His seminar course at the École had become a magnet for a new generation of thinkers exploring crossover ideas and soaking up findings from ethnography. Discussions ranged from linguistics to psychoanalysis, mathematics to atomic physics, but the core remained anthropology. Through structural analysis, Lévi-Strauss believed anthropology could become a kind of meta-science, capable of discovering not just the foundations of human cultural exchange, but deep laws that resonated through nature. In spite of career setbacks, he had a research program; it now even had a name. "If you had to pick a date for the birth of Lévi-Straussian structuralism," wrote his Swiss biographer, Denis Bertholet, "it would be 1952: the articles of that year, in the universal ambition that they bring, mark the moment when the suffix '-ism' can be legitimately added, in the history of thought, to the adjective 'structural.' "[34]

HIS GRAYING HAIR RECEDING, Lévi-Strauss was now in his mid-forties, hitting the middle-aged plateau. His youth had been disjointed, but ambitious. He had led the largest anthropological expedition of its time across Brazil and had lectured in São Paulo, New York and Paris. His kinship thesis had been published to wide acclaim. After a period of instability, his life was coming together again. From 1952, Lévi-Strauss mixed academic work with a new job, akin to his posting as cultural attaché in New York. Through Métraux, he was nominated as secretary-general of the International Social Science Council at UNESCO. The work was an empty ritual: "I tried to give the impression that an organization without goal or function had a reason for existing," Lévi-Strauss remembered, a task made more difficult by the generous budgets, which "had to be justified with a semblance of activity." After the breakup of his marriage to Rose-Marie Ullmo, Lévi-Strauss had begun a relationship with Monique Roman, whom he had met at Jacques Lacan's house. Born of an American mother and a Belgian father, she was in her late twenties—eighteen years his junior—and was attending his course at the Sorbonne.

Reintegrated into Parisian intellectual life, Lévi-Strauss was becoming well known in certain circles—a relatively small set of interested specialists who attended his courses and spoke at his seminars. A solid, if unspectacular, career beckoned, as a middle-ranking academic surrounded by a coterie of disciples. His way forward would be unconventional for its times. In a sense Lévi-Strauss was forced to circumvent the university system in order finally to dominate it.

TWO KEY PUBLICATIONS enabled Lévi-Strauss to reach beyond the academy and find a new audience for his ideas: the short pamphlet *Race et histoire* (1952) and, far more important, his memoir, *Tristes Tropiques* (1955). Together they gave a layman's version of what had been an involved, technical argument relayed largely in specialist journals. While *Race et histoire* drew Lévi-Strauss into a fiery and very public debate around some of the central tenets of anthropological orthodoxy, *Tristes Tropiques* fleshed out Lévi-Strauss's public persona, transforming him from a promising academic into a revered intellectual figure.

Race et histoire, commissioned by Alfred Métraux at UNESCO, was one of a series of pamphlets that formed a part of the UN's project to combat racism. It was a cultural relativist manifesto outlining positions that had been well rehearsed for many years in professional anthropological circles, but which were less known to the general public. Lévi-Strauss's main target was the nineteenth-century notion of cultural evolution, which had survived into the 1950s as the commonsense understanding of human history. This was the story of steady progression from primitive hunter-gatherer bands, through to more sophisticated agricultural settlements, then on to classical empires, culminating in the great European civilizations.

Aside from being highly conjectural, this version of events was merely a trick of perspective, argued Lévi-Strauss, the product of a distorted, ethnocentric vision. It was impossible to compare cultures, as each had specialized in different areas, working for solutions to different problems. Lévi-Strauss likened the process to the spin of a roulette wheel in a casino. The same numbers brought different yields, depending on the bets laid. Working their own systems, many cultures had succeeded where the West had failed. Inuits and the Bedouin had excelled at life in inhospitable climates; other cultures were thousands of years ahead of the West in terms of integrating the physical and the mental, with yoga, Chinese "breath-techniques" and "the visceral control of the ancient Maoris." Australian Aborigines, traditionally seen as at the bottom of the evolutionary ladder, had one of the most sophisticated kinship systems in existence. Polynesians had specialized in soilless agriculture and transoceanic navigation; philosophy, art and music had flourished in different ways around the globe.[35]

The counterattack came from Roger Caillois, a writer, sociologist and founding editor of the interdisciplinary journal *Diogène*. Superficially, Caillois's life had closely paralleled Lévi-Strauss's. In the interwar years he had mixed academia with surrealism, joining Bataille and Leiris in the short-lived experiment of the Collège de sociologie, set up to pursue Mauss's research into the sociology of the sacred, which combined surrealism and anthropology.[36] On the outbreak of the Second World War, Caillois found himself stranded in Argentina, where he taught and wrote. Like Lévi-Strauss, he had headed into the backlands, roving as far afield as Patagonia, subsequently writing eloquent accounts of his journeys. They met after the war in New York, when Lévi-Strauss, then cultural attaché, invited Caillois to give a talk. Both became acolytes of Dumézil; both developed a fascination for mythology. Their paths crossed again when they went head-to-head for Marcel Mauss's old chair, which Lévi-Strauss had ended up securing. Erudite, cultured, an intense thinker and poetic writer, Caillois could have been Lévi-Strauss's alter ego. "We ought to have got along," recalled Lévi-Strauss.[37]

But despite their similar formations, Caillois had come to radically different conclusions than Lévi-Strauss, which he explored in a critical review of *Race et histoire*, published in two parts in *La Nouvelle revue française*.[38] By the 1950s Caillois had cast off his youthful infatuation with surrealism, the irrational, the primitive, and was beginning to reassess his own sympathies. Surrealists and anthropologists like Lévi-Strauss saw their own society as sullied and hypocritical, and had naïvely sought purity, "safe at the opposite ends of the geographical spectrum."[39] For Caillois, Lévi-Strauss's veneration of preliterate cultures at the expense of the West was a question of inverse ethnocentrism—a twentieth-century disease of decadence and cultural malaise. Lévi-Strauss had perversely exaggerated the achievements of primitive societies. The complexities of aboriginal kinship systems said nothing about the aboriginal cultures themselves. What *was* an achievement, argued Caillois, was anthropology's attempts to model them. The West's openness to other cultures, the very existence of a discipline such as anthropology, was, for Caillois, a clear sign of superiority.[40]

In "Diogène couché," published in *Les Temps modernes*, Lévi-Strauss responded, launching a violent, thirty-three-page assault on Caillois. He reiterated his position, charging Caillois with crude ethnocentrism, accusing him of underestimating the mental efforts that went into constructing and sustaining so-called primitive cultures. Referring to his opponent as "M. Caillois" throughout, Lévi-Strauss pulled no punches. "America had its McCarthy and we have our McCaillois,"[41] he wrote, portraying Caillois as a dangerously paranoid apologist for the West. The debate—a classic progressive–conservative battle in the culture wars of 1950s France—rumbled on in the following issue, which published an exchange of letters between Caillois and Lévi-Strauss. "The Caillois–Lévi-Strauss controversy has been the big event in Parisian literary circles," Métraux wrote in a letter to the photographer and self-taught ethnographer Pierre Verger. "Lévi-Strauss's response is a masterpiece of reasoning, language and cruelty."[42]

Caillois's piece had clearly hit a nerve. "It made me very angry," Lévi-Strauss recalled.[43] Years later, Caillois remembered being shocked, rendered speechless by the vehemence of the counterattack. The aggressiveness was, indeed, out of character for Lévi-Strauss, but an undercurrent of defensiveness ran beneath the rhetoric. Perhaps the most wounding of all Caillois's criticisms was the accusation that Lévi-Strauss had been part of a group that was surrealist before being ethnographic. The implication was that Lévi-Strauss was an intellectual lightweight, following a poorly thought-out avant-garde vogue for the exotic, rather than a solid anthropological position.

Lévi-Strauss conceded that he was an "autodidact" where fieldwork was concerned, but distanced himself from the surrealists. He admitted to contributing articles to their magazines, but said that he had never really collaborated with them; he knew Breton, but their ideas were "completely different."

Maneuvering himself away from the avant-garde, Lévi-Strauss repositioned himself in far less controversial territory—back to the very French tradition of using primitive cultures as "tuning forks" in philosophical debates. His intellectual interest in the "primitive" was more classical, a part of a genealogy running from Montaigne and Rabelais and passing through Swift, Montesquieu, Rousseau, Voltaire and Diderot, "a tradition of Western thought that presses an exoticism, real or imaginary, into service for a social criticism." Contemporary fascination for the primitive was not merely a symptom of a twentieth-century *crise de conscience*, as Caillois had argued, but one that had produced classics such as *Essais*, *Discours sur l'origine de l'inégalité* and *Candide*. "I am not the person Caillois thinks I am," Lévi-Strauss concluded with a rhetorical flourish, writing that perhaps this person, "a wavering surrealist, an amateur ethnographer, a muddleheaded radical"—*surréaliste velléitaire, ethnographe amateur, agitateur brouillon*—was closer to Caillois himself.[44]

Lévi-Strauss was fighting for credibility, for gravitas in a small academic world that had already rebuffed him. He was trying to build his reputation as a serious academic, steering anthropology in a more rigorous, scientific direction. In this context, Caillois's charge of being a dilettante was wounding. But Lévi-Strauss would soon find that it was Caillois who was out of step with the mood of the nation. Its confidence destroyed by the years of occupation, France was about to suffer a further string of defeats, as the age of empire sped toward its conclusion.

Memoir

> A man lives two existences. Until the age of forty-five he absorbs the elements surrounding him. Then, all of a sudden, it's over; he doesn't absorb anything more. Thereafter he lives the duplicate of his first existence, and tries to tally the succeeding days with the rhythms and the odours of his earlier active life.
>
> Pierre Mac Orlan[1]

The French Empire, which had been in limbo through the occupation, had begun to unravel at the end of the Second World War. From the late 1940s on, there was unrest in Morocco, Cameroon, Madagascar and Algeria, with growing Vietminh resistance in French Indochina. In 1954, at Dien Bien Phu, a basin sunk into the hills of the modern-day Vietnamese–Laotian border, the French Empire went into retreat. After parachuting thousands of men in to secure a dilapidated Japanese-built airstrip, the French Expeditionary Forces were humiliatingly overpowered by Ho Chi Minh's army—pounded by artillery from the high ground and reduced to trench warfare in the jungle valleys. Months after losing Indochina, France faced rebellion in her North African *départements*. The National Liberation Front *maquisards* (guerrillas) launched attacks across Algeria, beginning the traumatic and drawn-out loss of what was then seen as an integral part of France itself. By the mid-1950s the colonial paradigm, which had shaped not just geopolitical arrangements, but French attitudes and culture, was beginning to fall apart.

Postwar France was gripped by a renewed sense of pathos and

disillusionment, but it was coupled with a growing interest in the non-Western cultures then emerging from beneath the imperial boot. Anthropologists became well-placed witnesses to this moment of revelation. Their field sites were at the margins of collapsing empires; the people they studied, after years relegated to bit parts in colonial sagas, were finding their voice. Culturally, the world was bending back on itself, rediscovering its own diversity, as one by one the imperial blocks began to disaggregate. The renaming of Lévi-Strauss's chair was symbolic of the shifting sensibilities. When he took up the post it was called Religions of Uncivilized Peoples (*Religions des peuples non civilisés*), a title that became less and less tenable. On several occasions Lévi-Strauss remembered having his interpretations challenged by the "uncivilized" people themselves—African students studying at the Sorbonne. He eventually succeeded in modernizing the chair's title to Comparative Religions of Peoples without Writing (*Religions comparées des peuples sans écriture*)—a firmer, more scientific designation, less likely to offend.

ONE OF THE many thinkers and writers who were sensing the changing mood was the geographer and ethnohistorian Jean Malaurie, a ruggedly handsome man with strong Gallic features, then in his late twenties. In the aftermath of the Second World War he had taken part in a series of scientific expeditions to Greenland. At around the same age as Lévi-Strauss when he had set off for Brazil, Malaurie had gone solo, traveling into the labyrinth of hummocks around Thule in the higher latitudes of the Arctic, in an expedition that had none of the trappings of Lévi-Strauss's adventures. "I landed in Thule on July 23, 1950 . . . after twenty-three days at sea," wrote Malaurie. "I immediately decided to spend the winter 150 kilometers farther north, in Siorapaluk: thirty-two inhabitants, six igloos . . . My equipment? There was none. I extracted permission from the Danish authorities to spend the winter there for one year once I was there."[2]

In spite of the remoteness of their territories, the Inuit were also living on the edge of empire. While traveling through the region by dogsled, Malaurie had stumbled across what at first appeared to be a monstrous mirage—a fenced-off compound housing an anonymous steel installation, the noise of machinery muffled by the snowfields. It turned out to be a top secret U.S. Air Force nuclear base, one of the many springing up as part of a developing Cold War logic. Even in these Arctic wastes, the West was on the move, bumbling blithely into Inuit territories, with no thought of the impact this might have. Although not trained as an ethnographer, Malaurie produced the first written genealogical records of these Inuit groups and became a passionate advocate of their culture.

On his return, Malaurie was out walking in Paris when, on the spur of the moment, he knocked on the door of the publishers Plon and proposed an account of his adventures. At the same time he put forward a new idea for a series of books to be called Terre humaine. His timing was perfect. Postwar, publishers in France were reworking their nonfiction lists, turning for inspiration to the new wave of the humanities to meet the needs of an expanding educated readership. In 1950 Gallimard launched Sartre and Merleau-Ponty's Bibliothèque de philosophie. The Bibliothèque de psychanalyse et de psychologie clinique and the Bibliothèque de sociologie contemporaine came out under the imprint Les Presses universitaires de France in the same year. Soon afterward Plon responded with two new collections: Recherches en sciences humaines (1952) and Civilisations d'hier et d'aujourd'hui (1953).[3]

Terre humaine would be subtly different from what had gone before. Malaurie envisaged a series that would be a collection of "*voyages philosophiques*" for the twentieth century, featuring modern-day savants on the move through the cultural hinterlands. The books would be intellectual but autobiographical, scientific yet engaged, feeding off the rich and largely unexplored literary terrain of indigenous cultures and ethnographic research.

By chance, Malaurie had come across Lévi-Strauss's complementary thesis on the Nambikwara while browsing in Paris's old university press library. He later confessed that he had found it boring, but while the ethnographic descriptions had left him cold, he had been captivated by the photographs—Lévi-Strauss's expressive images of the nomadic Nambikwara. Perhaps as a counterpoint to his own experiences in the Arctic, Malaurie looked to the tropics for one of the first books in the new series, asking Lévi-Strauss if he could write a nonacademic book about his experiences in Brazil.

Lévi-Strauss's *Tristes Tropiques* joined the collection's early titles along with Jean Malaurie's own *Les Derniers rois de Thulé*; Victor Segalen's docu-novel about his turn-of-the-twentieth-century experiences in Tahiti, *Les Immémoriaux*; and *Afrique ambiguë*, by anthropologist Georges Balandier. Later Malaurie mixed in the autobiography of Native American Don Talayesva, *Soleil Hopi*, for which Lévi-Strauss would write a preface, as well as Margaret Mead's *Sex and Temperament in Three Primitive Societies* and her controversial classic *Coming of Age in Samoa*, under the title *Moeurs et sexualité en Océanie*.

Tristes Tropiques was a book of loss, of mourning, a middle-aged lament for the passing of time. It came out of a particular period in Lévi-Strauss's personal life. On top of his divorce and related financial problems, his father, Raymond, had died in 1953. He had been hugely influential in Lévi-Strauss's early years, something that he would fully realize only much later. The cultural references that Raymond had imparted to his son would shape the latter part of Lévi-Strauss's career, and in interviews he would come back again and again to his experiences with his father.

Ironically, *Tristes Tropiques* represented a lowering of expectations around his career. Had he believed he was still in contention for the Collège de France, he later confessed, he would never have dared embark on something that could be seen as intellectually lightweight, but as it stood he felt he had nothing to lose. He had already dabbled with a more literary style of writing, with his abortive attempts at a novel. His notes from Brazil that had followed him around the world were still boxed up, a good deal of the material as yet unused. He was just entering middle age, trying to settle down and put his eventful past behind him. "I had a full bag that I wanted to unpack," he later said.[4]

Lévi-Strauss had also sensed that his academic work lacked a human dimension. In spite of his aloofness, he was, after all, flesh and blood. "I was sick of seeing myself labelled in universities as a machine without a soul," he told the historian François Dosse, with uncharacteristic feeling, "good only for putting men into formulas."[5] Nevertheless, he wrote *Tristes Tropiques* consumed by guilt, feeling that it was taking up time that should really have been devoted to proper academic work, like the second volume of his kinship studies, which he would never in fact write. This combination of guilt and liberation, the feeling that he was shirking his professional duties and the thrill that he might be burning his bridges once and for all produced an adrenal rush of activity. Over the winter of 1954–55, working at the astonishing pace of more than a hundred pages per month, he hammered through the first draft in "a permanent state of intense exasperation, putting in whatever occurred to me without any forethought."[6]

Written on a small German typewriter that Lévi-Strauss had picked up in a bric-a-brac shop in São Paulo, the resulting manuscript, held at the Bibliothèque nationale de France, is one continuous stream of words, with the occasional "*changer de page*" or "chapitre" typed midpage the only indication of a break in the narrative. As if working up a collage, Lévi-Strauss cut and pasted sections from old papers and notes onto the page, using strips of sticky tape, now brittle and yellowing with age. Whole chunks of his *petite thèse, La Vie familiale et sociale des Indiens nambikwara*, were included verbatim, stuck onto blank pages, modified only by replacing the academic *nous* with the more intimate *je*. Lévi-Strauss incorporated lectures, course notes and old articles. Chapter seventeen, for instance, which describes Lévi-Strauss's first disappointing fieldwork experiences among the Tibagy and the Kaingang in the state of Paraná, was culled from "Entre os selvagens civilizados" ("Among the Civilized Savages"), an article he had written for the culture supplement of the Brazilian national newspaper the *Estado de São Paulo*. Since his own notebooks on the Caduveo had disappeared during the war, parts of chapters eighteen and nineteen were lifted from his wife Dina's notes. And he filled out discussions of Nambikwara familial relations with an early Freudian interpretation of tribal dynamics, "The Social and Psychological Aspects of Chieftainship in a Primitive Tribe," published during the war in *Transactions of the New York Academy of Sciences*.

Many of the aphorisms that seem to crop up spontaneously were actually copied directly from a green notebook that Lévi-Strauss used to jot down ideas as they came to him, such as: "The tropics are less exotic, than out of date"; "Napoléon is the Mohammed of the West"; and "*Le moi est haïssable*" (The self is detestable). Above this last he wrote, in red, "*Pas de moi = il y a un* rien *et un* nous" (The absence of self = there is a nothingness and an us), which reappeared at the end of *Tristes Tropiques* as, "The self is not only hateful: there is no place for it between *us* and *nothing*."[7] (However, other interesting thoughts, like the cryptic "travel = the same and the reverse of a psychoanalysis," were left out.)[8] But there was much that was new, including a wealth of personal reminiscence, largely about Brazil, but also from his university days.

In between the spurts of speed-writing, some sections were labored over—particularly the often complex concluding sentences in which Lévi-Strauss tried to encapsulate his ideas on a given topic. In the preparatory notes he made for the book, there are five different versions of the last sentence in the section on Caduveo face painting, for instance. He ended up with a labored finale,[9] but perhaps he would have been better off with one of the versions he rejected—the less cumbersome and more lyrical "In this charming civilization the fashions of the female beauties evoke a golden age; laws are turned into poetry, and rather than be expressed in codes, are sung through their finery as they reveal their nudity."[10] But what is remarkable about the original manuscript is that it is in fact only lightly edited. Comments in crimson ballpoint and blue pencil are mainly minor tightening of language—*semble* becomes *est*, for instance, or redundant adverbs like *sans doute*, *complètement*, *profondément* are scored out, as are the odd flippant remarks. After a discussion of the erotic effect of Caduveo face designs, for example, Lévi-Strauss exclaimed, "Our powders and rouges pale in comparison!," but then decided against it.[11]

The extraordinary speed of production showed up in the finished product. The first edition was littered with misspelled Portuguese words, many of which were simply rendered phonetically. There were no notes or bibliography—a great shame in a book that drew liberally from such a wide range of sources. At times Lévi-Strauss fell prey to the errors that creep in when passages are lifted from old, dimly remembered notebooks. He had evidently forgotten that he had lightly fictionalized a number of anecdotes that he had planned to use in his novel, changing the names of protagonists. These episodes were reimported unchanged into *Tristes Tropiques*. And his thoughts on the relationship between Chopin and Debussy are remarkably similar to an exchange in *Sodome et Gomorrhe*, the fourth volume of Proust's *À la recherche du temps perdu*, although this may have been an intentional allusion.[12]

The upside was the fresh but slightly disorganized feel of stream-of-consciousness typing that still makes the book an infectious read. The central narrative—Lévi-Strauss's formation as an anthropologist, his posting in São Paulo and subsequent fieldwork in Mato Grosso—is constantly interrupted by pages on the idea of travel and travel writing, modernity's depressing uniformity, man's impact on his environment, the relative merits of world cities and religions. Sections of his aborted novel, the ideas for the play *L'Apothéose d'Auguste*, penned in desperation during a lull in fieldwork, stanzas of poetry that came to him in the Amazon, and thoughts on music crop up at intervals. At times the reader feels as if he is in a lecture theater, at others lumbering across the dusty savannah or tramping through the mulch of a tropical forest. By the end, as Lévi-Strauss takes on Islam, compares Buddhism to Marxism and muses on the ultimate futility of our quest for meaning, the reader seems to be inside Lévi-Strauss's head.

"*Je hais les voyages et les explorateurs*" (I hate traveling and explorers)—that first, posturing, deliberately provocative sentence announced the arrival of a new voice on the Parisian scene. The opening pages of *Tristes Tropiques* are a full-throttle rant against the whole genre of travel writing and the midcentury explorers and adventurers who entertained Parisian high society. For Lévi-Strauss they were frauds, evoking an exoticism that had long since disappeared, peddling stale genre prose like: "At five thirty in the morning, we entered the harbour at Recife amid the shrill cry of gulls, while a fleet of boats laden with tropical fruits clustered around the hull." The anthropologist, on the other hand, traveled only because he had to, wasting precious time hunting for truths—the myths, rituals or kin structures—that were hidden in the far-flung reaches of the world. The story of his adventures was merely "dross" obscuring his more scholarly findings.[13]

Yet at the same time, *Tristes Tropiques* is itself unquestionably a travel book of sorts, even as it parodies the genre. Perhaps there was an element of sly self-criticism in Lévi-Strauss's hierarchy between the anthropologist and the so-called explorer. We know from letters to the German anthropologist Nimuendajú that at times Lévi-Strauss felt like little more than a casual day-tripper himself: "I know absolutely nothing about the social organization of the Kaingang," he wrote in one. "I met them on what was in effect a tourist expedition, with no scope at all for work."[14] Even his longer expeditions have the weightless, itinerant feel of the explorer's restlessness that he excoriates in the first chapter of *Tristes Tropiques*. The sense of being constantly on the move, the descriptions of the rapidly changing environment and the mishaps—the herder Emídio's mutilated hand, Lévi-Strauss's own experiences of being lost on the savannah, the eye infection—are the staples of adventurers' tales.

In fact, *Tristes Tropiques* was a clever combination of travel writing and ethnography. One leavened the other in what was, after *L'Afrique fantôme*, Leiris's candid journal of his participation in Griaule's Dakar–Djibouti expedition, the first behind-the-scenes account of being an anthropologist. The ethnographer, Lévi-Strauss explained in an interview given following the book's publication,

> is like a photographer, condemned to use a telephoto lens; he only sees the natives, and he sees them in the minutest detail. Without renouncing all that, I wanted to enlarge the field, to admit the landscape, the non-primitive populations, the ethnologist himself at work or doubting, questioning himself about his profession.[15]

Like Leiris, Lévi-Strauss described the boredom and the uncertainties of the fieldwork experience, the false promises of the exotic and the realities of colonial frontiers. At the same time, *Tristes Tropiques* was hardly a wide-angled shot. What was missing were the others—Dina, Vellard and Castro Faria barely rate a mention; the drivers, the herders, the missionaries and the canoeists appear only fleetingly in what is often a more intimate drama between the anthropologist and "the savage." Sometimes it is as if Lévi-Strauss is alone in the field, communing with his informants, winkling out the secrets of their cultures.

The book has nevertheless become a landmark in anthropology. It was one of the first to blend confessional literature and ethnography, in what would become known as "reflexive" ethnography, a genre that would blossom from the 1960s onward. The impossibility of absolute objectivity in any scientific enterprise, acutely felt in the social sciences, brought ethnographers face-to-face with a philosophical dilemma, something that Lévi-Strauss grasped only after the fact. Again resorting to the camera lens analogy, he put a positive spin on a book that he had once seen as a distraction from his academic research:

> In retrospect, I must admit that in *Tristes Tropiques* there is a certain scientific truth which is perhaps greater than in our objective works because what I did was to reintegrate the observer into the object of his observation. It's a book written with a lens that's called a fish-eye, I think . . . It

> shows not only what is in front of the camera but also what is behind the camera. And so, it is not an objective view of my ethnological experiences, it's a look at myself living these experiences.[16]

A slow-burning pessimism, a lament at the progressive loss of our links—sensual, intellectual and cultural—to the world around us pervades the book. Its pathos caught the postwar mood perfectly, particularly in France. For Lévi-Strauss, globalization was creating a bleak world of architectural and cultural uniformity. Polynesian islands, once idylls of natural beauty, were being concreted over, while Asia's delicate network of local cultures was turning into vast gray suburbs. A world that from today's perspective seems relatively untouched was already sensing that the circle was closing. Man was soiling his own nest. "The first thing we see when we travel around the world," Lévi-Strauss wrote in despair, "is our own filth, thrown into the face of humanity."[17]

Anthropologists were but another aspect of Western expansion, their very presence a sign that the rot had already set in. By the time Lévi-Strauss's team had reached the Nambikwara, they were already cooking their meals in rusty jerry cans dumped by local motorboat operators. (Look closely at Lévi-Strauss's photographs of the Nambikwara and, in among the bows and arrows, gourds and woven baskets, there is also an assortment of smaller tins, planks of wood, bottles and enamel plates.)[18] Lévi-Strauss found himself "caught within a circle from which there is no escape." Centuries before, in a more diverse, culturally atomized world, travelers were exposed to untold riches, but through ignorance responded with indifference or active prejudice. Now, just as greater contact and interpenetration have opened these worlds up to us, they are disintegrating before our eyes, like parchments turning to dust in our hands.

More than a philosophy or a worldview, a whole style of thought was on display in *Tristes Tropiques* with Lévi-Strauss's trademark fascination with symmetry and inversion. The Buddhist sage and the Muslim prophet are polar opposites: "One is chaste, the other is potent, with four wives;

one is androgynous, the other bearded, one peaceable, the other bellicose, one exemplary and the other messianic."[19] Traveling from Europe to Brazil involved a threefold mutation—from the Old to the New World, from the northern to the southern hemisphere, from a temperate to a tropical climate; from being poor, he had become rich, prompting his transformation from the disciplined and thrifty to the spontaneous and profligate. A curious meal in the bush town of Rosário at the outset of the Serra do Norte expedition apparently consisted of half a chicken roasted and half cold; half a fish fried and the other half boiled.[20] Lévi-Strauss's mind was constantly fitting his experiences into geometric models, with axes, dimensions and inverse relationships. In *Tristes Tropiques* this comes across as a stylistic tic; in his more academic writings it was already becoming synonymous with structuralism as a method.

At the core of *Tristes Tropiques* was ethnography. Although many of the sections on the Nambikwara and the Bororo were reworkings of old material, the chapter on the Caduveo was a creative reinterpretation of what he'd seen on the Brazil–Paraguay borderlands fifteen years earlier. Casting his mind back to the Caduveo women and their strange arabesques, the interlocking designs that weaved across their necks and faces, Lévi-Strauss likened them to the playing-card characters in Lewis Carroll's *Alice's Adventures in Wonderland*. Like cards in a deck, the Caduveo patterns were characterized by similarity and difference, symmetry and asymmetry. It was a "hall of mirrors" effect—the inverted scrolls and arabesques refracting along axes, line playing off surface, angle contrasting with curve, pattern with background.

For Lévi-Strauss, these designs were not merely aesthetic inventions, passed down and perfected through the generations. They were subconscious meditations on structures found in traditional Caduveo social organization. This culture, a highly stratified system of intermarrying castes, which Lévi-Strauss compared to medieval European society, was in mourning for the loss of reciprocity to hierarchy, solidarity to division. The fissures and contradictions of their rigid social systems found expression in the subtle imbalances of the designs' alternating motifs. Caduveo art was in the last instance "a phantasm of society" expressing, at a subconscious level, the unease, the anxieties, the conflicts involved in being Caduveo.[21]

At the end of this strange yet somehow compelling analysis, Lévi-Strauss went one step further: parallels could be drawn between the formal properties of Caduveo art and Bororo hut plans. Although less dysfunctional than the Caduveo, the Bororo system had its own partially unresolved contradictions. It too was at once balanced and unstable, with its complicated combination of dual and tripartite social groupings. Lévi-Strauss's broader theoretical point was that structural echoes could be found in many aspects of social and cultural life—art, metaphysics, social systems, even the positioning of huts in a village. Again and again the human mind threw up similar relationships across domains that at first glance seemed completely unconnected.

What had previously been expressed in the hard-to-follow language of structural linguistics and technical kinship analysis had found its poetic expression. Shorn of their academic overlay, the ideas had a simple appeal. *Tristes Tropiques* hinted at a panhuman bond, even as it distanced Western thought from the output of indigenous cultures around the world. It showed indigenous culture in a new light, as creative but systematized, idiosyncratic yet ultimately of a piece.

DURING 1955 *TRISTES TROPIQUES* was unveiled to the public. A fifty-page extract first appeared in *Les Temps modernes* in August as "Des Indiens et leur ethnographe" (Indians and Their Ethnographer).[22] Taken from the middle of the book, the selection opened with a manifesto of the structuralist outlook:

> The customs of a community, taken as a whole, always have a particular style and are reducible to systems. I am of the opinion that the number of

> such systems is not unlimited and that—in their games, dreams or wild imaginings—human societies, like individuals, never create absolutely, but merely choose certain combinations from an ideal repertoire that it should be possible to define. By making an inventory of all recorded customs . . . one could arrive at a sort of table, like that of the chemical elements . . .[23]

Systems over individuals; instinct over creativity—this was hardly the kind of philosophical orientation likely to appeal to the journal's editors, among them Jean-Paul Sartre and Simone de Beauvoir. In the book itself, which appeared in October, Lévi-Strauss was more direct, taking calculated jabs at existentialism and the prevailing subjectivist philosophical mood. Existentialism's "overindulgent attitude towards the illusions of subjectivity," wrote Lévi-Strauss, reduced philosophy to "shopgirl metaphysics" (*métaphysique pour midinette*).[24] The core problem, as he saw it, was "understanding being in relationship to itself, not in relationship to oneself"—that is to say, mapping how facts in the world relate to one another rather than trying to grasp their particular import for us, how we perceive them or what we see as their significance. For Lévi-Strauss, existentialism agonized over the very material that should be filleted out and discarded. Even so, Sartre apparently liked *Tristes Tropiques* for the confessional intimacy of Lévi-Strauss's warts-and-all descriptions of fieldwork—what he saw as the revelation of the observer in the act of observing.[25]

Indeed, it was precisely Lévi-Strauss's grappling with his own "illusions of subjectivity" that made the book an unqualified success with the critics when it appeared in print in the autumn. The genre-bending mix of confessional, travelogue, philosophy and science brought forward comparisons to the great innovators of the past. Raymond Aron, writing in *Le Figaro*, likened *Tristes Tropiques* to Montesquieu's satirical epistolary novel *Lettres Persanes* (*Persian Letters*); *Combat* compared Lévi-Strauss to his boyhood hero Cervantes; while for the writer and critic François-Régis Bastide, Lévi-Strauss was the new Chateaubriand.[26]

For once nonfiction had trumped the novel as a vehicle for ideas and contemporary observation. *Tristes Tropiques* was avidly devoured not just by academics, but by artists like the playwright and key figure in the "theater of the absurd" Jacques Audiberti, who wrote congratulating him—the beginning of a long correspondence between the two. Even though, as a work of nonfiction, *Tristes Tropiques* was not eligible for France's most prestigious award for literary fiction, the Prix Goncourt, members of the academy issued a communiqué saying that they regretted they could not consider *Tristes Tropiques* for the 1955 prize. In an ironic twist, the following year Lévi-Strauss was offered another prize by the jury of the Golden Pen—for travel writing. He turned it down.

Tristes Tropiques's reputation soon spread beyond France. In 1957 the book appeared in Portuguese in Brazil, where the *Estado de São Paulo* gave it a glowing three-part review. As a historical memoir of Brazil in the 1930s, it was "one of the most remarkable studies ever written on contemporary Brazil," in a field in which impressionistic accounts written by foreigners predominated, although the piece went on to say that Lévi-Strauss was not beyond a form of European condescension in his more critical passages.[27] In the same year, although it had not yet been translated into English, the *Times Literary Supplement* gave the work a long front-page review; this was followed by another positive assessment in 1961 when the first English translation appeared under the title of *A World on the Wane*.[28] While in America, the critic Susan Sontag, writing in 1963 in the then recently launched *New York Review of Books*, hailed *Tristes Tropiques* as "one of the great books of our century." "It is rigorous, subtle and bold in thought," she continued. "It is beautifully written. And, like all great books, it bears an absolutely personal stamp . . ."[29]

Tristes Tropiques was certainly original in many respects, but Lévi-Strauss also drew heavily on his contemporaries. His memoir fit into a long tradition of French intellectuals leaving the metropolis behind for enlightenment on the road. It was the South American counterpart to André Gide's *Voyage au Congo* (1927), and owes much to Leiris's *L'Afrique fantôme* (1934). The tone of Paul Nizan's diatribe against French academia in *Aden Arabie* pervades Lévi-Strauss's much-cited early chapter "Comment on devient ethnographe" (rendered as "The Making of an Anthropologist" in the English edition). There are hints of Conrad and Proust, both of whom Lévi-Strauss greatly admired. His long passages on the geological impact of human settlement followed the writings of his friend and colleague the tropicalist geographer Pierre Gourou.

The French travel writer, novelist and professional flâneur Pierre Mac Orlan, whose books Lévi-Strauss had read and loved in his youth, provided another strand. Lévi-Strauss's explosive opening echoes Mac Orlan's *Petit manuel du parfait aventurier*—a long essay published in 1920, which took a philosophical look at the whole notion of travel. True exploration was at an end, Mac Orlan argued, dividing modern-day travelers into those driven by the need for conquest, fame or fortune and the more cerebral, contemplative type whose aim was to evoke a place, a people, a culture, rather than reach a destination. More generally, Mac Orlan's style of writing, his familiar, cosmopolitan tone, his combination of erudition and intimacy, his penchant for ports, backstreets and colorful lowlifes served as an unconscious template for Lévi-Strauss. After the publication of *Tristes Tropiques*, Lévi-Strauss was thrilled to receive a "particularly moving" letter of congratulation from Mac Orlan. "I knew I had written *Tristes Tropiques* with Mac Orlan in mind," Lévi-Strauss recalled after his retirement. "He probably liked my book because without realising it he found things in there that came from him."[30]

FOR MANY, *TRISTES TROPIQUES* was more than simply a mesmerizing read—it was life-changing. After reading it, Pierre Clastres switched from philosophy to anthropology and headed for South America. "I remember that Pierre Clastres was crazy about *Tristes Tropiques*, and had read it four or five times," recalled his friend and fellow convert Alfred Adler. The Belgian anthropologist Luc de Heusch, a student of Griaule's, had a similar revelatory experience. He had skimmed *Structures élémentaires* before setting off for fieldwork in Africa in the early 1950s. There he had set off on a Griaule-style quest, deep into the forests of the Belgian Congo. "In the utopian hope of gaining esoteric knowledge, I had myself initiated into a secret society, 'the masters of the forest.' But all the mysteries led to dead ends." He returned to France disillusioned. But he then read *Tristes Tropiques* and met Lévi-Strauss in his UNESCO office. "It was the beginning of a long dialogue," he recalled. "I might have given up ethnology, having been disappointed by fieldwork if, at this critical juncture, Lévi-Strauss had not revealed the possibility of a comparative study of 'archaic' societies." When he returned to Africa, de Heusch embarked on a structural analysis of Bantu myth.[31]

Jean Pouillon, the philosopher and close friend of Jean-Paul Sartre, was another of the many thinkers inspired by the book. After reading *Tristes Tropiques* he went back over all of Lévi-Strauss's published work, writing a laudatory summary—"L'Oeuvre de Claude Lévi-Strauss"—in *Les Temps modernes*.[32] (Intriguingly, in his review Pouillon referred to a forthcoming book by Lévi-Strauss entitled *Ethnologie et marxisme*, which never in fact appeared.) During this period Pouillon began attending Lévi-Strauss's seminars, before moving over to anthropology. By 1958 he was in Chad, savoring his own bittersweet experiences of ethnographic fieldwork.

The book had a crystallizing effect, drawing the disaffected into a new intellectual paradigm, as it evoked the brewing melancholy of a soon-to-be postcolonial France. Lévi-Strauss clothed new ideas with a world-weariness, giving them a gravitas that appealed to a certain type of intellectual. "I was sensitive to the pessimism, to this end-of-the-road aspect," remembered another of his future long-term collaborators, Michel Izard, about first coming across *Tristes Tropiques*.[33]

Through *Tristes Tropiques*, Lévi-Strauss was gathering acolytes, the foot soldiers of the coming structuralist revolution. But as his reputation grew, the critics circled. Caillois had attacked from the right; the historian Maxime Rodinson took him on from the left. Rodinson, a Jewish

Marxist historian specializing in the Middle East, had been radicalized early. As lower-middle-class tailors, his Russian émigré parents had joined the French Communist Party soon after its formation. They later perished in Auschwitz in 1943 while Rodinson was serving in Syria and Lebanon. In two articles for *La Nouvelle critique*, Rodinson picked up on what he felt to be Lévi-Strauss's ultimate political agnosticism. How could political progress be possible in a world of disparate cultural invention—each creation apparently as valid as the next? Coming from a Marxist perspective, Rodinson argued that anthropologists fetishized the trivial, putting games, material culture or rituals on an equal footing with core socioeconomic realities such as the division of property or labor. *Tristes Tropiques*'s relativist outlook, he concluded, denied the possibility of revolutionary change, a stance that would "bring desperation to Billancourt"—Paris's industrial hub, where the highly unionized Renault workers were fighting for better pay and conditions.

While parallels between French factory workers and Nambikwara nomads might seem far-fetched, many would share Rodinson's critique with more pointed examples from colonial conflict zones. In spite of Lévi-Strauss's diatribes against the West, his lofty philosophical tone refused political engagement. "Lévi-Strauss led us to this peaceful place," the anthropologist Alban Bensa told me. "It was a kind of escapism from the realities of twentieth-century indigenous life." Bensa, who has written classic ethnographies of the Kanak of New Caledonia, was one of the many anthropologists of the following generation who, like Rodinson, would come to question structuralism from a political perspective. He found its stillness and symmetry out of step with the violent late-twentieth-century world he was witnessing in New Caledonia. "Lévi-Strauss painted a perfect picture, of everything fitting into an overarching scheme. But when I started going into the field and seeing the effects of colonialism, I began to have my doubts."

In the 1950s, this strand of thought was typified by Georges Balandier, a key figure in the formation of anthropology in France. Like

Lévi-Strauss, Balandier had started out as a militant socialist; unlike Lévi-Strauss, his fieldwork in Africa on the eve of decolonization had radicalized him even further. Between 1946 and 1951, he worked in Senegal, Mauritania, Guinea, Gabon and Congo and became actively involved in the brewing emancipation movements. What he found there was not the wistful remnants of once great indigenous cultures, but grinding poverty and the political backlash against centuries of exploitation. Interviewed by historian François Dosse, he drew diametrically opposite conclusions to Lévi-Strauss's brand of hopeless pessimism:

> I can in no way accept the idea that in these societies myth shapes everything and history is absent, in the name of a notion in which everything is a system of relations and codes, with a logic of possible permutations that enables the society to maintain an equilibrium . . . societies are not produced, they produce themselves; none escapes history even if history is made differently and even if there are multiple histories.[34]

As colleagues and friends at UNESCO, Lévi-Strauss and Balandier were still on good terms in the 1950s, but would diverge thereafter. The more radical students—such as the left-wing writer and intellectual Régis Debray and anthropologists Marc Augé and Emmanuel Terray—attended Balandier's courses, forming a rift at the heart of the humanities in France. Decolonization, after all, was then being hotly debated as the struggle in Algeria intensified. While Balandier and his students protested against France's role in the war, Lévi-Strauss's interest in politics was declining—a radical position in itself, in an era in which political engagement was the sine qua non of the Parisian intellectual.

In France, colonialism—particularly in relation to the deteriorating situation in Algeria—had become the subject of passionate debate. Perhaps it was no coincidence that the year that *Tristes Tropiques* appeared Lévi-Strauss engaged in what would be his final high-profile political act.[35] He joined Jean-Paul Sartre, André Breton and Georges Bataille, among others, in signing a letter, published in November in *L'Express*, supporting the creation of a *comité d'action* (action committee) for peace in Algeria. But thereafter he shied away from political involvement. By the late 1950s he described political thinking as "an essentially emotional attitude," which had nothing to do with his role as a leading intellectual.[36] In 1960 he declined to participate in the high-profile "Manifeste des 121," a petition supporting Algerian independence, signed by a roll call of the era's leading lights.[37] Years later he would even forget that he had signed the 1955 letter.[38]

Even his rhetorical opposition to colonialism could have a conservative undertow. In 1956, he appeared to support the thinking behind Britain's catastrophic withdrawal from India, the aftermath of which he had witnessed firsthand, with this comment:

> Fifty years of modest, unprestigious research carried out by a sufficient number of ethnologists would have prepared Vietnam and North Africa for the solutions of the type that England managed in India—in a matter of months—thanks to the scientific effort that she had pursued for a century: maybe there is still time in black Africa and Madagascar.[39]

Politically, *Tristes Tropiques* may have pointed in the conservative direction in which Lévi-Strauss was drifting, but as a work of nonfiction, it was ahead of its time. Blurring the boundaries between serious academic literature, memoir and travel writing, he had created a hybrid that, although commonplace today, was rare in the 1950s, when the bulwarks between academic and popular writing were still fortified. This brought resentment from insiders, such as Paul Rivet, for whom the book was akin to a betrayal. He broke off contact with Lévi-Strauss, making peace only on his deathbed.[40] The disaffected, though, were far outnumbered by new readers, eager for a glimpse into the world of the professional anthropologist.

After the success of *Tristes Tropiques*, Lévi-Strauss was apparently still toying with the idea of continuing his literary writing career, perhaps as a journalist.[41] But it is difficult to imagine him sheering off at this point. If anything, his commitment to academia was strengthening. At the same time as he was fantasizing about feature writing, he was applying for funds from the Rockefeller Foundation to set up an anthropological institute (he was turned down), while continuing his courses at the École pratique des hautes études. In the winter of 1955–56 he returned to the more technical earlier work on kinship with a course entitled Prohibitions du Mariage.

In spite of his earlier rejections, through the second half of the 1950s his star began to rise once more. His financial problems now behind him, he moved back into the sixteenth arrondissement with his new wife, Monique Roman, into a solidly bourgeois apartment block where he lived until his death, and where I would meet him on a dark February morning half a century later. He installed his library, by then a formidable collection spanning the world, arranging his books not alphabetically or by theme, but geographically, with North America above Brazil, Africa under Europe. His new home was consecrated with the birth of his second son, Matthieu, in 1957. "My life had changed," recalled Lévi-Strauss.[42]

But the mere thought of Lévi-Strauss as a reporter or novelist is tantalizing. Sadly, *Tristes Tropiques* has remained a one-off. Other than the odd short essay, like his later reminiscences about wartime New York, he would never return to the genre. The passion that drove Lévi-Strauss to write *Tristes Tropiques* was extinguished as soon as it had served its purpose, just as its subject matter—his intense relationship with Brazil in the 1930s—had faded on his return to France.

Tristes Tropiques gallops to a close. As if receding into a mythical prehistory, the Bororo, Caduveo and Nambikwara disappear back into their remote forests and scrublands. The Brazilian backdrop changes abruptly to that of the Indian subcontinent, where Lévi-Strauss had recently traveled, the empty South American wastes giving way to the human density of the East. Days become centuries stretched into millennia, as Lévi-Strauss talks about all human history, world religions and philosophy.

He reserved his harshest judgment for Islam, a religion he saw as dangerously exclusive and xenophobic, incapable of seeing beyond itself and its own suffocating system. Its austerity, its combination of rigid rules, obsessive cleanliness and the marginalization of women made it "an ideal barrack-room religion."[43] Part of his revulsion had to do with an uneasy self-recognition. In Islam, Lévi-Strauss saw a reflection of certain tendencies in French thought: the same backward-looking orientation, the same blind faith in abstract solutions, the same dogged application of doctrine and a haughty disdain of other cultures.[44] Though himself a nonbeliever, he was not opposed to religion per se. "I get along better with believers than out-and-out rationalists," he told Didier Eribon. "At least the first have a sense of mystery—a mystery that the mind, it seems to me, is inherently incapable of solving."[45] But what he saw as Islam's doctrinaire approach rankled, and throughout his life he would air his dislike of the religion again and again, courting controversy in a progressively more multicultural, multifaith France.

In the final pages of *Tristes Tropiques*, Lévi-Strauss searched for an alternative. He returned to his stay in the Chittagong hill tracts, in a small, impoverished Buddhist village where the soft tolling of the gong mingled with the sounds of schoolchildren rote-learning the Burmese alphabet. Accompanied by village priests, he climbed barefoot through clayey soils up a hill to the *jédi*—a rudimentary pagoda composed of earthworks fenced off by bamboo. A thatched hut on stilts, with woven bamboo flooring, brass statues and a stag's head, served as a temple. After washing the mud from their feet, they went in. "A peaceful barn-like atmosphere pervaded the place and there was the smell of hay in the air," wrote Lévi-Strauss. The room was like "a hollowed-out haystack," and the muffled acoustics, the simplicity, the stillness drew him in as he observed the priests prostrating themselves before the shrine.[46]

Repelled by Islam, Lévi-Strauss found an intellectual kinship with Buddhism, which he saw as a corollary of his own philosophical outlook.[47] Like a Buddhist priest, he sought the erasure of the self and the dissolution of meaning. His structuralist method operated on a kind of a meditative loop of unanchored existence, endlessly combining and recombining elements, emptying them of their original significance. Buddhism was accepting of a paradox that underlined all human endeavor, summarized in Lévi-Strauss's unsettlingly convoluted formula: "Truth lies in a progressive dilating of meaning, but in reverse order, up to the point at which it explodes."[48] Both Buddhist and "savage" thought constantly edged toward this spiritual zone in which all distinctions between meaning and its absence fall away, where "fluid forms are replaced by structures and creation by nothingness."[49] The quest was one of total immersion, of unintellectualized embodiment. Like the seamless mixing of the religious and the everyday among the Bororo, who would conjure spirits with whirling bull-roarers in the men's house, where they also slept, worked and socialized, Buddhism appeared to integrate deep spirituality with everyday life, making each mentally attuned to the other.

The blend was seductive: on its own, structuralism could appear brutalist and reductive, but framed within Buddhism it took on an element of mystery. Just as Lévi-Strauss's raw materials—the dreamlike Pueblo myths, the colorful Bororo funerary rites, sensual body art and so forth—softened the blow of abstraction, so a hint of mysticism would help popularize his theories.

Yet his outlook could also be bleak. "The world began without man and will end without him," he wrote. Man's endeavors are merely a "transient effervescence," a fizzing chemical reaction destined to burn itself out, ending in sterility and inertia. Anthropology should be renamed "entropology," he concluded, since it is really recording a process of the breaking down, the dismantling of structures, as cultures like the Nambikwara disaggregate, losing their special forms and ideas.[50] The Nambikwara, as Lévi-Strauss had documented them, were already halfway there, scavenging on the edge of a degraded frontier.

"And yet I exist," Lévi-Strauss wrote, offering a glimmer of hope, only to go on, "not, of course, as an individual," but as a precarious stake "in the struggle between another society, made up of several thousand million nerve cells lodged in the anthill of my skull, and my body, which serves as its robot." There was no escape. From both the far-off vision of cosmological time to the intimacy of the self, all was infused with fatalism. Between the "transient effervescence" of human history and the "anthill" of Lévi-Strauss's skull there could be little hope, warmth or joy. In the end, the prose gathering pace for one last grandiose thought, all that we could hope for was direct, unmediated experience, the kind of raw sensuality that was still central to indigenous culture—the scent of a lily, the beholding of a precious stone, "or in the brief glance, heavy with patience, serenity and mutual forgiveness, that, through some involuntary understanding, one can sometimes exchange with a cat."[51]

The final chapters of *Tristes Tropiques* completed Lévi-Strauss's vision—a melancholic fusion of science, philosophy and asceticism. Just as his more academic work was looking forward with optimism to the new scientific horizons being opened up by linguistics and computing, so a backward-looking, romantic strain was merging with shades of Baudelaire, Mallarmé and Proust. This middle-aged bass note resonated through his mature work, introducing the hint of darkness and drama to an oeuvre that was finding its shape.

8

Modernism

At the middle of the century . . . an orientation away from mankind began. Once again one looked up to the stars and began an intensive measuring and counting.

KARLHEINZ STOCKHAUSEN[1]

IN THE MID-1930S, Lévi-Strauss had driven René Courtin's deteriorating Ford through the rust-colored earth of central Brazil. Out on the flats they had sped past a building site—"half vacant lot and half battlefield, bristling with electronic cable poles and survey posts." The future state capital, Goiânia, was being built from scratch on an empty plain.[2] By the late 1950s, a little to the east of Goiânia, architects had embarked on an even more ambitious project. Engineers marked out Brasília's *superquadras* onto a grid ruled into a low basin, a thousand kilometers from the coast. As the site was not yet connected by road, construction companies had to fly in thousands of tons of gravel, steel and machinery at exorbitant cost. Workers poured vast quantities of concrete, sculpting it into convex and concave forms, ramps and curved perimeters. By the end of the decade rows of ministry buildings lined the airplane-shaped design's central fuselage, a cascade of treeless lawns crisscrossed by multilane highways and overpasses. Later, geometric neighborhoods duplicated themselves down the wings.

Brasília was a peculiarly 1950s vision, built around clean lines and mathematical layouts. The era's models of tidy apartment blocks on stilts, sparse open spaces studded with evenly spaced shrubs, and cars whizzing along empty tarmac were spellbinding in miniature, but disorienting to scale. Architects Lúcio Costa and Oscar Niemeyer's original proposal had in fact been based on fifteen freehand sketches and a short statement. The detail—the population studies, economic or social-impact assessments, notions of how this blueprint would actually function as a living city—was absent. To this day, Brasília is a difficult city to walk around in.

In the mid-1980s, half a century after he had driven through the region, Lévi-Strauss stopped off in Brasília on a state visit with President Mitterrand. Remarkably, it was the first time he had been back to Brazil since his fieldwork days, not through lack of invitation or opportunity, but through an odd indifference to the country in which he had begun his career as an anthropologist and which had given him the raw material for his best-selling memoir. When I asked him what he had thought about Brasília, it was difficult to gauge any reaction, positive or negative. Probing a possible affinity between the ideas behind Brasília and structuralism, I met with Lévi-Strauss's hasty repudiation of any links between his own work and modernism. But what about his earlier association with the group of intellectuals that had formed around Mário de Andrade, a figure central to Brazil's nascent modernist movement in São Paulo? Lévi-Strauss was quick to clarify that he felt drawn to them for political, rather than artistic, reasons. They were a left-leaning oasis in an otherwise authoritarian desert, he explained.[3]

Yet Lévi-Strauss was of his time. He influenced and in turn was influenced by a specific cultural moment, a shifting of interests and orientations. In the 1950s a certain austerity reigned. Early modernism's hectic energy was dissipating, artistic expression cooling off into a more cerebral abstraction. It was a moment of stillness, of formal analysis, of simple furniture and anonymous suits. Echoes of the Lévi-Straussian turn toward disembodied systems were appearing across the arts. His blend of rationalism and mysticism, logic and enigma was in the air. A strain of thinkers, artists and musicians was delving into a more impersonal world of objects, colors and sounds and their relationships.

In a run-down studio in Paris, the composer Karlheinz Stockhausen was fiddling with primitive switchboards, shredding melody and cutting and splicing sounds, combining lifeless electronic noises into eerie soundscapes in his quest for "a structure to be realised in an Étude." Greek composer Iannis Xenakis was in Paris as well, composing a new kind of music that used models from the hard sciences to structure sounds spatially. Waveforms plotted on graph paper were converted into unsettling scores such as *Metastasis* (1953–55). Similarly, Pierre Boulez and Olivier Messiaen's serialism involved experiments with mathematical techniques of composition using abstract templates—grids of time codes, levels and pitch. As Alex Ross observed in his history of twentieth-century music, postwar avant-garde composition fit into a Cold War laboratory-experiment aesthetic. Gone were works named in the neoclassical fashion, the scherzos or sinfoniettas—"the archaic titles dropped from sight, replaced by phrases with a cerebral tinge: *Music in Two Dimensions*, *Syntax*, *Anepigraphe*. There was a vogue for abstracts in the plural: *Perspectives*, *Structures*, *Quantities*, *Configurations* . . . ,[4] as well as for high-tech parodies of tradition, such as Stockhausen's *Le Microphone bien tempéré* (1952).

In the visual arts, the baroque fantasies of the surrealists and expressionists gave way to a more distant, contemplative posture. On the canvases of Barnett Newman and Mark Rothko great blocks of color substituted visual narrative for rumination, while in France *art informel* was putting an abstract gloss onto improvisational techniques. Matter painting, the Color Field approach, Group Zero—Cold War art was emptying out content, delving back into an academic discourse around the very act of artistic expression. This was not the modernist optimism of the first-wave geometric abstract art—the Mondrians and the Maleviches—but rather a dimmed pensiveness, a trailing off. It referred not to some promised utopia, but to a mythic present, the mind in communion with itself.

French avant-garde fiction, which became known as the *nouveau roman*, was based on a similarly flattening effect. The novel's very substance—narrative timelines, plotting and believable characters with motivations—disappeared in a movement, as Alain Robbe-Grillet described it, away from "the old myths of depth" to "a flat and discontinuous universe where each thing refers only to itself."[5]

As the 1950s progressed, a new generation of thinkers was emerging in France. Sartre, de Beauvoir and Camus still dominated the scene in the aftermath of the Second World War, but they would soon be challenged by a different way of looking at the world. In 1953, the literary critic Roland Barthes published *Le Degré zéro de l'écriture* (*Writing Degree Zero*), which saw authentic writing as a constant battle against the stultifying effects of literary conventions. As Lévi-Strauss had already tried to demonstrate in the entirely different contexts of kinship and indigenous culture, in later books Barthes would go on to argue that absolute creativity was an illusion, writing being a game played out within the confines of the literary system. In 1954, the philosopher Michel Foucault was at Uppsala University in Sweden, scouring the Carolina Rediviva library's massive collection of seventeenth- and eighteenth-century medical texts for references as he began writing his thesis. His research would eventually result in *Histoire de la folie à l'âge classique* (later published in abridged form in English as *Madness and Civilization*), an epic study of the relationship between madness and reason through the ages. Foucault saw history less as a series of events than as a set of configurations, which would periodically rupture and metamorphose; madness became an arbitrary concept, drawing meaning only in relation to the shifting social mores of mainstream society. At the same time, Jacques Lacan was developing his heretical psychoanalytic work, reviving Freud through the prism of linguistics. The unconscious, Lacan argued, was "structured like a language."[6] As the self fragmented into chains of signifiers, Lacan continued his journey into the denser, more convoluted realms of the structuralist project.

Even history, a discipline that Lévi-Strauss had defined himself against, was moving in a more structuralist direction. Pioneered by the Annales school then headed by Fernand Braudel, Lévi-Strauss's former colleague at the University of São Paulo, the new history had stretched time out along "the calm, monotonous highways of the *longue durée*." Like a *nouveau roman*, incident and personality were eliminated; in their place were century-long trends: the rise and fall of food prices, glacial movements of population or gradual geopolitical realignment. Braudel wrote of "unconscious history," operating below the threshold of everyday experience at an imperceptibly slow pace. Constraints—of climate, geography, culture, mentality—could pen mankind into long periods of relative stasis.[7] This slow petrification fit the cultural mood of the 1950s like a glove. Once again man shrank before epic surroundings, entrapped in systems of which he was unconscious, yet dutifully replicating.

The fingerprints of Lévi-Strauss were all over these diverse projects. At different points, Lacan, Barthes, Foucault and Braudel openly acknowledged his impact on their thinking. Yet Lévi-Strauss always kept his distance, playing down any affiliation. In fact, with the exception of Lacan, with whom he remained a close friend (the Lévi-Strausses regularly dined with the Lacans in Paris and would visit their country house in Guitrancourt), he largely eschewed personal or intellectual contacts. Even with Lacan, his friendship was based more on the psychoanalyst's persona as a wealthy aesthete, art collector and bon vivant than as a theorist. Lévi-Strauss professed on several occasions not to understand Lacan's ideas. When he attended one of his seminars, he was impressed not so much by the content, but by the style:

> What was striking was a kind of radiant influence emanating from both Lacan's physical person and from his diction, his gestures. I have seen quite a few shamans functioning in exotic societies, and I rediscovered there a kind of equivalent of the shaman's power. I confess that, as far as what I heard went, I didn't understand. And I found myself in the middle of an audience that seemed to understand . . .[8]

For such an influential thinker, Lévi-Strauss trod a solitary path. "He was a lonely figure intellectually," Philippe Descola told me. "He cultivated close ties with Roman Jakobson and Georges Dumézil but was otherwise isolated."[9] And for someone who was profoundly interested in and moved by art and music, his eventual active disassociation from the avant-garde at midcentury is intriguing. In his academic work, traditional narratives were being broken apart, producing models that could be difficult to relate to the original subject matter. The resulting abstractions teetered between art and science. But the further Lévi-Strauss traveled down this route of methodological abstraction, the less he tolerated analogous experimentation in his own cultural milieu.

1955 WAS LÉVI-STRAUSS'S annus mirabilis. After the success of *Tristes Tropiques*, he returned to the academic side of his work with another landmark publication, "The Structural Study of Myth," which appeared in English in the *Journal of American Folklore*. Like Lévi-Strauss's article in *Word* on the application of linguistics to kinship, "The Structural Study of Myth" was a short think piece that laid the groundwork for decades of work. Just as the *Word* article broke the methodological ground for *Les Structures élémentaires*, so these twenty-odd pages provided the guiding ideas for Lévi-Strauss's magisterial *Mythologiques* quartet. The essay found him at his most radical, demonstrating a method that—although he would never admit it—cannot be dissociated from the prevailing late-modernist moment. It moves from narrative to abstraction, from literature to mathematics, deliberately disrupting a cornerstone of Western culture.

Myth was an area of growing interest for Lévi-Strauss. The telling of rambling stories peopled by strange animals, supernatural forces and the elements appeared to be deeply embedded in the human psyche. Individually, indigenous myths were chaotic, quirky narratives; collectively, common themes resonated. In one sense myths were dreamlike fantasies. In another, distilled through repetition, they became expressions of pure thought. With myth, Lévi-Strauss had an ample canvas on which to explore a subject that had fascinated him since his early contacts with Freud and the surrealists—the interplay between poetic expression and logic.

"The Structural Study of Myth" followed a familiar pattern: the statement of a perennial problem, the ridiculing of centuries of clumsy ad hoc theorizing, followed by a bold abstract solution, modeled on structural linguistics, which shifted the entire theoretical terrain. In the opening pages of the article, Lévi-Strauss briskly dispatched previous explanations. Notions that myths were metaphorical religions, collective dreams, reflections of actual social relations or fumbling protoscientific explanations reduced mythology to "idle play or a crude kind of philosophical speculation," doomed to end up as "platitude and sophism."[10] The core problem of past approaches was the attempt to read off sociological truths directly from the substance of a given myth. Once again, Lévi-Strauss drew the parallel to linguistics and its ill-fated attempts to pin certain sounds down to specific meanings—liquids to water, open vowels to large objects, and so forth. Only when words were detached from referents and language began being modeled as a formal system could real progress be made.

Following Saussure, Lévi-Strauss proposed breaking down mythic narratives into their constituent parts. These elements, which he coined "mythemes," were typically short summaries of narrative events (such as "sibling incest" or "brother and sister sacrificed") or characteristics of protagonists or things ("amorous" or "barren," "raw" or "cooked"). Once broken down into "mythemes," the analyst could order them into thematic columns, looking not just at discrete relationships between elements, but—again using a concept drawn from structural linguistics—"bundles of relations" (*paquets de relations*). Lévi-Strauss preempted criticism by stressing that he was applying linguistic theory to myth by way of analogy rather than direct correspondence. Myths, after all, were themselves made up of language; "mythemes," as short phrases, could not be analyzed in the same way as phonemes, mere fractions of words. Nevertheless, the carryover of ideas and concepts into a totally new field remained as ambitious and risky as ever.

To explain what at first reading seems bafflingly esoteric, Lévi-Strauss resorted to a Borgesian analogy. Alien archaeologists visit the Earth, post-apocalypse, and excavate a huge building, stacked with millions of pieces of paper bound in small, bricklike blocks and covered with ink symbols. They begin a long and painstaking analysis, eventually extrapolating an alphabet and key coordinates. The codes flow one way and one way only, they discover, from left to right and from top to bottom, in a flattened coil that—if stretched out—would form an almost endless string of sequences. But then the aliens come across a subset of papers, printed with sets of ruled horizontal lines plotted with squiggles, dots and arcs, which appear not to follow this iron rule. After trying and failing to decipher them, they realize that one line does not follow on from the next, but that the pieces of code have been stacked one upon the other; relationships, they realize, run up and down the page in a complex of harmony and dissonance.

The orchestral score became a favorite metaphor for Lévi-Strauss. The fact that its gridded staves, rigid time codes and keys could produce swirling, intensely romantic sounds was a paradox that fascinated him. By some mysterious process, logic was converted into emotion. Structurally, the score appealed to Lévi-Strauss's diagrammatic approach. The stacking up of different yet closely related elements down the score's page—the parts of the cello, the flute, the timpani and the bassoon, for instance—wending together to form an aesthetic whole, became for Lévi-Strauss a key image for an understanding of how culture was structured.

Read from left to right like a text, as the alien archaeologists had at first tried to do, the score became a juddering series of inversions, repetitions and thematic variations. In an imaginative leap, Lévi-Strauss found that this resonated structurally with the composition of mythic narrative, which abounded in echoing themes, unexpected plot twists and sudden reversals. If one could only read a myth vertically, in the same way as a musician reads a score, he reasoned, lining up the myth's narrative harmonies and counterpoints, uncovering its leitmotifs, its essence could be revealed.

With a theatrical flourish, Lévi-Strauss chose the central Western myth, Sophocles' *Oedipus Rex*, for his demonstration. Like a Brion Gysin cut-up, Lévi-Strauss spliced the myth into a collage of events and characters. From the fragments, certain themes emerged, which he ordered into a table of four columns. The myth could now be read in two directions. From left to right was the familiar narrative—*Oedipus*'s drawn-out realization of his horrific past. But Lévi-Strauss was more interested in the scorelike columns, where elements of the story were clustered in contrasting themes. The exercise was eccentric but riveting, the essay up to this point a virtuoso display of intellectual acrobatics and intuitive audacity.

The first column, which included Oedipus marrying his mother and Antigone contravening a ritual taboo by burying her brother, was said to represent an exaggeration of blood relations; the second, which had Oedipus killing his father and Eteocles slaying his brother, expressed an underrating of blood ties. Lévi-Strauss's explanation of the third and fourth columns, which were headed "Monsters being slain" (Cadmos killing the dragon and Oedipus the Sphinx) and "Lameness" (Oedipus's swollen feet at birth, his father Laios's "left-sided" posture) respectively, was more complicated. Difficulty in walking is recurrent in mythology in characters born from the earth, appearing in Pueblo and Kwakiutl myths, explained Lévi-Strauss; monsters are otherworldly. Hence the opposition was between the persistence versus the denial of man's earthly origins—a line of reasoning that the British anthropologist Edmund Leach later described as "vaguely reminiscent of an argument from *Alice through the Looking Glass*."[11]

In the closing pages Lévi-Strauss drew the strands together. The Oedipus myth was really about the fundamental conflict between the Greek religious theory that man, like plant life, was born of the earth, and the knowledge that humans result from blood relations in the union between a man and a woman. On the surface, *Oedipus Rex* told a story—the tragedy of a man who unwittingly marries his mother and kills his father—but underneath, at a deep structural level, the myth was a logical configuration—a portrait of the mind as it subconsciously ruminated on intractable social contradictions, in this case between religious belief and worldly realities.

Like Freud's *Interpretation of Dreams*, Lévi-Strauss's project was setting off in an increasingly idiosyncratic direction. How many theorists would have arrived at the same conclusions as his reading of *Oedipus*, even if they were trying to apply his own structuralist methods? Who, other than Lévi-Strauss, would have made the leap from the slaying of monsters to swollen feet to the earthly origin of man? Or from the binding of Oedipus's feet at birth to limping in Pueblo and Kwakiutl myths? And yet in his concluding remarks, this essentially interpretive exercise masqueraded as something far more exact, as if Lévi-Strauss was approaching myth as a scientist would a crystal or a gas, divining its behavior through experimentation. The logic of mythic thought, Lévi-Strauss concluded, "was as rigorous as that of modern science"—so rigorous, in fact, that it could be reduced to a single mathematical formula, the "genetic law of myth": $F_x(a) : F_y(b) \simeq F_x(b) : F_{a-1}(y)$.[12]

It is difficult to grasp Lévi-Strauss's own brief explanation of what this formula actually means, or see how it could be systematically applied. It seems, in fact, not to be a formula at all—in the sense of being a prescribed method for consistently achieving a given outcome—but rather a modeling of a narrative structure, using mathematical symbols as shorthand, in this case the "*torsion surnuméraire*" or "double twist": a kind of warped version of the simpler A is to B as C is to D (A : B :: C : D) that he had used in his analysis of the avunculate.[13] But followers of Lévi-Strauss need not have worried about the detail—they would wait ten years before the equation was even mentioned again in the second volume of the *Mythologiques* series, *Du miel aux cendres* (*From Honey to Ashes*). "It was necessary to quote it at least once more as proof of the fact that I have never ceased to be guided by it," Lévi-Strauss explained, in a curious allusion that has almost religious overtones.[14]

If one ignored his overblown claims to scientific rigor, though, the exercise did redefine problems in the field of mythology in an interesting and potentially productive way. Just as with kinship, it gave the analyst a point of purchase in an otherwise mystifyingly random field. In true Lévi-Straussian fashion, complex arguments had an ultimately simplifying effect. The abstract bundling into themes and oppositions meant that small variations in different versions of the same myth could be accounted for within the same overall structure. The search for the earliest or truest version was no longer necessary. Across continents, mythic elements endlessly combined and recombined, like the shuffling of genes down the generations. It was this type of epidemiological approach that Lévi-Strauss would spend much of the rest of his academic life exploring, as he took on myth in bulk, looking at hundreds of mythic variations sourced from across the Americas.

If the structural analysis of a single myth could seem arbitrary, the bulk approach felt far more convincing. Lévi-Strauss's analysis of four different versions of "La Geste d'Asdiwal" (The Story of Asdiwal), published the following year, took the argument into another dimension. Looking at the variations of a Pacific Northwest Coast Tsimshian myth compiled by Franz Boas, Lévi-Strauss found that the differences were systematic, and were themselves part of a structural logic. When the myth traveled from its source into neighboring cultures, it began to degrade. But at a certain point the myth would flip over, reconfiguring itself into an inverted form. He likened the result to optical projections in a light box. As the aperture is reduced, the image begins to blur until, at a pinpoint, the image clarifies, but is upside down and back to front.[15]

In Lévi-Strauss's mind, myth was almost like a living thing or a physical process. Like a crystal, "a myth grows spiral-wise until the intellectual impulse that produced it is exhausted," Lévi-Strauss wrote.[16] The idea that a poetic realm of jaguars and anteaters, rivers and stars dreamed up by small, low-tech indigenous groups could ape the symmetries found in natural phenomena and mathematical equations caught the imagination of a generation of scholars. This, and the avant-garde vitality of the splice technique, dazzled his contemporaries. *Tristes Tropiques* had given him a popular base outside the academy, just as the sheer originality of his ideas on myth was consolidating his position within it.

STRUCTURALISM'S GROWING APPEAL was not just intellectual. Lévi-Strauss's ideas became attractive at a particular political moment, a point of weakness and uncertainty on the French Left. For many progressive intellectuals, postwar France had been a period of political commitment to the French Communist Party and Marxism. Some, most famously Jean-Paul Sartre, had embraced Stalinism, even as reports of the regime's crimes were filtering out. In the mid-1950s, Lévi-Strauss still felt the need to refer to Marx, going as far as naming him in *Tristes Tropiques* as one of his key influences. "I rarely broach a new sociological problem," he wrote, "without first stimulating my thought by rereading a few pages of *The 18th Brumaire of Louis Bonaparte* or the *Critique of Political Economy*."[17]

But by the end of 1956, all this had changed. In March of that year, as the situation in Algeria deteriorated, the French Communist Party voted in favor of sending four hundred thousand troops to quell the dissent, a move that alienated many of its supporters. That June, Nikita Khrushchev's speech to the Twentieth Congress of the Communist Party was published in full in *Le Monde*. Khrushchev had accused Stalin of presiding over a reign of terror, involving the threatening and executing of his own party members, such as Comrade Eikhe, a loyal, long-term party member, executed in 1940 after being forced to sign a confession under torture. On top of these revelations, November saw the crushing of the Hungarian uprising. As Soviet tanks streamed through the streets of Budapest, the left-wing Western intelligentsia was thrown into crisis.

Although the French Communist Party would remain a potent political force, its credibility had sunk. Intellectuals fled the party as up-and-coming thinkers went in search of a new paradigm. It was "a kind of ceremonious massacre," remembered sociologist René Lourau, then twenty-three years old. "This made possible a clean sweep, a big breath of fresh air, a hygienic act."[18]

Lévi-Straussian structuralism rushed into the ensuing ideological vacuum—except that structuralism, as a detached, abstract science of culture, was itself a kind of vacuum. And that was precisely its appeal. Sloughing off the baggage of postwar politics, Lévi-Strauss offered a way out. Suddenly, arcane analyses of tiny South American tribes began to look attractive, even inspired. The new paradigm "let us stop being forced to hope for anything," as Michel Foucault later recalled.[19]

The fallout from the Left, and the impact of *Tristes Tropiques*, produced the next generation of anthropologists, as young, disaffected scholars were drawn into the orbit of Lévi-Strauss's developing program. Communist philosophers Alfred Adler, Michel Cartry, Pierre Clastres and Lucien Sebag quit the PCF in 1956 and began attending Lévi-Strauss's seminar courses at the Sixth Section. Before long, Sebag and Clastres were doing fieldwork in the Americas, while Adler and Cartry headed for Africa. Another key figure in the development of structural anthropology, Françoise Héritier, who would end up as Lévi-Strauss's successor at the Collège, made the move from history to anthropology, doing fieldwork in Upper Volta (present-day Burkina Faso), along with her future husband and collaborator, Michel Izard.

For the new converts, tracking the evolution of Lévi-Strauss's thought was not an easy task. Given his peripatetic early career, articles were now spread out through Brazilian, U.S., British, Dutch and French anthropological, sociological and linguistic journals, some available only in English. Feeling that these threads were now coming together into a coherent statement, Lévi-Strauss had already tried to draw them into an anthology, approaching the writer Brice Parain, who was then commissioning for

France's leading publisher, Gallimard, with the idea. He was turned down on the grounds that his thought "hadn't matured."[20] Parain would live to regret his decision. (He would later compound his mistake by rejecting another seminal thinker's early work—Michel Foucault's *Histoire de la folie*.) After the success of *Tristes Tropiques* at Plon, Lévi-Strauss had become hot publishing property, and Gaston Gallimard himself, founder of the publishing house, was called in to woo him. But the charm offensive was to no avail—Lévi-Strauss would remain loyal to Plon for the rest of his writing career.[21]

The resulting *Anthropologie structurale* (*Structural Anthropology*) (1958) brought together Lévi-Strauss's canon in one place for the first time. The classics were placed side by side, from Lévi-Strauss's groundbreaking early paper on kinship and linguistics to his essays on shamanism and psychoanalysis. There were the more recent explorations of myth and some earlier curiosities such as "The Serpent with Fish inside His Body," a short paper he had given in Paris at the end of the war, which drew parallels between an Andean myth and motifs on Nazca and Pacasmayo vases. At the last moment, Lévi-Strauss added in two postscripts to settle scores with his critics: Gurvitch and Rodinson, along with Jean-François Revel, who had recently published an attack on Lévi-Strauss in *Pourquoi des philosophes?* (*What Are Philosophers For?*).[22]

The dedication, strangely enough, was to Émile Durkheim, whose work Lévi-Strauss had repudiated in his youth as conservative and socially prescriptive; 1958 was the centenary of Durkheim's birth, and Lévi-Strauss paid homage as "an inconstant disciple" to the man who had fashioned the tools of modern anthropology. "There was something brilliant in the thought of Durkheim," he said later. "It was beautifully constructed, monumental."[23]

EARLIER IN HIS CAREER, it might have seemed as if Lévi-Strauss had suffered from bad timing. After Brazil, the war had disrupted his progress through the French academic system. On his return to France he had missed the postwar boat, repeatedly blocked by conservatives in the Collège de France. But in the final years of the 1950s, everything clicked. With *Anthropologie structurale*, Lévi-Strauss had loaded the more accessible *Tristes Tropiques* with the intellectual ballast he had patiently stored up through his academic career. His first forays into the world of indigenous mythology presaged a whole new body of innovative, challenging work.

Lévi-Strauss was finding his feet on the eve of the most radical theoretical and institutional upheaval in the humanities in postwar France. A massive expansion of higher education was already under way. The number of students gaining the baccalaureate rose sevenfold from the 1930s to the 1960s. As students poured into the university system, research boomed. In 1955, there had been just twenty social science research centers in France; by the mid-1960s, there would be more than three hundred.[24] The period of the *trente glorieuses*—three decades of unprecedented economic growth in France, spanning from 1945 to 1975—was reshaping the country, ushering in a more modern, technocratic ethos. In the shake-up, old-style scholarship would lose ground to sharper, more quantifiable methods. In the humanities this meant sociology and the new history's statistical approaches, along with abstract model-building in linguistics and psychoanalysis. In this new environment, Lévi-Strauss's stock was rising fast.

By the end of 1958, Lévi-Strauss was receiving the backing of Merleau-Ponty, a key bridging figure who was trying to reconcile the formal schemes of structuralism and phenomenology's excavations of the self. Merleau-Ponty had succeeded in creating the first chair in anthropology at the Collège de France[25]—a position designed specifically for Lévi-Strauss. The following year, Lévi-Strauss was put forward as a candidate while Merleau-Ponty aggressively lobbied fellow members of the Collège, trying to placate the more conservative wing. "Not only did he present it [Lévi-Strauss's candidacy], he devoted three months of his life to it, and he was not to live much longer," remembered Lévi-Strauss, who in gratitude kept a photo of Merleau-Ponty on his desk.[26] Again there was some opposition, but thanks to Merleau-Ponty's support, Lévi-Strauss, now fifty, entered the Collège on this, his third attempt, banishing forever what he would later describe as his "awkward past" (*passé aussi lourd*).[27]

HIS INAUGURAL ADDRESS, delivered in January 1960, opened with an old-fashioned riddle based on "the strange recurrence of the number 8, already well known from the arithmetic of Pythagoras, the periodic table of chemical elements and the law of symmetry of the medusa jelly fish." To these were added a series of dates: in 1858 the "engineers of social anthropology," Durkheim and Boas, were born; 1908 saw the creation of the world's first university chair for social anthropology, given to Sir James Frazer at the University of Liverpool; and in 1958, the Collège had finally created one in France. Lévi-Strauss, of course, had also been born in 1908—as had Merleau-Ponty, who was sitting in the audience and was apparently unhappy to be reminded of his age.[28]

Lévi-Strauss went on to place his work in the context of the greats, referencing, among many others, Saussure, Freud, Marx, Montesquieu, Spencer, Cuvier, Goethe, along with the usual roll call of anthropologists—Boas, Durkheim, Frazer, Mauss, Radcliffe-Brown, even Malinowski. He lingered over Mauss and his development of the almost mystical notion of the "total social fact"—"a foliated conception . . . composed of a multitude of distinct and yet joined planes . . . where body, soul, society, everything merges."[29]

While outlining his ideas on kinship and myth, he made his peace with history. The two met in slow motion. With the *longue durée*, history had almost come to a standstill. In a gesture of conciliation, Lévi-Strauss gave his crystalline structures minimal animation. "Structure itself occurs in a process of development . . . ," he said, citing Durkheim. "It is ceaselessly forming and breaking down; it is life which has reached a certain degree of consolidation . . ."[30]

He ended on a wistful note, lamenting the fact that the chair had not been created hundreds of years earlier, when Jean de Léry and André Thevet were writing about the Tupi, still padding barefoot through the forests and beaches of Rio de Janeiro's Guanabara Bay. (He later told Didier Eribon that this was also an allusion to the fact that he had been denied a chair a decade earlier.) "Men and women who, as I speak, thousands of miles from here, on some savannah ravaged by brush fire or in some forest dripping with rain," he wound up, "are returning to camp to share a meagre pittance and evoke their gods together." It was to these ragged groups, on the brink of extinction, that Lévi-Strauss as "their pupil, and their witness" dedicated his chair.[31]

He had entered a rarefied world of tradition and protocol. Merleau-Ponty eased him through the first rituals, providing a floor plan of the chamber where the professors met and reserving the chair next to him so that Lévi-Strauss was spared the embarrassment of sitting in someone else's place. But beyond the old-world ceremonials lay great opportunities in an elite institution devoted solely to the cultivation of the mind. As the 1960s dawned, Lévi-Strauss's only official duties were to present original courses every year, with the expectation (backed by resources) that he would set up his own research center.

His dominance in the 1960s and early '70s would rest not just on his originality and intellectual charisma, but on something far more prosaic—his skills as an institution builder at a time when the French academic system was opening up. As a student he had run a left-wing study group before becoming the personal secretary of the socialist *député* Georges Monnet. In New York he had been head of the École libre and cultural attaché at the French embassy. Back in Paris he was assistant director of ethnology at the Musée de l'Homme and secretary-general of UNESCO's International Social Science Council. Once elected to the Collège, he set about building up his own institutional empire.

Its beginnings were humble. Lévi-Strauss's research center, the Laboratoire d'anthropologie sociale, was initially housed in a building attached to the Musée Guimet in the sixteenth arrondissement on avenue d'Iéna, not far from the Musée de l'Homme. Inside the main building, thousand-year-old Indian, Cambodian and Japanese Buddha heads were on display, the fruits of the nineteenth-century Lyonnais industrialist Émile Guimet's collecting expeditions to India and the Far East. The serenity of the gallery space was far from the realities of Lévi-Strauss's ramshackle offices—the remains of an en suite bathroom that he shared with Jean Pouillon. "Pieces of pipe still stuck out of the walls, which were covered with ceramic tile," remembered Lévi-Strauss, "and I had what was left of the bathtub drain under my feet."[32]

An adjoining room was piled high with the Human Relations Area Files—a vast paper database covering hundreds of cultures that UNESCO had secured for France, produced by a conglomeration of U.S. universities. The files, which cross-indexed individual cultural features such as methods of food preservation (dried, smoked, pickled, and so forth), aspects of religious systems and kin terms, was a structuralist storehouse, perfect for Lévi-Strauss's style of work, saving hours of library research. With their emphasis on North America, the Area Files would be crucial as he began looking at the western hemisphere more and more as a single cultural block.[33] So bulky was the accumulation of files that there were fears that the floor would give way under them. Isac Chiva, a pioneer of French rural ethnography who would work closely with Lévi-Strauss as his deputy director at the Laboratoire, remembered their astonishment when Susan Sontag described their cramped rooms as "a large and richly endowed research institute" in her review of *Tristes Tropiques* for the *New York Review of Books* in the early 1960s.[34]

It was in these less than ideal surroundings that Lévi-Strauss met the then up-and-coming literary theorist Roland Barthes, who was looking for a supervisor for his thesis on fashion. Barthes later remembered being received by Lévi-Strauss on the landing on a pair of worn-out lawn chairs while his friend, the semiotician Algirdas Julien Greimas, waited anxiously in a café around the corner. Barthes returned to the café deflated—Lévi-Strauss had turned him down. The meeting, however, would turn out to be influential. During their talk, Lévi-Strauss suggested that Barthes read Vladimir Propp's *Morphology of the Folktale*, which was first published in the 1920s but had recently appeared for the first time in English translation. The book's proto-structuralist analysis of folktales would go on to have a major impact on the development of Barthes's ideas on "narrativity."[35]

Despite early similarities between their work, Lévi-Strauss grew progressively more skeptical of Barthes's project. "I never felt close to him," Lévi-Strauss later recalled, "and my feelings were confirmed later by the direction that his ideas took." In the 1970s, Lévi-Strauss was asked to write a preface to Barthes's book *S/Z*, a structuralist analysis of "Sarrasine," a short story by Balzac. When Barthes sent Lévi-Strauss a copy of the book, Lévi-Strauss replied with a short parody of the structuralist method, including male/female oppositions, a kin diagram and the conclusion that two characters in the short story, Filippo and Marianina, were in an incestuous relationship. Even though it was written as a joke, Barthes apparently took the analysis seriously, describing it as "stunningly convincing."[36]

The letter revealed a mischievous side to Lévi-Strauss, which undercut his reputation as a cold, analytical thinker. Toward the end of her life, Margaret Mead told anthropologist Scott Atran that although Lévi-Strauss appeared "aloof and frail," "he's more playful than he lets on and he'll outlive me by thirty years if a day."[37] (In the event, Lévi-Strauss survived Mead by thirty-one years.) But his practical jokes were not always shared by their intended targets. In the mid-1950s, André Breton was trying to develop a project on magic. He sent out questionnaires, which involved ranking pictures as more or less magical, to his friends, including Lévi-Strauss. By this stage skeptical of Breton's dilettantish interest in what he considered a serious anthropological subject, Lévi-Strauss ignored the questionnaire. When Breton sent it again, Lévi-Strauss gave it to his seven-year-old son, Laurent, to complete. Breton was furious, firing off a wounded letter to Lévi-Strauss and later sending him a copy of the resulting book, *L'Art magique*, with a brusque dedication to Laurent.[38]

HIS REPUTATION NOW ESTABLISHED, Lévi-Strauss was also benefiting from a quantum leap in the exposure of intellectual figures to the French public—the advent of arts programming on television. *Lectures pour tous* began broadcasting in March 1953. It ran on prime-time television, going on at nine thirty at night, on what was then the only station on air. Austere, studio-based interviews featured both well-established and up-and-coming thinkers, including the philosophers Gaston Bachelard and Raymond Aron, the philosophical historian Michel Foucault and the writer Albert Camus, as well as Lévi-Strauss himself. For the first time the broader public could actually see these people—from Bachelard's flowing beard and straggly white hair to Foucault's more severe balding pate—and construct a living image to fuse with the ideas.

In 1959 Lévi-Strauss was interviewed by Pierre Dumayet, discussing the book *Soleil Hopi*, for which he had contributed a preface.[39] Originally published by Yale University Institute of Human Relations in 1942 as *Sun Chief: The Autobiography of a Hopi Indian*, the book became one of the early editions in Plon's Terre humaine series. It followed the life of Don Talayesva, who had told his story to a Yale anthropologist for thirty-five cents an hour. Seated in a dark studio against the backdrop of what appears to be a semiabstract mural of billowing clouds, stars and serpents, Lévi-Strauss responded with efficiency to interviewer Dumayet's questions, situating Talayesva's account with overviews of the Hopi, their history and their contemporary problems. He came across as a highly literate technician. In a curious way this worked, as his relative formality played off against the exoticism of his subject matter.

Later that year, Lévi-Strauss gave a series of radio interviews to producer Georges Charbonnier, which were broadcast on Radiodiffusion-Télévision française (RTF) in the autumn.[40] In a new departure for Lévi-Strauss, the discussion broadened out from anthropology to contemporary culture, including some revealing discussions about modern art and music. As a young man Lévi-Strauss had been fascinated by the developing strands of modernism. But by now he was middle-aged, and disillusionment with modern art was setting in. For Lévi-Strauss, the great ruptures that had thrilled him in his youth had led nowhere. The path to abstraction had become a story of failure as modern art degenerated into a series of follies and empty aesthetic gestures.

In the Charbonnier interviews he sketched out how he saw this process unfolding. The first truly modern movement, impressionism, was an attempt to push past the studied, academicized representation of an object—the rule-bound conventions of the past—and represent reality "in the raw." For this it scaled back ambition, retreating from the grand, wide-angled landscapes to the more intimate portraits of rural and urban life—the haystacks, railway bridges and parks. But it was an essentially "reactionary revolution," "superficial and only skin-deep"—and it was merely trying to refine techniques of representation.[41] Cubism had provided the radical break. Cubist artists were genuinely revolutionary in their rediscovery of nonrepresentational aesthetic meaning—the patchwork of sensual and conceptual associations that hung around a given object.

Art critic Robert Hughes has said that cubism was based on the idea that "reality is not figure and void, it is all relationships, a twinkling field of interrelated events."[42] The statement has a structuralist flavor, and the fact that artists like Picasso had drawn inspiration from indigenous artifacts hinted at possible affinities. But as his thought developed, Lévi-Strauss became more and more skeptical of the movement. Whereas "primitive" art was a collective enterprise, embedded in the societies in which it was produced and fused with their ritual and religious lives, cubism was a contrived escape into an individualized aesthetic world. While artists like Picasso self-consciously juggled different styles, producing pastiches of previous ideas as they went, others were retreating into arid abstraction. The outlook was bleak. Across the arts, the West had reached an impasse. The fact that people were "deliberately and systematically trying to invent new forms . . . is precisely the sign of a state of crisis," Lévi-Strauss concluded. It was possible that the West was even entering an apictorial age in which art would disappear altogether.[43]

This was not to say that Lévi-Strauss believed that abstraction per se was always bad. A Mongolian shaman who daubed the walls of a sick person's house with a mural of semiabstract images representing various episodes from his dreams was an example of aesthetic creation of the highest order. But at the same time modern artists' attempts to return to this unself-conscious expression through experimentation were somehow reprehensible. "We have become divorced from abstract thought," he lamented. "This schism is light years away from the world of our so-called primitives for whom each color, each texture, each fragrance, each flavour is meaningful."[44]

Lévi-Strauss's own work straddled these contradictions. His criticisms of modern art were eerily similar to the attacks made against his own work—that it was too abstract, that it had become divorced from its context, that it was no more than self-absorbed aesthetic play. His attempts to model "primitive" culture verged on the self-conscious abstraction that he derided in modernism. Primitivism and Wagnerian romanticism, avant-garde cut-and-paste and preimpressionist landscape painters, classical illusions and modern linguistics—Lévi-Strauss mixed a fogeyish sentimentalism with an avant-garde sensibility. His personal aesthetic preferences, revealed during the Charbonnier interviews—Florentine Renaissance art, Poussin's epic landscapes, the romantic seaport images of the eighteenth-century French artist Joseph Vernet—were a sedately conservative list from such an experimental theorist and writer. When pressed, he evoked nature as his ultimate source of inspiration: "What made me a structuralist was less a viewing of the work of Picasso, Braque, Léger, or Kandinsky, than the sight of stones, flowers, butterflies or birds."[45]

The Charbonnier interviews also featured what would become one of Lévi-Strauss's best-remembered ideas—the distinction between "hot" and "cold" societies. In a long discussion, he described the differences between tribal and modern European societies.[46] "Primitive" societies lived at a figurative absolute zero. Rituals, kin structures and economies were set on rotations, like the tiny cogs inside a clock, their cultures existing on an eternal loop. "Hot" societies, by contrast, worked on the principle of the steam engine. Powered by "thermodynamic" differentials—between masters and slaves, lords and serfs, or the rich and the poor—they surged forward, spewing out energy. Against the gentle ticktock of tribal life, Lévi-Strauss's boiler room of modernity was continuously stoked up. The West was like a runaway train hurtling through billowing steam down the tracks of history.

The image was vivid and simple, illustrating an idea, drawn from cybernetic theory, that Lévi-Strauss had first aired at the close of *Tristes Tropiques*, when he had mourned the West's built-in drive to entropy, with its propensity to break down delicate cultures and exhaust the world's environment in its wake. Though presented with various caveats (for example, elements of the "hot" and the "cold" are inherent in all societies), it opened him up to the criticism that he was reifying primitive cultures, preserving them in an eternal freeze-frame of tradition—societies that, in many instances, were in fact undergoing drastic changes wrought by contact with the West. For Lévi-Strauss, this was missing the point. Of course all societies were undergoing change. It was their attitude to this fact that was the difference. While "primitive" societies denied or downplayed history's importance "with a dexterity we underestimate," the West focused compulsively on it.[47] (In a late interview he even suggested that the process was now reversing—primitive societies on fast-changing frontiers were "warming up," while France, with its focus on preserving its patrimony and returning to its roots, was cooling.)[48] Nevertheless, Lévi-Strauss's binary outlook, with the images of the steam engine and the clock, the primitive and the modern, "us" and "them," was reinforced, even as he insisted on the fundamental unity of humanity. It was a tension that would run through all his work as he tried to square the relativist and universalist wings of his thought.

Modernism and classicism, primitive and Western culture, science and art—these were the never fully resolved polarities of Lévi-Strauss's thought. Roman Jakobson had been comfortable with the affiliation between modernism and structuralist analysis, but Lévi-Strauss could never admit the obvious parallels. In his own assessments he was forthright, even extreme, in his preferences for primitive culture, Western classicism and contemporary science. But reading his oeuvre, the distinctions are never as clear. Perhaps Vincent Debaene, one of the editors of the Bibliothèque de la Pléiade edition of Lévi-Strauss's work, published on the eve of his hundredth birthday, was closest to the mark with the comment that Lévi-Strauss worked by marrying "formal classicism with methodological modernism."[49] And it was this odd combination that made his voice so distinctive, his ideas so unexpected. As he relaxed into his new life at the Collège, freed from the career anxieties that had dogged him since his return to Paris, these complexities blossomed into some of his most challenging and original work.

9

"Mind in the Wild"

> Ideas form a complete system within us, comparable to one of the natural kingdoms, a sort of bloom whose iconography will be traced by a man of genius who will pass perhaps as mad.
>
> Honoré de Balzac[1]

At the end of the First World War, the American anthropologist Ralph Linton was mobilized. He served in the exhausted battlefields of Champagne and Argonne in the 42nd Division during the final months of the Great War. While on duty, Linton noticed something that he had often read about in the ethnographies he had studied while doing his PhD thesis at Columbia University. As the fighting progressed, men began forging an almost spiritual identity with their division. They called it Rainbow because it was made up of units from twenty-six different states, with a spectrum of regimental colors. When they were asked to which division they belonged, they would answer, "I am a Rainbow." Rainbows became good omens—some soldiers actually claimed they saw them streaming across the sky every time they went into battle. They regarded themselves as special and distinct from other soldiers, so much so that when stationed near the 77th or Statue of Liberty division, they sewed the symbol of a rainbow onto their uniforms. By the end of the war many divisions had evolved in similar ways, wedding themselves to a symbol and imbuing it with spiritual significance, using it to mark themselves off from other groups. He concluded that something akin to tribal totemism was happening spontaneously on the battlefields of Europe.[2]

Linton's example, which Lévi-Strauss cited at the beginning of *Le Totémisme aujourd'hui* (*Totemism*), simplified what was in reality a hugely complex area of practice and belief. In the popular imagination, totems were seen as ritual emblems of indigenous groups—the hawk totem representing the hawk clan, for instance, just as the rainbow had stood symbolically for the 42nd Division. For most people, the phenomenon's most visible manifestations were the so-called totem poles—the magnificently carved cedar posts from North America that graced museums around the world.

Under serious ethnographic scrutiny, though, the concept became far more nuanced. Not only were totem poles misnomers (their purpose was, in fact, extremely varied—sometimes they were carved to represent myths, sometimes to commemorate important events or even to shame a person or group), but real totems, and the beliefs associated with them, were bewilderingly complex. Totems could be bears, kangaroos, eaglehawks, great rivers or mountains; but they could also be mosquitoes, oysters, shooting stars, bits of rope or even the act of laughing or vomiting. They were often linked to origin myths and ancestor cults and associated with food and marriage taboos, but as anthropologists had discovered there was no set pattern. Among the Tikopia, in the Solomon Islands, for instance, the eel was subject to such a strong taboo that even seeing it could induce vomiting; but another totem, the dolphin, would be carved up, cooked and shared out between clans if found stranded on the beach.[3] Examples like this proliferated through the ethnographic record in an array of apparently random attitudes and rules.

Just as with kinship and myth, totemism offered up an irresistible riddle for Lévi-Strauss. Regulations governing totems appeared to follow no clear logic. In a similar way to kinship and myth, there seemed to be a mismatch between the poetic efforts that went into the creation of these elaborate schemes and the unimaginative anthropological theories that purported to explain them. In the nineteenth century, totemism had been dismissed as superstition, a kind of primitive forerunner to true religion; in the twentieth, the functionalist school had tried to rationalize it, arguing that it fostered social cohesion or protected valuable animals or plants. Lévi-Strauss's approach would be typically abstract, delving once more into the inner logic of primitive thought.

The genesis of his interest in totemism had come from his intellectual mentor Georges Dumézil, who commissioned a short book on the subject for Presses universitaires de France's Myths and Religion series. The series was aimed at introducing specialist research to a broader audience; Lévi-Strauss's brief, to discuss a controversial issue in extended essay form, using a minimum of footnotes and a pared-down bibliography. Relying on the method he had begun using in the 1940s, Lévi-Strauss planned to use his first round of the seminars at the Collège as a dry run for the text, thinking aloud before refining his thoughts into the book.

Halfway through the academic year, though, he had already raced ahead of himself. An examination of totemic beliefs had become a springboard for a flood of philosophical ideas. He had moved from a patient assessment of the anthropological literature to forbiddingly abstract course titles, such as The Science of the Concrete and Categories, Elements, Species, Names. He wrote to Dumézil and asked for the commission to be extended into two volumes. Although taken aback, Dumézil agreed, on the condition that they include discreet references to totemism in the titles. On Lévi-Strauss's original manuscript for what would become *Le Totémisme aujourd'hui*, he wrote down a few suggestions: "*I. Le Totémisme aujourd'hui (ou bien) La Fin du totémisme. II. Derrière le totémisme (ou bien) Au-delà du totémisme*" [I. Totemism Today (or possibly) The End of Totemism. II. Behind Totemism (or possibly) Beyond Totemism.][4] In the end, Lévi-Strauss stuck to the original one-book commission, and the second volume took on a life of its own. Published separately by Plon, it became one of his most famous works: *La Pensée sauvage* (*The Savage Mind*).

The two books were intimately connected. At just over 150 pages of large type, *Le Totémisme aujourd'hui* is like a novella against the meatier *La Pensée sauvage*. The first book was a conceptual clearing of the way, a synthetic sifting through of previous anthropological theories; in the second Lévi-Strauss broke free with an explosion of new ideas. He has described *Le Totémisme aujourd'hui* as "a kind of historical and critical introduction" to *La Pensée sauvage*, and the two books—taken together—as a prelude to the *Mythologiques* quartet. Collectively they were "a break between two bursts of effort" as he drew breath between his earlier exploration of kinship systems and his later work on myth.[5]

In 2007, Lévi-Strauss told anthropologist Frédéric Keck that he had written *Le Totémisme aujourd'hui* "in a state of haste, precipitation, almost remorse."[6] Yet in tone, this is one of his calmest books. There is an above-the-fray coolness as he goes through the classical theories, discarding some outright, considering others at greater length, lamenting that a select few had touched on features of the system, only to fall at the final intellectual hurdle. His idea was to "retread pace by pace an itinerary which, even if it led nowhere, induces us to look for another route."[7] But after a meandering start, the course that Lévi-Strauss retraces is in fact remarkably straight, leading relentlessly on toward the intellect. By the book's end, the concept of totemism had vanished as abruptly as it had surfaced as an anthropological obsession in the late nineteenth century, dissolved back into the logical properties of the mind. For Lévi-Strauss, what anthropologists had avidly recorded was ultimately a mirage, a figment of their imaginations. "Up until now I had avoided tackling this nest of vipers," he told Gilles Lapouge of *Le Figaro littéraire* on the book's publication. "But sooner or later it was necessary to clean out the temple of ethnology, that is to say, to rid it of the notion of totemism."[8]

"Totemism is like hysteria . . . ," Lévi-Strauss opened the book, with characteristic melodrama. The two concepts had emerged in the nineteenth century at roughly the same time, and not by coincidence. For Lévi-Strauss, they had played a similar role as the flip sides of cherished

Western values, pitting primitive religion and neurosis against modernity and rationality. The idea of totemism reached its high-water mark in the first decades of the twentieth century with publications like Frazer's four-volume, twenty-two-hundred-page *Totemism and Exogamy*, which saw totemism as a superstitious protoreligion, and Freud's *Totem and Taboo*, an attempt to equate "primitive" peoples' totemic beliefs to those of neurotics. By 1920, French ethnographer Arnold van Gennep's *L'État actuel du problème totémique* (*The Current State of the Totemic Problem*) listed more than forty different theories of the phenomenon. And then the concept had gone into retreat. Unwieldy, difficult to define, totemism was subsequently "emptied of substance," "disincarnated," "liquidated."[9] Over the next decades it barely rated a mention in the leading anthropological textbooks. Like hysteria's cluster of neuroses and tics, assorted attitudes toward wallabies, bears, crabs or gusts of wind could no longer be nailed down to a single idea. Lévi-Strauss was fascinated by this process, as well as by the long tail of modern anthropologists who had returned to the different elements that had originally gone into the concept and tried to make sense of them.

The ethnographic record was vivid, especially among Australian Aborigines. Lévi-Strauss devoted a chapter to the work of A. P. Elkin, an Anglican priest and Australia's first professor of anthropology. At the end of the 1920s, Elkin had spent a year studying a variety of Aboriginal groups, traveling by lorry, packhorse, mule and motorboat from Broome up to the Drysdale River, through the Kimberley region in the north of Western Australia. This fieldwork, combined with library research on other regions, exposed Elkin to a huge variety of totemic beliefs and practices. He found that totems could be attached to every conceivable grouping—the moiety, subsection, clan and so on—as well as to dreams, to cults, to gender, to ancestor worship. Individuals could have their own personal totems and several further group totems. In northeastern South Australia, each person had matrilineal "flesh" totems, patrilineal "cult" totems, a dream totem and secret knowledge of his mother's brother's patrilineal cult totem. Among the Southern Aranda (central Australia) there were more than four hundred totems grouped into sixty different categories. While riveted by the detail that Elkin had managed to compile, Lévi-Strauss was disappointed by his conclusions. When Elkin tried to synthesize his findings, he was left with two rather vague ideas: totems expressed cooperation of man with nature, and continuity between past and present. The question that played on Lévi-Strauss's mind was why these peoples would need such rich intellectual systems to convey such bland propositions.

An intuitive solution proposed by Bronislaw Malinowski was that native peoples ritualized animals and plants to protect them because they were edible or useful to the group in some way. This "functionalist" approach was too neat for Lévi-Strauss, and he flooded the text with counterexamples culled from well-known ethnographies. The waterbuck, monitor lizard, various trees, certain diseases, hide, the red ant, monorchids, papyrus, durra-bird, gourd, rope—the list reads like an exercise in psychoanalytic free association, and yet for the Nuer of East Africa they were all considered totems. At the same time, plants and animals that were central to their diet and economy were treated with complete indifference. In central Australia, mosquitoes, flies and crocodiles commonly appeared as totems, even though they were seen as harmful. The less than convincing functionalist solution to this dilemma had been to say that they were venerated because they brought discomfort to their enemies. Lévi-Strauss was scathing: "In this respect it would be difficult to find anything which, in one way or another, positively or negatively (or even because of its lack of significance?), might not be said to offer an interest."[10] Endlessly adaptable, functionalist theories explained everything and nothing.

At the turn of the twentieth century, Oxford-educated Baldwin Spencer had teamed up with a stationmaster at the Alice Springs Overland Telegraph Station, Frank Gillen, who had little formal education, but an avid interest in Aboriginal culture and direct experience of their communities. In 1901–2 the pair mounted a major expedition across the desert plains of central Australia. They documented groups that had had only sporadic contact with Europeans, and produced some of the earliest film footage of native Australians—haunting black-and-white images of clay-daubed men performing ritual dances with bunches of dry foliage tied around their ankles, rhythmically pounding the desert sands.

Spencer and Gillen had come up with a different solution to the problem of "negative" totems. They had argued that Aborigines ritualized flies and mosquitoes and willed them to multiply because they were associated with periods of heavy rain. The idea had a functionalist flavor, but nevertheless reframed the argument in a suggestive way. The flies and mosquitoes had been transformed from "stimuli" to "signs," from natural objects to symbols. It was this more conceptual view of totemism that interested Lévi-Strauss. He praised a long line of anthropologists, including Raymond Firth and Meyer Fortes, who had looked at totemic complexes not in utilitarian terms, but as symbolic representations of human relations.[11] But again, this seemed too tidy. For Lévi-Strauss, the question that returned "like a Leitmotiv" whenever totemic systems were discussed was why specific animals or plants were chosen above others. Why the hawk rather than the eagle, the cassowary and not the emu, the wallaby rather than the kangaroo?

Once more he found his solution in the realm of logical abstraction. The choice of totems had nothing to do with utility or analogy—it was an expression of pure intellect. By way of an example, Lévi-Strauss returned to Radcliffe-Brown: not his earlier functionalist theories, but a lecture he had given in 1951, four years before his death. Looking cross-culturally, Radcliffe-Brown had noticed that totems relating to moieties were generally two species, often birds. In British Columbia opposing moieties were named eagle and raven. For certain Australian groups of the Darling River, it was the eagle-hawk and the crow; the white cockatoo and crow were used in Western Australia, and the white cockatoo and black cockatoo in Victoria. In eastern Australia, the bat and the night owl featured as male and female totems, respectively. The sea-eagle and the fish-hawk were common in Melanesia. Other pairs of animals were also used: two species of kangaroo, two types of bee, the coyote and the wildcat. Looking at the myths associated with these pairs, Radcliffe-Brown concluded that these choices were not so much about the animals themselves as their relationships—each pair expressed a kind of connected duality, a union of the similar, but different. The animals were related yet opposed, their structural pairing echoing the relationships between the moieties they represented, as a kind of yin and yang of indigenous thought.[12]

For Lévi-Strauss, Radcliffe-Brown's insight was fundamental. His change of emphasis from "animality" to "duality," as the French philosopher Henri Bergson had put it, lifted him "beyond a simple ethnographic generalisation—to the laws of language, and even of thought."[13] Indigenous peoples were involved in a conceptual game, building metaphysical models out of what they had readily at hand. It was not animals' individual characteristics that interested the native mind, but the way they contrasted, forming a code whose symbols were drawn from nature. On the one hand there are kinship relations; on the other there are relationships between animals and plants. In the system taken as a whole, "it is not the similarities, but the differences that resemble each other," Lévi-Strauss explained in a formula that somersaults in the mind. As such, totemism did not exist as a separate entity—a protoreligion; a primitive, utilitarian ritual—it was just one aspect of a highly abstract metaphorical style of thought. "Natural species are chosen not because they are 'good to eat' [*bonnes à manger*] but because they are 'good to think' [*bonnes à penser*]," Lévi-Strauss concluded with his much-quoted jibe against Malinowski.[14]

Le Totémisme aujourd'hui had all the tropes of Lévi-Strauss's distinctive style. The ethnographic detail wedded to logic, the unexpected shift from classical anthropological theories to linguistic models and, with his whimsical comparison between a passage from Henri Bergson and reflections of a Dakota wise man in the last chapter, the melding of French philosophy and native thought. The book also contained the clearest exposé of structuralism to date, signposted at intervals through the text. In the opening chapter Lévi-Strauss outlined the structuralist method, step by step: "(1) define the phenomenon under study as a relation between two or more terms, real or supposed; (2) construct a table of possible permutations between these terms; (3) take this table as the general object of analysis which, at this level only, can yield necessary connections . . ."[15] In this bald proposition, one can see both the inherent radicalism of the enterprise and its strangely alienated nature. Lévi-Strauss was fascinated by ethnographic minutiae, but only as the raw material for a second-order analysis.

Toward the middle of the book, he made explicit the intellectual step that set him apart from contemporary anthropological thinking, be it the British school of structural functionalism or the then emerging symbolic approaches. What was novel about Lévi-Strauss's outlook was a conceptual leap from figurative to formal analogy, from an actual to a structural resemblance. Like in his analyses of kinship, Lévi-Strauss was interested in comparing different *relationships*, not making one-on-one correspondences. A bear totem did not relate directly to a bear-clan; the clansmen were not in some metaphorical sense bearlike, as some anthropologists had argued. But contrasted against, say, a salmon totem of the neighboring clan, it made up one element of a cultural equation: bear is to salmon as bear-clan is to salmon-clan. His ultimate goal was to map out these "similarities between sets of differences," as he phrased it, using a Saussurian turn of phrase, similarities that could be as oblique, lateral and associative as the abstract art that he had disowned.

Anthropology's painstaking documenting of cultures was not an end in itself, Lévi-Strauss concluded. Its role was to trace the structural echoes that Lévi-Strauss believed reverberated through thought, cultural output, social relations and even the physical world. In so doing, he wrote as he drew *Le Totémisme aujourd'hui* to a close, anthropology would fulfill its role as a master discipline, integrating essence and form, method and reality.

WHILE LÉVI-STRAUSS was working on *Le Totémisme aujourd'hui*, material for *La Pensée sauvage* was coming together through his seminars at the Collège. The result was almost simultaneous publication. Just two months after *Le Totémisme aujourd'hui* appeared in March 1962, *La Pensée sauvage* came out to ecstatic reviews. Claude Roy, writing in *Libération*, called it "a major event in the history of modern humanism"; for Emmanuel Mounier, founder of the leading journal *Esprit*, which devoted an entire issue to the book in 1963, two "*événements philosophiques*" had appeared "back to back" (*coup sur coup*).[16]

The book's title was a double pun in French—*pensée* can mean both "thought" and "pansy"; *sauvage*, both "wild" (in the sense of "untamed") and "savage." *Sauvage* was at once an ironic reference to the derogatory nineteenth-century term for primitive and an allusion to the centuries-old French philosophical tradition typified by Rousseau and Montaigne, to which Lévi-Strauss saw himself as heir. Was there also a more contemporary reference to *l'esprit sauvage*—a theoretical term that had been used by the late Merleau-Ponty, to whom Lévi-Strauss dedicated the book? Whatever the case, Lévi-Strauss was being deliberately provocative: "I reprised the term 'savage' on purpose," he said in an interview after the book's publication. "It carries an emotive and critical weight, and I think that one shouldn't take the vitality out of problems."[17]

Pensée as "pansy" introduced a rustic, poetic touch. There was the idea of natural systems, and perhaps even a coded allusion to Lévi-Strauss's moment of revelation on the Maginot Line, when as a young conscript he had stopped to contemplate a bunch of dandelions. With *pensée* in the sense of "thought," it seemed as if he was joining the age-old philosophical debate on whether there were fundamental differences between "civilized" and "primitive" ways of thinking. For a Parisian intellectual audience in the early 1960s, the book would at first have appeared to be in the spirit of Lucien Lévy-Bruhl's earlier studies of *la mentalité primitive*.

But as Lévi-Strauss's argument unfurled, it became clear that *La Pensée sauvage* ultimately referred to something far more abstract and universal: not primitive thought, but a kind of untrammeled thinking, the mind running free. Taken together, the words in the title encapsulated all the elements of Lévi-Strauss's project—nature, culture and the intellect—in one sonorous expression.

In *La Pensée sauvage* Lévi-Strauss moved on from the simple dualities of *Le Totémisme aujourd'hui* into a world of extraordinary complexity. At its heart was the idea that "primitive" peoples were driven by the same disinterested intellectual curiosity as their modern counterparts. Whether in the deserts of central Australia and New Mexico or the forests of the Philippines and West Africa, indigenous groups gathered information systematically, scouring their environments and synthesizing what they found with a logical rigor. In the process, they had built up an encyclopedic knowledge, rich in detail. The Hanunóo from the southern tip of Mindoro Island in the Philippine archipelago named more than four hundred different animals, including sixty classes of saltwater mollusk; New Mexico's Tewa distinguished more than forty-five types of ground mushroom and ear fungus; while one ethnographer had recorded eight thousand animal and plant terms from a single informant in Gabon. Lévi-Strauss pulled examples from ethnographies from around the world of a knowledge that was poetic in its descriptive precision. The Tewa had forty different ways to describe the shape of a leaf; the Fang of Gabon could express subtle differences between "winds, light and colour, ruffling of water and variation in surf, and the currents of water and air."[18]

The exhaustive classification of plants and animals went far beyond the day-to-day needs of preliterate groups. Rummaging around their environment, "savages" observed, experimented, categorized and theorized, using a kind of free-form science. They combined and recombined natural materials into cultural artifacts—myths, rituals, social systems—like artists improvising with the odds and ends lying around their studio. The central image that Lévi-Strauss used to describe this process was that of the *bricoleur*—a tinkerer, an improviser working with what was at hand, cobbling together solutions to both practical and aesthetic problems. *La Pensée sauvage*—free-flowing thought—was a kind of cognitive bricolage that strived for both intellectual and aesthetic satisfaction. It was a very French idea, which brought together the artist and the atelier, the artisan and the dying crafts of a more creative age, an era that Lévi-Strauss experienced at first hand as a boy helping his father cobble together furniture in the living room of the rue Poussin apartment. "My father was a great *bricoleur*," Lévi-Strauss later recalled. "It was he that gave me the pleasure and the skill for bricolage."[19] As intellectual concepts, bricolage and the *bricoleur* were rich and evocative, and would prove influential in the years to come as a shorthand for a kind of off-the-cuff experimentation used in the visual arts, literature and philosophy.

La Pensée sauvage set out to explore the logic underlying bricolage, delving deeper into the realm of Saussurian linguistics of signs and symbols, binary oppositions and "relationships of differences" that Lévi-Strauss had deployed since listening to Jakobson lecturing in New York in the 1940s. There was now not even any need to invoke a range of plants and animals to build up a logical set of sufficient density. A single species could yield enough differences for the most intricate model. For the Osage (southern Sioux), the eagle is divided into the golden, spotted or bald eagle, by color and even by age. Through the eagle the Sioux were able to create a "three-dimensional matrix," a quotidian aspect of their environment becoming an "object of thought," a rich "conceptual tool."[20] Add a bear and a seal, and the permutations rose exponentially. Lévi-Strauss drew up the multiplying possibilities in a diagram that resembled a line drawing of a refracted crystal. "Species" and "individual" appear at the vortices; at its pivots are seal, bear, eagle, head, neck, feet. The intersections are given values: h1, h2, h3; f1, f2, f3; and so forth. The properties of what Lévi-Strauss called the "the totemic operator" were a distillation of structuralist rhetoric:

> The whole set thus constitutes a sort of conceptual apparatus which filters unity through multiplicity, multiplicity through unity, diversity through identity, identity through diversity. Endowed with a theoretically unlimited extension on its median level it contracts (or expands) into pure comprehension at its two extreme vortices, but in symmetrically reversed forms, and not without undergoing a sort of torsion.[21]

This was Lévi-Strauss at his most arcane, theoretical discourse at its most French. The model, as complex as it appeared, he went on to explain, represented "only a small portion of a cell," a "minute fraction" of the possibilities, given the potential numbers of individuals, species and parts of the body that could be analyzed. Modeling such a vast array of logical combinations was a task "reserved for ethnology of the next century," Lévi-Strauss concluded, which "could not be done without the aid of machines."

In *La Pensée sauvage,* Lévi-Strauss also returned to the Scottish biologist and mathematician D'Arcy Thompson's *On Growth and Form*, which he had read in the New York Public Library while writing his thesis, *Les Structures élémentaires de la parenté*. It was from D'Arcy Thompson that Lévi-Strauss elaborated on one of the keystones of structuralism—the idea of transformations. D'Arcy Thompson had shown that the form and structure of different species were mathematical transformations of each other. By warping a geometric grid, systematically elongating, squashing or tapering forms plotted onto its coordinates, a tapir's skull could be transformed into a horse's, a horse's skull into a rabbit's into a dog's. Antelope, rhinoceros and goat horns; teeth, tusks and seashells were but logarithmic transformations of each other.

Again Lévi-Strauss took only the flavor of these insights—the idea of mathematically generated patterns and the logic of form—applying them in his own idiosyncratic way. What he found, looking at the panorama of different ethnographic descriptions, was not so much a gradual evolution or seeping influences from neighboring cultures, but systemic structural change using the same overall symmetries and proportions. "I was soon to notice that this way of seeing was part of a long tradition," Lévi-Strauss recalled. "Behind Thompson was Goethe's botany, and behind Goethe, Albrecht Dürer and his *Treatise on the Proportions of the Human Body*."[22]

It MAY SEEM STRANGE that such a dense and technical book could become a landmark in French thought, but the first and last chapters—a stream-of-consciousness theoretical essay and a polemical attack on Jean-Paul Sartre, respectively—brought *La Pensée sauvage* to life for a broader readership. The first chapter was frenetic. One moment Lévi-Strauss was discussing Hanunóo plant classification, the next he was analyzing the ruff of a lace collar in a portrait of a woman by sixteenth-century French mannerist painter François Clouet and the inherent aesthetic qualities of miniatures. Lévi-Strauss interspersed references to Charles Dickens, the stage sets of silent-era French filmmaker Georges Méliès, Japanese gardens, the Sistine Chapel and cubism with ethnographic descriptions of a dozen different indigenous groups. "Art lies half way between scientific knowledge and mythical and magical thought," he declared at one point; "the painter is always midway between design and anecdote" at another. It may not always have been easy to follow, but his eclectic approach was compelling.

There was also a hint of the eccentric in *La Pensée sauvage*. The selection of illustrations ranged from the intriguing to the bizarre. There were Grandville's nineteenth-century drawings of humans with animal heads, taken from *Les Métamorphoses du jour* (1828–29), along with Charles Le Brun's seventeenth-century experimental sketches of crosses between human and animal physiognomy. The former were labeled, "The opposite of totemism: nature humanised," and the latter, "The opposite of totemism: man naturalised," though neither plate was discussed or even ever referred to in the text. More conventional were two carved stone *churinga*, sacred objects used in Aboriginal ancestor cults. But these were coupled with European-style outback landscapes painted by Australian Aborigines, which Lévi-Strauss described as "dull and studied water-colours one might expect of an old maid" and whose only raison d'être seemed to be a single throwaway comment in chapter three.[23]

In among the flotsam of Lévi-Strauss's mind was a philosophical set piece—an extended comparison between scientific and *sauvage* ways of thinking. Where scientific thought was analytical and abstract, breaking the world down into a series of discrete problems, *la pensée sauvage* sought a total solution. The scientist measured, weighed and modeled at a remove; the primitive dealt directly in the sensual experiences of his immediate surroundings, balancing them off against each other, ordering them into mytho-poetic formulae. In an interview for a documentary shot in the 1970s, Lévi-Strauss described the process of scientific research as a never-ceasing excavation—the breaking through of the surface reality in search of another analytical world behind, which would in turn yield a further world, and so on. "The progress in science consisted in reaching successive levels of more and more secret maps," Lévi-Strauss went on, "where explanations were found to the essence of the map we had." In contrast to this "constant probing, penetration," *la pensée sauvage* was all surface and no depth, taking the environment at face value, but nevertheless fashioning its elements into beautifully balanced and rigorously logical objects of the thought.[24] With this dichotomy, Lévi-Strauss was approaching the core of his own thinking—an amalgam of the sensual and the logical, which obsessed him throughout his career.

In the field he had jotted down tasting notes from the tropics, from the thirteen different flavors of honey that the Nambikwara gathered, whose aromas he likened to bouquets of burgundy, to appreciations of exotic fruits. The *araca* had "a turpentine taste with a fizz of faint acidity," crushed *açaí* produced a "thick raspberry-flavoured syrup" and the *bacuri* was "like a pear stolen from the orchards of Paradise." In the forest he had breathed in the chocolate aromas of decaying leaf litter, which made him think of how soil produces cocoa, and how the gravelly earth of Haute-Provence could beget both the floral scent of lavender and the pungency of truffles. It was there that the expedition team had spent three days cooking and eating, improvising haute cuisine in the depths of the forest, sampling hummingbird roasted on skewers *flambé au whiskey* and a ragoût of *mutum* (wild turkey) stewed with palm buds and served with a creamy sauce made from nut pulp *au poivre*. For all his intellectual austerity, his distrust of direct experience, Lévi-Strauss was alive to the senses.

Instead of fighting these apparent contradictions, he tried to fuse them. In doing so he believed he was solving a venerable philosophical problem: the relationship between abstract intellectual understanding and raw sensory perception, between the "intelligible" and "sensible," as Plato had framed it, or John Locke's "primary" and "secondary" qualities. A long line of thinkers, from the ancient Greek philosopher Democritus through to Galileo Galilei, René Descartes and Isaac Newton, had asked whether there was some fundamental distinction between qualities that exist independent of the observer—like geometric shapes, numbers, motion and density—and qualities that are subjective—colors, odors and textures, for instance. The idea of red, bitter or rough seemed fundamentally different from measurable, precisely definable entities like a circle, a square or the number three. While the West had marginalized "secondary qualities" in order to establish science, Lévi-Strauss argued that preliterate groups had transcended this debate, welding the sensual and the logical into a seamless whole.

For Lévi-Strauss, aesthetic sensation was the very currency of *la pensée sauvage*, but it was applied according to rigorous principles. Though freed to roam at will, untamed thinking had ended up producing a tidy collection of logical propositions, lining up elements in neat oppositions and inversions—fur versus feather, the smooth and the gritty, noise as against silence, fresh as opposed to putrid and so forth—that Lévi-Strauss would map out in a chapter titled "The Fugue of the Five Senses" in his next book, *Le Cru et le cuit* (*The Raw and the Cooked*).[25] The metaphor was less like the wilds of nature than a Parisian park, with its gravel squares, strips of lawn and rows of topiaried shrubs. His task was to analyze this strange fusion—a logical system built out of pure experience, a grammar of sound, odor and texture, a formal structure made up of perceptions of plants, animals and nature, of bears, seaweed, ants and shooting stars, which he termed "the science of the concrete" (*la science du concret*). "We have had to wait until the middle of this century for the crossing of long separated paths," he wrote as he wound up *La Pensée sauvage*.[26] Modern thought was engaging with that of the Neolithic, and human knowledge was at last coming full circle.

IT TOOK FOUR YEARS for *La Pensée sauvage* to appear in English translation. Rodney Needham, then still Lévi-Strauss's champion in Britain, gave the job to Sybil Wolfram, an Oxford University philosophy lecturer in her early thirties. Wolfram began work, but immediately fell out with Lévi-Strauss over criticisms he made of early drafts of the first two chapters. She almost left the project at this point, but the publishers persuaded her to complete the translation. When she handed in the script, Lévi-Strauss was damning: "I could not recognise my book as she had rendered it," he complained in a letter to the journal *Man*. For her part, Wolfram disassociated herself from the heavily edited version of her work that finally appeared in print, produced by several translators working under anthropologist Ernest Gellner, which she felt was "full of howlers, pieces of sheer nonsense, ungrammatical sentences, extreme infelicities, pointless substitutions, often resulting in absurdity and inaccuracy, the loss of allusions I have carefully preserved." Wolfram later joked, paraphrasing Lévi-Strauss, that the editing process had miraculously succeeded in "turning the cooked into the raw."[27]

The pairing was clearly no meeting of minds, as excerpts of their correspondence published in the Bibliothèque de la Pléiade edition of Lévi-Strauss's works reveal. Wolfram accused Lévi-Strauss of having "an inadequate knowledge of English," calling his suggestion of the word "structuration" a "revolting Americanism." At one point she sent Lévi-Strauss a long letter explaining the difference between "contingency" and "chance"; at another, she dismissed philosophical terms like *être* (being) and *devenir* (becoming) used as substantives as "meaningless metaphysical expressions." She found Lévi-Strauss's corrections infuriating. "If you do not mean what I put, then I do not understand what you mean," she wrote in exasperation.[28]

The title's wordplay produced further problems, with a range of possible permutations in English: *The Wild Pansy*, *Untamed Thinking* or Lévi-Strauss's own suggestion, *Mind in the Wild*. One of the editors proposed the academic-sounding *Natural Ideas—A Study in Primitive Thought*,[29] but the book would be published as *The Savage Mind*—a distortion of the original—minus the flowers on the front cover and the appendix, in which Lévi-Strauss had placed a series of historical descriptions of wild pansies. (Lévi-Strauss had the last word on the matter in the 2008 Pléiade edition, inserting a quote from Hamlet in English—"and there is pansies, that's for thoughts"—on the flyleaf.) Still the only version available in English, *The Savage Mind* does indeed have a clunky feel to it at times, but to be fair to the translators, taking Lévi-Strauss's punning philosophico-poetic prose into English was never easy, and was made more difficult by running disagreements with the author.

The Wolfram dispute underlines the enduring gulf between Lévi-Strauss and his British counterparts, Latin and Anglo-American intellectual sensibilities. Lévi-Strauss's elliptical, poetic style was indeed resistant to more literalist Anglo-American interpretations. His repeated use of hard science metaphors goaded critics who found it impossible to pin down the detail of his arguments and were indeed suspicious that his floral prose masked a lack of rigor.

Part of the problem was a lack of sensitivity to the context in which Lévi-Strauss was working. For him, ethnography worked in the service of ideas, a concept that was familiar to his French intellectual audience but which did not travel well across the Channel. In Britain the high-flown prose that came with the territory was seen as too intellectually showy, but even Lévi-Strauss was happy to admit in the last few pages of the book "there is a little rather false lyricism," though he never felt it discredited his ideas.[30]

In an interview in the early 1970s for the journal *Psychology Today*, Lévi-Strauss gave his interpretation of this French/Anglo-American divide:

> It happens that in France . . . philosophy makes up a sort of vernacular language that serves as a means of communication between the scientific world, the academic world, and the cultivated public on the one hand, and between different branches of research, on the other. This is not true for England or for the United States. I would even say that the philosophical aspect you point to in my work, which is perhaps attractive to some French readers, is a considerable source of irritation to the English and the Americans.[31]

The ease with which continental scholars moved between art and science was also alien to the more compartmentalized Anglo-American approaches. In the year that *La Pensée sauvage* was published, for instance, Lévi-Strauss joined forces with Roman Jakobson in a structural analysis of Charles Baudelaire's short poem "Les Chats." After much correspondence on the subject, the two men sat down together in Lévi-Strauss's study and coauthored an essay deconstructing the poem. A playful exercise, perhaps, but one which ended up being published in *L'Homme*, the house journal of the Laboratoire d'anthropologie, launched by Lévi-Strauss, Émile Benveniste and Pierre Gourou in 1961 as a French equivalent to *Man* in Britain and *American Anthropologist* in the United States.[32]

While British and American critics often seized on errors of scholarship and interpretation of sources, in France Lévi-Strauss was both attacked and lauded on strictly philosophical grounds. Some of the responses were as dense and theoretical as Lévi-Strauss's original work. In a debate between Lévi-Strauss and Paul Ricoeur, at that time one of France's leading philosophers, published in the 1963 *Esprit* devoted to a critical reading of *La Pensée sauvage*, Ricoeur told Lévi-Strauss:

> You salvage the meaning, but it is the meaning of non-meaning [*le sens de non-sens*], the admirable syntactical arrangement of a discourse that says nothing. I see you at that conjunction between agnosticism and a hyper-intelligence of syntax. This is what makes you at once fascinating and disturbing.[33]

Ricoeur described Lévi-Straussian structuralism as sometimes a "Kantianism without the transcendental subject"—that is to say, a disembodied version of the mental constraints that Kant argued gave shape to our perception of reality—at other times an "absolute formalism."[34] Lévi-Strauss had long fought against the tag "formalism," which he felt misinterpreted his position. As to "Kantianism without the transcendental subject," he liked the label, even adopting it in the first book of the *Mythologiques* quartet, *Le Cru et le cuit*, where he also cited approvingly another Ricoeur description of structuralism. Adrift from "the thinking subject," Lévi-Strauss's "categorising system" was "homologous with nature"—"It may perhaps be nature," Ricoeur concluded with an air of mysticism.[35]

By the end of the *Esprit* encounter, Ricoeur was fascinated by structuralism, but ultimately disillusioned:

> I see an extreme form of modern agnosticism. As far as you are concerned there is no "message" . . . you despair of meaning, but you console yourself with the thought that, if men have nothing to say, at least they say it so well that their discourse is amenable to structuralism.[36]

The vacuum of meaning, the absence of will, the erasure of the "subject"—at that time the focal point of philosophical thinking—these were aspects of structuralism that unsettled some.[37] But others, especially a new generation of thinkers who were at the beginning of their intellectual careers, were intrigued. Not only was Lévi-Strauss challenging the assumptions that had underpinned French thought for a generation, but he was proposing their radical opposites. Against the humanist orthodoxy, he was creating an intellectual space where people, himself included, were merely vessels for ideas, transition points of culture. These ideas had been aired to a mixed response through the 1950s. The time was now ripe for an assault on the philosophy of France's most famous thinker: Jean-Paul Sartre.

A philosopher who wrote of the nausea of being, the struggle for authenticity and personal freedom in a godless world; a very public intellectual whose private life became the stuff of legend; a onetime communist activist who ended up a Maoist sympathizer—it is hard to think of someone more at odds with Lévi-Strauss's ideas and persona. In public Lévi-Strauss praised Sartre as a great thinker who had "a prodigious capacity to express himself in the most diverse genres: theater, newspapers, philosophy, the novel."[38] Privately, Lévi-Strauss was scandalized by Sartre's outré lifestyle. While Lévi-Strauss was in America, Sartre's New York lover Dolorès Vanetti asked him if he liked Sartre. "How do you think I could like him after reading *She Came to Stay*?" he replied, referring to Simone de Beauvoir's first novel, *L'Invitée*, a fictionalized account of her ménage à trois with Sartre and her student Olga Kosakiewicz. "It's Sartre portrayed in his entirety and he comes over as a vile bastard." Dolorès duly passed on one of Lévi-Strauss's rare indiscretions to Sartre himself, who mentioned it in a letter to de Beauvoir. "Thanks a lot, my fine friend, for the portrait," Sartre added drily.[39]

In 1960, Sartre published the second of his great philosophical tracts, *Critique de la raison dialectique* (*Critique of Dialectical Reason*), sections of which had already appeared *Les Temps modernes*. Written in part as a response to Merleau-Ponty's criticisms of his work, it attempted the daunting task of marrying existentialism and Marxism into a coherent whole. On its publication, he sent a copy to Lévi-Strauss with the dedication "To Claude Lévi-Strauss. In testimony of a faithful friendship." He added that the book's "main questions were inspired by those which occupied you, and especially by the way you posed them."[40] Sartre had cited Lévi-Strauss approvingly several times during the course of *Critique de la raison dialectique*, including a chapter entitled "Structures—The Work of Lévi-Strauss," with examples drawn from *Les Structures élémentaires de la parenté*. There were even hints of structuralism's influence on Sartre, as he edged toward a more restricted, system-dominated view of freedom.

Assisted by Lucien Sebag and Jean Pouillon, Lévi-Strauss devoted his seminar at the École pratique des hautes études to an analysis of *Critique de la raison dialectique* over the winter of 1960–61, reading and rereading Sartre at the same time as he was writing *Le Totémisme aujourd'hui* and *La Pensée sauvage*. To the latter he ended up adding a final, relatively free-floating chapter—"History and Dialectic"—dealing specifically with Sartre's book. In the preface he described his critique "as a homage of admiration and respect."[41] But far from returning Sartre's compliment, Lévi-Strauss's assessment was brutal.

Densely woven with the jargon of another intellectual age, making some passages virtually incomprehensible to the modern-day nonspecialist reader, Lévi-Strauss attempted to bulldoze Sartre's entire project in the space of two dozen pages. His lines of attack were diverse: a defense of "analogical" primitive thought styles against Western dialectical reason; an attack on the solipsistic focus on the subject; more assaults on the primacy of history and Sartre's fundamentally ethnocentric outlook. At base many of the arguments were retreads of points he had already made in *Race et histoire* and *Tristes Tropiques*, but by now he had both refined and amplified his attack. His most cutting remarks were couched in anthropological Victoriana: Sartre's privileging of Western history over that of the Papuans was akin to "a sort of intellectual cannibalism much more revolting to the anthropologist than real cannibalism." His attempt to oppose the primitive and the civilized was an opposition that "would have been formulated by a Melanesian savage."[42] Lévi-Strauss felt he was now working on a far broader canvas than the Marxist/existentialist discourse of historical forces and the possibilities of personal emancipation. For Lévi-Strauss, Sartre, along with much of the Parisian intellectual elite, was engaged in a parochial debate about a few hundred years of Western mores and history. Bus stop queues, strikes, boxing matches—the examples from which Sartre built his "philosophical anthropology"—seemed provincial in comparison to structuralism's global reach.

Sartre, one of the era's most combative intellectuals who had often engaged his opponents in very public debate, gave no immediate response. He referred to the piece only several years later, after the structuralist boat had already sailed, lamenting that Lévi-Strauss had misunderstood his ideas and unfairly discredited historical research. Much later Lévi-Strauss would play down the controversy. "It was never much of a feud . . . ," he told a reporter at the *Washington Post*. "The Sartre disciples said that nothing can be known without history; I had to dissent. But it is not that I don't believe in history, I just feel there is no privilege for it."[43]

At the time, though, the significance of "History and Dialectic" was immense. There was a palpable sigh of relief in intellectual circles. Finally someone had dared to openly attack the man who had dominated French intellectual life for a quarter of a century. Sartre's rallying call for authenticity, commitment, acts of pure will in a time of gathering political disillusionment had begun to grate. With one sweeping gesture, Lévi-Strauss's challenge had broken the spell. To Sartre's "Hell is other people," Lévi-Strauss would retort, "Hell is ourselves." "Man is condemned to be free," wrote Sartre, but for Lévi-Strauss the whole idea of freedom was illusory.

Although Lévi-Strauss was only three years younger than Sartre, there was a sense that a generational shift was under way, a rupture of both style and substance. Power was passing from a chain-smoking, pill-popping haunter of Left Bank café society to a sixteenth-arrondissement aesthete.

Pitted against the image of the grandstanding intellectual was the sober technician, as sociologist Pierre Bourdieu recalled in an interview in the 1980s:

> It is true that philosophers like Sartre are still admirable and perhaps also important: the person who speaks when no one knows what to say—in times of crisis, etc.—but at the same time we were a bit tired of that kind of discourse, as prophets can also speak in the void, at the wrong time. So someone [that is, Lévi-Strauss] telling us, "See, we can understand, we can analyze, there are conceptual tools to understand things that seemed incomprehensible, unjustifiable, absurd"—I think that that was a very important thing.[44]

The promise of scientifically based humanities over philosophical rhetoric—though in reality Lévi-Strauss mixed both with abandon—was potent for young thinkers searching for a foothold in what had become a highly politicized activity. Technical terminology of "signs," "signifiers" and "oppositions," which had been road tested in linguistics, a discipline with true scientific pretensions, seemed more concrete than the interpretive terms from German philosophy like "ontotheology," "Dasein" and "noema" that they replaced. Like logical positivism after the First World War, structuralism offered to clean up philosophy, rid it of its vagueness and solipsistic reflections; but unlike logical positivism, it was built not on empiricism, but on high rationalism.

In his "ethnography" of French academic life, *Homo Academicus*, Bourdieu places Lévi-Strauss's attack on Sartre at the center of seismic changes in the intellectual ecology of the times. It signaled the rise of the social sciences, the ascendance of *anthropologie* (as opposed to the narrower, more specialized *ethnologie*) as a grand synthesizing discipline. Together with linguistics and history, anthropology was supplanting philosophy's unquestioned superiority. The journal *L'Homme*, along with the already well-established history periodical *Les Annales*, had begun overtaking *Les*

Temps modernes, which was "relegated to the status of purveyor of partisan, Parisian literary essays."[45] Seen in this light, Lévi-Strauss's continuing assault on the importance of history was a battle fought within a battle, a tussle for leadership within the newly emergent elite of the humanities.

THE PHILOSOPHICAL TIDE was turning. Once more, a clear choice was opening up between what writer and philosopher Alain Badiou defined as the two branches of twentieth-century French thought: the Bergsonian philosophy of "vital interiority, a thesis on the identity of being and becoming," and the Brunschvicgian philosophy of "the mathematically based concept"—or theories which took subjective experience as their point of departure as opposed to theories which looked at relationships between objects and concepts in the world. One sought meaning; the other, form. Lévi-Straussian structuralism, unambiguously pitched at the formal end of the spectrum, represented a radical break from the post–World War II orthodoxy.[46]

Ironically, given the severe, antihumanist tone of all his work, Lévi-Strauss's philosophical reflections threw up the image of a persona. He had set about delineating a style of thinking, but he ended up with a figure—not so much a noble savage as an indigenous bon vivant. A connoisseur and sensualist with a taste for avant-garde cut-up techniques, Lévi-Strauss's savage had an intuitive grasp of what Western thinkers had toiled for centuries to articulate. A logician of nature, he perceived "as through a glass darkly" (*comme à travers un nuage*) principles of interpretation that were only then becoming evident through the high tech of the times—simple computers and low-powered electron microscopes. A *bricoleur*, he recalled the ingenuity of the French artisan—a dying breed in an era of rapid, standardized industrialization.[47]

In the book's final pages, the presence of the figure behind *la pensée sauvage* was almost tangible, like an allegorical character in an ideas-driven novel, as Lévi-Strauss resorted to a string of metaphors and comparisons to explain how he saw the mysterious operations of "wild thought." He is glimpsed in the Aboriginal intellectual—a stock figure in Lévi-Strauss's writing since *Les Structures élémentaires*—scratching diagrams in the desert sands to represent his complex kinship systems, likened to a polytechnic professor demonstrating a mathematical proof on a lecture hall blackboard. In the final pages he reappears metaphorically, standing in a furnished room, surrounded by mirrors, each slightly off center, reflecting fragments of furniture and decoration that he has to piece together to somehow form a whole, like *imagines mundi*—the medieval allegories of continents with which scholars adorned maps and bibles.

Lévi-Strauss's savage was an amalgam of his own tastes and preferences—a mix of the eighteenth, nineteenth and twentieth centuries, of tradition and the avant-garde. It was his alter ego, fragments of who he was and who he wanted to be. The bond was intellectual. Perhaps he had been attracted to anthropology, he had mused in *Tristes Tropiques*, "because of a structural affinity between the civilisations it studies and my particular way of thinking."[48] Dreamed up in the library rather than the field, this persona bore little relation to the indigenous peoples he had actually met in the flesh and blood a quarter of a century before. When asked in 2005 by academic Boris Wiseman about his experiences as an ethnographer, Lévi-Strauss was frank:

> *Wiseman:* What in particular did you admire about the Caduveo?
>
> *Lévi-Strauss:* The ceramics and the body art—they were great artists.
>
> *Wiseman:* Did you admire their way of life?
>
> *Lévi-Strauss:* Not at all—they lived like poor Brazilian peasants.
>
> [. . .]
>
> *Wiseman:* Did you speak about France [to the Nambikwara]?
>
> *Lévi-Strauss:* Very little—the means of communication were very limited.
>
> *Wiseman:* Did you identify with the Indians you studied?
>
> *Lévi-Strauss:* No, not at all![49]

The image of the allegorical savage flickered faintly under the gloss of the intellect, pure thought, structure, but in the final pages of *La Pensée sauvage* it was snuffed out. The ultimate goal of the human sciences, wrote Lévi-Strauss, was "not to constitute, but to dissolve man." Four years later, in *Les Mots et les choses*, Foucault would add a lyrical touch to a similar idea: "Man is probably no more than a kind of rift in the order of things," he argued. "It is comforting, however, and a source of profound relief, to think that man is only a recent invention, a figure not two centuries old, a new wrinkle in our knowledge." Under a different configuration of knowledge, he concluded, in one of the most quoted lines from the era, "man would be erased, like a face drawn in sand at the edge of the sea."[50]

10

The Nebula of Myth

> Max Ernst built personal myths out of images borrowed from another culture . . . In the Mythology books I also cut up a mythical subject and recombined the fragments to bring out more meaning.
>
> CLAUDE LÉVI-STRAUSS[1]

WHEN LÉVI-STRAUSS FIRST TURNED his attention to the analysis of myth in the 1950s, he envisaged a machine—a "special device"—consisting of a series of upright boards two meters long and one and a half meters high on which cards containing mythic elements could be "pigeon-holed and moved at will." As the analysis moved into three dimensions, the cards would need to be perforated and fed through IBM equipment. The whole operation would require a substantial atelier, along with a team of dedicated technicians working to divine the "genetic law of the myth."[2]

A decade later, when he started on his famous myth tetralogy, he worked alone. Footage from the era has him crouched over his writing desk in his apartment, sitting in darkness, apart from a reading lamp lighting up piles of heavily annotated typescripts. Beside him, he stored his notes and references in a filing cabinet, with dividers marking off a hodgepodge of tribes, subject matters, animals and places: "sloth," "tapir," "Mexico," "California," "moon," "meteors," "weaving," "Kaingang," "Iroquois." He was now supplementing his anthropological reading with Diderot and d'Alembert's *Encyclopédie*, Alfred Brehm's zoology, Pliny and Plutarch, using an antique globe of the heavens to plot astronomical references. "Throughout the *Mythologiques* project I worked night and day nonstop," he told filmmaker Pierre Beuchot in a documentary shot soon after publication of the final volume, *L'Homme nu*. "I lost all idea of Saturdays or Sundays, of holidays, not allowing myself to let go of the thread . . . so that I could understand the structural properties of the content's smallest details."[3]

By the mid-1960s, thoughts of wooden boards, pigeonholes and computing cards had given way to something far more delicate and conceptual: a mobile of wire and thin strips of paper, looping and bending back on themselves. Lévi-Strauss would hang the mobiles from the ceiling in his office, and they turned gently as he worked through the logical possibilities they represented. On paper, the mobiles translated into notionally three-dimensional graphs of myth clusters. In one example four outer points represented "trusting guest," "wild virgin," "incestuous brother" and "adventurous husband"; along one axis ran "rolling head," "moon" and "rainbow"; along another, "moon," "spots" and "clinging woman." A dotted line ran diagonally across the axes, dividing the space into "(+) internal (–)" and "(–) external (+)" zones. Lévi-Strauss plotted myths (M_{393}, M_{255}, M_{401}, etc.) at various locations on the graph, according to their narrative properties.[4]

Almost half a century on, it feels strange to look back on such a quixotic enterprise and realize that it was the centerpiece of a theoretical movement that dominated the humanities at the time. For a period, Lévi-Strauss's myth mobiles were mainstream theory, at least in France. But as the enterprise went forward, it became clearer and clearer that this was a profoundly personal project, the outcome of one mind and a mass of material.

Ten years of thought, filtered through his seminar sessions on myth in the 1950s, had given Lévi-Strauss an ear for the dissonances and contrapuntal progressions of mythic narrative. The convoluted plots, the baroque and seemingly irrelevant detail, the way myths appeared to be propelled forward by sequences of rapid, not always fully connected events were by now music to his ears. "I read myths with joy," he told film critic Raymond Bellour, and he read many—several thousand—folding them into the logical models that evolved over a period of decades.[5]

Lévi-Strauss had theoretical reasons for choosing indigenous myth as his area of study. Myth represented the mind in the act of spontaneous creation, unfettered by reality. Unlike the kinship structures, whose models were tainted by all manner of sociological factors, myth was pure thought, a faithful reflection of the properties of the mind. In a certain sense myth *was* the mind, unveiled through its own impulsive workings.

The *Mythologiques* quartet was really one massive book, with four enormous chapters. *Le Cru et le cuit* (*The Raw and the Cooked*), *Du miel aux cendres* (*From Honey to Ashes*) and *L'Origine des manières de table* (*The Origin of Table Manners*) appeared in quick succession from 1964 to 1968. After a dramatic pause, *L'Homme nu* (*The Naked Man*) concluded the series at the end of 1971, the final *nu* echoing the opening *cru* of the first volume in sound, meaning and structural position. Lévi-Strauss worked fast, writing hundreds of pages a year, an urgency that he later attributed to his desire to finish the project before he died. He wanted to escape the fate of his intellectual hero, the founder of modern linguistics, Ferdinand de Saussure, who had spent decades studying Norse mythology but never published a word before his death. Bogged down in the limitless complexities of the subject, Saussure had only got as far as sketching his ideas in a collection of notebooks, which Lévi-Strauss later read on microfilm.[6]

Although at the beginning of the project Lévi-Strauss was only in his mid-fifties, a series of deaths of close colleagues had sharpened his sense of his own mortality. Two years after Merleau-Ponty had died of a massive stroke as he prepared a class on Descartes, Alfred Métraux committed suicide in 1963 at the age of sixty-one, after writing a long letter with references to friends, including Leiris and Lévi-Strauss. "It overwhelmed me as it did all his friends," Lévi-Strauss told Didier Eribon. "But now when I think back on it, it seems to me that his private life was a long preparation for suicide."[7] Two years later, on the eve of giving a series of talks for the Fondation Loubat on the cosmology of the Pueblo Indians, Lucien Sebag—a young, promising intellectual whom Lévi-Strauss had long been nurturing—also took his own life.[8]

THE *MYTHOLOGIQUES* WAS THE grand exposition of structuralism, an attempt, as Lévi-Strauss put it in the very first sentence of the first volume, "to show how empirical categories—such as categories of the raw and the cooked, the fresh and the decayed, the moistened and the burned, etc. . . . can . . . be used as conceptual tools with which to elaborate abstract ideas and combine them to form propositions." After the loose theorizing in *La Pensée sauvage*, Lévi-Strauss was ready to apply his ideas systematically, tracing the algebraic forms of a body of culture. He likened the native communities to a laboratory, his work an experiment designed "to prove that there is a kind of logic in tangible qualities, and to demonstrate the operation of that logic and reveal its laws."[9] It sounded like a process of distillation, of simplification, a conversion of chaos into order, as Lévi-Strauss liked to say, but in fact the *Mythologiques* series lifted his work to new levels of complexity. The mythic narratives were intricate, but Lévi-Strauss's analyses could be so difficult to follow that they had to be rendered in pseudo-mathematical formulae, used as shorthand for symbolic arrangements. By the third volume the arguments had become so involved that Lévi-Strauss admitted it took him several reads of a draft of *L'Origine des manières de table* before he fully understood his own line of reasoning.[10]

Peppered with allusions, quotes and epigrams from antiquity, the Enlightenment and the nineteenth century, from Virgil to Chateaubriand, from Balzac to Proust, the books gave off an air of erudition, tempered by the odd tongue-in-cheek aside. At the beginning of *L'Homme nu*, Lévi-Strauss slipped in a citation from *Playboy* magazine, a publication he apparently read and enjoyed, with the one-liner "Incest is fine as long as it is kept in the family."[11] Brooding chapter headings with a hint of science fiction—"The Instruments of Darkness," "The Harmony of the Spheres," "Echo Effects" and "The Dawn of Myths"—created a sense of intrigue. The quartet ran to more than two thousand pages, but the project did not end there. The so-called *petites mythologiques—La Voie des masques* (*The Way of the Masks*), *La Potière jalouse* (*The Jealous Potter*) and *Histoire de Lynx* (*The Story of the Lynx*)—would follow Lévi-Strauss into old age.

There were moments of humility. "However ponderous this volume may be," wrote Lévi-Strauss of *Le Cru et le cuit*, "it does not claim to have done more than raise a corner of the veil."[12] While he was working on the third volume, *L'Origine des manières de table*, he told Raymond Bellour that his contribution to the field was modest, amounting to no more than "the turning of a few pages of an immense dossier."[13] But there were also delusions of grandeur. He situated his work at the head of a vast historical process. As myth faded into the background, Lévi-Strauss argued, its function had been taken up by the classical music of Bach, Beethoven and especially Wagner. The avant-garde had subsequently degraded music's mythic content, leaving structuralism as the heir to a discourse going back millennia.

THE FIRST PAGES of *Le Cru et le cuit* stand at the very center of Lévi-Strauss's oeuvre as one of the most beguiling passages of writing in his career. After the freneticism of *La Pensée sauvage*, the *Mythologiques* series opened with a serenity, an inner calm. It was as if he had reached the plateau of his intellectual life, and was contented. Ideally positioned institutionally, he had found an open-ended project—a journey with no beginning and no end, as he put it—a limitless arena in which to practice his structuralist arts.

The idea was to analyze clusters of myths, linking up, comparing and superimposing them. Tracing a pattern resembling a rose curve—a mathematical formula that produced flowerlike figures—Lévi-Strauss would start with a single myth and move outward, taking in neighboring myths on all sides, analyzing a blossom of mythic material. Through the quartet he would inch northward, cluster by cluster, in an unbroken chain stretching the length of the Americas. The journey was not just geographical, but structural. Like D'Arcy Wentworth Thompson's mathematical transformations of the morphology of neighboring species,[14] each cluster represented a structural variation of the other, with some elements shifting, others inverting, still others dropping out altogether.

Axes of "guiding patterns" ran like ley lines through mythic thought, connecting up sets of myths. Nodes sprouted further axes, running perpendicular and intersecting with yet more axes at higher levels, like a coral reef forming on the ocean bed. "It follows that as the nebula spreads, its nucleus condenses and becomes more organised," wrote Lévi-Strauss, switching metaphors. "Loose threads join up with one another, gaps are closed, connections are established, and something resembling order is to be seen emerging from the chaos." He saw myth, en bloc, as a kind of substance. He described the proliferation of themes in myths as "irradiation," likening their splintering transformations to refracted light rays. Remoter myths were like a "primitive organism," "enclosed within a membrane," distending their protoplasm as they "put forth pseudopodia."[15]

This effusion of scientific vocabulary was enveloped in Lévi-Strauss's favorite metaphor—music—which he used to structure the text. The introduction to *Le Cru et le cuit* was in fact the "Overture," followed by chapter titles like "The Bird-Nester's Aria," "The 'Good Manners' Sonata," "The Opossum's Cantata" and "Well-Tempered Astronomy." When asked by the literary critic George Steiner in a BBC interview in the mid-1960s why he had called a chapter after a sonata, Lévi-Strauss brushed off the question saying that it was "a joke—because I found it so boring."[16] But in the "Overture" he gave a long, serious explanation.

Both myth and music transcended articulate expression with their timeless combinations of logic and aesthetics; they worked in tandem, posing and solving analogous structural problems. Striving for the "feeling of simultaneity" that orchestral music inspired when diverse parts fused into a whole, Lévi-Strauss modeled his book along the lines of a multipart composition with alternations in rhythm and key, variations on themes and contrasts between movements. More specifically, it was in opera—with its arias and instrumental ensembles, its alternating melodies and recitatives, its leitmotifs—that he had found a ready-made device for presenting the complexity of mythic discourse.

The ultimate model, though, was derived from his experiences as a child, when his father had taken him to the Opéra to hear Wagner's mighty Ring Cycle—a tetralogy, like Lévi-Strauss's own *Mythologiques*. At the time Lévi-Strauss had rejected Wagner's lush melodrama in favor of the new wave of modernism, but by middle age he was returning to Wagner's operas, and not just for aesthetic pleasure. He would listen to Wagner while he wrote, the music fusing with his own thinking about myth. Lévi-Strauss went as far as saying that Wagner was the "undeniable originator of structural analysis of myth."[17] Later he would cite a verse from Wagner's *Parsifal*, "*Du siehst, mein Sohn / zum Raum wird hier die Zeit*" (You see, my son / here time turns into space), as "probably the most profound definition ever given of myth."[18]

His use of the metaphor of music made for an experimental—one could even say modernist—text, whose sudden changes in style and genre, abrupt shifts between ethnography, analysis and transcripts of myths, did the reader no favors. In a long aside about *musique concrète* and serialism—the avant-garde movement that began in the 1920s with Arnold Schoenberg's twelve-tone compositional technique—Lévi-Strauss did, in fact, finally link his work to modernism, only to swiftly negate any affinity. There were similarities between serialism and structuralism; both shared "a resolutely intellectual approach, a bias in favor of systematic arrangements, and a mistrust of mechanistic or empirical solutions." It was precisely for this reason that special care was needed to distinguish the two. As a kind of formal idealism, serialism was actually "at the opposite pole" from structuralism, which Lévi-Strauss still insisted was a purely materialist science.[19]

Structuralism was, however, a strange kind of science, one that built its proofs out of poetic interpretations and refused definitive conclusions at every turn. At the end of the "Overture" Lévi-Strauss apologized for "these confused and indigestible pages," which he likened to esoteric sleeve notes on a record. Should the reader become discouraged, he urged him to return to its source, the indigenous myths themselves, "the forest of images and signs . . . still fresh with a bewitching enchantment."[20]

LÉVI-STRAUSS SET OFF on this marathon where he had begun, among the Bororo of Mato Grosso, Brazil. He had originally planned to start off in New Mexico with a series of Pueblo myths that he had run seminars on in the early 1950s, but he had found them too closed in on themselves. In 1957–58, when he had returned to the Bororo myths they had stood out as a natural departure point for future research. There was, of course, an elegiac undertone to the choice, drawing him back to his youth, when he had visited the Bororo as a twenty-seven-year-old aspiring anthropologist and felt the "giddiness" of the ethnographer's first moments in a recognizably anthropological setting: the clusters of virtually naked bodies smeared in paint, the thatched huts, the feather headdresses, the semiferal dogs and smoldering campfires. Then he had been more interested in the Bororo social organization, studying their circular hut plans, mapping a geometry of exchange and mutual obligation. Now he turned to the Bororo for M_1, "the key myth," and its variations (M_7–M_{12}), known as the bird-nester myths, the first and, as it subsequently turned out, pivotal links in a chain of analyses that would stretch across the western hemisphere, ending more than eight hundred myths later in the freezing Salish waterways of British Columbia.

His material came not from his own field notes, but from *I Bororos Orientali*, written by the Italian Salesian missionary Antonio Colbacchini in the 1920s. The book was of its time, with awkward photographs of indigenous people in the process of being Christianized—a Bororo woman in a full wedding dress, her bridegroom in a white suit, during a "Christian wedding"; three Bororo two-year-olds holding hands, dressed in ankle-length smocks over the caption "*Tre bambine salvate dall'infanticidio e allevate dalle Suore*" (Three children saved from infanticide and brought up by the nuns). Even so, the Salesian missionaries had been more sensitive than most to their exotic congregation, cultivating a profound interest in Bororo culture. Lévi-Strauss later jested that it could be said that the Salesians were converted by the Indians, and not the other way around.[21] Along with the missionary propaganda was a painstaking ethnography. Colbacchini included grammars, translations of color charts, notes on rituals and drawings of artifacts. Most important for Lévi-Strauss, he had transcribed more than one hundred pages of myths—some of them in the original language with a line-by-line parallel translation into Italian.[22]

M_1, "O xibae e iari" (The Macaws and Their Nest), was typical of the type of material Lévi-Strauss would be working with—a surreal series of non sequiturs, apparently superfluous incidents and sudden lurches into the fanciful. The hero steals some jingling bells made from the hooves of a wild pig and is helped by a large grasshopper; vultures chew off his buttocks, which are restored by a dough made from pounded tubers; and he later turns into a deer. The imagery is vivid—after the hero's father is eaten by carnivorous fish, all that remains are his bones on the bed of the lake, and lungs "in the form of aquatic plants" floating on the surface. At one point the hero awakes "as if from a dream," and indeed there is something dreamlike in the myth's woozy, surreal qualities. Seeping through Lévi-Strauss's analyses are echoes of a previous generation's obsessions: Freud's *The Interpretation of Dreams*, surrealism, free association and automatism. Significantly, M_1 even has Oedipal overtones—in the opening paragraph the "hero" rapes his mother while she collects palm fronds to make penis sheaths; toward the end he kills his father, impaling him on his deer horns.

The plot is complex, but the elements that would prove fundamental to the whole *Mythologiques* enterprise were as follows: after violating his mother, the boy is lured by his irate father up a cliff on the pretext of capturing macaws; there he is stranded and suffers great privations before he is rescued by vultures to return to his village and exact his revenge on his father. In the final scene, in one version of the myth, his vengeance extends to the whole village. He unleashes "wind, cold and rain" while spiriting his faithful grandmother away to a "beautiful and distant land."[23]

In this Freudian world, scatological references abounded. The loss of the hero's rectum in the opening myth was a hint of what was to come, from the widespread occurrence of the "anus stopper" to the role of vomiting, farting, defecating, menstruation and ejaculation in mythic narrative. Like Freud, Lévi-Strauss reveled in this kind of material; its multiple entrances and exits seemed built for structural analysis. The grandmother character in M_5 (The Original of Diseases) tries to kill her grandson by farting in his face while he sleeps, only to be skewered with a sharp-pointed arrow "plunged so deeply into her anus that the intestines spurted out." For Lévi-Strauss, this was an example of "triply inverted incestuous promiscuity"—grandmother instead of mother, back passage instead of front, aggressive woman rather than man.[24]

Lévi-Strauss rounded off the long and involved first chapter—a compendium of half a dozen myths, loosely connected ethnographic digressions, diagrams and pseudo-mathematical proofs—with what at first appeared to be a clear goal: "I propose to show that M_1 (the key myth) belongs to a set of myths that explain the origin of the *cooking of food*." But he then added, in parentheses, "although this theme is to all intents and purposes absent from it." Or rather, he went on to explain, the theme was "concealed" in the form of an inversion of myths from neighboring

Ge communities. The reference myth was, in fact, about the origin of rainwater, a reversal of the Ge cycle's origin of fire (hence cooking) myths. Perhaps it was appropriate, given the escalating complexity of his work, that the whole project was to be built around an absence, a negative example, which would form the crux of a riddle unfurling not just across the Americas, but through what Lévi-Strauss called "the curvature of mythological space."[25]

The rest of the book took on the first batch of 187 myths, submitting them to a pitiless analysis. The origin of cooking straddled the most elemental opposition of them all: nature/culture, as seen in the transformation of the raw (nature), through fire, into the cooked (culture), a central motif in indigenous mythology. Although he identified many other structural arrangements—oppositions related to each of the five senses, for instance, or to the heavenly bodies, or to north–south and east–west axes—it was this "gustatory code" which predominated, as it stood symbolically at the very birth of human society. In origin myths the raw/cooked polarity expressed not just man's passage from nature to culture, but also man's loss of immortality. Cooking processed the living into the dead; it involved the burning of wood—dead or rotten trees—on campfires, echoing death by natural causes; or the burning of a live tree, (tabooed in many hunter-gatherer groups as an act of aggression against the vegetable kingdom) often equated to death through violence.

Lévi-Strauss interpreted the terms loosely, as ideas that recurred metaphorically in many cultures in rituals at key times in the life cycle. In Cambodia, a "cooked" woman—one who had just given birth—slept on a raised bed mounted over a slow-burning fire; in contrast, girls were considered "raw" at the time of their first period, and were confined to the cool of the shade. Pueblo women, on the other hand, gave birth over hot sand—a symbolic "cooking" of the newborn baby.[26] The raw and the cooked spawned a whole complex of related oppositions in the "gustatory code," from the fresh and the decayed to the edible and the inedible, to different modes of cooking such as smoking, roasting and boiling, ideas that Lévi-Strauss would examine in later volumes of the *Mythologiques* quartet.

Once in place, these grids shaped Lévi-Strauss's interpretations of myths. Under his analytical gaze, the raw and the cooked, the moistened and the burned, fire and water spun out of the mythic matter, as if it were acted upon by some centrifugal force. Where oppositions did not obviously exist, they were creatively manufactured: rock and wood became "anti-foods"; ornaments, like bracelets and necklaces, were for Lévi-Strauss the "anti-matter of cooking," as they were made from the inedible parts of animals—shells, teeth and feathers.

Where, though, was this elaborate exercise actually leading? With all his formulae, graphs and arrows, Lévi-Strauss worked as if he were building up a case for a final proof. But any expectation of a definitive solution was undercut in the book's conclusion:

> Each matrix of meanings refers to another matrix, each myth to other myths, and if it is now asked to what final meaning these mutually significative meanings are referring—since in the last resort and in their totality they must refer to something—the only reply to emerge from this study is that myths signify the mind that evolves them by making use of the world of which it is itself a part.[27]

Promising science, Lévi-Strauss delivered a kind of Zen anthropology—the mind, myth, the universe were in structural communion, each overlapping, interpenetrating, each reflecting the other. There was no final solution, bar a sense of oneness, a demonstration of ultimate interconnectivity, a nirvana of thought and nature.

WHILE LÉVI-STRAUSS WORKED on the second volume of the quartet, he gave a long interview to the journalist Henri Stierlin for the television show *Personnalités de notre temps*, shot partly in the dilapidated offices of the Laboratoire d'anthropologie in the Musée Guimet and partly in the book-lined study of his sixteenth-arrondissement home. Now in his mid-fifties, dressed soberly in a dark suit, Lévi-Strauss was developing a certain fluency on camera. Sitting behind a small metal desk wedged into a corner in front of a tiled wall—the remnants of the bathroom—or standing in front of the rows of metal catalog drawers, he explained the work of the Laboratoire. In another segment, filmed in his study, Lévi-Strauss stood holding the lapel of his jacket in front of an ornate Indian mural and answered questions about how he became an anthropologist ("by chance") and whether man could really be studied scientifically. Studying mankind was like studying a mollusk, he explained—an amorphous, glutinous jelly that secretes a shell of perfect mathematical form, just as the chaos of humanity produced structurally perfect cultural artifacts. Lévi-Strauss left the sluglike body to the sociologists and psychologists, while the ethnographer's more elevated task was to fathom the geometric beauty of the shell. The scenes were interspersed with slow pans of the banks of archives that made up the Human Relations Area Files at the Laboratoire d'anthropologie, and of footage from Borneo of an indigenous woman lying down to have an ornate figure tattooed on her throat—not dissimilar to scenes that Lévi-Strauss had filmed among the Caduveo thirty years earlier. Brooding, dissonant music gave off an air of intrigue and intellectual gravity. It was interviews like this one that were beginning to establish the mystique of anthropology. Lévi-Strauss, as the only recognized figure outside academic circles, was emerging as the discipline's spokesperson, structuralism as the new vogue.

As abstruse as his academic books were becoming, Lévi-Strauss was a great simplifier of his ideas for the general public—ideas that were at root easy to grasp and philosophically satisfying. Myth is like a musical score, kinship a variation on a theme; culture is nature mediated by the mind; structuralism is the search for "hidden harmonies"; simplicity underlies complexity, order chaos, and so on. Indeed, it seemed that the more convoluted his written work became, the simpler his explanations.

His pithily titled short essays written for the *UNESCO Courier*—such as "These Cooks Did Not Spoil the Broth," "Witch-doctors and Psychoanalysis" and "Human Mathematics"—were clarity and accessibility exemplified.[28] Interviews in *Le Monde, Le Figaro littéraire, Le Nouvel Observateur, L'Express* and *Le Magazine littéraire* brought this pared-down version of Lévi-Strauss to wider and wider circles of readers.

As Lévi-Strauss immersed himself more and more deeply in the *Mythologiques* project, the theoretical seeds he had sown in the 1950s were bearing fruit in unexpected ways across diverse fields. He stood at the center of what appeared to outsiders to be a sudden coalescence of ideas.The watershed period was 1965 to 1967. The year 1965 saw the publication of French-Algerian philosopher Louis Althusser's structuralist rereadings of Marx, *Lire le capital* and *Pour Marx*. The following year came Foucault's "archaeology" of knowledge, *Les Mots et les choses*, with its disappearing face-in-the-sand conclusion, and Lacan's collection of papers, the nine-hundred-page *Écrits*. Despite their length and density—even impenetrability—both sold well. In 1967, the same year that Lévi-Strauss published his second volume of the *Mythologiques* quartet, *L'Origine des manières de table*, Roland Barthes's famous "The Death of the Author" piece appeared, an essay that echoed Lévi-Strauss's own claims that his books were "written through him" rather than positively authored, as well as his whole approach in the *Mythologiques*. Myths were authorless artifacts par excellence. Perhaps one day someone did think up elements of the fantastic stories to which Lévi-Strauss was devoting his life. But myths quickly evolved into unanchored cultural conversations, floating in the cognitive ether, as he explained with his contention that in the last instance "myths think one another" (*les mythes se pensent entre eux*).[29]

In *Système de la mode*, published the same year, Barthes attempted a structuralist take on fashion—the same project that Lévi-Strauss turned down years earlier. Not everyone was impressed; as the Brazilian writer José Guilherme Merquior, who attended Barthes's lectures, later wrote: "Some unkind wits went as far as suggesting that while it became more or less obvious that structuralism had failed to explain fashion, fashion might very well be able to explain structuralism."[30]

More promising were the structuralist readings of modern Western mythologies—not the operas of Wagner, but classic films. Raymond Bellour took the West's own mythemes—the shower scene in Hitchcock's *Psycho*, Melanie (Tippi Hedren) motoring across Bodega Bay in *The Birds*, Cary Grant's famous crop duster sequence in *North by Northwest*, or Philip Marlowe played by Humphrey Bogart talking to Vivian (Lauren Bacall) in a studio mock-up of a car journey in Howard Hawks's *The Big Sleep*. Bellour's frame-by-frame analysis looked at how the camera alternated between static and moving, distant and close, the speaker and the listener, short and long takes. With columns, diagrams and axes, he took Lévi-Straussian structuralism into new and fertile territory. Jim Kitses's *Horizons West* (1969) adopted the bulk approach in a study of the western, examining the works of directors like John Ford, Sam Peckinpah and Sergio Leone. Structured around contrasts between society and the frontier, civilization and wilderness, the genre was a natural target for structuralist analysis. Kitses teased out a series of key polarities—the West/the East, nature/culture, the individual/the community—which generated further oppositions: purity/corruption, self-knowledge/illusion and humanity/savagery. He looked at common motifs, such as the imperiled community, the outsider and the sacrifice. Like much of Lévi-Strauss's work, it was not so much the conclusions as the close analysis that was so revealing. Subjecting these overfamiliar scenes and genres to a detailed reading, breaking them apart into their constituent units and examining their hidden structural properties brought them to life in a new way.[31] It was almost like wandering through the director's subconscious.

Landmarks in linguistics and psychology were also appearing, with Piaget's *Le Structuralisme* and Noam Chomsky's *Language and Mind* both published in 1968, along with Payot's new edition of Saussure's famous *Cours de linguistique générale*. There were a slew of commentaries, PhD theses and books on structuralism, including Jean-Marie Auzias's *Clefs pour le structuralisme* and an edited collection of reflections from different disciplines, *Qu'est-ce que le structuralisme?* Literary journals ran special editions on the phenomenon, with *Les Temps modernes*, *L'Arc* and *Esprit* all devoting whole issues to the work of Lévi-Strauss. Everyone was turning toward the metaphor of language, anonymous matrixes, systems of interrelations, the logical, diagrammatic view of culture. "Structuralism was the air we breathed," remembered Anne-Christine Taylor, director of research at the Musée du quai Branly, whose doctoral research had been supervised by Lévi-Strauss in the 1970s.[32]

In July 1967, Maurice Henry's illustration in the literary journal *La Quinzaine littéraire* portrayed caricatures of Michel Foucault, Lévi-Strauss, Jacques Lacan and Roland Barthes as tribesmen in grass skirts, sitting together in a tropical forest. Foucault is smiling, explaining something; Lacan, bare-chested except for his trademark bow tie, looks on disapprovingly; Lévi-Strauss is engrossed in a sheet of paper, with Barthes leaning casually back on his hands. With an average age of more than fifty (Lacan was already in his mid-sixties), they were not exactly a new generation, but they were nevertheless at the intellectual vanguard. Henry captured the moment: a group of outwardly conservative, middle-aged men dealing in densely intellectualized exotica—a blend of tribal culture and psychoanalysis, literary theory and anthropology.

As structuralism peaked in the late 1960s, Stanley Kubrick's *2001: A Space Odyssey* was released. With its sense of anonymous mystery, its characters who seemed dimmed by their surroundings—ultimately dominated by a machine—and György Ligeti's frenetic but impersonal soundscape, it captured the awesome emptiness of a posthumanist world. It was also at around this time that early minimalist music arose, when composers like Terry Riley and Steve Reich broke away from the anguished dissonance that had long characterized modern music and started experimenting with new forms of expression. Looping melodies gradually falling out of step, repetition with periodic ruptures, the drone effect—it was the aural equivalent of the succession of similar-but-different models that appeared through the *Mythologiques* quartet, or the Caduveo tattoos, as they moved through their hundreds of subtle variations on a theme. At once modern and ancient, religious and atheistic, cold and romantic, the structuralist aesthetic signaled an easing off, a release of spiritual tension—not through a soothing reassurance, but as a result of being cast into the void.

ACCORDING TO THE HISTORIAN François Dosse, structuralism peaked as early as 1966, and by 1967 intellectuals were beginning to distance themselves from the label:

> Some players sought less-trodden paths in order to avoid the epithet "structuralist." Some even went so far as to deny ever having been structuralist, with the exception of Claude Lévi-Strauss, who pursued his work beyond the pale of the day's fashions.[33]

There were already rumblings of what would become known as post-structuralism, with Jacques Derrida's opening salvos against Lévi-Strauss and Foucault in *De là grammatologie* and *L'Écriture et la différence*, both published in 1967 (although many of the essays were in fact written much earlier). Dosse went on to argue that it was precisely at this moment of disaggregation that the media really picked up on the phenomenon.[34]

Uniquely, for a French anthropologist—indeed, for any anthropologist—Lévi-Strauss achieved global fame. English versions of his books were now appearing: the controversial translation of *La Pensée sauvage*, *The Savage Mind,* came out in 1966, and *The Elementary Structures of Kinship* was belatedly published in 1969, along with *The Raw and the Cooked. Newsweek* ran a piece, "Lévi-Strauss's Mind," on the publication of *The Savage Mind. Time* magazine responded with the essay "Man's New Dialogue with Man," the *New York Times* following with the more penetrating feature "There Are No Superior Societies," written by French-American writer and biographer Sanche de Gramont (aka Ted Morgan—an anagram of de Gramont). Lévi-Strauss went on American television, interviewed on NBC by Edwin Newman on the chat show *Speaking Freely*, and he appeared in *Vogue*'s "People Are Talking About . . ." photo-essay page, shot by Henri Cartier-Bresson. Meanwhile, honorary degrees flooded in—from Yale, Columbia, Chicago and Oxford—and Lévi-Strauss symposia spread through the world's universities. As one American anthropologist put it, by the late 1960s Lévi-Strauss "was as unavoidable at cocktail parties as cheese dip."[35]

For Lévi-Strauss, the exposure was a double-edged sword. It undoubtedly consolidated him institutionally. After securing funding from Braudel's Sixth Section and the CNRS, the Laboratoire d'anthropologie finally moved out of its shabby quarters in the Musée Guimet at the beginning of 1966 and into the Collège itself, taking up rooms that had hosted the chair in geology. The roomy offices, decked out with solid oak tables and antique mahogany cabinets in which Louis XVIII had stored his mineral collections, was like a dream come true for Lévi-Strauss. He was taken by its old-world feel, its "aura of a mid-nineteenth-century library or laboratory." It fit with his image of the hallowed wings and arcaded courtyards of the Collège, where great scholars had labored down the centuries. "That was how I saw the Collège de France I aspired to enter: the workplace of Claude Bernard, Ernest Renan . . . ," he remembered after his retirement.[36] Although the furniture was bequeathed to a stately home in Meudon, outside Paris, Lévi-Strauss oversaw the refurbishing of the woodwork and antique bookcases in his office. As his *Mythologiques* project moved up into North America, he pinned a three-meter-by-two-meter map of the United States behind his huge desk. As if in a war room, he could plot the coordinates of new myths on the march northward.

The Laboratoire grew into a major international research center, frequented by scholars from around the world, like the influential American anthropologist Marshall Sahlins, who spent the late 1960s in Paris. Its focus would always be anthropology, but it was seen as cutting-edge in the humanities and hosted interdisciplinary seminars, including sessions involving the emerging stars of post-structuralism: the Lithuanian semiotician Greimas, the writer on film Christian Metz, the Bulgarian-French literary critic Julia Kristeva and the cultural theorist Tzvetan Todorov.[37]

Lévi-Strauss's work was now being fueled by the field reports from the institute's scholars—a new generation of ethnographers, many born in the 1930s, when Lévi-Strauss was doing his own fieldwork. Before his suicide, Lucien Sebag along with Pierre Clastres had done fieldwork among the Guayaki, Euyaki and the Ayoré indigenous groups in Paraguay and Bolivia. Arlette Frigout was studying the Hopi in Arizona; another group—including Pouillon, Robert Jaulin, Isac Chiva, Ariane Deluz and Françoise Héritier—was bringing back data from field sites across Africa. From 1967, Maurice Godelier was in New Guinea studying the Baruya, a highlands tribe that had been in contact with outsiders only since the 1950s. It was an arrangement that Lévi-Strauss liked—"They are happy to spend a year in a tropical land, and I am happy to stay in Paris and write in my 'laboratory,' listening to classical music," he told writer Guy Sorman.[38] The Laboratoire's expansion greatly facilitated Lévi-Strauss's own work. He now had a large staff supporting the *Mythologiques* project—Pouillon transcribing his lectures, Isac Chiva along with Lévi-Strauss's wife, Monique, reading and correcting early drafts, and other researchers compiling myths.

But on an intellectual level, the sudden vogue for structuralism rankled. As soon as Lévi-Strauss hit the spotlight, he began publicly distancing himself from what he described as a "journalistic tic" of associating his work with the other thinkers—Lacan, Foucault, Barthes—with whom he was constantly being grouped.[39] Interviewed by de Gramont for the *New York Times* piece, he was forthright in his rejection of his new cult status:

> In the sense in which it is understood today by French opinion, I am not a structuralist . . . The best way to explain the current infatuation with structuralism is that French intellectuals and the cultured French public need new playthings every 10 or 15 years. Let's make one thing very clear.

> I have never guided nor directed any movement or doctrine. I pursue my work in almost total isolation, surrounded only by a team of ethnologists. As for the others, I don't want to name names, but to pronounce the name of structuralism in connection with certain philosophers and literary people, no matter how talented or intelligent they may be, seems to be a case of total confusion. I have the greatest admiration for the intelligence, the culture and the talent of a man like Foucault, but I don't see the slightest resemblance between what he does and what I do.[40]

The only true structuralists, according to Lévi-Strauss, were himself, the linguist Émile Benveniste and the mythographer and comparative philologist Georges Dumézil.[41] It was a strange choice. Although he clearly felt an intellectual kinship with Benveniste and Dumézil, who were colleagues and friends, Lévi-Strauss in fact rarely referenced them in his own work, which had an altogether more avant-garde flavor.

What Lévi-Strauss could not see was that the cult around him and his work was in part his own making. Not only was he appearing a great deal in the media, but his mature work introduced a mystical feel to what was already exotic material. Reading Lévi-Strauss—like reading parts of Foucault or Lacan—there was a sense of a prophet hinting at deep truths.[42] Lévi-Strauss may have felt that he was being crudely misrepresented. "Structuralism, sanely practiced, doesn't carry a message, it doesn't hold a master key, it doesn't try to formulate a new conception of the world or even mankind; it doesn't want to found a therapy or a philosophy," he told a journalist from *Le Monde*. But the very fact that he felt the need to deny any greater meaning to his work spoke volumes.

Even professional anthropologists were not immune to the charismatic aspects of Lévi-Strauss's thought. Claude Meillassoux remembered attending Lévi-Strauss's seminars at the height of the *Mythologiques* project:

> I went to Lévi-Strauss's courses at the Collège de France. He was the king who opened the door; the moment it seemed the philosophers' stone had

> been found, he shut the door again and took up another subject in the next seminar. Still, it was fascinating because he came up with intellectually stimulating comparisons and combinations.[43]

At his most expansive, Lévi-Strauss talked in vast tracts of time, about Nature with a capital *N*, universal modes of thought, Buddhism, the death of art and the elimination of the self. Yet in his own mind he was a mere artisan of cultural inquiry, a scholar patiently documenting and analyzing indigenous myth. The more he protested, the more commentators and critics saw the outlines of a unified discourse that cut across not just the humanities, but contemporary culture and politics.

Some saw the rise of structuralism as not simply the birth of a new intellectual movement, but a reflection of contemporary France. After the traumatic end of the war in Algeria, France had entered a period of stasis, headed by the elderly, sclerotically conservative General de Gaulle. Long buffeted by historical forces in the twentieth century, the country was returning to its provincial roots while quietly modernizing. Structuralism's closed, inert systems fit a time when French history was thinning out, cooling, slowing down; its appeals to science, mathematics and geometry suited a technocratic age. As de Gramont put it in the *New York Times*, "Despite pronouncements of General de Gaulle in both hemispheres, France no longer has much influence in world affairs. De Gaulle seems in fact to want to freeze history . . . perhaps he will be remembered as the first structuralist chief of state."[44]

The argument was given a political twist in a piece by François Furet writing for the left-liberal journal *Preuves*. Furet linked the rise of structuralism with the decline of Marxist political aspiration. Revolution was no longer in the air, de Gaulle's smothering orderliness having silenced the Left.[45] Sartre, finding his footing after the attacks in *La Pensée sauvage*, put it more strongly—structuralism was "the last barrier that the *bourgeoisie* can still erect against Marx."[46]

As THE 1960S WORE ON, Lévi-Strauss was drawn deeper and deeper into the *Mythologiques* project. His identification with his work was complete. He rose at five each morning and entered into a communion with the indigenous groups he was working on, inhabiting their world and their myths "as if in a fairytale."[47] The process was one of absolute immersion. "The myths reconstitute themselves through my mediation," Lévi-Strauss told Raymond Bellour. "I try to be the place through which the myths pass. I allowed myself to be entirely and totally penetrated by the matter of the myths. I mean the myths existed more than I did during that period."

Lévi-Strauss likened mythic elements to atoms, molecules, crystals and fragments of glass in a kaleidoscope, but in reality his method relied on intuition, flair and intellectual artistry—even chance. "You have to let the myth incubate for days, weeks, sometimes months," he said in the 1980s, "before suddenly something clicks."[48] He also spoke of making notes on cards and then dealing them out at random in the hope of finding unexpected correlations.[49] The artistic approach was seductive, but left many professional anthropologists—particularly Anglo-American ones—cold.

By the second volume of the *Mythologiques* quartet, *Du miel aux cendres*, some were losing patience. British anthropologist David Maybury-Lewis, then a professor at Harvard, was well placed to produce a critique of the evolving *Mythologiques* project. He was a Brazilianist who had done fieldwork among the Xavante and the neighboring Xerente in the mid-1950s—both Ge groups of central Brazil, closely related to the Bororo and squarely in the path of Lévi-Strauss's analytical sweep. Although sympathetic to the structuralist approach, in 1960 he had written a detailed criticism of Lévi-Strauss's essay "Do Dual Organizations Exist?" questioning him on both ethnographic and theoretical grounds, to which Lévi-Strauss had responded with a long and at times bruising rebuttal.[50]

In a review for *American Anthropologist* Maybury-Lewis described reading *Du miel aux cendres* as "one of the most exasperatingly onerous tasks I can remember assuming . . . What was pardonably experimental in *Le Cru et le cuit*," he went on, "becomes frankly irritating in its sequel." *Du miel aux cendres* was, indeed, a demanding book, which took Lévi-Strauss's arguments further and further away from commonsense interpretation. Extending his first-volume investigations into the origin of cooking, Lévi-Strauss injected two further symmetrically opposed elements, honey and tobacco. Honey as a foodstuff found ready-made in nature was "less than cooked," positioned at "the near-side of cooking"; tobacco, being "more than cooked"—in fact vaporized into ashes and smoke—occupied a structural position at the "far-side of cooking." They were sensually opposed, one wet and viscous, the other dry and crumbly, leading to further oppositions between rain and drought, glut and fasting. Honey, as nature's temptation, represented the descent to the earth; tobacco, through the wafting of smoke upward, the ascent to the heavens—hence the interplay in myths between high/low, sky/earth, world/heaven. As Lévi-Strauss struck out beyond the core of Amerindian myths he had examined in *Le Cru et le cuit*, another, more fundamental set of oppositions was appearing: the logic of forms. Container/contained, empty/full, inside/out were thematic—as seen, for example, in the proliferation of empty and filled gourds; or, in a more complex contrast, in the tree trunk stripped of its bark set against bamboo: one a solid cylinder, the other a hollow envelope; one with an outer absence, the other an inner void. *Du miel aux cendres* had more mathematical formulae and *pensée sauvage* logic, as well as moments of poetry: frog is to bee as wet is to dry, for instance.

But Maybury-Lewis was not convinced. Too often the oppositions felt forced, only tenuously grounded in the ethnography. Lévi-Strauss seemed more intent on closing his own logical circuits than on faithfully rendering the beliefs of the indigenous peoples he was covering. Part of the problem was his prose style, which glided over contradictions, assumptions and unlikely associative leaps, "just as a conjurer's patter distracts attention from what is really happening."[51]

Like Leach in his criticisms of *Les Structures élémentaires*, Maybury-Lewis's own fieldwork put him in a position to directly challenge Lévi-Strauss's use of central Brazilian ethnography. A key structural feature of central Brazilian mythology in the first two volumes of the *Mythologiques* quartet was the fact that the jaguar (who often appears as the keeper of fire, the ur-figure in the origin of cooking) has a human wife. Lévi-Strauss drew the feature from a parenthesis in one version of a Kayapó myth, and then went on to apply it to a whole string of other myths. But according to Maybury-Lewis, informants from the Kayapó, Apinayé, Xerente and Xavante peoples categorically denied the link, stating that the jaguar's wife was in fact a jaguar.

Aside from ethnographic nitpicking, Maybury-Lewis found the whole basis of the project unsatisfactory. Despite his invocations of science, Lévi-Strauss's propositions, as highly idiosyncratic interpretations, were essentially unprovable. So broad was his interpretive scope that a whole range of meanings could be elicited. As novelist John Updike wrote in the *New Yorker*, "With such a hunting license granted, parallels and homologies are easy to bag—child's play for a brain as agile as M. Lévi-Strauss."[52] But against his better judgment, Maybury-Lewis could not help feeling admiration for Lévi-Strauss's extraordinary project: "Even if these [ideas] are unprovable or unproven, this does not necessarily mean that they are inconsiderable or even implausible. This is why *Du miel aux cendres* is so tantalizing. There is so much that feels right."[53]

Rodney Needham, then professor of anthropology at Oxford University, was less forgiving of Lévi-Strauss's intuitive approach to research. An early supporter of his in Britain, Needham had already translated *Le Totémisme aujourd'hui* (published by Merlin Press as *Totemism* in 1964) when he began organizing the translation of *Les Structures élémentaires*, almost twenty years after its original publication. The process was laborious, involving two translators in Australia sending each chapter with queries about language, interpretation and sources back to Oxford for Needham to recheck against the French. Needham picked his way through Lévi-Strauss's five-hundred-page book, finding numerous discrepancies, mistranscribed quotes and errors in referencing. This was partly to do with Lévi-Strauss's whole style of operating—his encyclopedic approach and theoretical ambition, the scope of his projects and his intellectual avarice sometimes led to mistakes, a fact that he openly acknowledged. ("No claim is made that the work is free of errors of fact and interpretation," Lévi-Strauss had written disarmingly in the preface to the first edition; while in the second he had volunteered, "I admit to being an execrable proofreader . . . Once completed, the book becomes a foreign body, a dead being incapable of holding my interest.") But his on-the-hoof, ideas-driven method was anathema to Needham; an old-fashioned scholar, a stickler for correct referencing and ethnographic accuracy, he began to harbor doubts. "His scholarship was unreliable," he told me. "If you go back to the examples in the *Elementary Structures*, they were often wrong, or had the wrong interpretation—you couldn't send students back to Lévi-Strauss's works with any confidence."[54]

After the *Savage Mind* debacle, Lévi-Strauss had little to do with the translation process.[55] He did, however, find time to add a last-minute preface in which he criticized Needham's interpretation of his theories, reiterating comments he had made in the Huxley Memorial Lecture he had given in Oxford in 1965. The points he made might now seem arcane—the argument hinged on distinctions between prescribed and preferential marriage systems, theoretical rules and actual behavior. But for Needham its late appearance, in the final edit of a project to which he had devoted so much time and energy, was hurtful.

When I met Professor Needham shortly before his death in 2006 at his Holywell Street flat in the very heart of the Oxford colleges, he was still bitter, decades on. "I was going to read some Lévi-Strauss to prepare for our interview," he told me as we sat down in his meticulously laid-out apartment, plain but stylish with pared-down 1950s décor, "but I *recoiled* from it."[56] The dispute clearly ran deep—Needham lined the walls of his study with framed photos of intellectual greats, with the picture of Lévi-Strauss turned toward the wall. Once a champion of Lévi-Strauss and a key figure in the emergence of a British version of structuralism, Needham now felt Lévi-Strauss was a lush, self-conscious, grandiloquent writer. After their falling out, he wrote in the *Times Literary Supplement* that Lévi-Strauss should not be seen as a renowned exponent of structuralism, but as "the greatest Surrealist of them all."[57] When I asked Lévi-Strauss about Needham, he replied matter-of-factly, "He was kind and helpful in trying to popularize my ideas for the Anglo-Saxon world, but the way he did it misinterpreted my work, so I said so—the same goes for Leach."[58] But perhaps Lévi-Strauss's successor at the Collège de France, Philippe Descola, had a more convincing explanation: Lévi-Strauss did not like imitators, he told me, and repelled collaborations, even as he attracted them with the programmatic flavor of his research.[59]

Underlying the rifts were real differences in intellectual culture between Lévi-Strauss and his Anglo-American counterparts. It is indeed hard to imagine a British or American anthropologist producing a sentence like, "It is in the last resort immaterial whether in this book the thought processes of the South American Indians take shape through the medium of my thought, or whether mine take shape through the medium of theirs."[60] Lévi-Strauss's long period in the United States had not dimmed his essentially continental philosophical outlook. For all his appeals to the higher authority of the hard sciences, for all his use of metaphors drawn from physics, chemistry, astronomy and, most important, linguistics, his approach was becoming more literary and philosophical as he aged. So much so that when his American publishers, the University of Chicago Press, added the subclause "Introduction to a Science of Mythology" to each volume of the *Mythologiques* quartet, he was apparently very unhappy. The strictly scientific pretensions of his work were becoming less and less important to him. He was, after all, still using Jakobson's two-decade-old structural linguistic models as a blueprint for his own theories at a time when linguistics as a discipline was surging ahead.

Linguist Noam Chomsky, who had led the revolution, briefly touched on Lévi-Strauss's work in *Language and Mind* (1968), published at the height of French structuralism. Although sympathetic to his general orientation, Chomsky was dismissive of Lévi-Strauss's use of linguistics. Formal aspects of language identified by structural linguists like Jakobson were, for Chomsky, merely the epiphenomena of deeper rules—the generative grammar that he and his colleagues were then mapping out. "There is nothing to be said about the abstract structure of the various patterns that appear at various stages of derivation," he concluded. "If this is correct, then one cannot expect structuralist phonology, in itself, to provide a useful model for investigation of other cultural and social systems." The thought was ironic—could it have been that, for all Lévi-Strauss's insistence on breaking through surface realities and finding deeper structural truths, the linguistic model he chose represented a mere outer shell of appearance hiding the mechanics of language that were hidden at a deeper level still? It was not an idea that Lévi-Strauss ever stopped to contemplate. His coordinates had already been set and the pace of production was such that there was now no turning back.

Perhaps it is not surprising that one of Lévi-Strauss's most perceptive critics crossed both the Latin/Anglo-American and the anthropological/linguistic divides. French anthropologist Dan Sperber had studied under Georges Balandier and gone on to work with Rodney Needham in Oxford, as well as attending both Noam Chomsky's and Lévi-Strauss's seminars in the 1960s. As a young man he had been seduced by Lévi-Strauss and structuralism, and went on to Oxford to preach the word, but soon found Lévi-Strauss's theory wanting. "Its model didn't even work in its initial field, linguistics. Its claim to work for the rest of the universe was altogether doubtful," he told historian François Dosse.[61]

In one of the most penetrating critiques of Lévi-Strauss, Sperber concluded that although his instincts had been right, structuralism "was an uninspiring frame for an otherwise stimulating and inspired picture."[62] In the 1970s he began working from the ground up, blending contemporary advances in linguistics, cognitive psychology and neuroscience in his attempt to found a true science—what he called an "epidemiology" of ideas. Lévi-Strauss took no interest in his work, even though it had been directly inspired by the core questions that he had built his career around. "As for Sperber," he told Eduardo Viveiros de Castro in the 1990s, "I don't understand anything he writes! And this business about epidemiology, this seems to me such a return to the past."[63]

On the publication of *La Potière jalouse*—the second of the *petits mythologiques*, which he later wrote as companion pieces to the original quartet—Lévi-Strauss told Sperber that the book had been conceived as a response to his ideas. Sperber rushed out to buy a copy, but was disappointed to find there was not a single reference to his work. When I put this to Lévi-Strauss, he laughed. "That was a joke," he told me. "Sperber had criticized me for the fact that after introducing the canonic formula for myths $F_x(a) : F_y(b) \simeq F_x(b) : F_{a-1}(y)$"—first mentioned in his structural analysis of *Oedipus Rex*, then briefly alluded to in *Du miel aux cendres*—"I had never referred it again. In *La Potière jalouse* I mentioned it." In a final irony, in 2009 Dan Sperber became the first to receive the Prix Claude Lévi-Strauss, awarded for excellence in the social sciences.

Oblivious to criticism, Lévi-Strauss forged on and in early 1968 was finishing off his third *Mythologiques* volume, *L'Origine des manières de table*. By now he had clocked up more than five hundred myths, each taken apart, sifted for logical affinities and recombined into structural sets. He likened the process to the patient dismantling of the mechanisms of a clock—but this was a strange kind of clock, one whose cogs and wheels seemed to have been thrown together haphazardly, and whose ratios and symmetries became apparent only after exhaustive comparisons between scores of subtly different mechanisms. More plausibly, he described himself as like a photographer working in the darkroom of human consciousness, bringing out the myths' "latent, but hidden, properties."[64]

Ethnographically, Lévi-Strauss had crossed over into North America, leaving the jungles of the Amazon for the Midwestern prairie lands of the Plains Indians, a shift of focus that he described as "almost tantamount to exploring another planet." Conceptually, volume three added a feature that would complicate an already elaborate scheme: time. Taking his cue from the proliferation of myths involving canoe journeys, Lévi-Strauss moved from the spatial to the temporal. The logical relationships that he was now dealing in were ever-changing configurations between the "here" and the "there," near and far, the ebb and the flow, the rising and falling of water levels, and so forth.

Myths featuring canoe trips led on to journeys along rivers, to river crossings and floods, to discussions of stock mythic figures—the ferryman, "a semiconductor," carrying some people across and obstructing others[65]—and the "clinging woman," a curious character who attaches herself to the hero's back. He drew parallels between the sun and the moon and the steersman and the oarsman, both traveling together, but at a fixed distance apart—just like interrelated kin groups. The sun and the moon produced still more oppositions: summer and winter, nomadic and sedentary groups, hunting and cultivating, war and peace, as Lévi-Strauss began moving from simple oppositions to more complex quadripartite structures. Though now working in entirely different cultural milieu, he found that the North American "wives of the sun and moon" myth cycle was in fact a transformation of the original bird-nester series. A panoramic view across the Americas was now emerging, with "the bird-nester myths along a vertical axis, and the Moon's saga running horizontal."[66]

There was more rich scatological material, especially in Lévi-Strauss's ongoing examination of blockage and blocked characters, like M_{524}, a Guianan Taulipang just-so story explaining the origin of the anus. In the beginning neither men nor animals had anuses, but excreted through their mouths. A disembodied anus sauntered among them, taunting them by farting in their faces and then escaping. But they hunted him down, cutting him up into pieces and sharing him out among all animals—bigger or smaller, in accordance with the size of their orifice today. This is why all living creatures have an anus; otherwise they would be forced to excrete through the mouth or would burst, so the story ran.[67]

In a final section, which seemed strangely disconnected from the rest of the book, Lévi-Strauss reintroduced his famous "culinary triangle"—a gastronomic version of Jakobson's structural linguistics—which had first appeared in the journal *L'Arc* in 1965.[68] Using Jakobson's triangular model of sound distinctions, Lévi-Strauss substituted phonemes for "gustemes." Vowels and consonants became raw, cooked and rotted, which stood at the triangle's apexes, with air and water along two sides operating as mediators.

The argument was complex, examining all the various permutations of roasting, boiling and smoking within this scheme. Boiling was compared to rotting, for instance, as, mediated by water, it "decomposed" the raw; smoking, on the other had, was a slow and thorough form of cooking mediated by air, as opposed to the fiery, partial cooking of the roast. In a comparison between boiled and roasted dishes, he argued that while the former was often associated with homely frugality, roasting had a theatrical, ceremonial role. "Boiling provides a means of complete conservation of the meat and its juices," Lévi-Strauss concluded, "whereas roasting is accompanied by loss and destruction. Thus one denotes economy, the other prodigality; the latter is aristocratic, the former plebeian."[69] To demonstrate his arguments, he juxtaposed examples drawn from Aristotle, Diderot and d'Alembert's encyclopedia and the Marquis de Cussy with Guayaki, Kaingang, Maori and Jivaro ethnography in what was a tour de force of popular structuralism.

Through a process of constant recapitulation, he moved back and forth through his accumulating stock of myths, comparing, drawing parallels, finding new angles as he incorporated earlier material into later analytical developments. Everything is connected, he wrote in the foreword to *L'Origine des manières de table*, "M_{428} links up with M_{10} in *The Raw and the Cooked* . . . M_{495} coincides with a group of myths (M_1, $M_{7\text{-}12}$, M_{24})"—the Bororo and Ge series that began the whole project. As a result, the reader could just as well start with volume three and go on to volume one; "then, if still interested, he can embark on volume two."[70] You could even begin with volume two, Lévi-Strauss explained, then track back to volume one, finishing off with three, or take on volumes two and three in order, leaving volume one until last.

Every few hundred myths, Lévi-Strauss's argument took a new twist. Running in tandem with his geographical journey across the Americas was a conceptual one, a progressive adding of layers of logic—sensual, formal, spatial—that coursed through the mythic narratives. Comparing myth clusters, he saw that different indigenous groups had not just inverted specific mythic elements, but transposed them into completely new codes, from culinary to astronomical, sexual to cosmological. *L'Origine des manières de table* represented the most challenging step in the argument, as the point at which the temporal entered the equation. The relationships between the terms became relative, not absolute, oppositions, and in a kind of Native American modernist turn, the myths themselves were meditations on the very nature of these relationships. For Lévi-Strauss, stories about the moon, porcupine quills, the Pink River, a toad and an incontinent old woman were actually vehicles for thought about increasingly abstract properties—conjunction, disjunction and mediation.[71]

Lévi-Strauss had arrived at the outer limits of *la pensée sauvage*, the point at which "the science of the concrete" began admitting abstract thought. Up against the periphery, mythic thought began to degrade, its narrative collapsing into a series of short, repetitive episodes that Lévi-Strauss likened to the *roman-feuilleton*—the serialized novels issued in newspaper supplements, a kind of nineteenth-century equivalent to pulp fiction. For him, the ultimate heir to the collapse of mythic thought was the modern novel. Trapped inside tight genres, with repetitive characters and motifs, the novel fed off mythic elements ripped from their original context, as Lévi-Strauss explained with this lyrical image:

> The novelist drifts at random among these floating fragments that the warmth of history has, as it were, melted off from the ice-pack. He collects these scattered elements and reuses them as they come along, being at the same time dimly aware that they originate from some other structure, and that they will become increasingly rare as he is carried along by a current different from the one which was holding them together.[72]

Earlier, in conversations with Georges Charbonnier and in the "Overture" of *Le Cru et le cuit*, Lévi-Strauss had predicted the death of painting and the onset of a new, apictorial age. Avant-garde music, too, was drifting out of reach of the listener, like a heavenly body accelerating into the distance in an expanding universe.[73] Now the novel was fading away, sated on images stolen from the dawn of culture. Lévi-Strauss's vision was of a cultural apocalypse, an annihilation as severe as the environmental collapse that Western expansion was generating. This profound pessimism was wedded to a yearning for the failing powers of *la pensée sauvage*, a style of thought once dominant but now barely surviving in the crevices of modernity.

In the age of entropy, all that was left was to climb onto the treadmill of structural exegesis in an attempt to relive vicariously a purer, more integrated thought by unearthing its formal properties. And it was in this contemplative mood that Lévi-Strauss approached the fourth and final volume of the mighty *Mythologiques* project. Without warning, though, the spell of structuralist meditation was broken by a sudden irruption at the heart of French academic life.

Convergence

> In everything I have written on mythology I wanted to show that one never arrives at a final meaning. Does that ever happen in life?
>
> CLAUDE LÉVI-STRAUSS[1]

IN THE FIRST WEEKS of May 1968 the streets around the Collège de France became the stage for the famous *événements*. Near the offices of the Laboratoire d'anthropologie student groups carrying pipes and wooden planks and using garbage can lids as shields charged into rows of CRS riot police, in a boiling-over of dissatisfactions with an antiquated university system and the ultraconservatism of de Gaulle's France. Hails of cobblestones pelted the ranks of the police, with tear gas canisters streaming back in the other direction.

After nights of rioting, the atmospheric Latin Quarter was a mess. Protestors had dug up piles of cobblestones to be used as ammunition dumps, uprooted trees and pulled down fences. The remains of torched cars, tipped onto their sides, zigzagged down one street in a series of makeshift barricades. Throughout the *quartier* the walls were daubed with graffiti that would become famous: "*Sous les pavés, la plage*" (Under the cobblestones, the beach), "*La poésie est dans la rue*" (Poetry is in the streets) and "*J'ai quelque chose à dire mais je ne sais pas quoi*" (I have something to say, but I don't know what). Between the clashes students walked through the streets, putting up posters, holding sit-ins and convening discussion groups. By mid-May the Sorbonne was occupied, and in a separate dispute one-third of the French workforce was on strike, as de Gaulle's regime tottered. In the most theatrical way possible, historical forces had burst back on the scene, irrupting from within a grid of conservative repression.

The semiotician Algirdas Greimas remembered bumping into Lévi-Strauss as the protest movement got under way. "It's over," Lévi-Strauss told him. "All scientific projects will be set back twenty years."[2] In his youth, Lévi-Strauss would have been manning the barricades. Now, approaching his sixtieth birthday, he wandered around the occupied Sorbonne as a complete outsider, looking on with what he described as "an ethnographer's eye." He withdrew to his apartment, where he waited to be recalled by his colleagues at the Laboratoire. His only involvement was a meeting held with, among others, the liberal public intellectual Raymond Aron and the classicist Jean-Pierre Vernant, in which they passed a motion condemning the use of violence. "I found May 1968 repugnant," he later remarked. He was particularly upset by the wanton destruction in the streets in the Latin Quarter, the felled trees and desecrated buildings. To Lévi-Strauss, it was a return to a kind of mob rule. "I still have the *tripe* [guts] of a man of the left. But at my age I know it is *tripe* and not brain," Lévi-Strauss had said in 1967.[3] It now seemed that even in his *tripe* he was a conservative.

It was Sartre's moment—the only intellectual with the credibility to enter the occupied Sorbonne and, with the aid of a hastily improvised sound system, connect with the crowds of students who spilled out into the corridors and pavements. With the exception of Michel Foucault,[4] whose relative youth and growing sense of political engagement gave him kudos, the so-called structuralist thinkers were seen as a part of a discredited, elitist university system. This was no time for abstract analyses of myth or a semiology of narrative.

Barthes's and Greimas's students rebelled, setting up their own more politicized discussion groups. Barred from speaking during their own seminars, these great thinkers were reduced to answering questions when required. One day a student scrawled, "Structures don't take to the streets," across the blackboard; another day someone pinned up a poster reading, "Barthes says: structures don't take to the streets. We say: neither does Barthes"—a slogan that subsequently appeared on lecture-theater blackboards across the United States during Greimas's lecture tour in the autumn. A sensitive man who feared crowds and violent protest, Barthes was wounded by this sudden turn against him and his work, especially since he considered himself more authentically grounded in Marxism and the Left than his unruly students.[5]

Some felt a sense of schadenfreude at what they saw as the sudden exposure of the limitations of structuralist thought. The psychoanalyst Didier Anzieu, who had split from Lacan accusing him of obscurantism, felt vindicated, declaring: "It is not only a student strike in Paris . . . but a death warrant of structuralism as well." Later in the year *Le Monde* published a supplement entitled "*Le structuralisme, a-t-il été tué par Mai '68?*" (Has structuralism been killed by May '68?),[6] in which longtime Lévi-Strauss skeptic Georges Balandier wrote, "The whole idea of 1968 belied the structural world and structural man."[7] Much of this was in the broad brushstroke spirit of the times, with its sloganeering and political posturing, but May '68 did indeed jar with the feel of structuralism. France had been rocked by the return of the subject, the return of history writ large. Structuralism, broadly defined, along with the emerging post-structuralist thought, would remain dominant in the French academy in the years to come because those influenced by Lévi-Strauss had all risen to hold key positions in the university system, but the optimism around the project had been punctured.

Even Lévi-Strauss felt the turning of the tide:

> In the following months, I clearly sensed that the press and the so-called cultivated public which had hailed structuralism—wrongly moreover—as

> the birth of a philosophy of modern times turned abruptly away from it, with a kind of spite at having bet on the wrong horse. It's true, the May youth proved to be far removed from structuralism and much closer to positions, even though old ones, which Sartre defined right after World War II.[8]

But at the same time he welcomed the respite from the media frenzy that had enveloped structuralism in the run-up to May '68. He believed that his work existed on another plane entirely, floating high above the political squabbles of a changing France. May '68 was merely an inconvenience, an interruption, which, along with a bout of illness that he suffered the following year, had slowed the pace of his work on the *Mythologiques* project. As he began writing his fourth and final volume, his mind was elsewhere. "I was a monk," he said of the period.[9]

DEDICATED TO THE MEMORY of his father and to his mother (who, then eighty-five, had lived to see her son's success), *L'Homme nu* opened with a pan across the northwest of the United States. From the Rockies to the windswept Pacific coast of Oregon and Washington states, it glided over volcanic folds, Jurassic rock formations, deep gorges and basalt outcrops. From here, Lévi-Strauss's journey would work its way up the coast, crossing the border into British Columbia to straits and fjords around Vancouver Island. Over the course of the *Mythologiques* quartet, tropical forests had turned to prairies, the grasslands to estuaries and ocean passages. The jaguars, tapirs, parrots and monkeys that had peopled the central Brazilian narratives were by now grizzly bears, otters, salmon and woodpeckers. Although the characters had changed, they still trod the same structural pathways, hewn through the byways of a panhuman subconscious.

Based on lectures given at the Collège de France between 1965 and 1971,[10] *L'Homme nu* was a difficult book to write. After the third volume Lévi-Strauss had feared he would never finish the series, so complex had the analyses become. Each new strain of mythic thought begged anothe each set of myths posed fresh questions, suggesting further axes sheerin off in new directions. At the beginning of the Second World War, Lévi Strauss had criticized Marcel Granet's *Catégories matrimoniales et relation de proximité dans la Chine ancienne* for its overly elaborate attempts a modeling kin relations. Now he appeared to be falling into the same trap He had been striving to achieve order from chaos, but had found himsel stumbling through a set of interconnected chambers of logic, lost in maze of reason. If this was not to be a Sisyphean task—like Saussure Norse research—Lévi-Strauss had to be pragmatic. What eventuated wa a book brimming with ideas, some ambitious, all-encompassing sum maries of the *Mythologiques* project, others lightly sketched as notes fo further research.

As fragmentary and imperfect as the *Mythologiques* had been, by th end of *L'Homme nu* the mythic substance had begun to yield. By strang symmetry, the further Lévi-Strauss had traveled from his starting point i central Brazil, the more structurally similar the myths had become. As h moved up the Pacific coast from northern California to British Columbia from the Klamath-Modoc to the Salish indigenous groups, he began t make out a kind of structural convergence. The original Bororo bird nester myth with which Lévi-Strauss had led off the series reemerged, bu as with the analogy of optical projections through a light box that he ha used in relation to "La Geste d'Asdiwal," many of the "mythemes" ha flipped over.

In broad narrative outline, the original Bororo myth (M_1) and the Kla math variations (M_{530}, M_{531}), for instance, were uncannily similar. Bot told the story of a young man or a boy tricked into climbing to a hig place to capture birds. After being stranded, he is rescued by animals an returns to seek revenge on his deceiver. But in Lévi-Strauss's reading, eac element in the narrative had been inverted. In the Bororo myth the bird were macaws; in Klamath myth, eagles, a prototypical fruit-eating bir for a generic bird of prey. The boy in M_1 has his buttocks chewed off b vultures, while in the Klamath variation he is starved, hence privation through external aggression versus internal decay. In the South American myth he is saved by male cannibalistic vultures; in the North American ones his rescuers are harmless butterfly women. At the end of the Bororo myth the hero's revenge is to call on the rains, while in Klamath variations the hero summons a firestorm.[11] Taken together, the myths fit together like pieces of a puzzle.

Lévi-Strauss had begun thinking about the Bororo mythology more than a decade before he reached the fourth volume of the *Mythologiques*. When he had started on *Le Cru et le cuit*, the choice of the Bororo bird-nester story as the reference myth had been more or less arbitrary—an autobiographical coincidence that had led him to a complex of myths in central Brazil. Now he saw its significance, its pivotal place in the pan-American structures of mythic thought that he had been mapping over the last decade. A simple story of conflict between father and son had ended up containing "the whole system in embryo."[12] It was as if he had been driven by destiny, or a subconscious urge. "I now understand still more clearly why, of all the available American myths, this particular one should have forced itself upon me before I knew the reason why," he wrote. The wording is interesting: *forced itself upon me* [*s'est imposé à nous*]—again Lévi-Strauss was presenting himself as an inert receptor, his own mind a sounding board for mythic resonances.[13]

Through the tangle of mythic fibers, common themes were now being woven together. The passage from the southern to the northern hemisphere had yielded a transformation from a culinary to a vestimentary code. Raw became naked; cooked, clothed; preoccupations with the body's innards had transferred to its outer decorations. Even though the myths of the Pacific Northwest Coast dealt with a more sophisticated range of issues—bodily ornaments, trade, warfare, alliance through marriage—at a deep level all were formally analogous. In the end they revolved around perennial problems of a philosophical nature that the myths (and Lévi-Strauss himself) circled around, grappled with and meditated upon, without ever reaching definitive conclusions: the passage from nature to culture and the resulting separation of man from his natural surroundings, heaven from earth.[14]

Like a collapsing universe, the thousands of pages of analysis rushed toward a point of singularity. "Can we conclude," he wrote as he wound up his epic study, "that, throughout the entire American continent, there is only one myth, which all the populations have evolved through some mysterious impulse, but which is so rich in details and in the multiplicity of its variants that several volumes barely suffice to describe it?" The question was left begging, but hardly needed to be answered. For Lévi-Strauss, Amerindian myth was one vast conversation murmured from campfire to campfire across continents; a to-and-fro of images and sensations set in logical propositions, which twisted and turned in their passage across the Americas. The world of mythic thought was spherical—whichever direction one set out in, one would return to the starting point; all lines intersected, orbiting through mythological space. *La Pensée sauvage* had found its perfect mathematical form.

Nearing the finishing line, Lévi-Strauss switched from *nous* to *je*, from the densely analytical style of mythic exegesis to that of the nineteenth-century philosopher, with its reflections on art, music, its aphorisms and intellectual drama.[15] In the last pages he mounted a final defense of the method that he had pioneered, stressing its embeddedness in concrete, natural processes that modern science was revealing. Even sensory perception was ultimately rooted in logical operations. The scent of roses, leeks or fish was based on different combinations of the seven primary odors—camphoraceous (such as mothballs), musky, floral, peppermint, ethereal (like kerosene), pungent (such as vinegar) and putrid—which were linked to precise shapes of molecules docking with receptor-site counterparts.[16] The faculty of sight worked like a structuralist analysis in reverse: retinal cells, each specialized for particular stimuli, responded to one or other term of a binary opposition—up/down, upright/slanting, moving/still, dark/light and so on—sending the information back to the brain to be processed into an image. "Structural analysis, which some critics dismiss as a gratuitous and decadent game," Lévi-Strauss summed up, "can only appear in the mind because its model is already present in the body."

It is a curious paradox in all Lévi-Strauss's writing that at the very moment he evokes science in his defense, a kind of mysticism is not far behind. "Only its [structuralism's] practitioners can know, from inner experience," he wrote, "what a sensation of fulfilment it can bring, through making the mind feel itself to be truly in communion with the body."[17] It sounded like a religious epiphany—and who can doubt that, as he sat writing the last pages of the fourth and final volume of the *Mythologiques* tetralogy after half a lifetime lived in the rich imaginings of Amerindian minds, he would have experienced some sort of almost religious feeling of oneness, of intellectual euphoria?

THE SUMMER OF 1974 found Lévi-Strauss in an exclusive salon being fitted out in the ceremonial robes of the Académie française. Two tailors, one with a pincushion strapped to his arm and a tape measure draped around his neck, fussed around Lévi-Strauss's thin frame, fitting the famous *habit vert* wore by Academicians down the centuries. They helped him into a white waistcoat, followed by a fitted jacket with tails and heavily embroidered green lapels, and then a long black shoulder cape, fastening buttons, smoothing each item into place. The final touch was the bicorne—a cocked hat covered in black feathers—last fashionable in nineteenth-century military circles.

As he stood before the salon's antique mirrors, Lévi-Strauss looked wooden—awkwardly himself, rather than transformed by such a flamboyant outfit, just as he had in the many publicity shots that he had posed for over the years.

"I can't say I feel at ease," he told the fitters as he stood uncomfortably. "I'll have to practice wearing it."

"How do you feel? Strange?" asked a journalist off camera.

"A suffocating heat . . . that's all . . . I feel like a harnessed horse."

"Apart from feeling hot, how do you feel?" the journalist persisted.

"I like it," Lévi-Strauss replied without much conviction. "I think men should dress more gaily than they do now. After all, it's one of the rare occasions in our civilization when a man can dress like a woman."[18]

Jean-Paul Sartre had turned down the Légion d'honneur and refused the Nobel laureate on principle—the first to have done so. In contrast, Lévi-Strauss, now in his mid-sixties and already a member of the Légion d'honneur, positively relished taking up the Académie's twenty-ninth *fauteuil*, vacated by the death of writer Henry de Montherlant, and joining *les immortels* in one of France's oldest and most conservative intellectual institutions. For Lévi-Strauss, receiving the *épée* (ceremonial sword) was like being entrusted with a Bororo bull-roarer. The importance of tradition, ritual, ceremony, the preservation of culture, of language chimed with his own experiences as an anthropologist. With age he was becoming "more and more British," as his biographer put it, admiring Oxford and Cambridge, as well as a certain outdated image of England in general, as "a society that still knows how to leave a place for ritual."[19] (Or at least he liked the *idea* of traditions and rituals—he loathed actually attending ceremonial events, with their interminable speeches and empty protocol. After a presidential dinner at the Élysée Palace, Lévi-Strauss told a colleague that he had only accepted the invitation because he had to, and that he had not said a single word during the whole evening.)[20]

The previous year's only candidate and the first anthropologist ever to be put forward, Lévi-Strauss had edged in by three votes (sixteen out of a possible twenty-seven), helped by Roger Caillois, with whom he had battled in the 1950s. In a gesture of thanks, Lévi-Strauss asked Caillois to give the reception speech—normally a short, ritualistic heaping of praise on the incoming Academician. Instead, Caillois reserved the last part of his speech for an attack on Lévi-Strauss and structuralism. Alluding to their earlier feud, Caillois said that *Race et histoire* had "perhaps been written too quickly," but he saved his harshest words for structuralism:

> The structural method does not escape from the social sciences' original sin, which is to move little by little from plausible conjecture to a kind of inexcusable reductiveness [*déductivité*], infallible in all circumstances . . . It seems to me, however, that doubt has never ceased to torment you. You have been less and less inclined to go beyond pure description. You have taken to task those of your followers whose excesses have alarmed you. You have been frightened by the expansion of structuralism . . .[21]

In an interesting passage, Caillois defined structuralism as a kind of intellectual/spiritual antimatter: "a collection of intuitions or aspirations . . . which are not in fact a science, but without which science would hardly be conceivable; which are not in the least religious but which no religion ignores; which do not constitute a philosophy, being more abstract and limited." Structuralism was, rather, a product of a part-empirical, part-fanciful mind-set, "constantly on the lookout for echoes, reflections, harmonies which they sense constitute the framework of the universe."[22] According to Lévi-Strauss, Caillois's address was far milder than the written version he had submitted, but which he had subsequently been persuaded to tone down. One wonders, after this outburst, why Caillois had voted for Lévi-Strauss in the first place.

Many of Lévi-Strauss's colleagues at the Laboratoire d'anthropologie felt a certain resentment at his election, but for different reasons than Caillois's. The Académie française was, after all, a French gentlemen's club of letters (no woman had yet been admitted when Lévi-Strauss was elected)—a stuffy, elitist institution, which did not sit well with the generally progressive tone of the new discipline of anthropology. More and more, though, this was the man whom Lévi-Strauss was becoming. He now owned a substantial property in Lignerolles, Burgundy, with iron gates and a driveway leading up to a classically proportioned château where he spent his summers. After a hearty English breakfast of eggs, bacon and toast, he would go for long walks through the surrounding woodlands. In the afternoons, he would retire to his spacious living room, bathed in natural light from large windows and French doors, where he would catch up on his writing, go through a backlog of correspondence or browse through his seventy-two-volume early-nineteenth-century encyclopedia of the natural sciences.[23]

As he moved into old age, certain ideas that he had long harbored solidified. His fears of demographic explosion, the homogenizing of culture and environmental destruction were bound up in acid antihumanist and anti-Western rhetoric. "I think humanity is not that different from worms that grow inside a sack of flour and start poisoning themselves with their own toxins well before food and even physical space are lacking," he said on one occasion. On another, he likened the West to a virus, a "processor of a certain formula which it injects into living cells [that is, indigenous cultures], thereby compelling them to reproduce themselves according to a particular model." Humanism, an ideology that he had grappled with after the war, subjecting it to a critique that "gradually emptied it of its substance," became a particular target of Lévi-Strauss.[24] "I don't believe in God," he said in the *Time* magazine piece, "but I don't believe in man either. Humanism has failed. It didn't prevent the monstrous acts of our generation. It has lent itself to excusing and justifying all kinds of horrors. It has misunderstood man. It has tried to cut him off from all other manifestations of nature." And in an interview for *Le Monde*, he was more specific: humanism had culminated in colonialism, fascism and the Nazi death camps.[25]

Once more Lévi-Strauss found himself swimming against the tide, this time as a radical conservative. In 1971 he had been invited to give the inaugural lecture of UNESCO's International Year for Action to Combat Racism, in what the organization expected to be an uncontroversial reprise of ideas he had expressed in *Race et histoire* almost two decades before. But when Lévi-Strauss sent in the text to UNESCO forty-eight hours before the event, René Maheu, the director general, was dismayed. Lévi-Strauss used the address to question whether the fight against racism, as it had been conceived, was not feeding a process of cultural decay—"driving towards a world civilisation, itself likely to destroy the ancient individualism to which we owe the creation of the aesthetics and spiritual values which make our lives worthwhile."[26] Although vehemently opposed to racism, Lévi-Strauss trod a fine line, arguing that a degree of cultural superiority, even antipathy, between groups was necessary to maintain a distance that would preserve customs and ideas otherwise degraded through contact. The modern world's embrace of mutual acceptance and multiculturalism was snuffing out the sparks of creativity generated by cultural exchange. The obvious reference was to Count Gobineau's warnings about the dangers of miscegenation in his racist nineteenth-century tract *Essai sur l'inégalité des races*, a playful homage that was hardly appropriate for the opening of a campaign against racism.[27] Mortified, Maheu gave a long opening address in a desperate attempt take up some of Lévi-Strauss's allotted time.

Ever original, Lévi-Strauss continually wrong-footed his interlocutors, dashing the expectations that one would have for a leading French intellectual and critic of the West. In an interview in *La Nouvelle critique* in 1973 he shied away from taking a position on the Vietnam War, saying that the indigenous Montagnards were under just as much threat from the North as the South. He would later extend the argument, reassessing his earlier support for decolonization on the grounds that indigenous peoples were often worse off under newly independent regimes.[28] In May 1976, giving testimony before an Assemblée nationale law reform committee, he argued that the idea of liberty was completely relative. He attacked the 1948 Universal Declaration of Human Rights as irrelevant to the developing world, adding, referring to life in totalitarian states: "To undergo a regime of forced labour, food rationing, and thought control might even appear as a liberation to people deprived of everything."[29] Politically, his wartime Gaullist allegiance remained intact, and he would rejoice each time the conservatives won power. And in 1980 he opposed the election of the first woman into the Académie française, novelist Marguerite Yourcenar, saying that it ran against centuries of tradition.

Lévi-Strauss was losing touch with late-twentieth-century France. By the end of the 1970s, the backwash of decolonization was becoming more and more visible on Paris's street corners, in its shops and restaurants, changing the face of the city. The multiculturalism that had so fascinated him as a younger man in wartime New York now seemed like a threat to his own culture. Lévi-Strauss's neighborhood, the sixteenth arrondissement, had been prey to different forces, the gentrification that had wiped out the artist studios and *brocantes* of Lévi-Strauss's youth. In the mid-1950s, Lévi-Strauss had already been lamenting its demise in the pages of *Tristes Tropiques*: "Not long ago the sixteenth arrondissement was resplendent, but now its bright blooms are obscured by the sprouting of office blocks and apartment buildings which are gradually making it indistinguishable from the Parisian *banlieue*." By the 1980s, he was damning—"Now the area bores me," he told Didier Eribon.[30] Like his father before him, he deliberately withdrew into a hallowed past, into a France that no longer existed or, indeed, had ever existed.

This sense of withdrawal was echoed in his progressive retreat from intellectual debate. In 1974 Lévi-Strauss took part in a historic meeting of the age's intellectual giants, which has since become a landmark event in the cognitive sciences. The American anthropologist Scott Atran, then a graduate student at Columbia University in his early twenties, had the chutzpah to bring together an extraordinary collection of thinkers, from linguist Noam Chomsky to developmental psychologist Jean Piaget, from anthropologist Gregory Bateson to biologist Jacques Monod, along with Lévi-Strauss himself. Over the course of several days, in the atmospheric surroundings of the Abbaye de Royaumont, a thirteenth-century Cistercian abbey on the outskirts of Paris, these great minds debated the big questions that Lévi-Strauss had devoted his life to—the relationships between language, culture and the mind, rapprochements between philosophy and cognition, the search for human universals.

The debate was vigorous and stimulating, with Chomsky, then in his prime, in characteristic combative form, leading discussions on a range of topics and rebutting critics. But unlike at that other milestone in the cognitive revolution, the Bloomington conference in Indiana two decades earlier, Lévi-Strauss was strangely silent. "Lévi-Strauss sat patiently and said nothing as others spoke their piece or pontificated, or pleaded and shouted their oppositions," remembered Atran. "On the way to our last lunch, Noam Chomsky . . . walked up to Lévi-Strauss and said in a shy sort of way, 'Perhaps you remember me, when I sat in on your class at Harvard with Roman Jakobson?' Lévi-Strauss looked at Chomsky and said, 'I'm sorry, but no.' Those were the only words he would utter in the conference room." Much of the time he spent doodling, and his drawings—"of cats and other real and fantastical animals"—which he left behind on his desk, were fiercely fought over. The pathos of Atran's recollections is poignant. Lévi-Strauss's mind was as agile as ever when taking apart yet another set of Amerindian myths, but it seems that by his mid-sixties fresh intellectual perspectives were beyond him. Despite his subdued participation, he later lauded the Abbaye de Royaumont talks as the most important intellectual event of the second half of the twentieth century, but this fit into Lévi-Strauss's lifelong habit of flattering, but never truly engaging with, the work of his contemporaries.

Intellectually isolated, Lévi-Strauss's conservative instincts toward the arts were also hardening. Contemporary culture meant little to him. He disliked modern theater and rarely went to the cinema, preferring to watch old tapes of Hitchcock and Mizoguchi films at home. By retirement, his interest in art and music of the twentieth century had virtually fallen away as his devotion to nineteenth-century opera and painting deepened. The modern novel was dead, although in one concession to popular culture Lévi-Strauss liked reading American crime fiction—Erle Stanley Gardner's Perry Mason novels and Rex Stout's Nero Wolfe series.[31] As for rock bands and comics, "they don't hold any attraction for me," he said in the 1980s, "and that's an understatement!" He could worship the rawest indigenous artifacts, but maintained strict divisions between high and low culture in his own society. "To idolise the 'rock culture' or the 'comic strip culture' is to distort one meaning of culture for the benefit of another, to perpetrate a kind of intellectual swindle."[32]

And yet Lévi-Strauss still had a kind of radical appeal. Strands of his thought resonated with the Left, with students and academics. Through *Race et histoire* and *Tristes Tropiques*, Lévi-Strauss had brought twentieth-century anthropology's central idea—that all mankind shared a fundamental psychological unity—to a wide audience. "Whatever man is today," Lévi-Strauss told *Time* magazine, "man already was." It was a powerful message, one with potentially revolutionary implications for oppressed groups the world over. Although not involved politically in the defense of indigenous peoples, Lévi-Strauss did not shy away from making strong statements in the media, coruscating the West's (and by implication anthropology's) crimes, at a time when this line was still fresh and controversial. "It is because we have killed, exploited them for centuries that it was possible for us to look at them as mere things," he told George Steiner in the BBC interview in the mid-1960s. "We can study them as objects, because we have treated them as objects. There is no doubt that anthropology is the daughter of this era of violence."[33] He also preempted the environmental movement with his bleak prognoses for the future of the planet, beginning with his laments in *Tristes Tropiques* and continuing in his discourse on overpopulation and mankind's pillage of nature.

The evocative titles and the covers of his books gave off a countercultural charge. The cover of Plon's reissue of *Tristes Tropiques*, for instance, substituted one of Lévi-Strauss's fieldwork images for what had previously been an abstract drawing of a tattooed Caduveo woman. The new picture featured what looked like a teenage Nambikwara girl—although it is in fact a boy with long ruffled hair and full lips—wearing an elegant straw ornament piercing the nose. His head tipped back, his eyes glazed, he stares vacantly into the camera lens. Lévi-Strauss was unhappy with the change, but the image was potent. It spoke of youth and exoticism; it hinted at the erotic, striking a chord with the cultural upheaval of the times. Lévi-Strauss's classic, along with the rest of Plon's Terre humaine series, moved into the 1970s with a renewed appeal.

In *L'Homme nu* Lévi-Strauss had likened the study of American mythology to the weaving of giant fabric—a looping back and forth, a joining up of different-colored threads, in the hope of achieving a textural consistency. Long after finishing off the quartet, Lévi-Strauss continued his stitching and darning in his efforts to "reinforce weak spots," as he had put it, so that "the tiniest details, however gratuitous, bizarre, and even absurd they may have seemed at the beginning, acquire both meaning and function." The result was what he called his *petits mythologiques*, which appeared between 1975 and 1991, a collection of codas to his massive tetralogy. In *La Voie des masques* (1975), *La Potière jalouse* (1985) and *Histoire de Lynx* (1991) Lévi-Strauss not only filled gaps left in the *Mythologiques*, but integrated earlier work into the myth project.

La Voie des masques (the *voie* [way] echoing *voix* [voice]—another untranslatable title that was rendered *The Way of the Masks* in English), returned to one of Lévi-Strauss's favorite haunts while in exile, the halls of the American Museum of Natural History in New York. In among the totem poles were the rows of Northwest Coast Indian masks that Franz Boas had curated at the end of the nineteenth century. Carved in wood and painted in primary colors, the masks' bulging eyes, protruding tongues, hooked noses and O-shaped mouths had long interested Lévi-Strauss aesthetically. From the theatricality of the Kwakiutl's riot of color and form to the more subdued cobalt blue masks of the Bella Coola and the ruder primitivism of the Salish, these were striking images—a combination of the cathedral and the fairground, classical sculpture and carnival, as Lévi-Strauss described them.[34]

The book emerged from two visits to British Columbia, a region that had featured strongly in all his work, particularly in the last volume of the *Mythologiques*. He spent the month of February 1973 in and around Vancouver at the invitation of the University of British Columbia, and returned on a looser visit with his family in the summer of 1974. Accompanied by friend and colleague Pierre Maranda, Lévi-Strauss visited bric-a-brac shops and ethnographic boutiques, along with indigenous-run museums of Northwest Coast art.[35] In one, he was surprised to see the traditional masks he held in such great esteem displayed alongside a mask of Mickey Mouse fashioned from "papier-mâché or molded plastic."[36] He attended the famous potlatch ceremony—once a grand occasion of competitive gift-giving, which had formed the centerpiece of Marcel Mauss's *Essai sur le don*, but now withered to the exchange of little presents.

With the help of two psychiatrists at Vancouver General Hospital who had built up a rapport with British Columbia's indigenous groups, Maranda managed to get Lévi-Strauss into a night dance on the Musqueam reservation, an event normally barred to whites. The ceremony involved young indigenous men with drug and alcohol problems who had been seized from downtown Vancouver and Seattle and submitted to fasting and bathing in the glacial runs of the Frazer River. In the "winter dances" they completed their detoxification treatment by being guided by shamans through a rebirthing process. The long night of drumming and chanting left a deep impression on Lévi-Strauss—nine months later he wrote to Maranda from Paris that he was "still bowled over" by what he had witnessed. In his return trip the following summer, this time accompanied by his wife, Monique, and their son, Matthieu, he went to Harrison Springs, where he met members of the Salish people. Completely unaware of Lévi-Strauss's work, they talked unprompted about the importance of the "raw" and the "cooked" in their culture. During the first visit Lévi-Strauss had seen modern-day indigenous craftsmen re-creating the shapes and forms of their ancestors. In Victoria, Vancouver Island, he spoke to Nuu-chah-nulth carver Ron Hamilton in his workshop, in the midst of a series of half finished trunk-sized totem poles stretched out on a wood-chip covered floor. The scene, captured on camera for the Canadian documentary *Behind the Masks*, has a strong 1970s flavor to it. Hamilton, dressed in a thick woollen patterned sweater and jeans, sports a handlebar mustache and has long dark hair parted in the middle; Maranda wears a turtleneck sweater and suede trench coat and there is another figure in aviator glasses. In contrast, Lévi-Strauss's nondescript overcoat and scarf are unplaceable—he looks like someone who has stumbled onto a meticulously arranged film set. He quizzed Hamilton about the symbolism of the figures and their relationship to local mythology, in particular the different ways of carving the eyes on Tsonokwa masks, whether deep set or half-closed to signify blindness.

He was trying to analyze the masks structurally, in sets, just as he had done to myths in the *Mythologiques* series. Instead of "mythemes," Lévi-Strauss worked with aesthetic units—cavities versus protrusions; open versus half-closed eyes, bulging or sunken into their sockets; tongue visible versus tongue concealed; dark versus light hues; the use of feathers as against fur. In another virtuoso demonstration of his method, Lévi-Strauss found that the masks were in an inverted symmetrical relationship with the myths: when the message of neighboring myths was held constant, the plastic forms of the corresponding masks were inverted (sunken eyes becoming protruded, for example, or fur turning to feathers); and when the myths' message flipped over, the masks' formal properties were unchanged.[37]

"I myself feel the inadequacy of my work, because of its overly elliptical character," wrote Lévi-Strauss, responding to comments on *La Voie des masques* that Pierre Maranda had sent. "Since I have finished writing it, I have discovered new things: already enough material for a further chapter."[38] He did in fact get a chance to add this material in. Originally published in two slim, heavily illustrated volumes by the Swiss art imprint Éditions Albert Skira, it was later republished by Plon in a single volume with several additional chapters.

Lévi-Strauss still had drawers full of ideas, offcuts from the *Mythologiques* project, avenues never pursued, outlines of books he had never written. Nevertheless, he felt his work was nearing its end. Maranda remembers

Lévi-Strauss's telling him after the publication of *La Voie des masques* that this would be his last book. But after so many years at his desk, Lévi-Strauss found the idea of not writing existentially difficult. "Working doesn't make me any happier," he told Didier Eribon. "But at least it makes the time pass."[39]

IN DECEMBER 1977, Lévi-Strauss recorded the Massey Lectures, a series of five talks in English for the Canadian Broadcasting Corporation's program *Ideas*. "Once again I was forced to realise how poor my English was . . . ," he later lamented, "disgusted as I am even by my broadcasts in French."[40] He actually spoke English fluently, albeit with a slow delivery and a thick French accent, and in this case the simplifying effect of expressing himself in a second language worked in his favor. The lectures, published as *Myth and Meaning*, stand out as one of the clearest expositions of Lévi-Strauss's thought. In among the familiar ideas was a deflating humility. Structuralism was but a "very faint and pale imitation of what the hard sciences are doing." After ten books and scores of articles, his efforts boiled down to a simple and extremely modest claim: "My problem was trying to find out if there was some kind of order behind this apparent disorder—that's all. And I don't claim that there are conclusions to be drawn."[41]

When Lévi-Strauss finally retired in 1982, leaving behind him a career spanning half a century, structuralism was petering out. The following year he published his third and final book of essay compilations. *Anthropologie structurale deux* had come out in 1973, but this time around Lévi-Strauss felt he could not follow it up with a book entitled *Anthropologie structurale trois*. "The word 'Structuralism' had become so degraded and was the victim of such abuse that nobody knew what it meant," he told Eribon. "The word had lost its content."[42] The book, dedicated to Roman Jakobson who had died the previous year, ended up with the elegiac title *Le Regard éloigné* (*The View from Afar*).

Interviewed in 1985 by the anthropologist Bernadette Bucher, a former student of his, even Lévi-Strauss gave off a certain ambivalence about his chosen career. "If I may ask, what interests you at present?" Bucher floated, to which Lévi-Strauss responded:

> I don't know. Stage-setting. Once I had a chance to make stage sets, and I never had such fun in my life as when I was working on the stage, not only with carpenters and painters but technicians as well, setting the lightings and that sort of thing. I have a kind of repressed vocation for manual work and if I could . . . Anyway I am too old and there is no chance of anything of the kind coming up, so I will remain an anthropologist to the end of my life.[43]

Structuralism may have been on the wane, but Lévi-Strauss's reputation in France was stronger than ever. After the death of Jean-Paul Sartre in 1980, the literary magazine *Lire* asked six hundred intellectuals, politicians and students to nominate the three most influential contemporary thinkers. Lévi-Strauss topped the poll, followed by Raymond Aron and Michel Foucault, with Jacques Lacan and Simone de Beauvoir close behind. The first half of the 1980s swept away the competition. In February 1980, Roland Barthes died in the hospital after being struck by a delivery van as he crossed the rue des Écoles, near the Collège de France. The following year Jacques Lacan died at the age of eighty. Jakobson was the next to go, in 1982, followed by Aron in 1983, Foucault in 1984, Braudel in 1985 and Dumézil and de Beauvoir in 1986. As the 1980s drew to a close, Lévi-Strauss remained one of the only living representatives of an extraordinary postwar intellectual generation.

In October 1985, Lévi-Strauss returned to Brazil on a five-day state visit, accompanying the then president François Mitterrand. The entourage visited São Paulo and Brasília, where it was received by Brazilian president José Sarney. While in São Paulo, in among the stream of official meetings, dinners and photo opportunities, Lévi-Strauss managed to escape one morning, taking a taxi down to the Avenida Paulista in search of his old house on Cincinato Braga. The São Paulo he had known and loved in his youth, with its rolling hills and colonial architecture, had all but disappeared. Viaducts now connected the hilltops; highways filled in the ravines. Any sense of natural undulation had been eliminated by the high-rise blocks, fitted into the landscape like the levers of a lock over a key. The city, teeming with buses, trams and cars, had grown more than fifteenfold. Lévi-Strauss ended up stuck in a traffic jam and was forced to turn back.

In a trip organized by the national newspaper *Estado de São Paulo*, he was flown in a light aircraft from Rondonópolis in Mato Grosso out to the Bororo village where he had carried out fieldwork in the mid-1930s. Arriving over the site, the plane circled over half-cleared scrub, clumps of forest and a muddy river looping back and forth into the distance. Lévi-Strauss could just make out a group of Bororo huts set in a clearing when the pilot told him over the din of the engines that, although he could land, he would not be able to take off again. It was another abortive return to the past. Lévi-Strauss's only brush with the Bororo would be from above, as he peered down at the village. The aerial view was not unlike the bicycle-wheel-like plans he had reproduced in his books and articles; straggly dirt paths radiated from the longhouse at the hub out to the huts positioned around the rim. After half a century's absence, it seemed like an anticlimax. Another two decades on, I asked him if he was disappointed by Brazil. "No," he replied. "I was moved."[44]

For such an inquisitive mind, it seems extraordinary that Lévi-Strauss had never returned to Brazil, even to lecture or attend a conference, and that when he did return it would be in this stage-managed state visit as a representative of France, rather than on his own terms. In a similar way, he had waited until the very end of his academic career to visit British Columbia, another region whose art and ethnography he had heavily drawn on throughout his writing life. When he was there, he took a ferry across to Vancouver Island, and while surveying the forested coves from the deck he told Pierre Maranda, "the ecology is so important for me, and I think it plays such a part in the myth that there are a lot of things that should be not only seen but lived in, if I may say, so as to understand them."[45] The sentiment was there, but the desire to follow it through was somehow absent.

This lack of curiosity for firsthand cultural experiences was belied by his late fascination with Japan. Between 1977 and 1988 he visited Japan five times, giving talks but also setting aside time to explore the country. He described Japan as a kind of inversion of the West. Perched on the far eastern edge of the Eurasia continent, it mirrored France, which lay at the western margins of the land mass. With its sculptured landscapes layered with rice paddies, tea plantations, bamboo stands and cherry blossoms, and its ancient culture of stilted ceremony, Japan meshed with Lévi-Strauss's intellectual and aesthetic sensibility. A society of feather-light screens, lacquer masks, aestheticized ritual and self-denial—it was no wonder it attracted a series of structuralist thinkers, most famously Roland Barthes, but also Michel Foucault.

On his return from Brazil, Lévi-Strauss published the second installment of the *petites mythologiques*, *La Potière jalouse*, which he likened to ballet against the operatic tetralogy. Pithier and more playful, this was Lévi-Strauss enjoying himself with material that he had "kept in reserve" from the 1960s. During that period he had been working blind, moving from one cycle of myths to another on a voyage of intellectual discovery; now he had perspective and, working off a base of his past "proofs," he indulged in what he loved most—free-associating around big ideas and big thinkers.

The book revisited Freud, a reference point since he had discovered his work as a lycée student in the 1920s. Apart from the general theoretical thrust of Freud's work, throughout his career Lévi-Strauss had used specific Freudian concepts, such as inversion, displacement, secondary elaboration and transformation. Just as Freud would extrapolate from his primary sources with unexpected and revealing associations or metaphors (for instance, the theme of the legend of the labyrinth is really an anal birth, with the maze's winding paths being the intestines and Ariadne's thread the umbilical cord), so Lévi-Strauss made similar inventively lateral connections. As he put it, Freud's greatness lay in the fact that "he could think the way myths do," an ability that Lévi-Strauss also claimed for himself.[46]

A scatological joust with psychoanalysis, *La Potière jalouse* had the sloth and the goatsucker bird in South American Jivaro mythology as symbols of anal and oral retention and incontinence. Human jealousy became a form of psychological retention, the body akin to a potter's kiln, but for cooking excrement rather than clay. Freud's theories, Lévi-Strauss concluded, had already been invented by the Jivaro centuries before psychoanalysis was presented as a revolutionary technique in the West. "How wise are the Americans in calling psychoanalysts 'headshrinkers,'" Lévi-Strauss quipped, "thus spontaneously associating them with the Jivaro!"[47]

More seriously, he argued that the central mistake made by Freud—along with a long line of thinkers who had tried to decipher myths: Müller, Frazer and Jung—was to try to ascribe specific meanings to each element, interpreting each myth (or dream) in terms of a single code. For Lévi-Strauss, this was a hopeless task. Universals could not be sought at the level of surface imagery. The grist lay in the "mythemes" relationships to each other and in the interplay between different codes that myths simultaneously deployed. It was the invariant logic of these relationships that strung together a mass of baroque images and plots. Mythic thought floated free through space, twisting, turning and tumbling over, rotating, but never losing its overall structural shape, "free from the concern of anchoring itself to an outside, absolute reference, independent of all context."[48]

LÉVI-STRAUSS HAS OFTEN BEEN portrayed as a recluse, not least by himself—"I don't have much of a taste for socializing," he once said. "My initial instinct is to avoid people and go back home."[49] But as he turned eighty he gave a book-length interview to the writer and journalist Didier Eribon, which was published as *De près et de loin*. He had been impressed by a similar work on his mentor Georges Dumézil, *Entretiens avec Didier Eribon*, and indebted to Eribon "for enabling me to hear Georges Dumézil's voice from beyond the grave." (Dumézil had died in 1986, a year before the book was published.) Lévi-Strauss was also curious:

> What questions would I be asked, what aspects of my life and work would interest a young writer who might have been my son, or even my grandson? It was amusing, I confess, to discover how many of the events in which I had been involved or witnessed had taken on a legendary colouring for someone of a later generation. And so I made a rule not to evade any of the questions, even if they did not accord with the angle of vision from which I myself would have looked at the past.[50]

Although studiously avoiding his private life, Lévi-Strauss gave long and thoughtful answers to a wide range of questions about his life, work and ideas. Many of the answers had already been rehearsed in the scores of interviews that he had given to the press throughout his career. But at times he went further, talking frankly about his aesthetic preference for certain racial types (Japanese) over others, admitting his lack of patience for fieldwork, and lamenting his "hateful accent" in English and his general lack of talent for languages.[51]

When pressed, he spoke of his sense of his own Jewishness, not in religious or ancestral terms, but as a state of mind. Being a part of a traditionally persecuted group brought a heightened awareness and a sense that he would have to overachieve in order to have a chance to compete fairly. He was nevertheless fascinated by the idea of Israel. "I hesitated for a long time before going to Israel because re-establishing physical contacts with one's roots is an awesome experience." When, however, in the mid-1980s he finally made it, chairing a symposium at the Israel Museum on art and communication in preliterate societies, there was no resonance. His sense of connection had been "reduced to abstract knowledge" by the vast stretches of time between when his ancestors had left Palestine and when they had arrived in Alsace at the beginning of the eighteenth century.[52]

While on the Jewish question, Eribon brought up a letter Lévi-Strauss had written to Raymond Aron, and which subsequently resurfaced in Aron's published memoirs. In it, Lévi-Strauss expressed his support for the Palestinian cause, albeit while reiterating his dislike for Islamic culture. "It is obvious that I can't feel the destruction of the Indians as a fresh wound in my side," he had written, "and feel the opposite reaction when the Palestinian Arabs are involved, even if (as is the case) the brief contacts I have had with the Arab world have inspired within me a profound distaste." Lévi-Strauss explained the remark by saying that he had exaggerated because "I didn't want Aron to get the wrong idea about my attitude by attributing pro-Arab sympathies to me."[53]

During the Eribon interviews he described the outline of yet another work on indigenous myth that he was preparing, a companion piece to *La Potière jalouse*. He wondered out loud "whether it really is necessary to add another mythological proof to all the others," and said that the fact that he had not yet come up with a title was holding him back. "It's the title that gives the tone to the work," he explained.[54]

Published in 1991, *Histoire de Lynx* drew together the threads from fifty years of scholarship, knitting them into a tidy conclusion. In the 1940s and '50s Lévi-Strauss had grappled with the problem of dual systems of social organization—an example of which he had seen firsthand among the Bororo, with their symmetrically organized hut plans, which worked as blueprints for the exchange of rights, obligations, marriages and funerals.[55] In the 1960s he had considered, then set aside, a series of Salish myths involving fog and wind, the lynx and the coyote, and twins who progressively diverge. Now he realized that they were all in fact the same problem, differently stated. All fed in to a concept that had been thematic in his earlier work on kinship, the idea of an inherently unstable compact between reciprocity and hierarchy. This was the uneasiness at the heart of structuralism. Although cultural invention appeared poised on an equilibrium, a perfect balance of social and cultural symmetries, it always threatened to tip over into hierarchies of caste-like divisions.

On this disquieting note of cooperation masking inequality, of a superficial symmetry papering over structural discord, of concealed conflict, Lévi-Strauss ended his great myth enterprise. The detail, complexity and inventiveness of a project that now spanned two decades and some twenty-five hundred pages were undeniable. But by the 1990s Lévi-Strauss was virtually the only man left standing. Since the mid-1970s his followers had begun to drop off. The *petites mythologiques* were still popular—especially *La Potière jalouse*—but the ideas were no longer new, no longer cutting-edge. "The imaginative incitement is gone, and in its place there is the appearance of just going through the motions," wrote Needham of his late work.[56] For the wider public, Lévi-Straussian structuralism had become virtually like an intellectual brand—familiar, reliable, almost comforting. Like a gifted writer who had found his voice or a great painter hitting his stride, he was forgiven for turning out the same work over and over again, with slight variations of plot or palette.

A rump of interested scholars—mainly in France and Brazil—went on to pursue aspects of his work, but essentially Lévi-Strauss ended up as a one-man school, peddling a type of analysis that had become so utterly idiosyncratic that it was impossible to build on. The enormous energies he had devoted to modeling the world of myth have never been systematically followed up, a fact that one would imagine would have been at the very least disappointing, but as he reached the end of his life he appeared sublimely unconcerned about his legacy.

ASSESSING LÉVI-STRAUSS'S INFLUENCE is difficult. In the popular French imagination he will forever be associated with the Caduveo, the Bororo and the Nambikwara, peoples that he spent a matter of months studying more than seventy years ago; or with structuralism, an idea borrowed from structural linguistics circa 1940 and, despite the subsequent rapid advances in linguistics, never really renewed. He is also known as the master theoretician, but he denied that structuralism was even a theory, or a philosophy. It was a method of analysis, he said repeatedly, a tool for uncovering "hidden harmonies." He was known for his impenetrability, but the overall model that Lévi-Strauss worked with throughout his career was remarkably simple.

Responding to a query from British anthropologist Edmund Leach in the 1960s, Lévi-Strauss summarized his approach with a prosaic metaphor. Reality, he wrote, was like a club sandwich. It was composed of three similarly structured strata: nature, the brain and myth. Each of these elements cascaded from the other—the brain being merely one aspect of nature, and mythic thought a subset of mental function. These strata were separated by "two layers of chaos: sensory perception and social discourse."

Beyond the disorder of our first impressions, beyond the eccentricities of a living culture, were logical relationships—the symmetries, inversions and oppositions that Lévi-Strauss never tired of identifying. These structures underlined the order of all natural phenomena, be they crystals, organisms, language, kinship systems or the free flow of human thought in oral cultures as a shaman retold a myth for the thousandth time by a communal fire in the depths of the Amazon rain forest or on the North American prairies. "I am much closer to eighteenth-century materialism than to Hegel," concluded Lévi-Strauss, since the human brain's "laws of functioning are the same as the laws of nature."[57]

There was great breadth and scope to Lévi-Strauss's ideas, but they were fitted into this ultimately claustrophobic intellectual space. Throughout his career, ethnographic descriptions, mythic narratives and his own ideas folded back on one another in an endless process of self-reference. Fellow mythologist Wendy Doniger has likened Lévi-Strauss's way of thinking to the Klein bottle—a three-dimensional mathematical form made by sticking two inverted Möbius strips together, which Lévi-Strauss reproduces in *La Potière jalouse* to illustrate the structure of a myth. The comparison is apt. Mathematically generated but with an organic feel, the bottle's bulbous, undulating form is self-consuming and conceptually difficult to grasp. It has no true inner or outer surfaces. Like Lévi-Strauss's oeuvre, it eternally feeds back through itself.

What gave air to Lévi-Strauss's output, and introduced the lyricism that baffled his Anglo-American critics, was a profound interest in aesthetic expression and appreciation that ran in tandem with the cognitive side of his work. His lifelong quest to reconcile the "sensible" and the "intelligible"—that is to say, how raw sensory perception, which is an especially rich experience in oral cultures, relates to a more abstract intellectual understanding—added an artistic flavor to what could have been a dry academic exercise. In an interview with the film critic Raymond Bellour in the 1960s, he said that the whole myth project was really searching for answers to the perennial questions: What is a beautiful object? What is aesthetic emotion?—problems that preoccupied him more and more as his career progressed. In another interview, he elaborated:

> Myths are very beautiful objects and one never tires of contemplating, manipulating them or of trying to understand why one finds them so beautiful. And if I spend a long time in the study of myths, it's with the hope, upon dismantling these aesthetically admirable objects, that one could contribute in a way to understanding what the feeling of beauty is, and why we have the impression that a painting or a poem or a landscape is beautiful.[58]

This side of his work came to the fore in his last book, *Regarder, écouter, lire* (*Look, Listen, Read*), which largely broke free of Lévi-Strauss's obsessional exegesis of indigenous culture. Here was the classical side of his modernist/classicist matrix, moving through a history of aesthetic ideas and theories of sounds, colors and words via musings on the likes of Diderot, Rousseau, Proust, Poussin and a half-forgotten eighteenth-century proto-structuralist musicologist called Chabanon. The tone was conversational, studded with Lévi-Strauss's intriguing observations, such as, "In France we prefer a golden yellow," to which he added, quoting the eighteenth-century Jesuit intellectual Louis-Bertrand Castel, "leaving the English to a pure yellow which we find bland," and fascination for sensory crossover—from the eccentric invention of Castel's "ocular or chromatic clavichord" to concepts of "coloured hearing" and the meshing of musical and linguistic codes.[59]

STRUCTURALISM NEVER embedded itself in the popular culture the way existentialism did. It rather hung in the air, drifting on the winds of intellectual invention. Soaring over existentialism's anguished quest for authenticity, it claimed the high ground: the authentic would never be found in the petty, self-absorbed choices of the Left Bank intelligentsia because it already existed in the abstract workings of the mind. There was no use striving for it—it was all around us, it was in us, it *was* us. It had nothing to do with twentieth-century Western philosophy or a tortured soul in a garret—its essence has been effortlessly exercised since the human brain evolved and was set into intellectual play. If anything, Sorbonne-style philosophizing had blunted the mind, Western training polluting a purity of function.

Structuralism implied depth, but with its interplay of referentless signs, often felt more like a skidding along polished glass. The erasure of the self, atomized in an amalgam of blind structures, produced a floating sensation, unfocused but powerful. Lévi-Strauss, and the many who were influenced by him, brought a late-modernist vertigo as the reference points of the past—God, interior experience, the self, humanity—fell away into a void. Meaning as "an obscure vibration, a dim discharge of deeply enigmatic sense" lost its solidity.[60] Some have argued that structuralism was a reversion to a pre-Cartesian, prehumanist world of divine necessity, an ethnographic version of kabbalistic exegesis. But for others it was a return to something very different. In a fascinating exchange in *La Quinzaine littéraire* in April 1966, Michel Foucault gave his assessment as structuralism took off:

> *Question:* When did you stop believing in "meaning?"
>
> *Foucault:* The break came the day that Lévi-Strauss demonstrated—about societies—and Lacan demonstrated—about the unconscious—that "meaning" was probably only a sort of surface effect, a shimmer, a foam, and that what ran through us, underlay us, and was before us, what sustained us in time or space was the system.
>
> [. . .]
>
> *Question:* But then, who secretes this system?
>
> *Foucault:* What is this anonymous system without a subject, what thinks? The "I" has exploded—we see this in modern literature—this is the discovery of "there is." There is a *one*. In some ways, one comes back to the seventeenth-century point of view, with this difference: not setting man, but anonymous thought, knowledge without subject, theory with no identity, in God's place.[61]

One way to approach Lévi-Strauss is as he saw himself—as an *artiste manqué*, a man who would have loved to have been a painter like his father, or a musician, had he had the talent. In the Massey Lectures he remembered a conversation with the composer Darius Milhaud in the 1940s when they were both in exile in New York. Milhaud told him that he had first realized he would become a composer when, as a child, he was lying in bed falling asleep and heard an unfamiliar musical composition playing in his head—his first, subconscious efforts at composing. The conversation stuck, driving home the fact that musical talent was inbuilt, that whatever Lévi-Strauss did, he would never be able to fulfill his true desires.[62]

His experiments writing fiction, as a playwright or a poet, were quickly abandoned, but as a photographer he produced some memorable images—a powerful record of the lives of the Caduveo, Bororo, Nambikwara, Mundé and Tupi-Kawahib peoples. They were images captured at an important moment in history, as the Brazilian state moved to complete the long process that European colonialism had unleashed. But toward the end of his life, Lévi-Strauss was dismissive of the art. "I have never attached much importance to photography," he said in an interview for *Le Monde* in 2002. "I used to photograph, because it was necessary, but I always had the feeling that it was a waste of time, a waste of attention." And he was equally skeptical about the moving image in anthropology—"I have to confess, ethnographic films bore me."[63]

Saudades do Brasil, published in 1994, was in many ways the type of book Lévi-Strauss had once excoriated—an old-fashioned photo album of the returning explorer, with captions that sound as if they were written in the 1930s when Lévi-Strauss took the pictures. ("The attractiveness of the Nambikwara, notwithstanding their wicked reputation, is largely explained by the presence in their midst of very young women who were graceful despite their rather thick waists.")[64] In the prologue he spoke of the fact that in comparison to the smell of insecticide coming off his half-century-old notebooks, which instantly recalled his fieldwork experience, the photographs brought back nothing. The only sensation he felt as he leafed through the sixty-year-old prints was "the impression of a void, a lack of something the lens is inherently unable to capture."[65] But for anyone other than Lévi-Strauss, the images are richly evocative and reveal a keen eye for visual expression.

He eventually found his voice as a writer in *Tristes Tropiques*, but by this stage his course had been set. He would be a thinker, an academic, a trader in ideas. The inner artist would find expression not just in the way he wrote but in the ideas he produced, the way he pieced together, like a collage, the wealth of ethnographic material he had ingested. An analyst of form, Lévi-Strauss's own oeuvre was a hymn to proportionality;

if it were a painting, it would be one of the Poussin canvases Lévi-Strauss loved, an effortlessly fit-together composition of classical poise. The massive body of work he left behind was a kind of *pensée sauvage* of academia; roaming the libraries, he picked and mixed, throwing out memorable if speculative ideas—hot and cold societies, bricolage, the science of the concrete—as well as the strange and beautiful images found in the oppositions cooked up in the *Mythologiques* quartet. His grand theories about the human mind, culture and indigenous thought became more and more impressionistic—an operatic backdrop to the imagery of his work. Just as he did not have the patience for fieldwork, so he never stopped to examine systematically the implications of his own thinking. Instead, he kept moving forward, piling idea upon idea. While his powers of invention might have waned in old age, who could begrudge a thinker who produced something of the caliber of *Regarder, écouter, lire* in his mid-eighties?

The stature of Lévi-Strauss is such that even his harshest critics could not help but admire his output. American anthropologist Clifford Geertz, certainly no friend of the structural approach, put it well:

> Whatever becomes of circulating women, mythemes, binary reason, or the science of the concrete, the sense of intellectual importance that structuralism brought to anthropology, and most especially to ethnography . . . will not soon disappear. The discipline had worked its way into general cultural life before: Eliot read Frazer; Engels read Morgan; Freud, alas, read Atkinson; and in the United States, at least, just about everyone read Mead. But nothing like the wholesale invasion of neighboring fields (literature, philosophy, theology, history, art, politics, psychology, linguistics, and even some parts of biology and mathematics) had ever occurred . . . More than anything else he cleared a space that a generation of characters in search of a play rushed to occupy.[66]

In a world of ever more specialized areas of knowledge, there may never again be a body of work of such exhilarating reach and ambition.

Few thinkers have been so relentlessly inventive; even fewer have covered so much ground. Lévi-Strauss's inspired break from mainstream thought at midcentury changed the humanities forever. From the perspective of the early twenty-first century, an era left rudderless after the collapse of the "grand narratives" that drove thought through a good portion of the previous century, one can finally look back at Lévi-Strauss's extraordinary output with a sense of nostalgia for an age when thinkers still had intellectual space to work in, and were not forced down today's ever-narrowing corridors of knowledge.

Epilogue

> When I was six years old, my father gave me a beautiful Japanese print. It was, you might say, my first exotic experience with another culture. I still have that print. It is very old and in poor condition now—like me. All my life I have been seeking to understand the meaning in that print. Sometimes I think I have it.
>
> CLAUDE LÉVI-STRAUSS[1]

NOT MUCH REMAINS of the landscape through which Claude Lévi-Strauss traveled during fieldwork in the late 1930s in what are today Mato Grosso and Rondônia states. These dusty scrublands in the far west of Brazil are now at the agro-industrial frontier—a bleak landscape of cane fields and soya plantations, punctuated with hamlets of domed charcoal furnaces burning wood trucked in from the Amazon rain forests farther to the north. Backlit by vivid blue skies, little balls of dust roll along feeder roads through the plantations—the great road trains transporting produce for export—in an otherwise denuded landscape. Many of the strange *cerrado* orchards that had once dazzled the plains with spectacular mauve and yellow flowers have been plowed under.

The remains of Rondon's telegraph line snake through the secondary forests of the indigenous reservations, hundreds of porcelain adaptors lying scattered in the undergrowth. Descendants of the peoples that Lévi-Strauss struggled to understand in his fraught journey across the plateau now live marooned in clapboard settlements, subsisting from food packages delivered by indigenous agency officials. It is hard now to read through Lévi-Strauss's pocket-sized field notes without a sense of pathos, the pessimism that he was already expressing so well in *Tristes Tropiques* half a century ago.

Lévi-Strauss lived long enough to see his worst fears realized—the inexorable rise of the world's population, the wanton destruction of the environment, the wiping out of cultures that had taken millennia to develop and that he had spent his whole life trying to decipher. "This is not the world I knew, I liked, or can still conceive of," he said in old age, surveying contemporary realities. "For me it's an incomprehensible world."[2]

Longevity brought with it an ever-widening disjuncture. As far back as 1987, a *New York Times* reporter was describing Lévi-Strauss as "alert and nimble," as if it was a surprise that a seventy-nine-year-old was still in such good shape. On that occasion Lévi-Strauss had quipped that he was toiling at his "posthumous works."[3] But when he reached ninety, the years were beginning to weigh. He had by now largely stopped writing and no longer bothered to renew his passport. At a reception in his honor at the Collège de France, he spoke movingly of his current state of mind:

> Montaigne said that aging diminishes us each day in a way that, when death finally arrives, it takes away only a quarter of half of the man. But Montaigne only lived to be fifty-nine, so he could have no idea of the extreme old age I find myself in today. At this great age that I never thought I would attain, I feel like a shattered hologram.[4]

He described his life as a dialogue between the decrepit ninety-year-old man he had become and an ideal self who was still thinking about intellectual projects that would never see fruition. As he scaled the nineties, the dialogue continued. At ninety-two he said that old age was dimming his intellectual curiosity, but added that he was still reading prodigiously in both English and French—Jane Austen, Thackeray, Trollope and Dickens, as well as Balzac for "the fortieth time with complete enchantment."[5] But at the same time his sense of dislocation was deepening. Two years later, in an interview in *Les Temps modernes*, he was asked whether he thought about death. "Yes," he replied. "I'm not calling for death, but I don't have a place in this world anymore. It is a different world and I've finished my work here."[6]

A few months before his hundredth birthday, Lévi-Strauss became one of the few living authors to find a place in Gallimard's Bibliothèque de la Pléiade—a prestigious collection of annotated editions whose list includes French literary greats and heroes of Lévi-Strauss, such as Marcel Proust, Paul Verlaine, Charles Baudelaire and Arthur Rimbaud. Lévi-Strauss's choice of which works would go into the seven-book anthology was curious. There were the classics, like *Tristes Tropiques* and *La Pensée sauvage*, but he opted for his *petites mythologiques* over the centerpiece of his career, the monolithic *Mythologiques* quartet. The only trace of this great work was the inclusion of a short interview he gave Raymond Bellour, in which he explained the labyrinthine logic that had driven the first three volumes.[7] A further absence was Lévi-Strauss's PhD thesis, *Les Structures élémentaires de la parenté*, the reinterpretation of the field of kinship studies, which had established him as a leading thinker in postwar France. It was as if at the last moment he had chosen to excise the very heart of his life's work.

His hundredth birthday was celebrated across the world, but especially in France. President Nicolas Sarkozy visited him at his apartment; Arte, the Franco-German television station, devoted a day's programming to him, with France 3 featuring a live television debate between the young Columbia professor of French Vincent Debaene, one of the editors of the Pléiade edition, and the eighty-year-old anthropologist and longtime Lévi-Strauss critic Georges Balandier—one of the few dissenting voices on a day of effusive eulogies. Entrance was free for the day at the Musée du quai Branly, where a hundred scholars gathered in the Lévi-Strauss Auditorium to pay homage. By now confined to a wheelchair after breaking his femur, Lévi-Strauss did not appear publicly, but said that he felt there was little to celebrate about reaching such a morbid milestone. It is hard to imagine a similar outpouring for an intellectual, let alone an anthropologist, in America or Britain. But in France, Lévi-Strauss fit into a long tradition of the literary-philosophical thinker who has always occupied a special place in the soul of a nation.

Shortly before Lévi-Strauss died, Gilles de Catheu, a French doctor working with the indigenous peoples in Rondônia, visited him in his apartment. In a piece for the Brazilian newspaper *O Globo*, he described meeting a well-dressed, physically fragile, but intellectually alert Lévi-Strauss, sitting in his wheelchair behind his writing desk. They talked about the Mundé, the tribe Lévi-Strauss had briefly visited during the Serra do Norte expedition. As he left, de Catheu gave Lévi-Strauss a *marico*—an indigenous bag woven from *tucumã* palm fiber. "He held the *marico*, looking at the handles with interest," remembered de Catheu, "gently touching an object born of a thousand-year-old tradition with hundred-year-old hands . . . I have never seen so much happiness and emotion . . ."[8]

Lévi-Strauss died of heart failure two weeks later, just shy of his hundred and first birthday. When his death was announced on November 3, 2009, the tributes poured in once more, with wall-to-wall coverage on television, and *Le Monde* alone carrying half a dozen pages and three obituaries.[9] Among the thousands of homages, President Sarkozy hit a false note, writing in an official communiqué that Lévi-Strauss had been a "tireless humanist."[10]

A public funeral for such a revered intellectual figure would have attracted a grand procession through the streets of Paris, ending in a burial thronged by the great and good—politicians, intellectuals, students, as well as thousands of ordinary members of the public paying their respects to the last giant of mid-twentieth-century thought. But this was not Lévi-Strauss's style. By the time the news of his death broke, he had already been buried in a small cemetery near his château in Lignerolles. The ceremony was attended by close family—his wife, Monique, his two sons, Laurent and Matthieu, and two grandsons, along with the mayor of the town, Denis Cornibert. His last wishes were to be lowered into the grave in total silence. "That wasn't easy," recalled Cornibert.[11] A simple gold plaque reading CLAUDE LÉVI-STRAUSS—1908–2009 sits on the gravel burial mound. A stone's throw away from this bare grave are the forests where, in summers gone by, Lévi-Strauss would go out walking in the afternoons, hunting for wild mushrooms, bundling them into his scarf as he went.

ACKNOWLEDGMENTS

First and foremost I would like to thank my brother Hugo, whose contribution through many conversations and e-mail exchanges, as well as close readings of various drafts, was immense. I would also like to thank the late Professor Lévi-Strauss for meeting and corresponding with me, as well as allowing me access to his field notes and a manuscript of *Tristes Tropiques*. Professor Lévi-Strauss's family kindly granted permission to use fieldwork images from the 1930s, as well as family portraits. Of the many people who shared their thoughts on the work of Professor Lévi-Strauss I would like to thank the late Rodney Needham, Philippe Descola, Anne-Christine Taylor, Alban Bensa, Jean-Patrick Razon, Dan Sperber, Marcelo Fiorini, Stephen Nugent, John Sturrock, John Hemming and Eduardo Viveiros de Castro.

I am grateful for a research grant from The Society of Authors, which funded one of my trips to France. A traveling fellowship from the Winston Churchill Trust gave me the opportunity to visit the region where Lévi-Strauss carried out his fieldwork. Special thanks go to Alfeu França for enduring a five-thousand-kilometer drive along the potholed roads of the Brazilian central west during this trip. In Mato Grosso, my thanks go to Ivar Busatto, Anna Maria and José Eduardo da Costa and João dal Poz.

I would also like to thank my agent, David Godwin, who from the outset believed passionately in this book and whose enthusiasm drove the project forward. At Penguin, thanks go to my editor, Laura Stickney, for her astute comments and the fantastic work of the production editor, Noirin Lucas. My editor at Bloomsbury, Bill Swainson, provided invaluable input, and production editor Emily Sweet nurtured the manuscript into print in the UK. Staff at the Bibliothèque nationale in Paris, the British Library in London, along with the Museu do Índio and the Museu de Astronomia e Ciências Afins in Rio de Janeiro provided professional assistance throughout.

I wrote sections of this book in Brazil, where I enjoyed the attentive hospitality of Maria Alice França, Zenir de Paula, Laura and Edyomar Vargas de Oliveira Filho. In London, Leila Monterosso helped my family through a difficult but inspiring phase of our life in 2008. As ever, my family in Australia has been a source of constant encouragement. I am also grateful for the contribution of Helen and Paul Godard in Nîmes.

Finally, I would like to thank my wife, Andreia, for her unconditional love and support throughout the long and bumpy process that book writing entails. Our daughter, Sophia, appeared halfway through the writing of this book and over the last two years steered it to its conclusion.

NOTES

Introduction

1. Cited in Lévi-Strauss and Didier Eribon, *Conversations with Claude Lévi-Strauss,* Paula Wissing, trans. (Chicago: University of Chicago Press, 1991), p. 94 (hereafter Eribon, *Conversations*).
2. Claude Lévi-Strauss, *Tristes Tropiques,* John and Doreen Weighman, trans., (London: Picador, 1989), p. 277. This image, taken on Lévi-Strauss's earlier expedition among the Bororo, is reproduced in Claude Lévi-Strauss, *Saudades do Brasil: A Photographic Memoir,* Sylvia Modelski, trans. (Seattle: University of Washington Press, 1995), p. 87.
3. Lévi-Strauss's wife Dina had left the expedition earlier, having contracted a virulent eye infection at the beginning of the trip.
4. See "Cahiers du terrain—Mai 1938," Archives de Lévi-Strauss, Bibliothèque nationale de France.
5. Lévi-Strauss, *Tristes Tropiques* (Paris: Plon, 1971), p. 59.
6. Marc Augé, "Ten Questions Put to Claude Lévi-Strauss," *Current Anthropology,* vol. 31, no. 1, February 1990, p. 86.
7. Pierre Dumayet with Claude Lévi-Strauss, "Claude Lévi-Strauss à propos de *Soleil Hopi,*" *Lectures pour tous,* April 15, 1959, http://www.ina.fr/art-et-culture/litterature/video/I00014610/claude-levi-strauss-a-propos-de-soleil-hopi.fr.html.

8. Eribon, *Conversations*, p. 59. Lévi-Strauss quotes the expression of his friend and fellow Americanist Alfred Métraux.
9. Ibid., p. vii.
10. Alfred Métraux, *Itinéraires 1 (1935–1953): Carnets de notes et journaux de voyage* (Payot, 1978), p. 41.
11. Françoise Héritier in "Claude Lévi-Strauss était 'un passeur exceptionnel,'" *Le Monde*, November 4, 2009.
12. Lévi-Strauss, interview with the author, March 2005.
13. Lévi-Strauss, *Tristes Tropiques*, Picador, p. 71; Claude Lévi-Strauss, *Oeuvres*, eds. Vincent Debaene et al, Gallimard: Bibliothèque de la Pléiade, 2007, p. 47.
14. See Denis Bertholet, *Claude Lévi-Strauss* (Paris: Plon, 2003), p. 404.
15. Cited in David Pace, *Claude Lévi-Strauss: The Bearer of Ashes* (Boston: Routledge and Kegan Paul, 1983), p. 4.

1: Early Years

1. Marcel Fournier, *Marcel Mauss,* Jane Marie Todd, trans. (Princeton, N.J.: Oxford: Princeton University Press, 2006), p. 326.
2. Pablo Picasso cited in Françoise Gilot and Carlton Lake, *Life with Picasso* (Harmondsworth: Penguin, 1966), p. 257.
3. Marcel Mauss, *The Gift, Forms and Functions of Exchange in Archaic Societie,* Ian Cunnison, trans. (London: Cohen & West, 1954).
4. Mauss ran the institute along with the sociologist Paul Rivet and the philosopher and theorist on "primitive mentality" Lucien Lévy-Bruhl.
5. Fournier, *Marcel Mauss*, pp. 277–78.
6. Michel Leiris, *L'Âge d'homme* (Paris: Gallimard, 1946), pp. 189–90; translation from Colin Nettelbeck, *Dancing with de Beauvoir: Jazz and the French* (Carlton, Victoria: Melbourne University Press, 2004), p. 113.
7. James Clifford, *The Predicament of Culture: Twentieth Century Ethnography, Literature and Art* (Cambridge, Mass., and London: University of Harvard Press, 1988), pp. 117–51.
8. See Vincent Debaene, "Les Surréalistes et le Musée d'ethnographie," *Labyrinthe*, vol. 12, 2002 (http://labyrinthe.revues.org/index1209.html), for a discussion on this point.
9. Claude Lévi-Strauss in the documentary film by Pierre-André Boutang and Annie Chevallay, *Claude Lévi-Strauss in His Own Words* (*Claude Lévi-Strauss par lui-même*), Arte Éditions, 2008, time code 33:43.
10. From a 1973 interview with Jean-José Marchand for L'Office de Radiodiffusion-Télévision française (l'ORTF), reprinted in *Lévi-Strauss: l'homme derrière l'oeuvre*, ed. Emile Joulia, (Paris: Éditions Jean-Claude Lattès, 2008), p. 167.

11. Lévi-Strauss, *Tristes Tropiques*, Picador, p. 300.
12. Lévi-Strauss in Eribon, *Conversations*, p. 6.
13. Levi-Strauss in Boutang and Chevallay, *Claude Lévi-Strauss in His Own Words*, 32:08.
14. Lévi-Strauss in Eribon, *Conversations*, pp. 93–94.
15. Ibid., p. 93.
16. Ibid., p. 172.
17. Claude Lévi-Strauss, *The View from Afar*, Joachim Neugroschel and Phoebe Hoss, trans. (Oxford: Basil Blackwell, 1985), p. 275.
18. Lévi-Strauss is referring here to Romains's twenty-seven volume *Les Hommes de bonne volonté* (1932–46) novel cycle, set around the time of Lévi-Strauss's childhood. The characters—the philosopher Pierre Jallez and the politician Jean Jerphanion—become friends as students at the École normale supérieure in the first volume and then reappear throughout the novels as commentators, discussing contemporary events and French society, in letters and on long walks through Paris.
19. Lévi-Strauss, *Tristes Tropiques*, Picador, p. 494.
20. Claude Lévi-Strauss, *The Raw and the Cooked: Introduction to a Science of Mythology 1*, John and Doreen Weightman, trans. (Chicago: University of Chicago Press, 1983), p. 15.
21. Interview with Jean-José Marchand for l'ORTF in *Lévi-Strauss: l'homme derrière l'oeuvre*, ed. Joulia, p. 174.
22. Vauxcelles had coined the terms *fauvisme* and *cubisme* ("Braque reduces figures, houses to geometric schemes, to cubes") along with the less memorable *tubisme* to describe Léger's tubular style, but was an arch-skeptic of modernism. He was cool toward Lévi-Strauss's topic, but nevertheless encouraged him to write.
23. Lévi-Strauss in Eribon, *Conversations*, p. 172.
24. Ibid., p. 5.
25. Bertholet, *Claude Lévi-Strauss*, p. 28.
26. Claude Lévi-Strauss interview with Philippe Simonnot, "Claude Lévi-Strauss: un anarchiste de droite," *L'Express*, October 17, 1986.
27. Lévi-Strauss in Eribon, *Conversations*, p. 8.
28. See the interview with Jean-José Marchand for l'ORTF, reprinted in *Lévi-Strauss: l'homme derrière l'oeuvre*, ed. Joulia, pp. 170–71.
29. Cited in Bertholet, *Claude Lévi-Strauss*, p. 27.
30. Although not at that point integrated into the Sorbonne.
31. Claude Lévi-Strauss interview with Jean-José Marchand, Arte France TV, 1972. In a more acerbic mood, he told a *Time* magazine journalist in the 1960s that he had chosen philosophy "not because I had any true vocation for it, but because I had

sampled other branches of learning and detested them, one and all," in "Man's New Dialogue with Man," *Time*, June 30, 1967.

32. Lévi-Strauss in Boutang and Chevallay, *Claude Lévi-Strauss in His Own Words*, 31:25.
33. Bertholet, *Claude Lévi-Strauss*, p. 31.
34. Claude Lévi-Strauss, "Autoportrait," *Le Magazine littéraire*, hors-série no. 5, 4e trimestre, 2003, p. 8; Eribon, *Conversations*, p. 8.
35. Lévi-Strauss in Eribon, *Conversations*, p. 15.
36. Bertholet, *Claude Lévi-Strauss*, p. 49.
37. Ibid., pp. 56–57.
38. Claude Lévi-Strauss, signed Georges Monnet, "Picasso et le Cubisme," *Documents*, Picasso special edition, 1929–30, pp. 139–40.
39. Fournier, *Marcel Mauss*, p. 285.
40. A. A. Akoun, F. Morin and J. Mousseau, "A Conversation with Claude Lévi-Strauss," *Psychology Today*, vol. 5, 1972, p. 83.
41. Bertholet, *Claude Lévi-Strauss*, p. 42; *Lévi-Strauss: l'homme derrière l'oeuvre*, ed. Joulia, p. 169.
42. Lévi-Strauss quoted in 1929 in Bertholet, *Claude Lévi-Strauss*, p. 44.
43. Lévi-Strauss, *Tristes Tropiques*, Picador, p. 64.
44. Lévi-Strauss in Eribon, *Conversations*, p. 12.
45. Ibid., p. 11.
46. Ibid., p. 10.
47. Ibid., p. 13.
48. Pierre Dreyfus would go on to become CEO of Renault and serve under François Mitterrand as minister for industry.
49. Lévi-Strauss in Boutang and Chevallay, *Claude Lévi-Strauss in His Own Words*, 34:23.
50. Lévi-Strauss, *Tristes Tropiques*, Picador, p. 69; Richard Fortey, "Life Lessons," *Guardian*, April 7, 2005.
51. "three sources of inspiration" in Lévi-Strauss, *Tristes Tropiques*, Picador, p. 71; "*trois maîtresses*" in *Tristes Tropiques* in Lévi-Strauss, *Oeuvres*, p. 46.
52. Claude Lévi-Strauss, "Ce que je suis," *Le Nouvel Observateur*, June 28, 1980, p. 16.
53. Paul Nizan, *Aden Arabie,* Joan Pinkham, trans. (New York and London: *Monthly Review Press*, 1968), pp. 61, 65.
54. Véronique Mortaigne, "Claude Lévi-Strauss, grand témoin de l'Année du Brésil," *Le Monde*, February 22, 2005.
55. Bertholet, *Claude Lévi-Strauss*, p. 71.
56. See James A. Boon, *From Symbolism to Structuralism* (Oxford: Blackwell, 1972), p. 144.
57. Lévi-Strauss, *Tristes Tropiques*, Picador, pp. 55–56.
58. Jean Maugüé, *Les Dents agacées* (Paris: Éditions Buchet/Chastel, 1982), p. 76.

59. Quoted in Thomas E. Skidmore, "Lévi-Strauss, Braudel and Brazil: A Case of Mutual Influence," *Bulletin of Latin American Research*, vol. 22, no. 3, 2003, p. 345.
60. Lévi-Strauss, *Tristes Tropiques*, Picador, p. 21.
61. France Antarctique was an attempt to establish a French Protestant colony in Rio de Janeiro's Guanabara Bay in 1555. The colony collapsed in religious acrimony before being routed by the Portuguese in 1560.
62. Bertholet, *Claude Lévi-Strauss*, p. 100.
63. Lévi-Strauss in Eribon, *Conversations*, p. 12.
64. Claude Lévi-Strauss, *Myth and Meaning* (London: Routledge, 2006), p. 47.

2: Arabesque

1. Lévi-Strauss, "Postscript to Chapter XV," *Structural Anthropology*, Claire Jacobson and Brooke Grundfest Schoepf, trans. (Harmondsworth: Penguin, 1968), p. 332.
2. Lévi-Strauss, *Tristes Tropiques*, Picador, p. 75.
3. Ibid., p. 87.
4. Maugüé, *Les Dents agacées*, p. 81.
5. Lévi-Strauss, *Tristes Tropiques*, Picador, pp. 77–84.
6. Ibid., p. 96.
7. Ibid., p. 106.
8. Lévi-Strauss, interview with the author, March 2005. "O Estrangeiro," © 1989 by Caetano Veloso, is used by kind permission of Terra Enterprises, Inc.
9. Lévi-Strauss, *Tristes Tropiques,* Picador, p. 104.
10. Ibid., p. 113.
11. Claude Lévi-Strauss, *Saudades de São Paulo* (São Paulo: Companhia das Letras, 1996), p. 18.
12. Ibid., p. 43.
13. Oscar Niemeyer, *The Curves of Time: The Memoirs of Oscar Niemeyer* (London: Phaidon, 2000), p. 62.
14. "A Frenchman feels at home in Brazil," wrote Louis Mouralis, a French travel writer who visited the northeast and São Paulo in the early 1930s; the "language is spoken widely; culture, assimilated unevenly but often well, is topic of conversation; customs and everyday opinions similar, with a more marked Iberian accent." In *Brazilian Mosaic: Portraits of a Diverse People and Culture*, ed. G. Harvey Summ (Wilmington, Del.: SR Books, 1995), p. 102.
15. Lévi-Strauss, interview with *L'Express*, trans. Peter B. Kussell, in *Diacritics*, vol. 1, no. 1, Autumn 1971, p. 45.
16. Peter Fleming, *Brazilian Adventure* (London: World Books, 1940), p. 71.

17. Lévi-Strauss, *Saudades do Brasil*, p. 22.
18. Lévi-Strauss, *Saudades de São Paulo*, pp. 25, 51, 71, 80.
19. Lévi-Strauss, *Tristes Tropiques*, Picador, p. 138; Lévi-Strauss, *Saudades do Brasil*, p. 20.
20. Maugüé, *Les Dents agacées*, p. 102.
21. Lévi-Strauss in Eribon, *Conversations*, p. 23.
22. Fournier, *Marcel Mauss*, p. 291.
23. Lévi-Strauss in Eribon, *Conversations*, p. 20.
24. Fernanda Peixoto, "Lévi-Strauss no Brasil: a formação do etnólogo," *Mana*, vol. 4, no. 1, 1998, pp. 90–91.
25. Ibid., pp. 88–89.
26. Lévi-Strauss, interview with *L'Express*, in *Diacritics*, p. 45.
27. Braudel cited in Thomas E. Skidmore, "Lévi-Strauss, Braudel and Brazil," p. 345.
28. These included Sérgio Milliet, Rubens Borba de Moraes, Paulo Duarte and Mário de Andrade.
29. Dina was also the driving force behind the founding, with Andrade, of the Ethnographic and Folklore Society.
30. Cited in Dorothea Voegeli Passetti, *Lévi-Strauss, Antropologia e arte: minúsculo–incomensurável* (São Paulo: Editora da Universidade de São Paulo, 2008), pp. 85, 93.
31. Ibid., p. 82.
32. Lévi-Strauss, *Tristes Tropiques*, Picador, p. 150.
33. Ibid., pp. 150–54.
34. Lévi-Strauss in Eribon, *Conversations*, p. 21.
35. Lévi-Strauss, *Tristes Tropiques*, Picador, p. 197.
36. Ibid., p. 200.
37. Ibid., pp. 200–202.
38. Ibid., pp. 204–5.
39. Lévi-Strauss, *Saudades do Brasil*, p. 21.
40. Variously spelled Caduveu, Kaduveu, Kaduveo; I use Lévi-Strauss's spellings for indigenous names throughout.
41. Dina Lévi-Strauss, "*Tristes Tropiques*: Docs préparatoires 2/10, récit du voyage São Paulo–Porto Esperança par Dina Lévi-Strauss," Archives de Lévi-Strauss, Bibliothèque nationale de France, p. 2.
42. Ibid., p. 1.
43. Lévi-Strauss, *Oeuvres*, p. 1724.
44. Now a separate state, Mato Grosso do Sul.
45. Dina Lévi-Strauss, "*Tristes Tropiques*: Docs préparatoires," p. 3.
46. Re: Dina's illness, which is not mentioned in *Tristes Tropiques*, see Lévi-Strauss, "Note sur les expéditions," *Oeuvres*, p. 1724.

47. Dina Lévi-Strauss, "*Tristes Tropiques*: Docs préparatoires," p. 10.
48. Ibid., p. 14.
49. Lévi-Strauss, *Tristes Tropiques,* Picador, p. 221.
50. Ibid., p. 239.
51. "Lettres à Mário de Andrade," *Les Temps modernes*, no. 628, August–October 2004, p. 257.
52. Boris Wiseman, *Lévi-Strauss, Anthropology and Aesthetics* (Cambridge: Cambridge University Press, 2007), p. 137.
53. Lévi-Strauss, *Tristes Tropiques,* Picador, pp. 216–17.
54. Lévi-Strauss, "Le Coucher de soleil: entretien avec Boris Wiseman," *Les Temps modernes*, no. 628, p. 4.
55. Ibid., p. 275.
56. Lévi-Strauss in Boutang and Chevallay, *Claude Lévi-Strauss in His Own Words*, 15:30.
57. Lévi-Strauss, *Tristes Tropiques*, Picador, p. 278–79.
58. Lévi-Strauss, interview with the author, February 2007.
59. Lévi-Strauss, *Tristes Tropiques*, Picador, p. 279.
60. Ibid., p. 283.
61. See footnote in Claude Lévi-Strauss, "Contribution à l'étude de l'organisation sociale des Indiens Bororo," *Journal de la Société des Américanistes*, vol. 28, no. 2, 1936, pp. 275–76.
62. Lévi-Strauss in Boutang and Chevallay, *Claude Lévi-Strauss in His Own Words*, 22:50.
63. Lévi-Strauss, *Tristes Tropiques,* Picador, p. 318.
64. Ibid., p. 320.
65. In the documentary film *À propos de Tristes Tropiques*, by Jean-Pierre Beaurenaut, Jorge Bodanzky and Patrick Menget, L'Harmattan et Zarafa Films, 1991.
66. Up until the middle of the twentieth century Mato Grosso was sometimes spelled with two *t*'s.
67. Lévi-Strauss in Eribon, *Conversations*, p. 21.
68. Cited in Luís Donisete Benzi Grupioni, *Coleções e expedições vigiadas: os etnólogos no Conselho de Fiscalização das Expedições Artísticas e Científicas no Brasil*, Hucitec/ANPOCS, 1988, p. 137.
69. Lévi-Strauss, "Contribution à l'étude de l'organisation sociale des Indiens Bororo," pp. 269–304.
70. Cited in Bertholet, *Claude Lévi-Strauss*, p. 95.
71. Lévi-Strauss in Eribon, *Conversations*, p. 24.
72. Grupioni, *Coleções e expedições vigiadas*, p. 150.
73. Lévi-Strauss cited in Bertholet, *Claude Lévi-Strauss*, p. 90.

74. Lévi-Strauss cited in Grupioni, *Coleções e expedições vigiadas*, p. 124.
75. Lévi-Strauss, *Saudades do Brasil*, p. 56.
76. Maugüé, *Les Dents agacées*, pp. 118–19.
77. Lévi-Strauss, *Tristes Tropiques*, Picador, p. 158.
78. Maugüé, *Les Dents agacées*, p. 121.
79. Lévi-Strauss, *Boletim da Sociedade de etnografia e folclore*, no. 2, 1937, p. 5.
80. Maugüé, *Les Dents agacées*, p. 121.
81. Ibid., p. 111.
82. Lévi-Strauss in *Le Magazine littéraire*, no. 223, October 1985, p. 20.
83. Lévi-Strauss in Eribon, *Conversations*, p. 54.

3: Rondon's Line

1. Lévi-Strauss, *Tristes Tropiques*, Picador, p. 355.
2. Ibid., pp. 325–28.
3. On the extraordinary story of the building of the Rondon line, see Todd A. Diacon, *Stringing Together a Nation: Cândido Mariano da Silva Rondon and the Construction of a Modern Brazil, 1906–1930* (Durham, N.C.: Duke University Press, 2004).
4. Lévi-Strauss, *Tristes Tropiques*, Picador, p. 357.
5. Grupioni, *Coleções e expedições vigiadas*, pp. 142–46.
6. Castro Faria interview, *Acervo Histórico de Luiz de Castro Faria*, Museu de Astronomia e Ciências Afins, Rio de Janeiro, 1997.
7. Cited in Luiz de Castro Faria, *Um outro olhar: diário da expedição à Serra do Norte*, (Rio de Janeiro: Ouro Sobre Azul, 2001), p. 17.
8. In Bernardo Carvalho, *Nine Nights*, (London: Vintage Books, 2008), p. 33.
9. Grupioni, *Coleções e expedições vigiadas*, p. 152.
10. Castro Faria, *Um outro olhar*, p. 43.
11. Ibid., p. 50.
12. Ibid., p. 51.
13. Lévi-Strauss, *Tristes Tropiques*, Picador, p. 345.
14. Luiz de Castro Faria interview, 1997.
15. Letter to Rivet, June 17, 1938, sent from Utiariti, in *Critique*, no. 620–21, January–February 1999, reproduced between pages 96 and 97. Forty thousand francs was the equivalent of around twenty thousand dollars in today's money.
16. Lévi-Strauss, *Tristes Tropiques*, Picador, p. 346.
17. Castro Faria, *Um outro olhar*, p. 59.
18. Lévi-Strauss, *Tristes Tropiques*, Picador, p. 351.
19. Castro Faria, *Um outro olhar*, p. 63.

20. Lévi-Strauss, "Lettres à Mário de Andrade," p. 260.
21. Lévi-Strauss, *Tristes Tropiques*, Picador, p. 354; Castro Faria, *Um outro olhar*, p. 68.
22. Lévi-Strauss cited in *Les Temps modernes*, no. 628, pp. 260–61.
23. Castro Faria, *Um outro olhar*, p. 73.
24. Lévi-Strauss, *Tristes Tropiques*, Picador, p. 363.
25. Ibid., p. 374.
26. See Lévi-Strauss, *Saudades do Brasil*, p. 126.
27. Lévi-Strauss, *Tristes Tropiques*, Picador, pp. 374, 427.
28. Castro Faria, *Um outro olhar*, p. 85.
29. That is, fire, water, earth, sun, moon, wind, night; small, big, near, far, much, pretty, ugly. Lévi-Strauss also included Portuguese vocabulary, a language he was still struggling with. On one page he writes, "*Nombre d'expressions employées pour dire: on = 'o homen,' 'o camarada,' 'o collega* [*sic*]*', 'o negro,' 'o tal,' 'o fulano*'" ("Number of expressions used to say 'one' [in the sense of 'you']"); on another there is: "*Arroz-sem-sal (riz-sans-sel). On prononce 'Rossemsal*'" ("Rice without salt, pronounced 'Rossemsal'"). Claude Lévi-Strauss, "*Tristes Tropiques*: Docs préparatoires 4/10 souvenirs," Archives de Lévi-Strauss, Bibliothèque nationale de France, pp. 100, 104.
30. Lévi-Strauss's field notes are now kept in his archive in the Bibliothèque nationale de France in Paris. Excerpts have been published in Lévi-Strauss, *Oeuvres*, pp. 1617–26.
31. Cited in Bertholet, *Claude Lévi-Strauss*, p. 116.
32. See "Cahiers du terrain," Archives de Lévi-Strauss, Bibliothèque nationale de France, boxes 4–6.
33. Castro Faria, *Um outro olhar*, pp. 88, 93.
34. Ibid., p. 85; Castro Faria, "Mission Tristes Tropiques," *Libération*, September 1, 1988.
35. Grupioni, *Coleções e expedições vigiadas*, p. 152.
36. Castro Faria, *Um outro olhar*, pp. 102, 109–10.
37. "*Route très longue et sans intérêt . . . une longue et pénible traversée de forêt sèche*": Claude Lévi-Strauss, "Cahiers du terrain," Campos Novos (2e quinzaine août 1938), Archives de Lévi-Strauss, Bibliothèque nationale de France.
38. Lévi-Strauss, *Tristes Tropiques*, Picador, pp. 492–93.
39. Lévi-Strauss describes the play in *Tristes Tropiques*, pp. 495–500; the text has been published in Gallimard's Bibliothèque de la Pléiade edition *Oeuvres*, pp. 1632–50.
40. Lévi-Strauss, *Tristes Tropiques*, Picador, p. 493.
41. Ibid., pp. 495–500.
42. Robert F. Murphy and Buell Quain, *The Trumaí Indians of Central Brazil*, J. J. Augustin, 1955, pp. 103–6.
43. Alfred Métraux, *Itinéraires 1 (1935–1953): carnets de notes et journaux de voyage*, Payot, 1978, p. 41.

44. Letter from Buell Quain to Heloísa Alberto Torres, August 2, 1939, in Mariza Corrêa and Januária Mello, eds., *Querida Heloísa: cartas de campo para Heloísa Alberto Torres*, ed. (Unicampo, 2008), p. 84.
45. Ibid., p. 103.
46. The multiple interpretations have been spun together in Bernardo Carvalho's mesmerizing fictionalized account *Nine Nights* (London: Vintage Books, 2008).
47. Murphy and Quain, *The Trumaí Indians*, p. 2.
48. *Tristes Tropiques*, Picador, p. 393.
49. Ibid., pp. 389–90.
50. Castro Faria, *Um outro olhar*, p. 131; Lévi-Strauss, *Oeuvres*, p. 1727.
51. Lévi-Strauss, *Tristes Tropiques*, Picador, p. 416.
52. Ibid., pp. 421–22.
53. Ibid., p. 449.
54. Ibid., p. 435.
55. Ibid., pp. 434, 221.
56. Ibid., p. 436.
57. Ibid., p. 451.
58. "*Impressionante. Ossos esmigalhados, nervos expostos, dedos partidos*": Castro Faria, *Um outro olhar*, p. 174.
59. Reproduced in *Le Magazine littéraire*, no. 223, 1985, p. 56.
60. Reproduced in Marcel Hénaff, "Chronologie," *Le Magazine littéraire*, no. 311, 1993, p. 17; compare Lévi-Strauss, *Saudades do Brasil*, p. 191.
61. Lévi-Strauss, *Tristes Tropiques*, Picador, pp. 456–57.
62. Lévi-Strauss, *Oeuvres*, p. 1767.
63. Lévi-Strauss, *Tristes Tropiques*, Picador, pp. 471–72.
64. Castro Faria, *Um outro olhar*, p. 185.
65. In the 1950s Lévi-Strauss spent one week studying two villages in the Chittagong hill tracts in what was then western Pakistan, and in the 1970s he made two short visits to British Columbia—but it would be stretching it to define these trips as ethnographic fieldwork.
66. Lévi-Strauss cited in *Les Temps modernes*, no. 628, p. 263.
67. See Lévi-Strauss, interview for *L'Express*, in *Diacritics*, p. 47.
68. "Claude Lévi-Strauss in "Conversation with George Steiner," *BBC Third Programme*, October 29, 1965.
69. Lévi-Strauss in "Le Coucher de soleil," p. 6; Eribon, *Conversations*, p. 45.
70. Lévi-Strauss in Eribon, *Conversations*, pp. 44–45.
71. Lévi-Strauss, *Tristes Tropiques*, Picador, pp. 492–93.
72. Castro Faria, "Mission Tristes Tropiques."

73. Lévi-Strauss, interview with the author, February 2007.
74. Lévi-Strauss, *The Raw and the Cooked*, p. 8.
75. Alban Bensa, interview with the author, January 2008.
76. Alfred Métraux, *Itinéraires 1*, p. 42.
77. In fact, counting all his expeditions, Lévi-Strauss left only 328 out of a total of 1,200 artifacts behind in Brazil—perhaps fortunately, for while his collections have been well preserved in Paris, the rest have languished uncataloged in the Museu de Arqueologia e Etnologia da Universidade de São Paulo, where some pieces have simply disintegrated. See Elio Gaspari, "Parte da coleção de Lévi-Strauss virou pó," *Folha de São Paulo*, November 11, 2009. When I visited USP in 2005, staff at the museum were unable even to locate Lévi-Strauss's collection.
78. Lévi-Strauss, *Tristes Tropiques*, Plon, p. 29, my translation; the translation in *Tristes Tropiques*, Picador, p. 34, has the racist-sounding "half-naked nigger boys" for the far milder "*une bande de négrillons à demi nus*" of the original.

4: Exile

1. Denis de Rougemont, *Journal des Deux Mondes* (Paris: Gallimard, 1948), p. 91. With the exception of the last phrase, "bitter yet cleansing wind," the translation is taken from Jeffrey Mehlman, *Emigré New York: French Intellectuals in Wartime Manhattan, 1940–1944* (Baltimore and London: John Hopkins University Press, 2000), pp. 62–63.
2. "*Il respira profondément . . . de façon très vague, Paul Thalamas pensa à Berkeley et à la célèbre théorie par laquelle l'évêque anglais prétend prouver, par la différence entre les dimensions apparentes de la lune au zénith et sur l'horizon, la relativité de nos impressions visuelles*": Lévi-Strauss, *Oeuvres*, pp. 1628, 1630.
3. Lévi-Strauss in Eribon, *Conversations*, p. 91.
4. Lévi-Strauss in Bertholet, *Claude Lévi-Strauss*, p. 121.
5. Ibid., p. 121.
6. Bertholet, *Claude Lévi-Strauss*, p. 122.
7. Lévi-Strauss, interview with the author, February 2007.
8. "*la bouffonnerie la plus totale*": Bertholet, *Claude Lévi-Strauss*, p. 122.
9. Interview with Lévi-Strauss, Jérôme Garcin, *Boîte aux lettres*, France 3, 1984.
10. Jean Rouch in Lucien Taylor, "A Conversation with Jean Rouch," *Visual Anthropology Review*, vol. 7, no. 1, Spring 1991, p. 95.
11. Lévi-Strauss in Eribon, *Conversations*, p. 25.
12. Gaston Roupnel in Fernand Braudel, *On History* (Chicago: University of Chicago Press, 1982), p. 7.

13. Conditions could be harsh. In Gurs, camp officials worked out that "Uncle Raaf," which was cropping up with increasing frequency in letters to relatives, was a code word for hunger, and had all references cut by the censor. Richard Vinen, *The Unfree French: Life under the Occupation* (London: Allen Lane, 2006), p. 142.
14. Lévi-Strauss in Eribon, *Conversations,* p. 26.
15. Lévi-Strauss, interview with the author, February 2007.
16. Lévi-Strauss in Eribon, *Conversations,* p. 99.
17. Lévi-Strauss, *Tristes Tropiques,* Picador, p. 24.
18. Lévi-Strauss, *Oeuvres,* pp. 1734–35.
19. This is according to Lévi-Strauss himself, in an interview with the author, February 2007.
20. Victor Serge cited in Martica Sawin, *Surrealism in Exile and the Beginning of the New York School* (Cambridge, Mass., and London: MIT Press, 1995), p. 120.
21. Lévi-Strauss, *Tristes Tropiques,* Picador, p. 25.
22. Ibid.
23. Victor Serge cited in Mark Polizzotti, *A Revolution of the Mind: The Life of André Breton* (London: Bloomsbury, 1995), p. 494.
24. Victor Serge cited in Lévi-Strauss, *Oeuvres,* p. 1736.
25. Lévi-Strauss, *Tristes Tropiques,* Picador, p. 26.
26. Lévi-Strauss, interview with the author, February 2007.
27. Lévi-Strauss, *Tristes Tropiques,* Picador, pp. 25–26.
28. See Claude Lévi-Strauss, *Look, Listen, Read* (New York: Basic Books, 1997), pp. 143–51; "*prise de conscience irrationelle*": Claude Lévi-Strauss, *Regarder, écouter, lire* (Paris: Plon, 1993), p. 141.
29. Breton in Polizzotti, *Revolution of the Mind,* p. 496.
30. Lévi-Strauss, *Tristes Tropiques,* Picador, pp. 27–28.
31. Ibid., p. 26.
32. Claude Lévi-Strauss in Paul Hendrickson, "Behemoth from the Ivory Tower," *Washington Post,* February 24, 1978.
33. Polizzotti, *Revolution of the Mind,* p. 497.
34. Lévi-Strauss, *Tristes Tropiques,* Picador, p. 39; Lévi-Strauss, *Oeuvres,* p. 1736.
35. Lévi-Strauss, *Tristes Tropiques,* Picador, p. 40.
36. Lévi-Strauss, *The View from Afar,* pp. 259–60.
37. Ibid., p. 259.
38. Ibid., p. 263.
39. Claude Lévi-Strauss, "Anthropology: Its Achievements and Future," *Nature,* vol. 209, no. 5018, January 1966, p. 10.
40. Lévi-Strauss in Tom Shandel, *Behind the Masks,* National Film Board of Canada, 1973.

41. Claude Lévi-Strauss, *The Way of the Masks* (London: Jonathan Cape, 1983), p. 10.
42. Waldberg in Bertholet, *Claude Lévi-Strauss*, p. 133.
43. This, according to the recollections of Claudine Herrmann—who was tutored by Lévi-Strauss in New York and ended up working for him, typing up his index cards for "a fantastic salary of three dollars an hour"—in *Lévi-Strauss: l'homme derrière l'oeuvre*, ed. Joulia, pp. 20–21.
44. See picture inset between pages 264 and 265 in *Claude Lévi-Strauss*, ed. Michel Izard, (Paris: L'Herne, 2004).
45. Lévi-Strauss, *The View from Afar*, p. 260.
46. Sawin, *Surrealism in Exile*, p. 185.
47. Interview with Lévi-Strauss, *Boîte aux lettres*.
48. Lévi-Strauss in Eribon, *Conversations*, p. 31.
49. Waldberg in Bertholet, *Claude Lévi-Strauss*, p. 142.
50. Ibid., p. 143.
51. Bill Holm and Bill Reid, *Indian Art of the Northwest Coast: A Dialogue on Craftsmanship and Aesthetics*, (Houston: Institute of the Arts, Rice University, 1975), pp. 9–10.
52. Lévi-Strauss, *The View from Afar*, pp. 260–61.
53. *VVV: Poetry, Plastic Arts, Anthropology, Sociology, Psychology*, no. 1, 1942, p. 2.
54. Claude Lévi-Strauss, "Indian Cosmetics," *VVV*, no. 1, 1942, pp. 33–35.
55. Claude Lévi-Strauss, "Souvenir of Malinowsky [*sic*]," *VVV*, no. 1, 1942, p. 45.
56. Lévi-Strauss in Eribon, *Conversations*, p. 36.
57. Claude Lévi-Strauss, *The Scope of Anthropology*, (London: Jonathan Cape, 1967), p. 44.
58. Lévi-Strauss in Eribon, *Conversations*, p. 38.
59. Ibid., p. 30.
60. Peter M. Rutkoff and William B. Scott, *New School: a History of the New School for Social Research* (New York: Free Press, 1986); Claus-Deiter Krohn, *Intellectuals in Exile: Refugee Scholars and the New School for Social Research* (Amherst: University of Massachusetts Press, 1993); Emmanuelle Loyer, *Paris à New York: intellectuels et artistes français en exil (1940–1947),* (Paris : Grasset, 2005).
61. Isabelle Waldberg in Patrick Waldberg, *Un amour acéphale: correspondance 1940–1949* (Paris: Éditions de La Différance, 1992), pp. 184–85.
62. Lévi-Strauss, *The View from Afar*, p. 102.
63. The Marx comparison is taken from Robert Parkin, "Structuralism and Marxism," in *One Discipline, Four Ways: British, German, French and American Anthropology* (Chicago: University of Chicago Press, 2005), p. 209.
64. Lévi-Strauss in Eribon, *Conversations*, p. 43.

65. Lévi-Strauss, *The View from Afar*, p. 267.
66. See, for instance, Jerry Fodor and Massimo Piattelli-Palmarini, *What Darwin Got Wrong* (London: Profile Books, 2010).
67. Lévi-Strauss in Eribon, *Conversations*, p. 41.
68. François Dosse, *History of Structuralism*, vol. 1, *The Rising Sign, 1945–1966* (Minneapolis, Minn., and London: University of Minnesota Press, 1997), p. 53.
69. Bengt Jangfeldt, "Roman Jacobson in Sweden 1940–41," *Cahiers de l'ILSL*, no. 9, pp. 141–49; Andrew Lass, "Poetry and Reality: Roman O. Jakobson and Claude Lévi-Strauss," in *Artists, Intellectuals and World War II: The Pontigny Encounters at Mount Holyoke College, 1942–1944*, ed. Christopher Benfey and Karen Remmler (Amherst: University of Massachusetts Press, 2006), pp. 173–84.
70. Lévi-Strauss, "Cahiers du terrain," Archives de Lévi-Strauss, Bibliothèque nationale de France, boxes 4–6; "*langue semble différente*": "Cahiers du terrain," Campos Novos (2e quinzaine août 1938), box 6.
71. Lévi-Strauss, interview for *L'Express*, in *Diacritics*, p. 47.
72. Lévi-Strauss in Eribon, *Conversations*, p. 114.
73. Roman Jakobson, *Six Lectures on Sound and Meaning* (Hassocks: Harvester Press, 1978), p. 19.
74. Ibid., p. 20.
75. Ibid., p. 66.
76. Lévi-Strauss in ibid., "Preface," p. xiii.

5: Elementary Structures

1. Lévi-Strauss, "The family," in *Man, Culture and Society*, Harry L. Shapiro, ed. (Oxford: Oxford University Press, 1971), p. 357.
2. Fournier, *Marcel Mauss*, p. 345.
3. Lévi-Strauss in Jean-Marie Benoît, "Claude Lévi-Strauss Reconsiders: From Rousseau to Burke," *Encounter*, no. 53, July 1979, p. 20.
4. Denis de Rougemont, *Journal des deux mondes* (Paris: Gallimard, 1948), pp. 151–53.
5. Lévi-Strauss, *Structural Anthropology*, vol. 1, pp. 226, 257.
6. Ibid., p. 261.
7. Lévi-Strauss in *Le Magazine littéraire*, no. 223, October 1985, p. 23.
8. Mehlman, *Emigré New York*, p. 133.
9. Lévi-Strauss in Eribon, *Conversations*, p. 5.
10. Lévi-Strauss, *Oeuvres*, p. 1689.
11. Ibid., p. 46.
12. Lévi-Strauss, "Autoportrait," p. 13.

13. Maurice Merleau-Ponty, *The Phenomenology of Perception* (London: Routledge and Kegan Paul, 1962), pp. 91–93.
14. Mehlman, *Emigré New York*, p. 184.
15. Ibid., p. 181.
16. Lévi-Strauss in Eribon, *Conversations*, p. 45.
17. Claude Lévi-Strauss, "L'Analyse structurale en linguistique et en anthropologie," *Word: Journal of the Linguistic Circle of New York*, vol. 1, no. 2, August 1945, pp. 1–21, reprinted in *Structural Anthropology*, vol. 1, pp. 31–54.
18. Lévi-Strauss, *Structural Anthropology*, vol. 1, pp. 34, 46.
19. That is, societies in which descent is traced through the mother.
20. For Lévi-Strauss, the maternal uncle was a structural shorthand for a "wife-giver"—a role that could fall to others in the group. See his clarification of this point in Claude Lévi-Strauss, *Structural Anthropology*, vol. 2, Monique Layton, trans. (Harmondsworth: Penguin, 1978), p. 83.
21. Lévi-Strauss, *Structural Anthropology*, vol. 1, p. 42.
22. Thanks go to my brother Hugo for this sentence.
23. Lévi-Strauss, *Structural Anthropology*, vol. 1, p. 50.
24. Annie Cohen-Solal, "Claude L. Strauss in the United States," *Partisan Review*, vol. 67, no. 2, 2000, p. 258.
25. Lévi-Strauss, *The Way of the Masks*, p. 10.
26. Lévi-Strauss in Eribon, *Conversations*, p. 48.
27. Lévi-Strauss in Bertholet, *Claude Lévi-Strauss*, p. 162.
28. Claude Lévi-Strauss, "The Use of Wild Plants in Tropical South America," *Handbook of South American Indians: Physical Anthropology, Linguistics and Cultural Geography of the South American Indians*, vol. 6, ed. Julian Steward (Washington: Government Printing Office, 1963), pp. 465–86.
29. Cohen-Solal, "Claude L. Strauss in the United States," pp. 258–59.
30. Lévi-Strauss, *The View from Afar*, p. 266.
31. Entry dated March 13, 1947, in Métraux, *Itinéraires 1*, p. 171.
32. Lévi-Strauss in Eribon, *Conversations*, p. 56.
33. Cited in James Atlas, *Bellow: A Biography* (London: Faber & Faber, 2000), p. 138.
34. Michel Foucault in David Macey, *The Lives of Michel Foucault* (London: Hutchinson, 1993), p. 33.
35. Lévi-Strauss cited in Bertholet, *Claude Lévi-Strauss*, p. 180.
36. In Fournier, *Marcel Mauss*, pp. 349, 423.
37. *Le Magazine littéraire*, no. 223, October 1985, p. 23.
38. Lévi-Strauss, *The Elementary Structures of Kinship*, James Harle Bell, John Richard von Sturmer, and Rodney Needham, trans. (London: Eyre and Spottiswoode, 1969),

p. 125. Lévi-Strauss cites Australian anthropologist W. E. H. Stanner, though selectively. When Stanner began fieldwork in the Daly River settlement in the Northern Territory in 1932, he wrote: "I was impressed by their genuine bewilderment and the comical expressions they wore when they found, after a vain attempt to work out the terms by clear marks in the soil, that they could not remember." See Melinda Hinkson, "The Intercultural Challenge of W. E. H. Stanner's First Fieldwork," *Oceania*, vol. 75, no. 3, March–June 2005, p. 198.

39. Lévi-Strauss, *Elementary Structures*, p. xxiii.
40. Ibid., p. 12. Or, as he later put it: "The incest prohibition is thus the basis of human society; in a sense it *is* the society," in "The Scope of Anthropology," *Structural Anthropology*, vol. 2, p. 19.
41. Mauss, *The Gift*, pp. 77–78.
42. Lévi-Strauss, *Elementary Structures*, p. 454.
43. Ibid., p. 51.
44. Subsequently rephrased by Lacan as, "It's not the women, but the phalluses that are exchanged," in Dosse, *History of Structuralism*, vol. 1, p. 118.
45. Lévi-Strauss in Eribon, *Conversations*, p. 105. Cf. a clear statement to the contrary in Lévi-Strauss's early piece for the linguistic journal *Word* ("L'Analyse structurale"): "In human society, it is the men who exchange women, and not vice versa," in Lévi-Strauss, *Structural Anthropology*, vol. 1, p. 47.
46. Lévi-Strauss, *Elementary Structures*, p. 124.
47. Ibid., p. 443.
48. Ibid., p. 497.
49. Simone de Beauvoir, "L'être et la parenté," cited in *Le Magazine littéraire*, hors-série no. 5, 4e trimestre, 2003, p. 60.
50. Ibid., p. 63. The *la* refers to *oeuvre.*
51. Georges Bataille, *Eroticism*, Mary Dalwood, trans. (London: Penguin, 2001), pp. 200–201.
52. According to American anthropologist Robert F. Murphy, "*Les Structures* was issued in a printing so limited that it was soon exhausted. Those in libraries either fell apart (the work was miserably manufactured) or were stolen, and the few remaining copies were treasured by their owners the way bootlegged copies of Henry Miller used to be," in "Connaissez-vous Lévi-Strauss?" *Saturday Review*, May 17, 1969, pp. 52–53, reprinted in *The Anthropologist as Hero*, ed. E. Nelson Hayes and Tanya Hayes (Cambridge, Mass., and London: MIT Press, 1970), p. 165.
53. Dosse, *History of Structuralism*, vol. 1, pp. 18–19.
54. Non-French-speaking anthropologists did, however, have an English summary of *Elementary Structures*, written by the Dutch anthropologist Josselin de Jong, who,

independently of Lévi-Strauss, had been toying with the same ideas in relation to ethnographic data in Indonesia.

55. In Stanley J. Tambiah, *Edmund Leach: An Anthropological Life* (Cambridge: Cambridge University Press, 2002), pp. 114–15.
56. From Cambridge University Anthropological Ancestors interviews at http://www.dspace.cam.ac.uk/handle/1810/25. The specifics of the argument are highly complex. See Leach's original article, "The Structural Implications of Matrilineal Cross-Cousin Marriage," *Journal of the Royal Anthropological Institute*, vol. 81, 1951, pp. 166–67; and Tambiah's summary in *Edmund Leach*, p. 117.
57. Edmond Leach, "Claude Lévi-Strauss—Anthropologist and Philosopher," *New Left Review*, vol. I/34, November–December 1965, p. 20.
58. Lévi-Strauss, *Elementary Structures*, p. 49, footnote 5. Lévi-Strauss was responding to a similar criticism made by David Maybury-Lewis.
59. See Arthur P. Wolf and William H. Durham, eds., *Inbreeding, Incest, and the Incest Taboo* (Stanford: Stanford University Press, 2004), p. 5.
60. See Maurice Godelier's *Métamorphoses de la parenté* (Paris: Fayard, 2004); and Jack Goody's review, "The Labyrinth of Kinship," *New Left Review*, vol. I/36, November–December 2005.
61. Claude Lévi-Strauss, "Entretien par Raymond Bellour," in Lévi-Strauss, *Oeuvres*, p. 1659.
62. Lévi-Strauss, *Elementary Structures*, p. xxvii.
63. See, for instance, Claude Lévi-Strauss, *The Raw and the Cooked*, p. 10: "In *Les Structures*, behind what seemed the superficial contingency and incoherent diversity of the laws governing marriage, I discerned a small number of simple principles, thanks to which a very complex mass of customs and practices . . . could be reduced to a meaningful system."

6: On the Shaman's Couch

1. Claude Lévi-Strauss, "Witch-doctors and psychoanalysis," *UNESCO Courier*, no. 5, 2008, pp. 31–32.
2. "Claude Lévi-Strauss: A Confrontation," *New Left Review*, vol. I/62, July–August 1970, originally published as "Réponse à quelques questions," *Esprit*, no. 322, November 1963.
3. Claude Lévi-Strauss, "The Sorcerer and His Magic," in *Structural Anthropology*, vol. 1, pp. 167–85.
4. Claude Lévi-Strauss, "The Effectiveness of Symbols," in ibid., pp. 186–205.
5. Lévi-Strauss, "Witch-doctors and Psychoanalysis," pp. 31–32.

6. Lévi-Strauss, *Structural Anthropology*, vol. 1, p. 204.
7. Claude Lévi-Strauss, *An Introduction to the Work of Marcel Maus,* Felicty Baker, trans. (London: Routledge and Kegan Paul, 1987), p. 45.
8. Claude Lefort, "L'Échange et la lutte des hommes," *Les Formes de l'histoire* (Paris: Gallimard, 1978), p. 17; originally published in *Les Temps modernes*, no. 64, February 1951, pp.1400–17.
9. Lévi-Strauss, *The Scope of Anthropology*, p. 50.
10. Lévi-Strauss in Eribon, *Conversations*, p. 49.
11. Jonathan Judaken, *Jean-Paul Sartre and the Jewish Question* (Lincoln, Neb.; Chesham: University of Nebraska Press, 2006), p. 69.
12. Lévi-Strauss in Eribon, *Conversations*, p. 50.
13. Lévi-Strauss, *Tristes Tropiques*, Picador, p. 165.
14. Ibid., p. 166.
15. Ibid., pp. 175, 176.
16. Claude Lévi-Strauss, "Kinship Systems of the Chittagong Hill Tribes (Pakistan)," *Southwestern Journal of Anthropology*, vol. 8, no. 1, Spring 1952, pp. 40–51; "Miscellaneous Notes on the Kuki of the Chittagong Hill Tracts, Pakistan," *Man*, vol. 51, December 1951, pp. 167–69.
17. Lévi-Strauss, *Oeuvres*, p. 1689.
18. Lévi-Strauss, *Tristes Tropiques*, Picador, p. 169.
19. Ibid., pp. 161–62.
20. Ibid., p. 179.
21. Lévi-Strauss in Eribon, *Conversations*, p. 50.
22. Ibid., p. 102.
23. Claude Lévi-Strauss, *Anthropology and Myth: Lectures 1951–1982*, Roy Willis, trans. (Oxford: Basil Blackwell, 1984), p. 2.
24. For an account of Descola's ordeal, see Philippe Descola, *The Spears of Twilight: Life and Death in the Amazon Jungle*, Janet Lloyd, trans. (London: HarperCollins, 1996), pp. 22–23.
25. Philippe Descola, interview with the author, February 2007.
26. Lévi-Strauss, *Anthropology and Myth*, p. 199.
27. Lévi-Strauss, *Structural Anthropology*, vol. 1, p. 71. The notion that the brain might be made up of separate, semi-independent functions has in fact gained adherents since Lévi-Strauss ridiculed the idea in the 1950s; see Jerry Fodor's *The Modularity of Mind: An Essay on Faculty Psychology* (Cambridge, Mass.; London: MIT Press, 1983).
28. Lévi-Strauss, *Structural Anthropology*, vol. 1, p. 70.
29. For tools, for instance, he proposed a scheme of analysis that involved three layers of differences: the way the tool was used (to strike, rub or cut); its leading edge

(sharp, blunt or serrated); and how it was manipulated (with perpendicular, oblique or circular movements). Lévi-Strauss, in *An Appraisal of Anthropology Today*, Sol Tax et al., eds. (Chicago: University of Chicago Press, 1953), p. 293.

30. Ibid., p. 294.
31. Ibid., p. 321.
32. Ibid., pp. 349–52.
33. Elisabeth Roudinesco, *Jacques Lacan & Co: A History of Psychoanalysis in France, 1925–1985*, (Chicago: University of Chicago Press, 1990), p. 560.
34. Bertholet, *Claude Lévi-Strauss*, p. 209.
35. Claude Lévi-Strauss, *Race et histoire* (Paris: Gonthier, 1968), pp. 46–50.
36. At the Collège, the sacred had been conceived not so much in religious terms, but as anything that inspired a heightened sensitivity, whether it was awe, fear or fascination. In keeping with Bataille's own intellectual obsessions, eroticism and death were thematic. The group was dedicated to resacralizing society, fusing it with the human energies that modernity had bleached out. Caillois became obsessed with the image of the female praying mantis, twisting her head back to devour her mate, an image he likened to the femme fatale in fiction—a woman luring her partner to his death.
37. Lévi-Strauss in Eribon, *Conversations*, p. 85.
38. Roger Caillois, "Illusion à rebours," *La Nouvelle revue française*, no. 24, December 1954, pp. 1010–24; and no. 25, January 1955, pp. 58–70.
39. In Claudine Frank, ed., *The Edge of Surrealism: A Roger Caillois Reader* (Durham, N.C., and London: Duke, 2003), p. 48.
40. Caillois, "Illusion à rebours," pp. 67–70.
41. Claude Lévi-Strauss, "Diogène couché," *Les Temps modernes*, no. 110, 1955, p. 1214.
42. Alfred Métraux in Bertholet, *Claude Lévi-Strauss*, p. 219.
43. Lévi-Strauss in Eribon, *Conversations*, p. 85.
44. Lévi-Strauss, "Diogène couché," pp. 1218–19.

7: Memoir

1. Pierre Mac Orlan, *La Vénus Internationale* (Paris: La Nouvelle Revue Française, 1923), pp. 236–37.
2. Jan Borm, *Jean Malaurie: un homme singulier* (Paris: Éditions du Chêne, 2005), pp. 53, 56.
3. Vincent Debaene, "Atelier de théorie littéraire: La collection Terre humaine: dans et hors de la literature," *Fabula*, March 1, 2007: http://www.fabula.org/atelier.php?La_collection_Terre_humaine%3A_dans_et_hors_de_la_litt%26eacute%3Brature.

4. Lévi-Strauss, *Le Magazine littéraire*, no. 223, October 1985, p. 24.
5. Dosse, *History of Structuralism*, vol. 1, p. 130.
6. "Auto-portrait de Claude Lévi-Strauss," in *Claude Lévi-Strauss*, éditions inculte, 2006, p. 183; originally published in a special edition of the journal *L'Arc* dedicated to the work of Lévi-Strauss, see *L'Arc*, no. 26, 1965.
7. Lévi-Strauss, *Tristes Tropiques*, Picador, p. 543.
8. "*Voyages = même chose et contraire d'une psychoanalyse*": "*Tristes Tropiques*: Docs préparatoires 10/10 carnet vert," Archives de Lévi-Strauss, Bibliothèque national de France, p. 56.
9. Lévi-Strauss, *Tristes Tropiques*, Picador, p. 256: "In this charming civilisation, the female beauties trace the outlines of the collective dream with their make-up; their patterns are hieroglyphics describing an inaccessible golden age, which they extol in their ornamentation, since they have no code in which to express it, and whose mysteries they disclose as they reveal their nudity."
10. Lévi-Strauss, *Oeuvres*, p. 1695.
11. "*Que sont nos poudres et nos rouges à côté!*": "*Tristes Tropiques*: vol. 2 de la dactylographie," Archives de Lévi-Strauss, Bibliothèque nationale de France, p. 200.
12. Lévi-Strauss, *Oeuvres*, pp. 1746, 1769.
13. Lévi-Strauss, *Tristes Tropiques*, Picador, p. 15–16.
14. Lévi-Strauss cited in Grupioni, *Coleções e expedições vigiadas*, p. 150.
15. Cited in Pace, *Claude Lévi-Strauss*, pp. 20–21.
16. Lévi-Strauss in Boutang and Chevallay, *Claude Lévi-Strauss in His Own Words*, 1:04:50.
17. Lévi-Strauss, *Tristes Tropiques*, Picador, p. 43.
18. Tragically, much later the Nambikwara would suffer the side effects of cooking food in empty drums of DDT.
19. Lévi-Strauss, *Tristes Tropiques*, Picador, pp. 534–35.
20. Ibid., p. 348.
21. Lévi-Strauss, *Tristes Tropiques*, Picador, 1989, p. 256.
22. Claude Lévi-Strauss, "Des Indiens et leur ethnographe," *Les Temps modernes*, no. 116, August 1955, pp. 1–50.
23. Lévi-Strauss, "Des Indiens et leur ethnographe," *Les Temps modernes*, no. 116, August 1955, p. 1; translation from Lévi-Strauss, *Tristes Tropiques*, Picador, p. 229.
24. "shopgirl metaphysics": Lévi-Strauss, *Tristes Tropiques*, Picador, p. 71; "*métaphysique pour midinette*": Lévi-Strauss, *Tristes Tropiques*, Plon, p. 63.
25. This is according to Jean Pouillon, Sartre's friend and fellow editorial board member of *Les Temps modernes*; see Dosse, *History of Structuralism*, vol. 1, p. 7. Despite the

apparent disjuncture, *Les Temps modernes* would continue to publish essays by Lévi-Strauss, as well as commentaries on his work.

26. For a summary of reviews of *Tristes Tropiques* in the French press, see Dosse, *History of Structuralism*, vol. 61, p. 133; Bertholet, *Claude Lévi-Strauss*, p. 219.
27. Lévi-Strauss, *Oeuvres*, p. 1717.
28. John Peristiany, "Social Anatomy," *Times Literary Supplement*, February, 22 1957; David Holden, "Hamlet among the Savages," *Times Literary Supplement*, May 12, 1961.
29. Susan Sontag, "A Hero of Our Time," *New York Review of Books*, vol. 1, no. 7, November 28, 1963.
30. Lévi-Strauss in Eribon, *Conversations*, p. 59.
31. Interview with Luc de Heusch by Pierre de Maret, *Current Anthropology*, vol. 34, no. 3, June 1993, pp. 290–91.
32. Jean Pouillon, "L'Oeuvre de Claude Lévi-Strauss," *Les Temps modernes*, no. 126, July 1956, pp. 150–73.
33. Dosse, *History of Structuralism*, vol. 1, p. 137.
34. Ibid., p. 266.
35. Lévi-Strauss did intervene on one further occasion in 1968. He joined more than a hundred other academics, including Michel Leiris, Louis Dumont, Maxime Rodinson and Georges Balandier, in signing an open letter to the Brazilian military dictator, General da Costa e Silva, denouncing the atrocities suffered by the Brazilian indigenous peoples after a string of accusations of torture and murder were made against the Serviço de Proteção aos Índios (Indian Protection Service).
36. Georges Charbonnier, *Conversations with Claude Lévi-Strauss*, John and Doreen Weightman, trans. (London: Jonathan Cape, 1969), p. 13.
37. These included avant-garde musician Pierre Boulez, actress Simone Signoret, writer Marguerite Duras and Lévi-Strauss's colleagues and friends Jean Pouillon and Michel Leiris.
38. Bertholet, *Claude Lévi-Strauss*, p. 230.
39. Ibid.
40. Lévi-Strauss in Eribon, *Conversations*, p. 59.
41. "After *Tristes Tropiques* there were times when I imagined that someone in the press was going to ask me to travel and write," he later confessed, in Eribon, *Conversations*, p. 159.
42. Lévi-Strauss cited in Bertholet, *Claude Lévi-Strauss*, p. 220.
43. Lévi-Strauss, *Tristes Tropiques*, Picador, p. 529.
44. Ibid., p. 530.
45. Lévi-Strauss in Eribon, *Conversations*, p. 7.

46. Lévi-Strauss, *Tristes Tropiques*, Picador, p. 539.
47. See I. Strenski, "Lévi-Strauss and the Buddhists," *Comparative Studies in Society and History*, vol. 22, 1980, pp. 3–22.
48. Lévi-Strauss, *Tristes Tropiques*, Picador, p. 542; Lévi-Strauss, *Oeuvres*, 2007, p. 442.
49. Lévi-Strauss, *Tristes Tropiques*, Picador, p. 541.
50. Ibid., p. 543.
51. Ibid., p. 544.

8: Modernism

1. Karlheinz Stockhausen cited in Ivan Hewett, "Karlheinz Stockhausen Obituary," *Guardian*, December 7, 2007.
2. Lévi-Strauss, *Tristes Tropiques*, Picador, p. 157.
3. Lévi-Strauss, interview with the author, March 2005.
4. Alex Ross, *The Rest Is Noise: Listening to the Twentieth Century* (London: Fourth Estate, 2008), p. 392.
5. Kristin Ross, *Fast Cars, Clean Bodies: Decolonization and the Reordering of French Culture* (Cambridge, Mass.; London: MIT Press, 1995), p. 2.
6. Dosse, *History of Structuralism*, vol. 1, p. 105.
7. Fernand Braudel, *On History*.
8. Lévi-Strauss in Elisabeth Roudinesco, *Jacques Lacan & Co*, p. 362.
9. Lévi-Strauss, interview with the author, February 2007.
10. Lévi-Strauss, *Structural Anthropology*, vol. 1, p. 207.
11. Edmund Leach, *Claude Lévi-Strauss* (London: Fontana/Collins, 1974), p. 65.
12. Lévi-Strauss, *Structural Anthropology*, vol. 1, p. 228.
13. In 1969, Lévi-Strauss told Canadian researcher Pierre Maranda that he "has never seen it as anything more than 'a drawing' to illustrate the 'double twist' which is translated with respect to the passage from metaphors to metonymies and vice versa," in Elli K. Maranda and Pierre Maranda, *Structural Models in Folklore and Transformational Essays* (The Hague and Paris: Mouton, 1971), p. 28.
14. This point is taken from Dan Sperber, "Claude Lévi-Strauss Today," *On Anthropological Knowledge* (Cambridge: Cambridge University Press, 1985), pp. 65–66. For Sperber, in using the words "never ceased to be guided" by his formula, Lévi-Strauss "sounds not like a scientist but rather like a transcendental meditator claiming to be guided by his mantra."
15. Lévi-Strauss, "The Story of Asdiwal," *Structural Anthropology*, vol. 2, p. 184.
16. Lévi-Strauss, *Structural Anthropology*, vol. 1, p. 229.
17. Lévi-Strauss, *Tristes Tropiques*, Picador, p. 70.

18. Dosse, *History of Structuralism*, vol. 1, p. 160.
19. Foucault in ibid., p. 160.
20. Lévi-Strauss in Eribon, *Conversations*, p. 68.
21. Although later Gallimard managed to publish a collection of essays and commentaries, as well as reissue *Race et histoire* for its Folio collection; see Raymond Bellour and Catherine Clément, eds., *Claude Lévi-Strauss* (Paris: Gallimard, 1979); Claude Lévi-Strauss, *Race et histoire* (Paris: Gallimard, 1987). At the end of Lévi-Strauss's life, Gallimard also published a collection of his works in the prestigious Bibliothèque de la Pléiade, see Claude Lévi-Strauss, *Oeuvres*, eds. Vincent Debaene et al. (Paris: Gallimard, 2007).
22. Like his attacks on Caillois, these were rhetorical salvos. He dismissed the sociologist Georges Gurvitch, who had branded his attempts to mathematically model social relations "a complete failure," as unqualified to comment on advances in anthropology. A similar ploy was used against Jean-François Revel, while Rodinson's Marxist critique was batted straight back with the taunt "My conception is infinitely closer to Marx's position than his," based on a somewhat selective reading of *Das Kapital*. Lévi-Strauss, *Structural Anthropology*, vol. 1, p. 338; Pace, *Claude Lévi-Strauss*, pp. 96–99.
23. Beatriz Perrone Moisés, "Entrevista: Claude Lévi-Strauss, aos 90," *Revista de antropologia*, vol. 42, no. 1–2, 1999.
24. See Kristin Ross, *Fast Cars, Clean Bodies*, p. 186.
25. Despite the subject matter of his work, Marcel Mauss had occupied the sociology chair.
26. Lévi-Strauss in Eribon, *Conversations*, p. 60.
27. Lévi-Strauss in Eribon, *Conversations*, p. 61; Claude Lévi-Strauss and Didier Eribon, *De près et de loin* (Paris: Éditions Odile Jacob, 1988), p. 90.
28. Lévi-Strauss, "The Scope of Anthropology," *Structural Anthropology*, vol. 2, pp. 7–8; Eribon, *Conversations*, p. 61.
29. Lévi-Strauss, "The Scope of Anthropology," pp. 6–7.
30. Ibid., p. 17.
31. Ibid., p. 32.
32. Lévi-Strauss in Eribon, *Conversations*, p. 63.
33. The Area Files were not without their critics. Margaret Mead apparently described the catalogs as "instant anthropology like instant coffee," cited in Isac Chiva, "Une communauté de solitaires: le Laboratoire d'anthropologie sociale," in *Claude Lévi-Strauss*, ed. Izard, p. 74.
34. Isac Chiva, "Une communauté de solitaires: le Laboratoire d'anthropologie sociale," p. 68; Susan Sontag, "The Anthropologist as Hero," in *The Anthropologist as Hero*, ed. Hayes and Hayes, p. 186.

35. See Louis-Jean Calvet, *Roland Barthes: A Biography*, Sarah Wykes, trans. (Cambridge: Polity Press, 1994), pp. 129–30.
36. The letter was later printed at the end of *Claude Lévi-Strauss*, ed. Raymond Bellour and Catherine Clément, pp. 495–97. Lévi-Strauss's account is in Eribon, *Conversations*, p. 73; Barthes's "stunningly convincing" is cited in Dosse, *History of Structuralism*, vol. 2, *The Sign Sets, 1967–present*, Deborah Glassman, trans. (Minneapolis, Minn.; and London: University of Minnesota Press), 1997, p. 115.
37. Scott Atran, "A Memory of Lévi-Strauss," International Cognition and Culture Institute, November 4, 2009, http://www.cognitionandculture.net/index.php?option=com_content&view=category&id=67:scott-atrans-blog&layout=blog&Itemid=34.
38. Lévi-Strauss in Eribon, *Conversations*, p. 34.
39. Pierre Dumayet with Claude Lévi-Strauss, "Claude Lévi-Strauss à propos de *Soleil Hopi*."
40. The interviews were later published as Georges Charbonnier, *Entretiens avec Claude Lévi-Strauss* (Paris: Plon, 1969); English version: Georges Charbonnier, *Conversations with Claude Lévi-Strauss* (London: Jonathan Cape, 1969).
41. Charbonnier, *Conversations with Claude Lévi-Strauss*, pp. 69–70.
42. Robert Hughes, "The Artist Pablo Picasso," *Time*, June 8, 1998.
43. These comments were mild in comparison to what was to come. Later Lévi-Strauss accused modern artists of polluting their sources of inspiration. In an interview for the review *Arts* about a new exhibition of Picasso at the Grand Palais, Paris, in 1966, he described the movement as something akin to "what the Americans call 'interior decoration,' a sort of accessory to the furnishings"; see Lévi-Strauss, *Structural Anthropology*, vol. 2, pp. 277, 283.
44. Lévi-Strauss, interview for *L'Express*, in *Diacritics*, p. 50.
45. Lévi-Strauss, *Structural Anthropology*, vol. 2, p. 278.
46. Charbonnier, *Conversations with Claude Lévi-Strauss*, pp. 32–42.
47. Claude Lévi-Strauss, *The Savage Mind* (London: Weidenfeld and Nicolson, 1966), p. 234.
48. See Eduardo Viveiros de Castro, "Entrevista: Lévi-Strauss nos 90, a antropologia de cabeça para baixo," *Mana*, vol. 4, no. 2, 1998, p. 119.
49. Vincent Debaene in Lévi-Strauss, *Oeuvres*, p. xxxiv.

9: "Mind in the Wild"

1. Honoré de Balzac in Claude Lévi-Strauss, *The Savage Mind* (London: Weidenfeld and Nicolson, 1966), p. 130.

2. Claude Lévi-Strauss, *Totemism*, Rodney Needham, trans. (Harmondsworth: Penguin, 1973), p. 76.
3. Ibid., p. 97. The dolphin is, however, taboo for one specific lineage of the Tafua clan, the Korokoro.
4. Lévi-Strauss, *Oeuvres*, p. 1775.
5. Lévi-Strauss, *The Raw and the Cooked*, p. 9.
6. "*dans un état de hâte, de précipitation, presque de remords*," Lévi-Strauss, *Oeuvres*, p. 1777.
7. Lévi-Strauss, *Totemism*, p. 83.
8. Bertholet, *Claude Lévi-Strauss*, p. 262.
9. Lévi-Strauss, *Totemism*, p. 72.
10. Ibid., p. 134.
11. Ibid., p. 146. Fortes, for instance, had drawn parallels between the Tallensi's highly complex totemic system and their ancestor cult. The Tallensi viewed their ancestors as "restless, elusive, ubiquitous, unpredictable, aggressive," just like the crocodiles, snakes or leopard that featured in their totemic system.
12. Ibid., pp. 155–61.
13. Ibid., p. 163.
14. Ibid., p. 162; *Le Totémisme aujourd'hui* in Lévi-Strauss, *Oeuvres*, p. 533.
15. Lévi-Strauss, *Totemism*, p. 84.
16. Lévi-Strauss, *Oeuvres*, pp. 1792–93.
17. Ibid., p. 1777.
18. Lévi-Strauss, *The Savage Mind*, pp. 3–9.
19. Lévi-Strauss in Boutang and Chevallay, *Claude Lévi-Strauss in His Own Words*, 34:23.
20. Lévi-Strauss, *The Savage Mind*, p. 149.
21. Ibid., p. 153.
22. Lévi-Strauss in Eribon, *Conversations*, p. 113.
23. Speaking of the Australian Aborigines, Lévi-Strauss said that in some respects they were "real snobs . . . as soon as they were taught the accomplishments of leisure, they prided themselves on painting the dull and studied watercolours one might expect of an old maid," in Lévi-Strauss, *The Savage Mind*, p. 89.
24. Lévi-Strauss in Boutang and Chevallay, *Claude Lévi-Strauss in His Own Words*, 1:10:00.
25. Lévi-Strauss, *The Raw and the Cooked*, pp. 147–63.
26. Lévi-Strauss, *The Savage Mind*, p. 269.
27. See exchange in Claude Lévi-Strauss and Sybil Wolfram, "The Savage Mind," *Man*, vol. 2, no. 3, New Series, September 1967, p. 464; M. Estellie Smith, "Sybil Wolfram Obituary," *Anthropology Today*, vol. 9, no. 6, December 1993, p. 22.

28. Lévi-Strauss, *Oeuvres*, pp. 1799–1801.
29. Ibid., p. 1800, note 2.
30. "Claude Lévi-Strauss: A Confrontation," *New Left Review*, p. 72. The penultimate chapter, for instance, entitled "Le Temps retrouvé," concludes with a diagram representing Australian Aboriginal ritual—a triangle whose apexes represent VIE (±), RÊVE (+) and MORT (–), a kind of *structuralisme à la Proust*.
31. A. A. Akoun, F. Morin and J. Mousseau, "A Conversation with Claude Lévi-Strauss," p. 79.
32. " 'Les Chats' de Charles Baudelaire," *L'Homme*, vol. 2, no. 1, 1962, pp. 5–22.
33. "Claude Lévi-Strauss: A Confrontation," *New Left Review*, p. 74.
34. Bertholet, *Claude Lévi-Strauss*, p. 279.
35. Lévi-Strauss, *The Raw and the Cooked*, p. 11.
36. "Claude Lévi-Strauss: A Confrontation," *New Left Review*, p. 74.
37. For critic Jean Lacroix writing in *Le Monde*, *La Pensée sauvage* represented "the most rigorously atheistic philosophy of our time," while over two issues of *Les Temps modernes* in 1963 he subjected Lévi-Strauss's ideas to a Marxist critique; Dosse, *History of Structuralism*, vol. 1, p. 234.
38. Claude Lévi-Strauss interview with Philippe Simonnot, "Claude Lévi-Strauss: un anarchiste de droite," *L'Express*. http://www.lexpress.fr/informations/archive-claude-levi-strauss-un-anarchiste-de-droite_714140.html.
39. Letter from Sartre to de Beauvoir, February 1946, in Jean-Paul Sartre and Simone de Beauvoir, *Lettres au Castor et à quelques autres*, vol. 2, (Paris: Gallimard, 1983), p. 335.
40. Lévi-Strauss, *Oeuvres*, p. 1778.
41. Lévi-Strauss, *The Savage Mind*, p. xxi.
42. Ibid., pp. 257–58, 249.
43. Lévi-Strauss in Paul Hendrickson, "Behemoth from the Ivory Tower."
44. Pierre Bourdieu, in *Réflexions faites*, Arte France, March 31, 1991.
45. Pierre Bourdieu, *Homo Academicus*, Peter Collier, trans. (Stanford: Stanford University Press, 1988), p. xxi.
46. Alain Badiou, "The Adventure of French Philosophy," *New Left Review*, vol. I/35, September–October 2005, p. 68.
47. This idea is taken from J. G. Merquior, *From Prague to Paris: A Critique of Structuralist and Post-Structuralist Thought* (London: Verso, 1988), p. 89.
48. Lévi-Strauss, *Tristes Tropiques*, Picador, p. 64.
49. Lévi-Strauss, "Le Coucher de soleil," p. 4.
50. Michel Foucault, *Les Mots et les choses: une archéologie des sciences humaines* (Paris: Gallimard, 1966), p. 398.

10: The Nebula of Myth

1. Lévi-Strauss in Eribon, *Conversations*, p. 35.
2. Lévi-Strauss, *Structural Anthropology*, vol. 1, pp. 228–29.
3. Claude Lévi-Strauss in Boutang and Chevallay, *Claude Lévi-Strauss in His Own Words*, 1:15:00.
4. Claude Lévi-Strauss, *The Origin of Table Manners: Introduction to a Science of Mythology 3*, John and Doreen Weightman, trans. (London: Jonathan Cape, 1978), p. 102.
5. Lévi-Strauss, "Entretien par Raymond Bellour," in *Oeuvres*, p. 1657.
6. Lévi-Strauss in Eribon, *Conversations*, p. 132.
7. Ibid., p. 36.
8. Sebag had been undergoing psychoanalysis with Lacan when he fell in love with Lacan's daughter Judith. After Lacan ended the sessions, Sebag shot himself in the face.
9. Lévi-Strauss, *The Raw and the Cooked*, p. 1.
10. Sanche de Gramont (aka Ted Morgan), "There Are No Superior Societies," in *The Anthropologist as Hero*, ed. Hayes and Hayes, p. 16; originally published in the *New York Times Magazine*, January 28, 1968.
11. Claude Lévi-Strauss, *The Naked Man: Introduction to a Science of Mythology 4*, John and Doreen Weightman, trans. (London: Jonathan Cape, 1981), p. 25; De Gramont, "There Are No Superior Societies," p. 17.
12. Lévi-Strauss, *The Raw and the Cooked*, p. 31.
13. Lévi-Strauss, "Entretien par Raymond Bellour," in *Oeuvres*, p. 1664.
14. "Claude Lévi-Strauss in Conversation with George Steiner," *BBC Third Programme*. In this interview with the BBC in 1965, Lévi-Strauss made this link explicit, telling Steiner that while mythic structures recurred, there might be "several species" of myths.
15. Lévi-Strauss, *The Raw and the Cooked*, pp. 3–6.
16. "Claude Lévi-Strauss in Conversation with George Steiner," *BBC Third Programme*.
17. Lévi-Strauss, *The Raw and the Cooked*, p. 15.
18. Lévi-Strauss, *The View from Afar*, p. 219.
19. Lévi-Strauss, *The Raw and the Cooked*, p. 27.
20. Ibid., pp. 31–32.
21. Lévi-Strauss in Boutang and Chevallay, *Claude Lévi-Strauss in His Own Words*, 20:10.
22. D. Antonio Colbacchini, *I Bororos Orientali: "Orarimugudoge" del Matto Grosso (Brasile)*, Torino, 1925. Just as Lévi-Strauss was finishing the final draft of *Le Cru et*

le cuit, another important Salesian source became available, the first volume of the *Enciclopédia Boróro*, forcing him to delay publication until he had had a chance to read it and incorporate it into his analyses.

23. Lévi-Strauss, *The Raw and the Cooked*, p. 37.
24. Ibid., pp. 59, 64.
25. Claude Lévi-Strauss, *From Honey to Ashes: Introduction to a Science of Mythology 2*, John and Doreen Weightman, trans. (London: Jonathan Cape, 1973), p. 469.
26. Lévi-Strauss, *The Raw and the Cooked*, 1970, p. 335.
27. Ibid., p. 340.
28. Now collected in "Claude Lévi-Strauss: The View from Afar," *UNESCO Courier*, no. 5, 2005, http://unesdoc.unesco.org/images/0016/001627/162711e.pdf.
29. See Boris Wiseman's interesting discussion on this point, linking this idea with similar sentiments expressed by the symbolist poets Stéphane Mallarmé and Paul Valéry, in *Lévi-Strauss, Anthropology and Aesthetics* (Cambridge: Cambridge University Press, 2007), pp. 202–3.
30. Merquior, *From Prague to Paris*, p. 128.
31. Also important was the work of Christian Metz, who introduced a Lacanian semiotic approach to film studies.
32. Anne-Christine Taylor, interview with the author, February 2007.
33. Dosse, *History of Structuralism*, vol. 2, p. xiii.
34. Ibid., pp. xiii–xiv.
35. Murphy, "Connaissez-vous Lévi-Strauss?" p. 165.
36. Lévi-Strauss in Eribon, *Conversations*, p. 76.
37. Bertholet, *Claude Lévi-Strauss*, p. 291.
38. Guy Sorman, "Lévi-Strauss, New Yorker," *City Journal*, vol. 19, no. 4, November 6, 2009.
39. Lévi-Strauss, "Entretien par Raymond Bellour," in *Oeuvres*, p. 1662.
40. De Gramont, "There Are No Superior Societies," pp. 9–10. Lévi-Strauss would later question the quality of Foucault's scholarship and would even go on to vote against Foucault's entry into the Collège.
41. This, according to a letter he sent to Catherine Backès-Clément on May 30, 1970; see Bertholet, *Claude Lévi-Strauss*, p. 316.
42. Psychoanalyst Didier Anzieu expressed it well in relation to Lacan, who he felt was trapping students in an "unending dependence on an idol, a logic or a language, by holding out the promise of fundamental truths to be revealed but always at some further point, and only to those who continue to travel with him," in a review of *Jacques Lacan* by Elisabeth Roudinesco (Cambridge: Polity Press, 1997), by Richard

Webster, "Lacan Goes to the Opera" *New Statesman* (1996), vol. 126, November 7, 1997, p. 44(2).

43. Cited in Dosse, *History of Structuralism*, vol. 1, p. 271.
44. De Gramont, "There Are No Superior Societies," p. 18.
45. François Furet, "Les Intellectuels français et le structuralisme," *L'Atelier de l'histoire*, Flammarion, 1982, pp. 37–52; originally published in *Preuves*, no. 92, February 1967.
46. Dosse, *History of Structuralism*, vol. 1, p. 325.
47. Boris Wiseman and Judy Groves, *Introducing Lévi-Strauss and Structural Anthropology* (Cambridge: Icon Books, 2000), p. 132.
48. Lévi-Strauss in Eribon, *Conversations*, p. 133.
49. Ibid., p. viii.
50. See David Maybury-Lewis, "The Analysis of Dual Organizations: A Methodological Critique," *Bijdragen tot de Taal-, Land- en Volkenkunde*, vol. 116, no. 1, 1960, pp. 17–44; Claude Lévi-Strauss, "On Manipulated Sociological Models," in ibid., pp. 45–54. Both are available online at http://www.kitlv-journals.nl/.
51. David Maybury-Lewis, "Science or Bricolage?" in *The Anthropologist as Hero*, ed. Hayes and Hayes, pp. 162, 154–55.
52. This was in relation to a review of the following volume, *The Origin of Table Manners*, in the *New Yorker*, July 30, 1979, p. 85.
53. Maybury-Lewis, "Science or Bricolage?," pp. 161–62.
54. Needham, interview with the author, February 2006.
55. Needham puts it more strongly: "Professor Lévi-Strauss formally declined to examine the translation before it went to press, and has likewise abstained from reading the proofs," *The Elementary Structures*, 1969, p. xviii.
56. Needham, interview with the author, February 2006. The last-minute preface was compounded by other perceived slights—Needham said that when he wrote to Lévi-Strauss to let him know that he had burned all their correspondence, Lévi-Strauss wrote back saying that was fine, since there was nothing of any value there anyway. Needham said that, in person, he found Lévi-Strauss cold and not very forthcoming. When Lévi-Strauss came to Oxford to receive an honorary degree, Needham said, he never thanked anybody; he simply arrived, collected the degree and left—a description that does not tally with other people's (including my) experiences with Lévi-Strauss. He was reserved and could be taciturn, depending on the circumstances, but he always made a point of being courteous.
57. Jeremy MacClancy, "Obituary: Rodney Needham, Oxford Social Anthropologist and Champion of Structuralism," *Independent*, December 13, 2006. Part of the problem was Needham's own extreme sensitivity and eccentricities, which produced

many rifts in his working life. After a dispute with colleagues, he moved his library out of the anthropology department and never set foot there again, teaching instead out of All Souls and relaying messages into the department via the porter.

58. Lévi-Strauss, interview with the author, February 2007.
59. Ibid.
60. Lévi-Strauss, *The Raw and the Cooked*, p. 13.
61. Dosse, *History of Structuralism*, vol. 2, p. 15.
62. Sperber, *On Anthropological Knowledge*, p. 69.
63. Viveiros de Castro, "Entrevista: Lévi-Strauss nos 90," p. 120.
64. Lévi-Strauss, *From Honey to Ashes*, p. 473.
65. Lévi-Strauss, *The Naked Man*, p. 291.
66. Ibid., p. 515.
67. Lévi-Strauss, *The Origin of Table Manners*, pp. 474–75.
68. Claude Lévi-Strauss, "Le triangle culinaire," *L'Arc*, no. 26, 1965, pp. 19–29.
69. Lévi-Strauss, *The Origin of Table Manners*, p. 484.
70. Ibid., pp. 15–16.
71. Ibid., p. 469.
72. Ibid., p. 131.
73. Lévi-Strauss, *The Raw and the Cooked*, p. 26.

11: Convergence

1. Claude Lévi-Strauss in Eribon, *Conversations*, p. 142.
2. Cited in Dosse, *History of Structuralism*, vol. 2, p. 144.
3. "Man's New Dialogue with Man," *Time*.
4. Although Foucault was not in Paris during the May '68 protests (he was working at the University of Tunis), on his return he would become actively involved in the protest movement, siding with students at the newly established university, Paris VIII at Vincennes, where he was head of the philosophy department.
5. Calvet, *Roland Barthes*, pp. 163–70.
6. "Le structuralisme, a-t-il été tué par Mai '68?" *Le Monde*, November 30, 1968.
7. Georges Balandier cited in François Dosse, *History of Structuralism*, vol. 2, p. 152.
8. Lévi-Strauss, interview for *L'Express*, in *Diacritics*, p. 45.
9. Bertholet, *Claude Lévi-Strauss*, p. 283.
10. Except for lectures given over the 1968–69 academic year, in which Lévi-Strauss examined Salish mythological themes involving fire/water and fog/wind, which he would cover later in *Histoire de Lynx* (1991).
11. Lévi-Strauss, *The Naked Man*, p. 35.

12. Ibid., p. 624.
13. Ibid., p. 510; "*nous comprenons pourquoi c'est lui, entre tous les mythes américains disponibles, qui s'est imposé à nous avant même que nous en sachions la raison*," *L'Homme nu* (Paris: Plon, 1971), p. 458.
14. Lévi-Strauss in Eribon, *Conversations*, pp. 136–37.
15. The reason he gave for having used *nous* was to reduce the subject to "the insubstantial place or space where anonymous thought can develop, stand back from itself, find and fulfill its true tendencies and achieve organisation, while coming to terms with the constraints inherent in its very nature," in Lévi-Strauss, *The Naked Man*, p. 625.
16. Lévi-Strauss was drawing on the work of American scientist J. E. Amoore in the 1950s. In fact Amoore argued that only the first five smells were based on the molecule shape-receptor model; the last two, putrid and pungent, were recognized by their electrical charge. Other models of the perception of smell have since been proposed, including Luca Turin's vibration theory, which forms the basis of Chandler Burr's popular nonfiction book *The Emperor of Scent* (Random House, 2003).
17. Lévi-Strauss, *The Naked Man*, p. 692.
18. Lévi-Strauss in Boutang and Chevallay, *Claude Lévi-Strauss in His Own Words*, 1:24:00.
19. Lévi-Strauss in Eribon, *Conversations*, p. 84.
20. Pierre Maranda, "Une fervente amitié," in *Claude Lévi-Strauss*, ed. Michel Izard, p. 56.
21. "Réponse de M. Roger Caillois au discours de M. Claude Lévi-Strauss," Académie française, June 27, 1974, http://www.academie-francaise.fr/immortels/discours_reponses/caillois.html.
22. Ibid.
23. See Maranda, "Une fervente amitié," p. 55; Bertholet, *Claude Lévi-Strauss*, pp. 397–98.
24. Claude Lévi-Strauss letter to Denis Kambouchner, cited in "Lévi-Strauss and the Question of Humanism," in *The Cambridge Companion to Lévi-Strauss*, ed. Boris Wiseman (Cambridge: Cambridge University Press, 2009), p. 37.
25. Bertholet, *Claude Lévi-Strauss*, p. 369.
26. Cited in Pace, *Claude Lévi-Strauss: The Bearer of Ashes*, p.193.
27. Count Gobineau was a thinker whom Lévi-Strauss greatly admired and whose ideas he had used in both *La Pensée sauvage* and *L'Homme nu*. Lévi-Strauss believed that Gobineau had been wrongly overlooked for holding views that, although unacceptable today, were commonplace in his own time. See Lévi-Strauss's discussion in Didier Eribon, *Conversations*, pp. 145–63.
28. Cited in Pace, *Claude Lévi-Strauss*, pp. 193–94.
29. Lévi-Strauss, "Reflections on Liberty," *The View from Afar*, p. 280.

30. Lévi-Strauss, *Tristes Tropiques*, p. 106; Eribon, *Conversations*, p. 3.
31. According to Maranda, in "Une fervente amitié," p. 54.
32. Lévi-Strauss in Eribon, *Conversations*, p. 165, translation modified.
33. "Claude Lévi-Strauss in Conversation with George Steiner," *BBC Third Programme*.
34. Lévi-Strauss, *The Way of the Masks*, pp. 5–8.
35. Pierre Maranda, an anthropologist interested in the structural approach, had met Lévi-Strauss several times in the 1960s, and in 1968 ended up working at Lévi-Strauss's invitation as an associate director of studies at the École pratique des hautes études en sciences sociales; see his homage to his long friendship with Lévi-Strauss in Maranda, "Une fervente amitié," pp. 52–75.
36. Lévi-Strauss, *Saudades do Brasil*, p. 17.
37. For a brief and lucid demonstration of this, see Lévi-Strauss's discussion of a comparison between the Salish and the Kwakiutl masks and myths in Tom Shandel, *Behind the Masks*, National Film Board of Canada, 1973.
38. Maranda, "Une fervente amitié," p. 57.
39. Lévi-Strauss in Didier Eribon, *Conversations*, p. 95.
40. Lévi-Strauss, *The View from Afar*, p. 235.
41. Claude Lévi-Strauss, *Myth and Meaning* (London: Routledge, 2006), pp. 7, 9.
42. Lévi-Strauss in Didier Eribon, *Conversations*, p. 91.
43. "Bernadette Bucher with Claude Lévi-Strauss, 30 June 1982," *American Ethnologist*, vol. 12, no. 2, 1985, pp. 365–66.
44. Lévi-Strauss, interview with the author, March 2005.
45. Lévi-Strauss in Tom Shandel, *Behind the Masks*.
46. Claude Lévi-Strauss, *The Jealous Potter* (Chicago and London: University of Chicago Press, 1996), p. 190.
47. Ibid., p. 186.
48. Ibid., p. 206.
49. Lévi-Strauss, "Le Coucher de soleil," p. 12. In an earlier interview, Lévi-Strauss was more direct: "I am by temperament somewhat of a misanthrope"; see A. A. Akoun, F. Morin and J. Mousseau, "A Conversation with Claude Lévi-Strauss," p. 82.
50. Lévi-Strauss in Augé, "Ten Questions Put to Claude Lévi-Strauss," p. 85.
51. Lévi-Strauss in Eribon, *Conversations*, pp. 87, 151.
52. Ibid., pp. 156–57.
53. Ibid., p. 151.
54. Ibid., p. 94.
55. See Lévi-Strauss, "Do Dual Organizations Exist?" *Structural Anthropology*, vol. 1, pp. 132–63. In a complex analysis he found that features previously dismissed as anomalies in so-called dual-organization societies were integral to their structure. He

went on to argue that there were really two different types of dualism, diametric and concentric, mediated by a ternary structure.

56. Rodney Needham, "The birth of the meaningful," *Times Literary Supplement*, April 13, 1984.
57. Cited in Tambiah, *Edmund Leach*, p. 253.
58. Lévi-Strauss in Boutang and Chevallay, *Claude Lévi-Strauss in His Own Words*, 1:15:00.
59. Lévi-Strauss, *Oeuvres*, pp. 1572–73.
60. Merquior, *From Prague to Paris*, p. 191.
61. Cited in Didier Eribon, *Michel Foucault* (London: Faber and Faber, 1992), p. 161.
62. Lévi-Strauss, *Myth and Meaning*, p. 47.
63. Claude Lévi-Strauss, "Entretien," *Le Monde*, February 22, 2005.
64. Lévi-Strauss, *Saudades do Brasil*, p. 142.
65. Ibid., p. 9.
66. Clifford Geertz, *Works and Lives: The Anthropologist as Author* (Stanford: Stanford University Press, 1988), pp. 25–26.

Epilogue

1. Lévi-Strauss cited in Paul Hendrickson, "Claude-Lévi Strauss: Behemoth from the Ivory Tower," *Washington Post*, February 24, 1978.
2. Claude Lévi-Strauss in Didier Eribon, "Visite à Lévi-Strauss," *Le Nouvel Observateur*, no. 1979, October 10, 2002: http://tempsreel.nouvelobs.com/actualite/opinion/00030882.EDI0001/visite-a-levi-strauss.html.
3. James M. Markham, "Paris Journal: A French Thinker Who Declines a Guru Mantle," *New York Times*, December 21, 1987.
4. Lévi-Strauss, *Oeuvres*, p. lvii.
5. Claude Lévi-Strauss in Didier Eribon, "Visite à Lévi-Strauss."
6. Lévi-Strauss in "Le Coucher de soleil: entretien avec Boris Wiseman," *Les Temps modernes*, no. 628, August–October 2004, p. 17.
7. Lévi-Strauss, "Entretien par Raymond Bellour," in *Oeuvres*, pp. 1654–55.
8. Gilles de Catheu, "Saudades do Brasil," *O Globo*, November 7, 2009.
9. There were a few dissenting voices, including a piece in the left-wing magazine *Marianne* questioning his position on race and his attitude to Islam; see Philippe Cohen, "Lévi-Strauss sans formol," *Marianne*, November 4, 2009.
10. "Tous les anthropologues français sont les enfants de Claude Lévi-Strauss," *Le Monde*, November 3, 2009.
11. "Les obsèques de Claude Lévi-Strauss ont déjà eu lieu," *Le Point*, November 3, 2009.

Further Reading

1. Claude Lévi-Strauss and Didier Eribon, *Conversations with Claude Lévi-Strauss*, Paula Wissing, trans. (Chicago: University of Chicago Press, 1991).
2. Georges Charbonnier, *Conversations with Claude Lévi-Strauss*, John and Doreen Weightman, trans. (London: Jonathan Cape, 1969).
3. Claude Lévi-Strauss, *Myth and Meaning* (London: Routledge, 2006).
4. Pierre-André Boutang and Annie Chevallay, *Claude Lévi-Strauss in His Own Words* (*Claude Lévi-Strauss par lui-même*), Arte Éditions, 2008; Tom Shandel, *Behind the Masks*, National Film Board of Canada, 1973.
5. Edmund Leach, *Claude Lévi-Strauss* (London: Fontana/Collins, 1974).
6. David Pace, *Claude Lévi-Strauss: The Bearer of Ashes* (Boston: Routledge and Kegan Paul, 1983).
7. François Dosse, *History of Structuralism, vol. 1, The Rising Sign, 1945–1966* (Minneapolis, Minn., and London: University of Minnesota Press, 1997); *History of Structuralism, vol. 2, The Sign Sets, 1967–present* (Minneapolis, Minn., and London: University of Minnesota Press, 1997).
8. Boris Wiseman and Judy Groves, *Introducing Lévi-Strauss and Structural Anthropology* (Cambridge: Icon Books, 2000).
9. Dan Sperber, "Claude Lévi-Strauss Today," in *On Anthropological Knowledge* (Cambridge: Cambridge University Press, 1985).
10. Clifford Geertz, "The Cerebral Savage: On the Work of Claude Lévi-Strauss," in *Works and Lives: The Anthropologist as Author* (Stanford: Stanford University Press, 1988).
11. Howard Gardner, *The Mind's New Science: A History of the Cognitive Revolution* (New York: Basic, 1987); John Sturrock, *Structuralism* (London: Fontana, 1993); J. G. Merquior, *From Prague to Paris: A Critique of Structuralist and Post-structuralist Thought,* (London: Verso, 1988); Boris Wiseman, "Claude Lévi-Strauss," in Christopher John Murray, ed., *Encyclopedia of Mòdern French Thought* (New York; London: Fitzroy Dearborn, 2004); http://www.routledge-ny.com/ref/modfrenchthought/levistrauss.PDF.
12. Claude Lévi-Strauss: *The Anthropologist as Hero*, ed. E. Nelson Hayes and Tanya Hayes (Cambridge, Mass., & London: MIT Press, 1970).
13. Claude Lévi-Strauss, *Tristes Tropiques*, John and Doreen Weightman, trans. (London: Picador, 1989).
14. Claude Lévi-Strauss, "New York in 1941," in *The View from Afar*, Joachim Neugroschel and Phoebe Hoss, trans. (Oxford: Basil Blackwell, 1985).
15. Claude Lévi-Strauss, *Saudades do Brasil: A Photographic Memoir*, Sylvia Modelski, trans. (Seattle: University of Washington Press, 1995).

16. Claude Lévi-Strauss, *The Raw and the Cooked: Introduction to a Science of Mythology 1*, John and Doreen Weightman, trans. (London: Jonathan Cape, 1970); Claude Lévi-Strauss, *The Naked Man: Introduction to a Science of Mythology 4*, John and Doreen Weightman, trans., (London: Jonathan Cape, 1981).
17. Claude Lévi-Strauss, *The Savage Mind* (London: Weidenfeld and Nicolson, 1966).
18. Lévi-Strauss, *The Elementary Structures of Kinship*, James Harle Bell, John Richard von Sturmer and Rodney Needham, trans. (London: Eyre and Spottiswoode, 1969).
19. Lévi-Strauss, "The Structural Study of Myth" in *Structural Anthropology*, vol. 1, (Harmondsworth: Penguin, 1968).
20. Claude Lévi-Strauss, "The View from Afar," *UNESCO Courier*, no. 5 (2008): http://unesdoc.unesco.org/images/0016/001627/162711E.pdf.
21. Denis Bertholet, *Claude Lévi-Strauss* (Paris: Plon, 2003).
22. Frédéric Keck, *Lévi-Strauss et la pensée sauvage* (Paris: Presses universitaires de France, 2004); Frédéric Keck, *Claude Lévi-Strauss, une introduction* (Paris: Pocket, 2005); Frédéric Keck and Vincent Debaene, *Claude Lévi-Strauss : L'homme au regard éloigné* (Paris: Gallimard, 2009).
23. Claude Lévi-Strauss, *Oeuvres* (Paris: Gallimard: Bibliothèque de la Pléiade, 2007).

FURTHER READING

Approaching the work of Claude Lévi-Strauss can be daunting. He was a prolific writer, active for over half a century, publishing several hundred essays and more than a dozen books—seven on mythology alone—throughout his long career. In the 1980s a book-length bibliography of secondary sources was published; since then, another library of Lévi-Strauss-related material has appeared with a late surge of publications to commemorate his centenary. Sheer quantity is at times matched by a density of ideas and material—indeed, some stretches of *The Elementary Structures of Kinship* and the *Mythologiques* quartet are not for the fainthearted.

But for someone often considered an intellectual elitist, Lévi-Strauss had a popular touch, especially in the many interviews, radio broadcasts and documentary films in which he participated over the years. He was extremely articulate, effortlessly delivering potted summaries of his most demanding books. There was also an autobiographical strain to his work, which often interweaved incidents from his life with own thinking, the two sometimes merging into a kind of vital essence. And for readers unfamiliar with French, all of Lévi-Strauss's books and most of his essays have been translated into English.

Of the many interviews he gave, Didier Eribon's book-length *Conversations with Claude Lévi-Strauss* is by far the most comprehensive and searching.[1] Divided into three parts, it covers his early travels; the rise of structuralism; and his ideas on art, politics and culture. Lévi-Strauss's late 1950s radio interviews with Georges Charbonnier have also been published in book form.[2] In this encounter, Lévi-Strauss talked at length about contemporary art and music. On the subject of myth, the Massey lectures, later published as *Myth and Meaning*, are as clear as the originals are opaque.[3] A good compilation of his television interviews, as well as a highly watchable feature documentary, is Pierre-André Boutang and Annie Chevallay's *Lévi-Strauss: In His Own Words*; while the Canadian Film Board's documentary, *Behind the Masks,* which covers his first trip to British Columbia in the 1970s, gives a flavor of his method, featuring a short lecture summarizing his analysis of myths and masks.[4]

One of the best summaries of his ideas in English is Edmund Leach's *Claude Lévi-Strauss*, which, in a series of essays, takes the reader step-by-step through the complexities of Lévi-Strauss's arguments.[5] Also interesting is David Pace's *Claude Lévi-Strauss: The Bearer of Ashes*, a critical assessment of the development of his ideas.[6] François Dosse's two-volume narrative account of the era, *History of Structuralism*, contextualizes Lévi-Strauss's work and the enormous influence he had over his contemporaries.[7] For a witty, bare-bones summary, replete with cartoon figures of Lévi-Strauss expounding his theories in speech bubbles, Boris Wiseman and Judy Groves's *Introducing Lévi-Strauss and Structural Anthropology*, offers a rapid, but by no means trivialized, introduction to Lévi-Strauss.[8]

French anthropologist Dan Sperber's "Claude Lévi-Strauss Today," which combines admiration and skepticism in the right measure, is one of the most balanced and intelligent essay-length assessments of his work.[9] Coming from a more literary perspective, American anthropologist Clifford Geertz's "The Cerebral Savage: On the Work of Claude Lévi-Strauss" is a critique of what he calls Lévi-Strauss's "infernal culture machine," ending up questioning whether Lévi-Strauss's theories represent "science or alchemy."[10] Good chapter-length summaries of Lévi-Strauss's work can also be found in Howard Gardner, *The Mind's New Science: A History of the Cognitive Revolution*; John Sturrock, *Structuralism*; J. G. Merquior, *From Prague to Paris: A Critique of Structuralist and Post-Structuralist Thought*; and Boris Wiseman's entry in the *Encyclopedia of Modern French Thought*.[11] Published in 1970, *Claude Lévi-Strauss: The Anthropologist as Hero* brings together an interesting selection of short review pieces by Susan Sontag, David Maybury-Lewis and Sanche de Gramont among others, written at the height of Lévi-Strauss's fame.[12]

For those wishing to return to the original works, Lévi-Strauss's classic memoir, *Tristes Tropiques*, remains by far the most accessible and enjoyable entry point into his oeuvre.[13] The narrative follows his early years as a disillusioned university student, through to his discovery of anthropology and fieldwork in Brazil. Strangely, it skips over his crucial period of exile in New York, though this gap was partially filled by a short, descriptive essay on his first impressions on arriving in Manhattan in the third volume of his essay anthologies, *The View from Afar*.[14] For a visual companion piece to *Tristes Tropiques*, the coffee-table book, *Saudades do Brasil* showcases Lévi-Strauss's formidable talents as a field photographer.[15]

In his academic works, certain key chapters stand out as accessible encapsulations of his ideas. Lévi-Strauss often began and ended his books with clarity; it is the following through of the argument, demonstrated by hundreds of examples, that can be a slog for the general reader. The "Overture" and the "Finale" of the *Mythologiques* series, for instance, summarize the project in lucid prose; the intervening two thousand pages, though, require high levels of concentration to hold on to all the strands of Lévi-Strauss's argument while remembering the twists and turns of an ever-accumulating stock of mythic material.[16] Similarly, *The Savage Mind* begins with a statement of key notions—the importance of disinterested classification, bricolage and the science of the concrete—but then drifts into complex ethnographic applications of these ideas.[17] The same could be said of *The Elementary Structures of Kinship*, which opens with a general discussion of the fundamental distinction between nature and culture and the power of the incest taboo, before becoming overladen with kinship diagrams and ethnographic minutiae.[18]

Lévi-Strauss is certainly easier to manage at essay length. "The Structural Study of Myth," his classic early demonstration of his method using Sophocles' *Oedipus Rex,* is a key reference point.[19] For an easy overview of some of his more general ideas, Lévi-Strauss wrote short, popularizing essays for the *UNESCO Courier*, covering discussions on the illusory notion of the "primitive," the relationship between shamans and psychoanalysis and structural analyses of cooking, that are now available online.[20]

For readers of French, the options are virtually limitless. However, a few of the more recently published titles stand out. Denis Bertholet's 2003 biography, *Claude Lévi-Strauss*, is a detailed overview of his life and ideas.[21] Frédéric Keck has written a series of clear introductions to Lévi-Strauss's work, including *Lévi-Strauss et la pensée sauvage*; *Claude Lévi-Strauss, une introduction*; and, with Vincent Debaene, *Claude Lévi-Strauss: L'homme au regard éloigné*.[22] The Bibliothèque de la Pléiade edition of *Oeuvres*, published when Lévi-Strauss was ninety-nine, is a fitting conclusion to his life and work.[23] It contains not just the bulk of his oeuvre, but previously unpublished material from Lévi-Strauss's recently opened archive at the Bibliothèque nationale in Paris, including excerpts from his aborted novel, the first acts of a play he wrote in Brazil and his field notes. All this is presented with the Bibliothèque de la Pléiade's customary gravitas, from the almost weightless Bible paper and soft leather cover to the pale pink flyleaves and the gold-embossed "Claude Lévi-Strauss Oeuvres" on the spine.

INDEX

Abbaye de Royaumont talks, 320–21
Académie française, 315–17, 319
Adler, Alfred, 216, 237
Africa, 16–17, 19–20, 34–35, 217, 219, 237, 254, 294
  Dakar-Djibouti expedition to, 40, 88–89, 167, 209
African-Americans, 19, 33
Afrique fantôme, L' (Leiris), 209, 215–16
Afro-Brazilians, 51, 56, 57, 86, 114
Agamben, Giorgio, 12
Alquié, Ferdinand, 36
Althusser, Louis, 289
Alvarenga, Oneyda, 96
Amado, Jorge, 57
Amaral, Tarsila do, 56–57
"Analyse structurale en linguistique et en anthropologie, L'" (Structural Analysis in Linguistics and Anthropology) (Lévi-Strauss), 157–60
Andrade, Mário de, 57–58, 62, 66, 83, 90, 91–92, 96, 109, 118, 226, 354*n*
Andrade, Oswald de, 56–57
Anthropologie structurale (*Structural Anthropology*) (Lévi-Strauss), 237–38, 239
anthropology:
  Anglo-American, 17–18, 40, 55, 74, 88, 110, 165, 174–75, 265–67, 297–303
  CLS on progress of, 195–97
  cultures as changed by, 110
  French, 5, 17–20, 34, 35, 39–41, 74, 88–89, 165–66, 218, 237
  linguistics and, 129, 193–97
  of 1930s vs. nineteenth century, 1–2, 3, 88–89
  North American, 42–43, 242, 250, 281, 304
  physical, 55–56, 57, 75, 112, 138
  solitary cultural immersion of, 2, 3, 75, 87–89, 96, 99, 101, 110, 112
  surrealism and, 199
Anthropophagy (Amaral), 56–57
anti-Semitism, 23, 78, 117, 120–23, 186
Anzieu, Didier, 310, 376*n*
Apothéose d'Auguste, L' (*The Apotheosis of Augustus*) (Lévi-Strauss), 98–99, 101, 208
Aragon, Louis, 35
Aron, Raymond, 214, 244, 309, 327, 332
Art magique, L' (Breton), 243–44
Atran, Scott, 243, 320–21
Audiberti, Jacques, 215

Augé, Marc, 4, 174, 219
Aurignacian culture, 77
Australian Aborigines, 263, *373n*, *374n*
  kinship system of, 122, 168, 172, 198, 274
  totemism of, 253–55
Auzias, Jean-Marie, 290–91
avant-garde, 3, 13, 15, 17, 18–19, 25–26, 27, 33–35, 44, 56, 200–201, 228, 280, 282–83, 307

Babeuf, Gracchus, 30
Bachelard, Gaston, 244
Badiou, Alain, 12, 273
Baker, Josephine, 19, 34
Balandier, Georges, 205, 218–19, 302, 310, 343, *369n*
Balzac, Honoré de, 13, 28, 32, 243, 249, 342
Barthes, Roland, 12, 228, 229, 242–43, 289–90, 291, 309–10, 327, 329
Bastide, François-Régis, 214
Bastide, Paul Arbousse, 55
Bataille, Georges, 18, 33, 34, 173, 199, 219–20, *367n*
Bateson, Gregory, 320–21
Bayet, Albert, 167
Beiços de Pau, 87, 90
Belgian Workers Party, 27, 30
Bellour, Raymond, 278, 280, 290, 297, 335, 343
Bellow, Saul, 164
Benedict, Ruth, 99, 137–38, 139
Benoît-Lévy, Jean, 157
Bensa, Alban, 112, 218
Benveniste, Emile, 167, 186, 196, 267, 295
Berger, Gaston, 161, 186
Bergson, Henri, 39, 164, 256, 273
Bertholet, Denis, 196–97
Beuchot, Pierre, 277
Bibliothèque de la Pléiade, 177, 248, 266, 343, *371n*
binary pairs, 148, 153, 247–48, 260, 314–15
Blum, Léon, 30
Boas, Franz, 42–43, 55, 131, 235, 240, 323
  CLS relationship with, 138–39
  death of, 139
  fieldwork of, 138, 181
  Northwest Coast motifs described by, 152
Bogatyrev, Petr, 143
Boggiani, Guido, 65
Bolivia, 2, 80, 81, 109, 294
Borges, Jorge Luis, 146, 174, 232
Bororo, 2, 47, 62, 68–75, 79, 83, 91, 92, 112, 123, 177, 212, 328
  artifacts collected from, 71, 73–74
  bartering for artifacts with, 75
  body paint of, 68, 69, 70, 283
  bull-roarers of, 73, 116, 223
  film footage of, 72–73
  funerals of, 71, 72, 192
  huts of, 70, 72, 283
  kinship system of, 71–72, 74, 122, 170, 332
  material culture of, 8, 68, 69, 73–74, 116
  men of, 68–69, 71, 223, 328
  myths of, 69, 71, 283–86, 306
  ritual music of, 70
  tobacco crop of, 70–71
  village layout of, 71–72, 74, 170, 213, 283, 328, 332
Bouglé, Célestin, 31, 41, 42, 123
Boulez, Pierre, 227, *369n*
Bourdieu, Pierre, 272
brain, 11, 193, 335, *366n*
Brancusi, Constantin, 17
Brasília, 7–8, 225–26, 327–28
Braudel, Fernand, 42, 54, 55, 56, 229, 327
Brazil, 1–3, 7–8, 9, 14, 41–43, 45, 47–78, 79–114, 123, 125, 129, 137, 181, 215, 341–42
  CLS's preliminary reading on, 42–43
  CLS's state visit to, 327–29
  degraded indigenous cultures of, 43, 52, 60–61, 64, 65, 68, 327–28
  Depression's effect on, 52
  eighteenth-century gold rush in, 50
  folk music of, 57, 84
  Ge linguistic group of, 72, 79–80, 82, 84, 285–86, 297
  journey to, 47–49, 116
  miscegenation in, 55–56
  modernism in, 52, 56–57, 225–26
  modernization of, 51–52
  Nazi-styled Integralists in, 52, 78
  pioneer zone colonization projects of, 58–59
  political turbulence in, 52, 78, 113
  press of, 73–74, 75, 85

Brazil, CLS's first fieldwork in, 7, 14, 33, 40–41, 58–77, 86, 120, 155, 225
academic response to, 73–75
bartering for artifacts in, 15, 61, 63–64, 75
brevity of, 74–75
clothing worn for, 66, 70, 76
early disillusioning experiences of, 59–61
equipment and supplies for, 63–64
Fazenda Francesa and, 63–64, 67–68
film footage of, 8, 66–67, 72–73
financing of, 62
hardships of, 66, 69, 77
indigenous artifacts collected by, 8, 9, 64, 71, 73–74, 77
see also Bororo; Caduveo
Brazil, CLS's 1938 fieldwork in, 1–3, 79–114, 117, 344
bartering for artifacts in, 2, 83, 95, 102, 116
boa constrictors and, 2
brevity of, 109–12
bureaucratic hurdles surmounted by, 83, 84–85, 113–14
canoes in, 104, 105
capuchin monkey acquired in, 54, 104–5, 107
clothing worn for, 1, 87, 90
CLS's depressive episode in, 97, 99
CLS's field notes of, 2, 3, 94–95, 96, 97–98, 107, 115, 137, 143–44, 263–64, 357*n*
CLS's preliminary reading for, 82–83
drawings of, 94, 95, 107, 132
equipment and supplies for, 1–2, 85, 87–88, 94, 104, 109
ethnographic team of, 83–85, 87, 96, 104, 105–6, 108–9, 111–12
eye infections contracted in, 96–97
financing of, 82–83, 88
game hunting in, 90, 104
goal of, 79–80
hardships of, 90, 94–95, 103
hired crew of, 87, 90, 104, 105–6
indigenous artifacts collected in, 83, 88, 93, 95, 109, 114, 115–16
material culture as focus of, 95, 109
and natives' hostile actions, 83, 87, 91
outbound journey of, 89–92
pack animals of, 87, 88, 89, 104, 109
photographs of, 1–2, 90, 93, 94, 107, 115, 205, 322–23, 338
return trip of, 108–9
river crossings in, 91
route of, 80
scale of, 87–89, 110
shooting accident in, 106–7, 132
subsequent evaluations of, 109–12
telegraph line and, 79, 80–81, 83, 86–87, 88, 89, 90–91, 92, 97, 101, 104, 105
see also Nambikwara
Breton, André, 9, 20, 34–35, 124, 125, 186, 191, 219–20
CLS's relationship with, 126–28, 133, 201, 243–44
in Greenwich Village, 133, 135, 136
indigenous artifacts collected by, 134, 135
spontaneous creativity doctrine of, 127
on Voice of America, 151
Brillouin, Léon, 157
Brown, Al, 20
Brunschvicg, Léon, 164, 273
Bucher, Bernadette, 327
Buddhism, 222–23
Burma, 170, 175, 222–23

Caduveo, 2, 47, 62, 63–68, 73–75, 85, 92, 102, 112, 155, 177, 207, 274, 354*n*
film footage of, 8, 66–67
material culture of, 8, 64, 65, 67, 68, 73
nineteenth-century depictions of, 65
painted facial patterns on women of, 3, 8, 65–66, 67, 68, 136, 152–53, 169, 207, 212–13
social organization of, 212–13
wall-less huts of, 64, 67
Cahen, Léon, 29, 30, 45
Caillois, Roger, 199–201, 217, 316–17, 367*n*, 371*n*
Cain, Julien, 161
Camus, Albert, 12, 126, 161, 228, 244
Capitaine Paul-Lemerle, 125–28
Carlebach, Julius, 135
Carlu, Jacques, 160
Caro-Delvaille, Henry, 24, 123
Cartel des gauches, 30
Cartry, Michel, 237

Castel, Louis-Bertrand, 336
Castro Faria, Luiz de, 1, 2, 84–109
 on CLS's fieldwork, 111
 field diary of, 84, 86, 88, 89, 90, 91, 94, 95, 97, 106–7, 108
 Quain encountered by, 85–86
Céline, Louis-Ferdinand, 33
Centre national de la recherche scientifique (CNRS), 165, 293
Cervantes, Miguel de, 24, 214
Césaire, Aimé, 136
Chamson, André, 32
Charbonnier, Georges, 244–48, 307
"Chats, Les" (Baudelaire), 267
Chicago, Ill., 162–63
China, ancient:
 art of, 152–53
 kinship system of, 121–22, 312
Chirac, Jacques, 9
Chiva, Isac, 242, 294
Chomsky, Noam, 290, 302, 320–21
Cinna (Corneille), 98–99
Clastres, Pierre, 216, 237, 294
"*Claude Lévi-Strauss detestou a Baía de Guanabara*" (Veloso), 49
Clouet, François, 262
Colbacchini, Antonio, 284
"cold" vs. "hot" societies, 247–48
Collège de France, 5, 6, 11, 71, 161, 191, 205, 237, 308, 342, 367*n*, 376*n*
 CLS's admission to, 238–43, 248
 CLS's inaugural address to, 240–41
 CLS's rejections by, 185–87, 189
 CLS's research center at, *see* Laboratoire d'anthropologie sociale
 CLS's seminars at, 251, 258, 295–96, 311
Collège de sociologie, 199
Comité France-Amérique, 42
communism, 30, 52, 78, 236–37, 269
Companie des transports maritimes, 125, 126
Comte, Auguste, 55, 81
Condamine, Charles Marie de la, 88
Conrad, Joseph, 27, 33, 88, 181, 216
Constructive Revolution movement, 32
"Contribution à l'étude de l'organisation sociale des Indiens Bororo" (Lévi-Strauss), 74
Corneille, Pierre, 98–99
Cornibert, Denis, 344–45
Costa, Lúcio, 226
Cours de linguistique générale (Saussure), 147–48, 290
Courtin, René, 76–77, 120, 155, 225
Cresson, André, 29
cross-cultural comparisons, 55, 152–53, 255–56
Cru et le cuit, Le (*The Raw and the Cooked*) (Lévi-Strauss), 26, 268, 278, 280–87, 298, 306, 307, 313, 324
 Bororo myths in, 283–86
 conclusion of, 287
 English version of, 292
 inversions and oppositions in, 264–65, 285–87
 orchestral music metaphor in, 281–83
 raw/cooked polarity in, 285–87
 scatalogical references in, 285
cubism, 25, 26, 33, 245, 262
cultural evolution, 122, 172, 198
cultural relativism, 198–201, 218
cybernetics, 132, 194, 247
Czechoslovakia, 142–43

da Cunha, Mário Wagner Vieira, 57–58
Dakar-Djibouti expedition, 40, 88–89, 167, 209
Darwin, Charles, 142
Davy, Georges, 166
Déat, Marcel, 30
"Death of the Author, The" (Barthes), 289
Debaene, Vincent, 248, 343
de Beauvoir, Simone, 12, 43–44, 161, 162, 214, 228, 269, 327
 CLS's impression of, 36
 Structures élémentaires reviewed by, 172–73
Debray, Régis, 219
Debussy, Claude, 26, 208
de Catheu, Gilles, 344
De Gaulle, Charles, 140, 157, 296, 308–9
 American supporters of, 150–51, 153–54
de Gramont, Sanche, 292–93, 294, 296
Degré zéro de l'écriture, Le (*Writing Degree Zero*) (Barthes), 228
de Heusch, Luc, 216–17
de la Tour, Maurice Quentin, 21

Delay, Jean, 161
Deleuze, Gilles, 36
Deluz, Ariane, 294
de Montherlant, Henry, 316
Denmark, 143, 203
De près et de loin (Eribon), 4, 331
Derain, André, 16
Derrida, Jacques, 292
de Saint Phalle, Niki, 195
Descola, Philippe, 191, 230, 301
Dickens, Charles, 13, 27, 262, 342
"Diogène couché" (Lévi-Strauss), 200–201
Documents, 33–34, 136
"Do Dual Organizations Exist?" (Lévi-Strauss), 297, 380*n*-81*n*
Doniger, Wendy, 335
Dosse, François, 206, 219, 292, 302
Dostoyevsky, Fyodor, 27, 33
Dreyfus, Pierre, 37, 352*n*
dualism, 152–53, 167, 169, 255–56, 259, 380*n*-81*n*
Duchamp, Marcel, 133
Dumas, Georges, 41–42, 55, 123
Dumayet, Pierre, 5, 244
Dumézil, Georges, 166, 174, 186, 190, 199, 230, 351, 295, 327, 331
Du miel aux cendres (*From Honey to Ashes*) (Lévi-Strauss), 234–35, 278, 297–99, 303
Durkheim, Emile, 17, 31, 55, 164, 166, 167, 192, 238, 240
Duthuit, Georges, 135

École coloniale, 18
École des beaux-arts, 21
École des hautes études commerciales, 21
École normale supérieure, 6, 28–29, 30, 31, 40, 351*n*
École pratique des haute études, 17, 18, 161, 180–81, 190, 196
  CLS's chair of religious studies at, 189–93
  CLS's seminars at, 237, 270
"Effectiveness of Symbols, The" (Lévi-Strauss), 181–83
Elkin, A. P., 253–54
Emergency Rescue Committee, 124
Endless Column (Brancusi), 17
Engels, Friedrich, 27
"Enigma of Incest, The" (Bataille), 173
Eribon, Didier, 4, 6, 111, 121, 139, 156, 187, 191, 222, 241, 279, 326, 331–32
Ernst, Max, 9, 124, 133, 134–35, 136, 186, 276
Escarra, Jean, 167
Essai sur le don (*The Gift*) (Mauss), 17, 168–69, 184–85, 324
Estado de São Paulo, 50, 206–7, 215, 328
Étudiant socialiste, 31, 35
  "Livres et revues" section of, 33
evolution, 142
  cultural, 122, 172, 198
exchange, types of, 169, 188
existentialism, 12, 156, 165, 173, 214, 270, 336

fairy tales, 55
Fang, 259
Faral, Edmond, 186
Fazenda Francesa, 63–64, 67–68
Febvre, Lucien, 181
Fédération des étudiants socialistes, 31
figurines, 65
  Karaja clay dolls, 77
Fiji Islands, 85
Firth, Raymond, 255
folk music, 57, 84
Fondation Loubat lecture series, 186, 279
Ford, Gordon Onslow, 133
Fortes, Meyer, 255, 373*n*
Foucault, Michel, 12, 165, 228, 229, 237, 238, 244, 275, 289, 291, 292, 309, 327, 329, 337, 376*n*
Fournier, Marcel, 15
France:
  Chamber des députés of, 30, 31
  CLS's hundredth birthday celebration in, 343–44
  colonial empire of, 16, 34–35, 40, 52–53, 201, 202–3, 217, 218–20, 236
  ethnographic displays in, 15–16, 19–20
  higher education expanded in, 239
  intellectual elite of, 28–29, 36, 40
  political Left in, 29–32, 236–37, 296, 310, 322
  postwar publishing in, 204
  press of, 12, 111, 289
  Third Republic of, 44
  trente glorieuses period in, 239
  TV arts programming in, 244–48

France, in World War II, 117, 118–26, 149–55, 165
Allied liberation of, 153–54
CLS's flight from, 9, 10, 23, 48, 122–26; *see also* Lévi-Strauss, Claude, as exile in New York City
CLS's military service in, 118–20
épuration sauvage in, 154–55
German occupation of, 119–25, 149–50, 155, 186
Jewish question in, 121, 122, 149–50, 186
Maginot Line of, 118, 130, 194, 258
postoccupation tensions in, 157
refugees from, 119–20, 121, 123–26
Resistance in, 120, 123, 126, 150, 151
Vichy government of, 120–23, 128, 150, 160
France Antarctique, 43, 353*n*
Francis I, King of France, 185
Frazer, Sir James, 10, 171, 240, 253
1928 lecture of, 35
Free French, 140, 151
French Committee of National Liberation, 154
French Communist Party, 30, 236–37
French realist films, 54
French Revolution, 28, 30
Freud, Sigmund, 12, 27, 39, 45, 147, 167, 174, 176, 179, 180, 181, 183, 228, 231, 234, 240, 253, 284–85, 329–30
Freyre, Gilberto, 57
Frigout, Arlette, 294
Fry, Varian, 124
"Funes the Memorious" (Borges), 146
Furet, François, 296

Gallimard, 177, 204, 237–38, 343, 371*n*
Geertz, Clifford, 339
Gellner, Ernest, 265
geology, 38–39, 45, 147
"Geste d'Asdiwal, La" (The Story of Asdiwal) (Lévi-Strauss), 235, 312
Gide, André, 28, 215
Gillen, Frank, 254–55
Gobineau, Count, 319, 379*n*
Godelier, Maurice, 294
Gorky, Arshile, 133
Gourou, Pierre, 216, 267
Gracchus Babeuf et le communisme (Lévi-Strauss), 30
Granet, Marcel, 10, 121–22, 142, 169, 190, 312
Great Britain, 12, 17–18, 58, 154, 174–77, 257, 265–67, 316
Expeditionary Force of, 118, 119
India and Pakistan partitioned by, 187
withdrawal from India of, 220
Greenland, 203–4
Greimas, Algirdas Julien, 242–43, 294, 309–10
Griaule, Marcel, 40, 88–89, 167, 209, 216
Gris, Juan, 16
Groupe des onze (Group of Eleven), 31–32, 38
Groupe socialiste interkhâgnal, 30
Guayaki, 84, 294, 305
Guggenheim, Peggy, 133, 134
Guilbaud, Georges, 196
Guillaume, Paul, 16–17
Guimet, Émile, 242
Gurvitch, Georges, 184–85, 238, 371*n*

Haka Chin, 175–76
Hamilton, Ron, 324–25
Handbook of South American Indians, 137, 162
Hanunóo, 259, 262
Hare, David, 136
Hegel, Georg Wilhelm Friedrich, 27, 164–65
Heidegger, Martin, 156, 165
Henry, Maurice, 291
Héritier, Françoise, 6, 237, 294
Herrmann, Claudine, 361*n*
Histoire de la folie à l'âge classique (Foucault), 228, 238
Histoire de Lynx (*The Story of the Lynx*) (Lévi-Strauss), 280, 323, 332–33, 378*n*
Histoire d'un voyage fait en la terre du Brésil, L' (Léry), 43, 50
Homme, 267, 272–73
Homme nu, L' (*The Naked Man*) (Lévi-Strauss), 277, 278, 279–80, 311–15, 323
Homo Academicus (Bourdieu), 272
Hopi, 134, 192, 244, 294
"hot" vs. "cold" societies, 247–48
Hourcade, Pierre, 42
Hpalang, 175
Hughes, Robert, 245
Hugo, Victor, 32
humanism, 173, 258, 269, 273, 318, 344
Humboldt, Alexander von, 88

Husserl, Edmund, 145, 156, 161, 165
Hyppolite, Jean, 164–65

I Bororos Orientali (Colbacchini), 284
Immémoriaux, Les (Segalen), 205
impressionism, 33, 245
incest taboo, 27, 122, 167, 168, 169, 172, 173, 179
  modern view of, 177–78
India, 187–89, 220, 221–22
"Indian Cosmetics" (Lévi-Strauss), 136–37
Interpretation of Dreams, The (Freud), 174, 234, 284
Inuit, 135, 138, 198, 203–4
"irrational awareness," 127
Islam, 222, 223, 332, 381*n*
Israel, 332–33
Izard, Michel, 217, 237

Jakobson, Roman, 11, 129, 142–48, 153, 154, 158, 163, 164, 165, 166, 168, 176, 180, 194, 230, 248, 267, 301–2, 305, 327
Jakobson, Svatava, 143
Japan, 24, 329, 331
Jaulin, Robert, 294
Jaurès, Jean, 27
jazz bands, 19, 133
Jeune République, La, 30
Jivaro, 183, 305, 330
Journal de la Société des Américanistes, 74, 84
Journal of American Folklore, 230
Jouvet, Louis, 54
Jubiabá (Amado), 57

Kachins, 175–76
Kahnweiler, Daniel-Henry, 26
Kaingang, 60–61, 65, 73, 206, 209, 305
Kanak, 190, 218
Kant, Immanuel, 27, 31, 156, 165, 196, 268
Karaja, 76–77, 86
Keck, Frédéric, 252
Kermode, Frank, 176
Khrushchev, Nikita, 236
kinship systems, 11, 55, 56, 119, 129, 132, 142, 145, 146–48, 152, 157–60, 166, 178–79, 184, 188, 190, 194, 199, 213, 221, 252, 333
  of Australian Aborigines, 122, 168, 172, 198, 274
  avunculate relationship in, 158–60, 234
  of Bororo, 71–72, 74, 122, 170, 332
  classical Chinese, 121–22, 312
  cognition in, 160
  mathematical symmetry of, 122
  in matrilineal vs. patrilineal societies, 158–59, 253–54
  models for, 143–44, 159, 168, 170
  moieties in, 71–72, 74, 122, 147, 170, 255–56
  totemism and, 255–56
  of Tupi-Kawahib, 107–8
  women as reciprocal gifts in, 168–72
  see also incest taboo; *Structures élémentaires de la parenté, Les*
Kirchoff, Paul, 163
Kitses, Jim, 290
Klamath-Modoc, 312–13
Koestler, Arthur, 124
Kojève, Alexandre, 165, 190
koro, 61
Koyré, Alexandre, 144, 154, 166
Krahô, 100
Kris, Ernst, 144
Kristeva, Julia, 294
Kroeber, Alfred, 43, 137, 194
Kubrick, Stanley, 291
Kuki, 47, 188
Kwakiutl, 138, 181, 233, 323–24, 380*n*

Labiche, Eugène, 24
Laboratoire d'anthropologie sociale, 6–7, 191, 241–43, 267, 287–88, 308, 309, 317
  expansion of, 293–94
  Human Relations Area Files at, 242, 288, 371*n*
Lacan, Jacques, 12, 166, 180, 183–84, 187, 196, 197, 228, 229, 289, 291, 310, 327, 375*n,* 376*n*
Lam, Wifredo, 125
Landes, Ruth, 86
Language and Mind (Chomsky), 290, 302
Laporte, Yves, 161
Lapouge, Gilles, 252
Laugier, Henri, 155
Lautréamont, Comte de, 61
Lazareff, Pierre, 151
Leach, Edmund, 174, 175–77, 178, 233, 299, 301, 334

Le Brun, Charles, 262
Le Corbusier, 160
Leenhardt, Maurice, 190
Lefort, Claude, 177, 185
Lefranc, Georges, 30
Léger, Fernand, 26, 56, 351*n*
Leiris, Michel, 19, 34, 40, 166, 172, 199, 209, 215–16, 369*n*
Leroi-Gourhan, André, 165
Léry, Jean de, 43, 50, 61, 241
Lettres Persanes (Montesquieu), 214
Lévi-Strauss, Claude:
  aesthetic preferences of, 246
  American crime fiction read by, 321
  appearance of, 4, 113
  background of, 20–23, 44
  birth of, 16, 21
  country château of, 317–18, 344–45
  death of, 12, 344
  funeral of, 344–45
  humor of, 5, 43–44, 243–44, 279–80, 303
  Jewish roots of, 4, 9, 20, 21, 22–23, 331–32
  marriages of, 13–14
  old age of, 342–44
  personality of, 5–6, 10, 43–44, 58, 96, 113, 127, 134, 144, 157, 243, 377*n*
  photographs of, 4, 5–6, 10
  play written by, 98–99, 101, 208
  popular culture rejected by, 321–22
  self-description of, 3
  self-education of, 10–11
  self-effacement of, 4–5
  unfinished novel of, 116–17, 205, 208
Lévi-Strauss, Claude, as anthropologist:
  aesthetic sensibility of, 127, 136, 142, 152, 335–36
  anti-Western rhetoric of, 61, 211, 218, 247–48, 306–7, 318, 322
  camera owned by, 8, 53
  caricature of, 291
  ceremonial events disliked by, 310
  coherent theoretical outlook of, 184
  conservative opinions of, 318–22
  culture universals derived by, 3, 11, 322
  doctoral thesis of, 85, 115, 132, 137, 143–44, 147, 163, 166–67, 343
  global fame of, 12, 292–93, 294
  historical approaches rejected by, 137
  influence of, 12, 334–40
  intellectual *trois maîtresses* of, 39, 45, 147
  journalism career considered by, 41, 189, 221
  lecture style of, 191–92, 251
  method of, 3, 75, 110–11, 116
  philosophical orientation of, 70, 103, 111, 116, 156, 267, 301–2, 313–14
  political involvement avoided by, 219–20
  progressive isolation of, 14, 229–30, 320–21, 331
  prose style of, 4–5, 44, 48, 256, 266–67, 298–99
  public persona of, 3–6, 7, 198
  racism as viewed by, 318–19
  retirement of, 326
  "sensible" vs. "intelligible" sought by, 263–65, 314–15, 335
  stature of, 339–40
  theoretical radicalism of, 158
  TV art programming interviews of, 244–48
Lévi-Strauss, Claude, as exile in New York City, 9, 10, 11, 14, 122–48, 149–55, 180, 186, 191, 194, 337
  antique Tuscan sideboard purchased by, 136
  ethnographic materials brought by, 125, 129
  French surrealist emigrés and, 124, 128, 132–36, 151, 164
  at New York Public Library, 141–42, 155, 162, 163, 164, 169, 174, 261
  teaching positions of, 123, 130, 132, 137, 139–41, 145, 157
  transatlantic journey of, 124–29
  on Voice of America, 151–52
  see also New York, N.Y.
Lévi-Strauss, Claude, in early years, 20–45
  abortive political campaign of, 37
  agrégation passed by, 35–37, 40, 156
  anti-Semitism encountered by, 23
  artistic sensibility of, 20, 24–25, 29, 32, 44
  astrology book purchased by, 37
  avant-garde influence on, 25–26, 27, 33–34, 44
  Cahen's assessment of, 29, 45
  childhood of, 22–28
  dissertation of, 31
  extended family of, 22, 37
  Frazer's 1928 lecture missed by, 35

Freud's influence on, 27, 39, 45
hiking of, 38–39
law studies of, 29, 30–31, 35, 44–45
literature read by, 27–28, 32
at Lycée Condorcet's *hypokhâgne,* 28–29, 30
at Lycée Janson de Sailly, 25, 27, 28, 36, 43
military service of, 37, 43
miniature Japanese furniture collected by, 24
musical interests of, 24, 25–26, 29, 44
philosophy studies of, 29, 30, 31, 35, 38, 40, 44, 351*n*-52*n*
political idealism of, 27, 29–32, 35, 37, 38, 43, 78, 151, 157
reality vs. analytical subtext in thinking of, 38–39, 45
at Sorbonne, 29, 30–31, 35–37, 43
teaching career of, 37–38, 41, 43, 115, 121
Lévi-Strauss, Dina Dreyfus, 14, 29, 47, 73, 354*n*
ethnography course taught by, 57–58, 113
eye infection contracted by, 96–97
fieldwork of, 1, 62, 63, 64, 66–67, 70, 81, 87, 90, 111–12, 117, 207
fieldwork techniques taught by, 57, 94
in French Resistance, 123
marital relationship of, 57–58
marital separation of, 117–18
in São Paulo, 54, 56, 57, 63, 76, 112
teaching career of, 37–38
wedding of, 37
Lévi-Strauss, Emma Lévy, 21–22, 23, 24, 120, 122, 123, 149, 152, 155, 311 Lévi-Strauss, Laurent, 14, 162, 243–44, 344–45
Lévi-Strauss, Matthieu, 14, 221, 324, 344–45
Lévi-Strauss, Monique Roman, 14, 197, 221, 294, 324, 344–45
Lévi-Strauss, Raymond, 21–27, 32, 120, 122, 123, 149, 152, 155, 160, 260, 282, 311
abandoned silk farm purchased by, 38
bourgeois lifestyle of, 22
CLS painted by, 21
death of, 205
Exposition coloniale Madagascan pavilion decorated by, 34, 38
financial problems of, 22, 26–27, 29, 37, 44
modernism as ruinous to, 26–27, 44
at São Paulo, 54
in World War II, 120, 122, 123, 149, 152, 155
Lévi Strauss, Rose-Marie Ullmo, 14, 161–62, 187, 197
Lévy, Rabbi, 22–23
Lévy-Bruhl, Lucien, 258, 350*n*
Lewisohn, Ludwig, 33
Lewitzsky, Anatole, 150
linguistics, 11, 57, 129, 165, 166, 179, 184, 196, 228, 239, 272, 290, 302, 334
anthropology and, 129, 193–97
sound analysis in, 145–46, 158, 231
see also structural linguistics
Linton, Ralph, 137–38, 139, 249–50
Lipkind, William, 86
Livingstone, David, 66
Loewenstein, Rudolph, 144
logical positivism, 272
Lomax, John, 57
Lourau, René, 237
Lowie, Robert, 10, 40–41, 45, 55, 74, 84, 123, 137, 138, 178, 194

Mac Orlan, Pierre, 202, 216
Maheu, René, 318–19
Malaurie, Jean, 203–5
Malinowski, Bronislaw, 2, 87–88, 96, 240
CLS's tribute to, 137
functionalist approach of, 254, 256
Mallarmé, Stéphane, 32, 224, 376*n*
Manifesto antropófago (*Cannibalist Manifesto*) (Andrade), 56–57
Maori, 198, 305
tattoos of, 152–53, 169
Marajó, 8, 68
Maranda, Pierre, 324–26, 329, 370*n*, 380*n*
Margueritte, Victor, 32
Maritain, Jacques, 151, 154
Marseilles, 124–25, 171
Martinique, 125, 128
Marx, Karl, 27, 31, 39, 45, 141, 147, 174, 176, 236, 240, 289, 296, 371*n*
Marxism, 39, 218, 236, 270, 310, 371*n*
masks, 16, 34, 152, 169, 323, 325, 380*n*
sxwaixwe, 131–32
Massey Lectures, 326, 337
Masson, André, 124, 133

matrilineal societies, 158–59, 253–54
Matta, Roberto, 133, 135
Maugüé, Jean, 42, 76–77, 78
Mauss, Marcel, 17–19, 20, 34, 41, 74, 150, 166, 190, 193, 199, 324, 350*n*, 371*n*
  CLS's portrayal of, 184–85
  fieldwork seminars of, 10, 18, 40
  material culture emphasized by, 57, 109
  reciprocity thesis of, 168–69
  "total social fact" idea of, 240
  in World War II, 150
Maybury-Lewis, David, 297–99
Mead, Margaret, 12, 138, 139, 194, 195–96, 205, 243, 371*n*
Meillassoux, Claude, 295–96
Méliès, Georges, 262
Mendoza, 47–49, 50–51, 116
Merleau-Ponty, Maurice, 36, 156–57, 177, 186, 204, 239–40, 241, 258, 270, 278
Merquior, José Guilherme, 289–90
Mesquita, Júlio, 50–51
Messiaen, Olivier, 227
Metastasis (Xenakis), 227
Métraux, Alfred, 6, 34, 40, 100, 112, 113, 123, 198, 200
  CLS's relationship with, 137, 163, 187, 197
  suicide of, 278–79
Metz, Christian, 294, 376*n*
Mexico, 19, 40, 139, 155, 181
  French exiles in, 124
  Gualupita terra-cotta figurines of, 77
Meyerhof, Otto, 124
Micheau, Jeanine, 155
Milhaud, Darius, 337
Milliet, Sérgio, 83, 354*n*
mind, human, 11–12, 141, 174, 193, 234, 256, 278
  unconscious, 127, 134, 166, 180–84, 228, 229
missionaries, 3, 20, 52, 82
  Jesuit, 91, 101
  native's murders of, 83, 91
  Salesian, 68, 71, 281, 375*n*-76*n*
Mitterrand, François, 7, 226, 327, 352*n*
modern art, 16–17, 26, 33–34, 36–37
  CLS's criticism of, 245–46, 372*n*
  cubism, 25, 26, 33, 245
  impressionism, 33, 245
modernism, 7–8, 11, 13, 20, 25–27, 28, 44, 127, 134, 142, 160, 225–48, 282, 351*n*
  of avant-garde fiction, 228
  Brazilian, 52, 56–57, 225–26
  in history, 228–29
  late, 225–30, 336–37
  in music, 227, 245
  in visual arts, 227
modesty, 93
Monbeig, Pierre, 55
Monnet, Georges, 31, 32, 33, 78, 241
Monod, Jacques, 320–21
Montaigne, Michel Eyquem, Seigneur de, 163, 201, 258, 342
Mont-de-Marsan, 37, 189
Montesquieu, 214, 240
Morgan, Lewis Henry, 167
morphology, 142, 152–53
Morphology of the Folktale (Propp), 243
Motherwell, Robert, 133
Mounier, Emmanuel, 258
Mundé, 3, 47, 105, 108, 112, 344
Murphy, Robert, 101, 364*n*
Musée de l'ethnographie, 15–16, 17, 40
  Exposition coloniale at, 34–35, 38
  Exposition du Sahara at, 19–20
Musée de l'Homme, 9, 15–17, 62, 78, 82–83, 109, 115–17, 134, 139–40, 149–50, 160, 165–66, 172, 187, 241
  CLS's indigenous artifacts collection at, 115–16, 117, 150
  Indiens du Matto Grosso exhibition at, 73–74
  1937 Exposition internationale des arts et techniques dans la vie moderne at, 115
Musée national d'Histoire naturelle, 18
music, 11, 24, 25–26, 29, 44, 337
  avant-garde, 280, 282–83, 307
  of Bororo, 70
  folk, 57, 84
  minimalist, 291–92
  modernism in, 227, 245
  of Nambikwara, 3, 92, 94
  orchestral, as metaphor, 232–33, 281–83
  of Tupi-Kawahib, 108
mythemes, 231, 235, 290, 312–14, 325, 330
Mythologiques quartet (Lévi-Strauss), 71, 183, 193, 230, 234–35, 252, 268, 276–87,

289, 293, 294, 295, 297–307, 311–15, 323–24, 325, 339, 343
myths, 11, 119, 131, 134, 159–60, 170, 180–84, 190, 192–93, 194, 199, 230–36, 238, 239, 250, 252, 256, 276–307, 311–15, 329–30, 332–33, 334, 335
as authorless, 289
bird-nester, 283–86, 304, 312–13
Bororo, 69, 71, 283–86, 306, 312–13
CLS's mathematical formula ("genetic law") of, 234–35, 276, 303
clusters of, 277, 281, 306
convergence of, 312–14
culture variations of, 235
fairy tales and, 55
inversion in, 235, 285–86, 306, 312–13, 325
jaguar's wife as element in, 299
language and, 183
in modern films, 290
modern novel and, 306–7
Oedipus, 27, 233–34, 285–86
oppositions in, 243, 256, 264–65, 286–87, 298, 304, 306
psychoanalysis and, 182–84
scatological material in, 285, 304–5, 330
walking difficulty as element of, 233

Nambikwara, 1, 5, 47, 87, 89, 91–97, 105, 109–10, 112, 123, 147, 150, 162, 172, 177, 204–5, 211, 274, 322–23, 338, 368*n*
amorous play of, 93
CLS rescued by, 103
CLS's thesis on, 166, 167
as CLS's ur-culture, 103
curare arrow poison of, 92, 95
eye infection contracted by, 96–97
honey types gathered by, 263–64
internecine feuds of, 97
intertribal meeting of, 101–3
kinship system of, 122
language of, 91, 92, 95, 105
material culture of, 8, 92–93, 95, 97, 102, 104, 116
monkeys kept by, 93, 104, 107
murderous attacks by, 83, 91, 101
music of, 3, 92, 94
nakedness of, 91, 92, 93
pidgin communication with, 86
tobacco smoked by, 108
"writing" experiment on, 102–3
Napoléon III, Emperor of France, 21
Nathan, Marcel, 27
Nazi Germany, 9, 10, 15, 23, 48, 113, 117–26, 318
anti-Semitism of, 78, 117, 120–23
Brazilian Integralists and, 52, 78
Czechoslovakia invaded by, 143
France occupied by, 119–25, 149–50, 155, 186
labor camps of, 150
racism of, 55, 121, 140
refugees from, 78, 114, 116, 121, 140, 143
Needham, Rodney, 174–75, 176–77, 265, 299–301, 302, 333, 377*n*-78*n*
"Ne visitez pas l'Exposition coloniale" manifesto, 34–35
Newman, Barnett, 227
New York, N.Y., 115, 129–48, 149–57, 180, 186, 191, 194, 337
American Museum of Natural History, 131–32, 323–24
Barnard College, 140–41
CLS's feeling of indebtedness to, 163–64
CLS's French cultural attaché appointment in, 155, 160–64, 197, 199
collector's items available in, 135–36
Columbia University, 85–86, 99–100, 137–39, 140, 249, 320
École libre des hautes études de New York, 139–40, 144–45, 152, 153–54, 155, 157
French political schisms in, 150–51, 153–54
French refugees in, 124, 128, 130, 132–36, 138–39, 150–51, 164
Greenwich Village, 132–36, 149, 153
Hunter College, 140
multiculturalism of, 130
Museum of the American Indian, 135
New School for Social Research, 123, 130, 132, 137, 139
1952 Wenner-Gren anthropology symposium in, 193–97
Office of War Information in, 151–52
psychoanalysts in, 144
urban landscape of, 130–31

New York Public Library, 141–42, 155, 162, 163, 164, 169, 174, 261
Niemeyer, Oscar, 52, 226
Nimuendajú (Curt Unckel), 74–75, 79, 82, 83–84, 106, 209
Nizan, Paul, 40, 55, 216
Noces, Les (Stravinsky), 25–26, 108
Nunberg, Herman, 144

Oddon, Yvonne, 150
Odoevsky, Vladimir, 145–46
Oedipus, myth of, 27, 233–34, 285–86
Oedipus Rex (Sophocles), 233–34, 303
Offenbach, Jacques, 21
On Growth and Form (Thompson), 142, 261–62
O País do Carnaval (Amado), 57
Origine des manières de table, L' (*The Origin of Table Manners*) (Lévi-Strauss), 278, 279, 280, 289, 303–7
overpopulation, 189, 322

Pacific Northwest Coast, 134–35, 138, 161, 181, 235
  CLS's visits to, 323–26, 328–29
  masks of, 131–32, 152, 169, 323, 325
  myths of, 312–14
  totem poles of, 134, 250, 323, 324–25
Pakistan, 187–89, 358*n*
Panama, 181–82
Parain, Brice, 237–38
Paraná Plantations Limited, 58
Paris:
  Allied liberation of, 153, 154
  Belle Epoque music halls of, 19
  Bibliothèque nationale de France, 2, 116, 206, 357
  Bourse, 21, 26
  Café de Flore, 18–19
  Directory of Cultural Relations of, 155–56
  Grand Palais, 8, 31
  Institute du monde arabe, 6
  intellectual refugees from, 124
  Jardin des plantes, 6
  Lycée Henri-IV, 6, 115, 120–21
  Lycée Louis-le-Grand, 30
  multiculturalism of, 320
  Musée de Cluny, 21
  Musée de l'Homme, *see* Musée de l'ethnographie; Musée de l'Homme
  Musée du Quai Branly, 9–10, 20, 74, 291, 343
  Musée Guimet, 241–42
  1968 student protest movement in, 308–11
  Opéra, 21, 23, 24, 282
  Palais de Chaillot, 15–16, 160
  Palais du Trocadéro, 15–16, 19–20, 34
  postwar conditions in, 164
  Rosenberg's gallery, 26
  Wildstein Gallery, 73
  in World War II, 117, 124, 150
Parti communiste français (PCF), 30, 236–37
Patrie humaine, La (Margueritte), 32
patrilineal societies, 158–59, 253–54
Pelléas et Mélisande (Debussy), 26
Penn, Irving, 4
Pensée sauvage, La (*The Savage Mind*) (Lévi-Strauss), 12, 251–52, 258–75, 279, 343
  bricoleur image in, 259–60, 273
  critics of, 268–69
  English version of, 265–67, 292, 300
  illustrations selected for, 262–63
  intellectual understanding vs. sensory perception in, 263–65
  philosophical aspect of, 267, 268–69, 273
  prose style of, 266–67
  puns in title of, 258–59, 266
  Sartre attacked in, 262, 269–73
  structuralism in, 260–62
Pétain, Henri Philippe Omer, 150
Petit manuel du parfait aventurier (Mac Orlan), 216
Petrullo, Vincenzo, 86
Phänomenologie des Geistes (Hegel), 164–65
Phénoménologie de la perception, La (*The Phenomenology of Perception*) (Merleau-Ponty), 156–57
phenomenology, 12, 164–65, 239
"Philosophical Postulates of Historical Materialism with Specific Reference to Karl Marx, The" (Lévi-Strauss), 31
physical anthropology, 55–56, 57, 75, 112, 138
Piaget, Jean, 167, 290, 320–21

Picasso, Pablo, 4, 34
  CLS on, 26, 33, 245–46
  photograph of, 16
  West African mask acquired by, 16
"Picasso and Cubism" (Lévi-Strauss), 33
Piéron, Henri, 186
Pinto, Estevão, 85
Plon publishers, 204, 238, 244, 251, 322–23, 325
Pollock, Jackson, 133
Polynesians, 198–99, 211
positivism, 80, 82
  logical, 272
post-structuralism, 292, 294, 310
Potière jalouse, La (*The Jealous Potter*) (Lévi-Strauss), 27, 183, 280, 303, 323, 329–30, 332, 333, 335
Pouillon, Jean, 217, 242, 270, 294, 369*n*
pre-Columbian artifacts, 16
  see also Pacific Northwest Coast
Primitive Peoples of Mato Grosso, Brazil (Petrullo), 86
Primitive Society (Lowie), 40–41
primitivism, 57, 65, 127, 180, 201, 245–46
Prix Claude Levi-Strauss, 303
Prix Goncourt, 215
Propp, Vladimir, 243
Proudhon, Pierre-Joseph, 27
Proust, Marcel, 4, 41, 208, 216, 224, 336, 343
psychoanalysis, 110, 133, 137, 144, 147, 166, 176, 180–84, 193, 196, 207, 228, 239, 310, 330
  shamanic cures vs., 181–83
  totemism and, 252–53
Pueblo Indians, 192, 233, 279, 283, 286
Puerto Rico, 128–29

Quain, Buell, 85–86, 87, 94, 99–101
  health concerns of, 86, 100
  suicide of, 100–101
Quesalid, 181

Race et histoire (Lévi-Strauss), 197–201, 270, 316, 318, 322
Radcliffe-Brown, Alfred, 158–60, 171, 240, 255–56
Radiodiffusion-Télévision française (RTF), 244–45
reciprocity, 168–72
Redfield, Robert, 162–63, 194
reflexive ethnography, 210–11, 214
Regard éloigné, Le (*The View from Afar*) (Lévi-Strauss), 326
Regarder, écouter, lire (*Look, Listen, Read*) (Lévi-Strauss), 335–36, 339
religion, 17, 189–93, 203, 222, 233–34
Religious Life of Primitives seminars, 181, 190, 196
Revault d'Allonnes, Olivier, 174
Revel, Jean-François, 238, 371*n*
Ricoeur, Paul, 268
Rio de Janeiro, 52, 53, 78, 81, 130
  CLS's first impressions of, 49–50
  France Antarctique colony in, 43
  Guanabara Bay of, 49, 50, 241, 353*n*
  Museu Nacional, 62, 63, 83, 84–85, 100, 113–14
  Quain in, 99–101
Rivers, William, 171
Rivet, Paul, 19–20, 34, 78, 82–83, 88, 116, 138–39, 150, 165, 220, 350*n*
Rivière, Georges-Henri, 19–20
Robbe-Grillet, Alain, 228
Rockefeller Foundation, 123, 161, 221
Rodinson, Maxime, 217–18, 238, 369*n*
Romains, Jules, 25, 351*n*
Rondon, Cândido, 80–82, 92, 108, 111
  telegraph line constructed by, 81–82, 341
Rondon Commission, 82, 106
Roosevelt, Franklin Delano, 151
Roosevelt, Theodore, 82
Roquette-Pinto, Edgar, 82, 111
Ross, Alex, 227
Rothko, Mark, 227
Rouch, Jean, 119
Rougemont, Denis de, 115, 151
Roupnel, Gaston, 120
Rousseau, Jean-Jacques, 27, 43, 103, 163, 201, 258, 336
Roy, Claude, 258

Sahlins, Marshall, 293
Saint-Exupéry, Antoine de, 150
Saint-Simon, Comte de, 31
Salish, 131–32, 283, 312, 323–24, 332–33, 378*n*, 380*n*

São Paulo, 51, 52–61, 62, 63, 76–78, 109, 112, 114, 226, 327–28, 353*n*
CLS's description of, 53
CLS's photographs of, 53–54
CLS's residence in, 54, 58
Culture Department of, 57, 62, 83
industrialization of, 53
sociological analysis of, 56
São Paulo, University of, 41–43, 50–51, 52–58, 62, 83, 112, 123
CLS's sociology course at, 41, 55–56, 57–58, 112
French mission's elitist attitude at, 54–55, 56
Sapir, Edward, 138
Sarkozy, Nicolas, 343, 344
Sarney, José, 327–28
"Sarrasine" (Balzac), 243
Sartre, Jean-Paul, 12, 14, 151, 156, 161, 165, 172, 204, 214, 217, 219–20, 228, 236, 296, 316, 327
CLS's attacks on, 262, 269–73
1968 student protests and, 309
outré lifestyle of, 269
Saudades do Brasil, 107, 338
Saudades de São Paulo, 53
Saussure, Ferdinand de, 11, 145, 147–48, 165, 166, 231, 240, 278, 290
Saussure, Raymond de, 144, 180, 181
Schaeffner, André, 34
Sebag, Lucien, 237, 270, 279, 294, 375*n*
Section française de l'Internationale ouvrière (SFIO), 30, 31, 32, 38
Segalen, Victor, 205
Seghers, Anna, 125
Seligmann, Kurt, 134, 135
Serge, Victor, 124, 125–26
serialism, 227, 282–83
"Serpent with Fish inside His Body, The" (Lévi-Strauss), 238
Seyrig, Henri, 154, 155
shamans, 180–83, 190, 246, 334
childbirth incantation of, 181–82
rebirthing ritual of, 324
Shannon, Claude, 132, 194–95
Silz, René, 62–68, 83–84
Sioux, 260
Smadja, Henri, 126, 128
smell, sense of, 314, 379*n*
socialism, 27, 29, 30, 31, 35, 37, 78
Société de géographie, 30
Société des Américanistes, 42
sociology, 55–56, 57–58, 112, 139, 152–53, 239
Durkheimian, 17, 55, 166
positivist, 55
Soleil Hopi (Talayesva), 205, 244
Sontag, Susan, 215, 242
Sophocles, 233–34
"Sorcerer and His Magic, The" (Lévi-Strauss), 181
Sorman, Guy, 294
Sousa Dantas, Luís de, 42
Soustelle, Jacques, 40, 151
Soviet Union, 30, 115, 125, 126, 142–43, 236–37
Speer, Albert, 15, 115
Spencer, Baldwin, 254–55
Sperber, Dan, 302–3
"Split Representation in the Art of Asia and America" (Lévi-Strauss), 152–53
Staden, Hans, 43
Steiner, George, 281, 322, 375*n*
Steward, Julian, 194
Stiealin, Henri, 287–88
Stockhausen, Karlheinz, 225, 227
Strauss, Isaac, 21
Strauss, Léa, 22
Stravinsky, Igor, 25
structuralism, 3, 4, 9, 12, 14, 59, 71–72, 163–64, 194–95, 196–97, 175, 225–48, 267, 270, 271, 272, 279–83, 305, 326–27, 333, 336–40
Buddhism and, 223
and CLS's dandelion structure revelation, 118–19, 142, 194, 258
communism and, 236–37
critics of, 217–18, 238, 246, 268–69, 297–303, 310, 316–17, 335
as formalism, 268, 273
history and, 240
humanities as moving toward, 184–85, 228–30
of human mind, 141
influence of, 236–38, 287–96, 322–23
Japan and, 329
method of, 257, 314
modernism and, 7–8, 11, 13, 20, 225–30, 282–83

1968 student protest movement and, 308–11
orchestral score as metaphor of, 232–33, 281–83
in *Pensée sauvage,* 260–62
philosophical basis of, 118–19
serialism vs., 282–83
splice technique and, 233, 236
subjectivity vs., 214
in *Totémisme aujourd'hui,* 256–57
transformations in, 261–62
in *Tristes Tropiques,* 211–14, 217–19
structural linguistics, 142–48, 157–60, 166, 168, 170, 194–95, 213, 301–2, 334
basic tenets of, 145–47
phonemics in, 129, 146, 231, 305
phonetics in, 145, 148
splitting technique and, 152–53
"Structural Study of Myth, The" (Lévi-Strauss), 230–36
Structures élémentaires de la parenté, Les (*The Elementary Structures of Kinship*) (Lévi-Strauss), 10–11, 147–48, 160, 162, 166–79, 188, 217, 270, 299, 343
academic sources of, 162, 166, 169, 174, 175–76
citations in, 167
English version of, 174, 292, 299–300
envisaged second volume of, 178, 190
evolving views on, 177–79
final paragraph of, 171–72
geographical area included by, 166, 171
impact of, 172–77
inaccuracies in, 175–76, 300
incest taboo principle of, 167, 168, 169, 172, 173, 177–78, 179
kin diagrams in, 170
kinship analyses in, 170–71, 172
as landmark publication, 174, 178
limited first edition of, 174, 364*n*
nature/culture divide in, 178
preface of, 168
prose style of, 171
reciprocal gift-giving principle of, 168–72
reviews of, 172–73, 175–76, 185
standard criticism of, 177
Suor (Amado), 57
surrealism, surrealists, 9, 11, 13, 17, 20, 34–35, 43, 56, 61, 73, 142, 151, 180, 199, 200–201, 231, 284
"automatic," 127
French, in New York City, 124, 128, 132–37, 164
parlor games of, 133
VVV journal launched by, 136–37
Suyá, 99
symbolic thought, 181–83, 184, 190, 255, 256, 257
symbolist movement, 13, 26, 28, 32, 56, 376*n*
Système de la mode (Barthes), 289–90
S/Z (Barthes), 243

taboos, 250, 286
see also incest taboo
Talayesva, Don, 205, 244
Tales of Charles Perrault conference, The, 55
Tanguy, Yves, 34–35, 90, 132, 135
Taylor, Anne-Christine, 291
Temps modernes, Les 172, 177, 185, 200, 213–14, 217, 269, 272–73, 291, 343
Terray, Emmanuel, 174, 219
Terre humaine book series, 204–5, 244, 323
Thevet, André, 43, 241
Third Congress of Socialist Students of France, 31
Thompson, D'Arcy Wentworth, 141–42, 261–62, 281
Tibagy, 60, 65, 206
Todorov, Tzvetan, 294
Torres, Heloísa Alberto, 84–85, 100
Totem and Taboo (Freud), 167, 253
totemism, 17, 27, 55, 119, 249–57, 373*n*
anthropological theories of, 250–51, 252–53, 254, 255–56, 257
of Australian Aborigines, 253–55
choice of, 255–56
complexity of, 250
dualism in, 255–56
in ethnographic record, 253–56
functionalist approach to, 251, 254, 255, 256
kinship systems and, 255–56
negative, 254, 255
as symbols, 255, 256
taboos linked to, 250
in World War I military divisions, 249–50
Totemism and Exogamy (Frazer), 253

Totémisme aujourd'hui, Le (*Totemism*) (Lévi-Strauss), 250, 251–57, 258, 259, 270, 299
totem poles, 134, 250, 323, 324–25
Tristes Tropiques (Lévi-Strauss), 3, 4, 7, 8, 14, 22–23, 33, 40, 66, 75, 87, 94, 103, 123, 187, 198, 205–24, 238, 239, 242, 247, 270, 274, 320, 322–23, 338, 343
  as anthropological landmark, 210–11
  aphorisms in, 207
  Breton described in, 127–28
  Buddhism as viewed in, 222–23
  central narrative of, 208
  contemporary accounts similar to, 215–16
  critical success of, 214–15, 220, 230
  critics of, 217–20
  English version of, 39, 215, 216
  ethnography in, 209–11, 212–13
  first draft of, 205–8
  impact of, 216–17, 237
  Islam as viewed in, 222, 223
  journey to Brazil in, 47–49
  Marx in, 236
  opening pages of, 209, 216
  pessimistic tone of, 211, 217, 219, 223–24, 342
  philosophical tone of, 218
  reflexive ethnography in, 210–11, 214
  structuralism in, 211–14, 217–19
  sunset described in, 48, 116
  symmetry and inversion in, 211–12
  as title of CLS's uncompleted novel, 116–17
  as travel book, 209
Trobriand Islands, 2, 159, 170
Trotsky, Leon, 33
Trubetskoy, Nikolai, 145
Trumaí, 99, 101
Tsimshian, 131, 235
Tupi, 1, 43, 78, 79, 80, 86, 106, 241
Tupi-Kawahib, 47, 106–8, 112, 162
Tupinambá, 43, 50, 61
2001: A Space Odyssey, 291
Tyler, Edward, 10

UNESCO, 187, 198, 217, 219, 289, 318–19
  Human Relations Area Files of, 242
  International Social Science Council at, 197, 241
United States:
  CLS's family connections in, 123
  folk music of, 57
  Foreign Agents Registration Act of, 154
  nuclear air bases of, 204
  Office of Strategic Services (OSS) of, 157
  press of, 12
  Vichy government recognized by, 150
Unckel, Curt (Nimuendajú), 74–75, 79, 82, 83–84, 106, 209
Updike, John, 299
Uppsala University, 228
urucu dyes, 83, 93, 97, 106

Vanetti, Dolorès, 151, 269
van Gennep, Arnold, 55, 253
Vargas, Getúlio, 52, 78, 113
Vauxcelles, Louis, 26, 351*n*
Vellard, Jean, 1, 2, 83–84, 86, 87, 96, 108, 109
  curare poison experiment of, 95
  harsh methods employed by, 84
  illnesses of, 105, 112
  indigenous artifacts collected by, 114
Veloso, Caetano, 49
Verger, Pierre, 200
Vernant, Jean-Pierre, 309
Vernet, Joseph, 13, 246
Versailles, 22–23, 26
Vie familiale et sociale des Indiens Nambikwara, La (*The Family and Social Life of the Nambikwara*) (Lévi-Strauss), 166, 167, 204–5, 206
Villa-Lobos, Heitor, 57
Vivieros de Castro, Eduardo, 303
Vlaminck, Maurice de, 16
Voice of America, 151–52
Voie des masques, La (The Way of the Masks) (Lévi-Strauss), 132, 280, 323–26
von den Steinen, Karl, 85, 129
Voyage au bout de la nuit (Céline), 33
Voyage au Congo (Gide), 215
VVV, 136–37

Wagley, Charles, 86, 100
Wagner, Richard, 13, 24, 282
Waldberg, Isabelle, 140
Waldberg, Patrick, 133–34, 140, 151

Wauters, Arthur, 27
Weaver, Warren, 195
Weil, André, 172
Weil, Simone, 36, 172
Wenner-Gren Foundation, 193–97
Wiener, Norbert, 194
Wiseman, Boris, 274
Wolfram, Sybil, 265–66
Word: Journal of the Linguistic Circle of New York, 158–60, 168, 178, 230
Workers' International Bureau, 31
World War I, 18, 19, 22–23, 25, 26, 30, 118, 123, 249–50, 272
World War II, 13, 23, 117–48, 149–57, 190, 199, 202
  Allied European campaign of, 153, 154
  see also France, in World War II; Nazi Germany
writing, 102–3

Xenakis, Iannis, 227
Xerente, 84
Xingu, 86, 99–100, 162

Yale University, 244
Yourcenar, Marguerite, 319

Žižek, Slavoj, 12
Zola, Émile, 32
Zuni, 134, 192